Afterimage of Empire

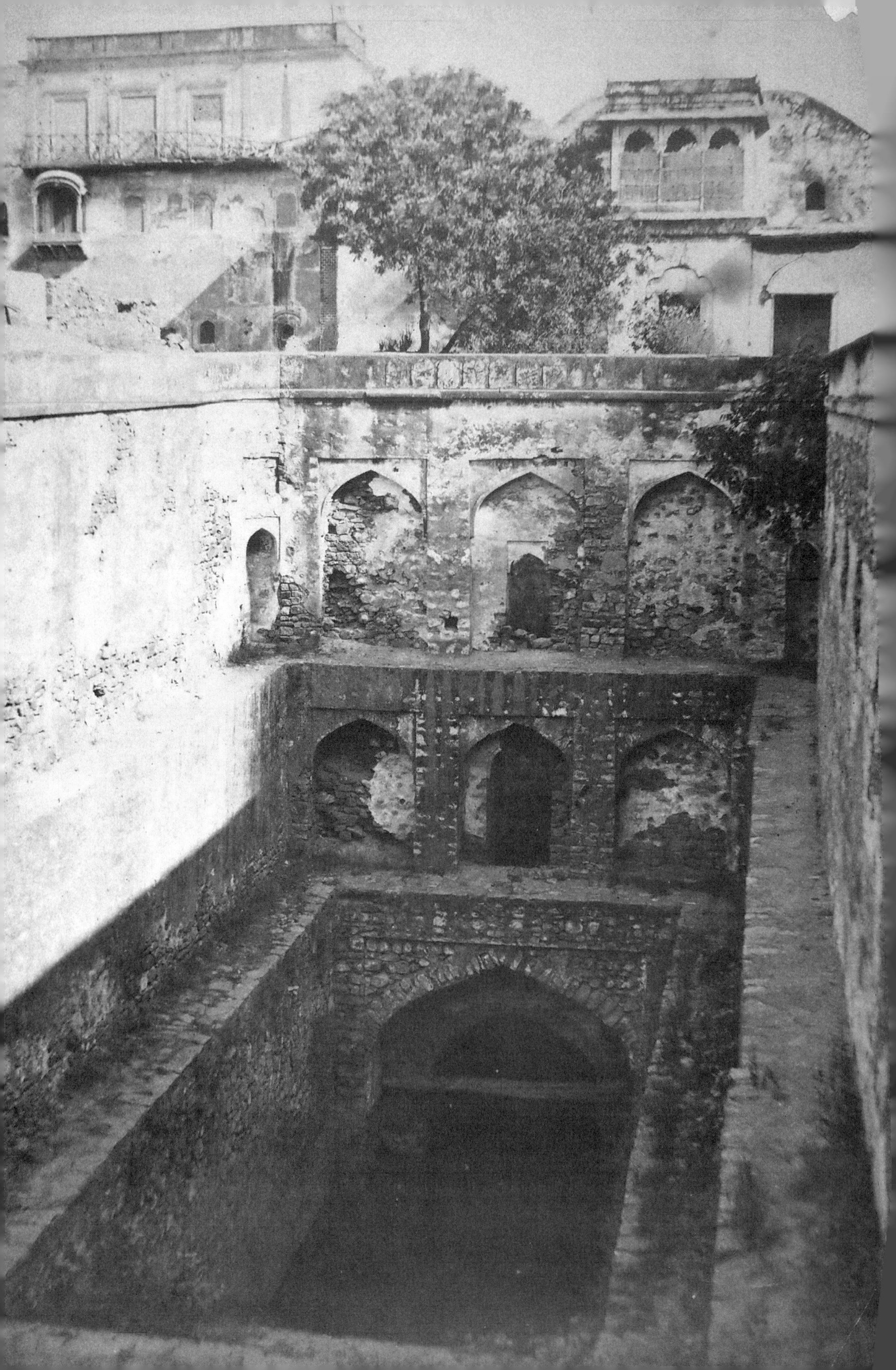

Afterimage of Empire

PHOTOGRAPHY IN NINETEENTH-CENTURY INDIA

Zahid R. Chaudhary

MINNESOTA

University of Minnesota Press
Minneapolis
London

This publication is made possible in part from the Barr Ferree Foundation Fund for Publications, Princeton University.

Portions of the Introduction and chapter 2 were previously published as "Phantasmagoric Aesthetics: Colonial Violence and the Management of Perception," *Cultural Critique* 59 (2005): 63–119.

Published by the University of Minnesota Press
111 Third Avenue South, Suite 290
Minneapolis, MN 55401-2520
http://www.upress.umn.edu

Library of Congress Cataloging-in-Publication Data

Chaudhary, Zahid R.
Afterimage of empire : photography in nineteenth-century India / Zahid R. Chaudhary.
p. cm.
Includes bibliographical references and index.
ISBN 978-0-8166-7748-1 (hardback)
ISBN 978-0-8166-7749-8 (pb)
1. Photography—India—History—19th century. I. Title.
TR103.C49 2012
770.954—dc23
2011047428

Printed in the United States of America on acid-free paper

20 19 18 17 16 15 14 13 12 10 9 8 7 6 5 4 3 2 1

For Chaudhary Muhammad Rafiq (1933–2009)
and Razia Begum Rahman

The formation *[Bildung]* of the five senses is the work of all previous history.

—Karl Marx, *Economic and Philosophical Manuscripts of 1844*

Contents

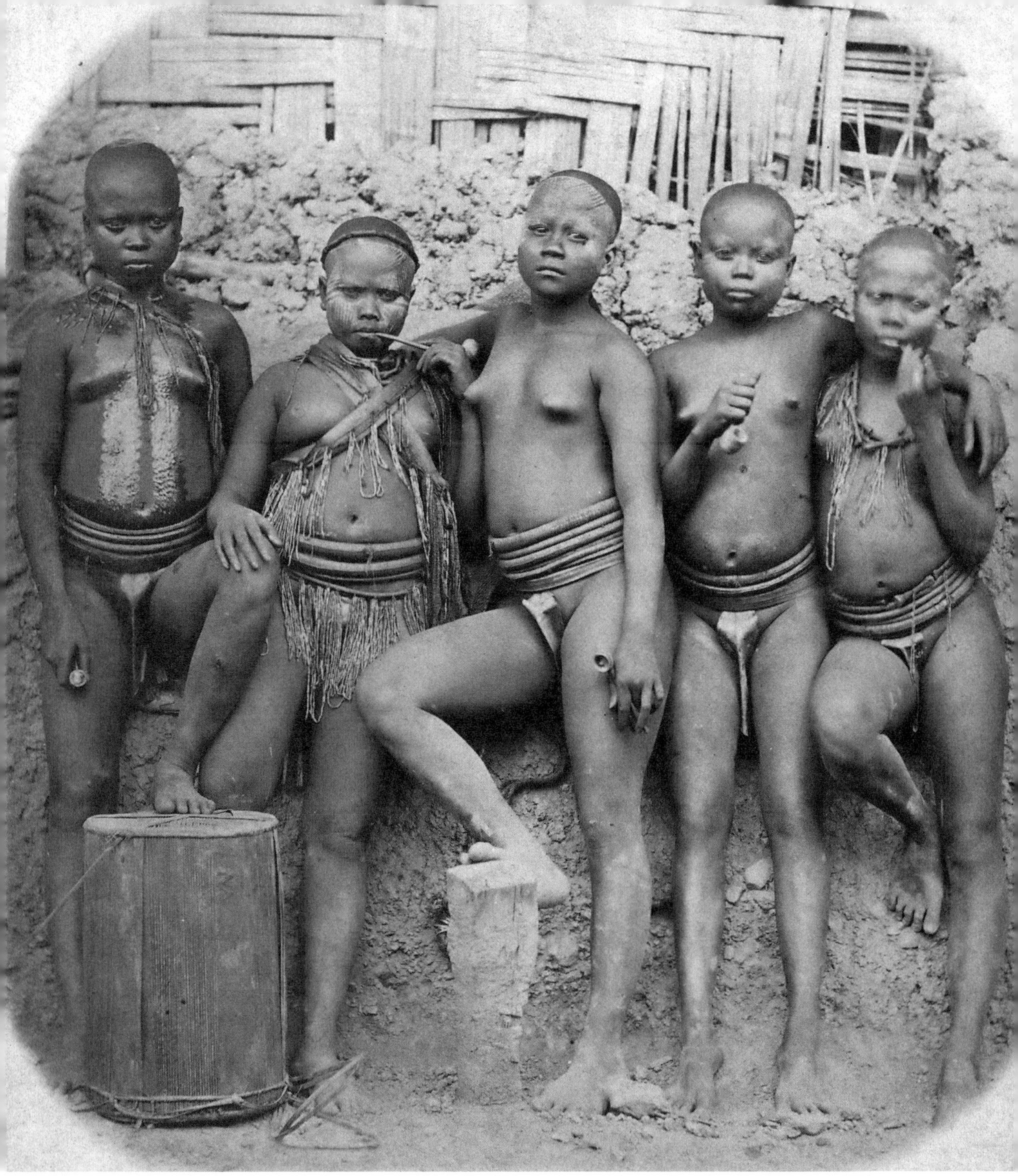

Figure I.1. G. E. Dobson, *Group of Five Young Andamanese Women,* 1872. RAI5759. Courtesy of the Royal Anthropological Institute of Great Britain and Ireland.

INTRODUCTION

Sensation and Photography

The body is our anchorage in a world.

—Maurice Merleau-Ponty, *Phenomenology of Perception*

Just as the mode of existence of human collectives changes over long historical periods, so too does their mode of perception.

—Walter Benjamin, "The Work of Art in the Age of Its Technological Reproducibility"

Persuasion

How might we reorient our understandings of colonial representations if we shift our focus to that interface between bodies and world that is the precondition for making meaning? In *Afterimage of Empire* I argue that, following the well-traveled routes of global capital, photography arrives in India not only as a technology of the colonial state but also as an instrument that extends and transforms sight for photographers and the body politic, British and Indian alike. Such perceptual transformations are congruent not only with the technomaterial changes within photographic practice but also with transformations at the level of aesthetic form. These transformations show that while *sensing* the world is inseparable from, though not identical with, *making sense* of it, the traffic between sense perception and ideation is historically conditioned.

The global dissemination of photography in the 1800s has had irreversible effects on the modern formation of the senses. A viewer's relationship to a photograph at first involves sight, only in order to set sight itself within the play of other sensate experiences: smell, hearing, touch, taste, but also embodied experiences of memory, desire, pleasure, and pain. While such experiences cannot be dissociated from the sensory and affective experience of older mimetic forms, such as novels or poems, photography at this early juncture did not require textual or elite–aesthetic literacy as its condition of reception.[1] So its reach qualitatively and quantitatively increased over the course of the nineteenth century. In the early era of photography, observers viewed this new medium's aesthetic potential with enthusiasm and skepticism in equal measure. This period is pivotal in assessing the formative contribution of photography to the history of sensate experience—of the aesthetic, in its root sense. I assume that a key aspect of early photography is not simply to represent or to produce images but to help form a newly technologized body on a mass scale across diverse social formations. If, following Marx, the "formation *[Bildung]* of the five senses is the work of all previous history,"[2] then in this study I understand photography as establishing a new *Bildung* that is global in scope. The cultural, material, and economic contradictions and effects of capitalism take an especially acute form in the colonies, and photography's negotiation with this terrain in India is particularly instructive, not only for a genealogy of colonial visual culture, but also for theories of photographic practice. What the *colonial* history of the medium may have to teach us about the making of the modern perceptual apparatus, of the links between perception and meaning, and of the transformation of aesthetic experience itself, is the primary focus of this book.

An anecdote from colonial history serves to show the subtle dance between sensing and making sense, framing and persuasion. On October 15, 1869, while visiting London, Syed Ahmed Khan, an Indian Muslim reformer and essayist, wrote a long and detailed letter to the secretary of the Scientific Society at Allygurgh. The letter later appeared in Urdu and in English translation in the *Allygurgh Institute Gazette.* In the context of a discussion of the English treatment of Indians, he writes:

> In the India Office is a book in which the races of all India are depicted in pictures and in letterpress, giving the manners and customs of each race. Their photographs show that the pictures of the different manners and customs were taken on the spot, and the sight of them shows how savage they are—the equals of animals. The young Englishmen who, after passing the preliminary Civil Service examination, have to pass examinations on special subjects for two years afterwards, come to the India Office preparatory to starting for India, and, desirous of knowing something of the land to which they are going, also look over this work. What can they think, after perusing this book and looking at its pictures, of the power and honour of the natives of India? One day Hamid, Mahmud [Khan's sons], and I went to the India Office, and Mahmud commenced looking at the work. A young Englishman, probably a passed civilian, came up, and after a short time asked Mahmud if he was a Hindustani? Mahmud replied in the affirmative, but blushed as he did so, and hastened to explain that he was not one of the

> aborigines, but that his ancestors were formerly of another country. Reflect, therefore, that until Hindustanis remove this blot they shall never be held in honour by any civilized race.[3]

The book in question is the eight-volume *The People of India* (1868–75), an ethnographic magnum opus complete with 486 albumen prints. Khan's original letter is more specific about certain details, noting that the Englishman's question was asked "with evident feeling of contempt" and that Mahmud "felt deeply ashamed."[4] Hence the desire to distance oneself from India, even as an Indian, and to rely on an alternate genealogy that, in Mahmud's case, goes back to Herat, to the Husaini Syeds who arrived in India in the seventeenth century. Of course, condensed within this search for an alternative genealogy are the race and class anxieties of an educated Indian who is traveling in London and has just learned to view himself from an English point of view. It is worth noting, however, that in spite of being shocked at the parade of tribals and "native" types, Khan is perfectly persuaded by the civilizational discourse upon which *The People of India* depends. His emphatic rejection of the volume speaks paradoxically to photography's powers of persuasion. On the one hand, Khan and his son Mahmud are not at all convinced that *The People of India* is representative of the people of India; photography in this volume has ostensibly failed in its ideological mission. On the other hand, the sense of shame that leads Mahmud to disown his connection to India speaks of a deeper and far more profound persuasion that India is in fact a place to which it would be shameful to belong. Photography cannot, of course, be wholly credited with this persuasion: the number of sources for such a worldview for an elite Indian subject in the nineteenth century is no doubt overdetermined. But photography can, it seems, be credited with the power to summon such shame from its depths, to give visible shape to the murky and half-apprehended notions of one's own place in the world. This, too, is a form of persuasion, all the subtler for being uncannily familiar and all the more powerful for being "objectively" true.

And yet such forms of persuasion have their own unforeseen effects. As invested as Syed Ahmed Khan is in civilizational discourse—in this very letter he condemns Indians for being uncivilized—his writings on Indian education, gender, and Muslim identity constitute an alternate narrative of improvement and self-making that is not neatly contiguous with the English civilizing mission for India. There is nothing predetermined about photography's persuasive powers, in other words. Moreover, in the circuit of power and knowledge where the images from *The People of India* circulated, it is clear that persuasion at the level of discourse does not assume a subject who is doing the persuading. This might seem an unlikely claim to make for a volume commissioned by the colonial state and fueled in part by the enthusiasm of Governor-General

Lord Canning and his wife for photography. A certain kind of Saidian-derived postcolonial reading practice would describe British representations of colonized people as part of a growing archive of overarching rationality in which the colonized subjects figure as "other," and English subjects figure as fully human.[5] Certainly *The People of India* and much colonial photography in India lend themselves to such a reading, a reading whose argumentative tracks are by now very familiar, usually taking this course: discourse creates its object; Western knowledge creates the non-West as a one-dimensional figure of difference; Western knowledge is, in turn, one-dimensional itself; the Western subject, like the non-Western one, is trapped in this discursive production that relies on binary terms in which the West occupies the privileged place of the binary.[6] The persuasive power of this line of thinking is indisputable and is easily at hand when faced with an archival object like *The People of India,* which seeks to fix and define "natives" in the service of colonial management.[7] But this line of thinking can also be a kind of machinery that produces an identical result, no matter how intractable the material.[8] Nevertheless, pursuing it briefly is worthwhile, if only to demonstrate how, precisely, the present work is written at the limits of such a methodology.

Between Sensation and Intellection

The photographic archive left from the days of the British Raj in India consists of a perhaps predictable range of representations: landscapes, buildings (standing and in ruins), the indigenous populations (individuals and groups, living and dead), and the British engaged both in "high tea" and in war. The history of photography in India begins almost concurrently with its inception in Europe; it became available in India within a year of Louis Jacques Daguerre's experiments in 1839 but proliferated widely on the subcontinent only after 1857. Thus I situate the history of photography in India in the context of the seismic upheaval that was the Sepoy Revolt of 1857–58, in which Indian recruits in the British army rebelled against their superiors. The constitutively tense tripartite relation among photographer, camera, and represented colonial subject or object was produced, for the most part, in the aftermath of the Sepoy Revolt.

Immediately after the last rebels were hanged and shot in 1858, direct crown rule replaced the rule of the East India Company, and Charles John Canning, the first viceroy, began encouraging army officers to take cameras on their travels to photograph the people of India and to deposit copies of the plates with him. This was the beginning of the first state-sanctioned archival photographic practice in India. In 1863 John William Kaye of the Secret and Political Department in eastern Bengal, expanded Canning's project to photograph systematically all of the communities of India, in preparation for the eight-volume *The People of India*. The rhetoric of the preface to the first volume turns on the capacious notion of interest:

> The great convulsion of 1857–58, while it necessarily retarded for a time all scientific and artistic operations, imparted a newer interest to the country which had been the scene, and to the people who had been the actors in these remarkable events. When, therefore, the pacification of India had been accomplished, the officers of the Indian services, who had made themselves acquainted with the principles and practices of photography, encouraged and patronized by the Governor-General, went forth and traversed the land in search of interesting subjects.[9]

In addition to the imputation that photography is at once scientific and artistic (the latter being a most important "supplement" to, and a potential contradiction of, the former), the word *interest* in this passage serves as a sort of ideological pivot: the violent revolt imparted a newer interest to India, requiring that officers travel the land in search of interesting subjects. The logical circularity of this fundamental proposition would have required little explanation for the nineteenth-century British consumer, to whom *The People of India* was chiefly directed and for whom such "interest" was wholly unproblematic and naturalized. For us the words *interest* and *interesting* are overdetermined by notions of (ethical) concern and (psychological and economic) investment, both of which are at once key players in the domain of knowledge and contain within themselves barely concealed traces of fear for all manner of loss, from the economic to the psychological. The newest technological apparatus for the articulation of this nexus of concern–investment–knowledge was the camera, with which the army officers planned to "shoot" their interesting subjects.

It was in this conjuncture, then, that photography in India came to have its most extensive and profound application.[10] It entered the ever-expanding archive of Empire, taking its place beside the more or less fetishized archaeological and ethnographic artifact in the public museum or in the bourgeois interior with its unique form of private appropriation, consumption, and ideological reproduction. *The People of India* formally launched the genre of anthropological photography on an unprecedented scale on the vast subcontinent. Its aim was to "preserve" rapidly disappearing forms of life, in the process giving full reign to the photographers' primitivist aesthetics and simultaneously building taxonomies of castes and professions. Detective surveillance was never far away: here we are reminded that the German word for "enlightenment," *Aufklärung*, means also "surveillance"—another constitutive feature of its "dialectic," in the sense of Adorno and Horkheimer, and not the least of its darker side.

It is in light of this discursive context that we can enter into the chiaroscuro world of colonial photography. Figure I.1, from the *People of India,* is a photograph taken by G. E. Dobson: *Group of Five Young Andamanese Women,* from 1872. Three years later, in a paper published in the *Journal of the Anthropological Institute,* Dobson wrote that the central female figure was from the Andamanese Orphan School on Ross Island, whom he had seen frequently in the school or in the church "dressed in white." Yet his photograph representing her "destitute of clothes, shaved, and greased with a mixture of olive-coloured mud and fat" was clearly more appropriate, insofar as Dobson's concern and interest were to stage the authentic primitiveness he imagined to lie beneath the mere veneer of superimposed British civilization.[11] In a double move, Dobson "represents" the fear that civilization itself is fragile, as easily stripped as a Sunday dress. The truth of the authentic primitiveness revealed here could be represented only through an imposed phantasmagoria of naked flesh, mud-caked faces, and the requisite wooden vessel—turned upside down, with the primitive foot resting on it, as if to suggest a momentary refusal of labor.

In a similar vein, a lithograph based on a photograph by Tosco Peppé of two Juang girls (Figure I.2), also reproduced in *The People of India,* shows us two women, "wild timid creatures" whom Peppé had "immense difficulty in inducing to pose before [him]."[12] Convinced that this was "almost their last appearance in leaves," Peppé insisted on capturing them in their "natural state" lest the onslaught of civilization destroy the image.[13] The frame of this photograph gives us a view of what is no doubt intended to convey a natural scene: the two women standing virtually nude against a wooden wall, while one woman innocently toys with the bead necklace close to the other woman's breast and indicates the other woman's genitals with her free hand. This is the fantasy of primitive innocence, when forbidden knowledge remained as-yet undiscovered. The positioning of a "primitive" woman's hands near the breast and genital area of another "native" is meant not to detract but to add to the cold scientific racial truth invested in the anthropological photograph. But if this frame presents us with a view of the natural habitat of the primitive, then why does the primitive figure seem radically not-at-home in it? The immense difficulty with which Peppé induced these women to pose before him has left an imprint on the photograph itself, in the glare with which the molested woman on the right stares out at us. Dressed, posed, and captured, these Juang girls have had foreignness imposed on them. The colonial forms of knowledge intervening in the lifeworlds of these two figures frame them with forms radically foreign to the two figures, not only because the concept of the "primitive" itself marks the site of the colonizer who produces this concept, but also, more literally, because these two women normally wear Manchester saris rather than leaves and beads.[14] This intervention, in turn, secures the photographer

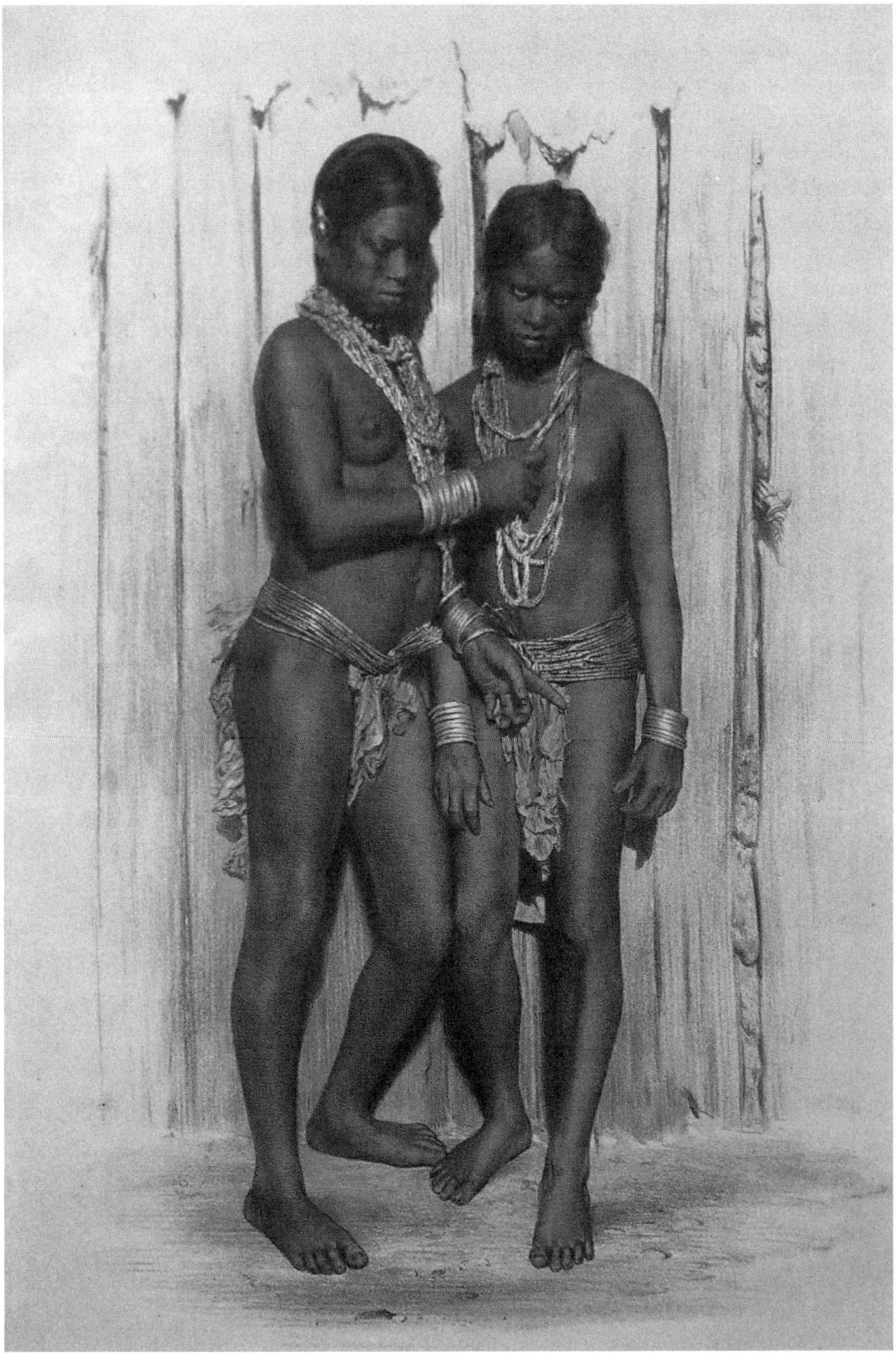

Figure I.2. Two Juang girls. Lithograph based on a photograph by Tosco Peppé. From Edward Tuite Dalton's *Descriptive Ethnology of Bengal,* 1872. The Alkazi Collection of Photography.

in the certainty of his own foreignness to *this* scene, distinguishing him from the undifferentiated primitiveness surrounding him in India.

These photographs record the radical transformations (epistemic, political, and economic) in social relations that pass under the sign of the colonial encounter. Such transformations are of a piece with the logic of the colonial scene of technological reproduction. For example, Benedict Anderson notes that central to the historical consolidation of the colonial state are the powers offered by the age of technological reproduction; print and photography allowed the possibility of "infinite reproducibility" of the sites (archaeological, cartographic, racial) of state imaginings. While this process remained politically "unconscious" at the level of statecraft, "it was precisely the infinite quotidian reproducibility of its regalia that revealed the real power of the state":[15]

> Through technologies such as the census, the map, and the museum (all of which are buttressed by the technological reproducibility of their knowledge), the colonial state did not merely aspire to create, under its control, a human landscape of perfect visibility; the condition of this "visibility" was that everyone, everything, had (as it were) a serial number. This style of imagining did not come out of thin air. It was the product of the technologies of navigation, astronomy, horology, surveying, photography and print, to say nothing of the deep driving power of capitalism.[16]

In the case of India, it is important to remember that these technologies become central not only to the colonial state but also to forms of private capital that only partly overlap with the colonial state. Colonial photography produces a visibility that legitimates and records the "value" of the colonial effort in the same frame as it measures the colonial subject. It aids in the production of regularities, showing us ghostly series of racial forms, sublime vistas of foreign lands, or history distilled into picturesque ruins. Walter Benjamin writes, "With regard to countless movements of switching, inserting, pressing, and the like, the 'snapping' of the photographer had the greatest consequences. Henceforth a touch of the finger sufficed to fix an event for an unlimited period of time. The camera gave the moment a posthumous shock, as it were."[17] Like the factory clock that is the figure of the temporality of shock in Benjamin's account, photography inserts shock into the very time frozen in the photographic image. The photograph, a material and transportable image of "reality," allows the scene within the frame to be defamiliarized anew in each context in which the photograph is discovered. If photography makes the reality of the depicted scene commutable across time and space, then the reality we witness in these images is not accessible in any unmediated way. Not only have we been able to read these photographs against the grain, but also the meaning of what we see in the frame will constantly shift, since the transportable "reality" that photographs produce continually changes character with respect to the conditions in which that reality is read.

Here we come across an insurmountable limit to colonial discourse analysis, and the specific limit, in our case, is made possible by the medium specificity of photography itself. We cannot pursue a Saidian-derived methodology of reading colonial photographs, because the phenomenology of the photographic image prevents us from doing so in good faith. The "posthumous shock" that the camera gives to the historical moment preserved in the colonial archive undoes the fixity of that archive's narratives about the "native." If the rhetoric of photography is such that we are persuaded by it at some unconscious level, then the forms of specific persuasions are not predetermined. Put simply, photography can just as easily fail as succeed when pressed into the service of a particular ideological agenda. This is because photographs inevitably record more than the photographer's intention; certain details and contingencies recorded by the camera and yet unseen in their own time can either buttress or undo the aims of any project that mobilizes photography.[18] In spite of photography's use as one technology among others of colonial control and discipline, it is a medium that itself resists control. This has been the case since its inception; the modern proliferation of increasingly mobile and "uncontrollable" digital photography is simply a corollary to this fundamental phenomenological aspect of the medium.

This aspect of photography is paradoxical, since it hinges on a play of the visible and the invisible: certain details in photographs become legible only under certain historical conditions. On the one hand, the photograph shows too much, in fact more than we can see, and by that same logic, something we cannot apprehend is inevitably present in every photograph, something beyond the reach of our sight, bound as we are to the horizon of our own present perceptions. Walter Benjamin referred to this dimension of visuality as the "optical unconscious," and no doubt certain details make themselves manifest to the camera lens in a way that the naked eye is incapable of seeing. As Benjamin reminds us, the camera does not necessarily render the contents of such an unconscious visible (though it might); rather, it allows us to conceive of such a zone in the same way that psychoanalysis allowed us to conceive of the instinctual unconscious.[19] Two interrelated implications are present here: objects in the world necessarily give rise to concepts,[20] and the transformations in perceptual apparatus that are indexed by visual technologies such as photography necessarily transform the conceptual apparatus. In addition, Benjamin's use of the term *unconscious* signals that all may not be as it appears to the consciousness that receives the photographic image. Even as images began to proliferate faster and farther over the course of the nineteenth century, the visible was not necessarily the same as the fully manifested. It is not that we must simply await the historical manifestation of what remains invisible now or that with greater clarity (new instruments, new stances) we can access what remains invisible, but rather, like the unconscious itself, an absolute otherness exists at the heart of the visible itself, an otherness to which photography alerts us. Maurice Merleau-Ponty, in a fragment to his posthumously published book, *The Visible and the Invisible,* puts it best in his discussion of touch: "The untouchable is not a touchable that happens to be inaccessible; the unconscious is not a representation that happens to be inaccessible. The negative here is not a *positive that is elsewhere* (something transcendent). It is a true negative."[21] So if photography allows us to make visible the infinitely small steps involved in the flap of a bird's wing, such a visibility only points to a field of the heretofore unknown, invisible, and unconscious.[22]

The senses constantly come up against their limits, and the invention of photography showed, retrospectively and sometimes triumphantly, the "poverty" of vision that predated it. But the senses may also inhibit perception itself. As the inventor of the unconscious argues in *Beyond the Pleasure Principle,* blocking stimuli is as important to the human sensorium as allowing stimuli to penetrate. Here, Sigmund Freud's unease with phenomenological understandings of consciousness is worth considering. In other words, if perception is excentric—the senses extend outward toward the world—then a reverse tendency simultaneously occurs in which consciousness serves as a kind of armor against, rather than an entry point for, the world. If, as one phenomenological axiom would have it, our being in the world is commensurate with our being datives for the ways in which the world manifests itself to us, then this capacity to arm ourselves against the world challenges the founding assumptions of the phenomenological understandings of the self. Insofar as it extends sense perception, the camera, I argue, encompasses both aspects of consciousness: it functions both as a sensory prosthetic and as an armor against the world.

While the camera-as-prosthesis extends sight, the means of arranging the scene necessarily relies upon previous habits of looking. In addition to our historical positioning, the *form* of the composition, too, can serve to block out aspects of the scene even as it presents it. Chapter 3 details the picturesque aesthetic as one aesthetic form that serves as a kind of armor against the world it seeks to sense. There, to make sense of the world means necessarily to keep certain elements from becoming available to sensation. Aesthetic forms must restrict the presencing of objects in the world in order to make these objects manifest. In that respect, aesthetic forms are similar to the phenomenological understanding of habit. Habit is critical to the business of perception, because it is what allows us to filter out objects from consciousness in order to get through the day; if every object were subjected to our attention we could never move forward. Habit straddles the boundary between sensation and judgment. Edmund Husserl, while insisting that one of the aims of phenomenology is to recognize our own habits as habits and therefore see the world afresh, provides a subtle account of the work that habits perform for us:

> If, in an act of judgment, I decide for the first time in favour of a being and a being-thus, the fleeting act passes; but from now on *I am abidingly the Ego who is thus and so decided,* "I am of this conviction." That, however, does not signify merely that I remember the act or can remember it later. This I can do, even if meanwhile I have "given up" my conviction. . . . As long as it is accepted by me, I can "return" to it repeatedly, and repeatedly find it as mine, habitually my own opinion or, correlatively, find myself as the Ego who *is* convinced, who, as the persisting ego, is determined by this abiding *habitus* or state.[23]

The acquiring of habit, although indispensible, necessarily entails, for Husserl, a continual reaffirmation and recognition of the newly habituated self, which is the same as recognizing a familiar judgment as one's own. Like aesthetic forms, habits can be cultivated, improvised upon, assumed, made invisible, and be subjected to scrutiny.

If Husserl's example of habit is the judgment, Merleau-Ponty reminds us that judgments, intellection, making sense, are all matters of the body, particularly where habit is concerned:

> It is the body which understands in the acquisition of habit. This way of putting it will appear absurd, if understanding is subsuming a sense datum under an idea, and if the body is as an object. But the phenomenon of habit is just what prompts us to revise our notion of "understand" and our notion of the body. To understand is to experience the harmony between what we aim at and what is given, between the intention and the performance—and the body is our anchorage in a world.[24]

The body is the pivot between sensation and intellection; we learn by doing and responding, and the acquisition of skills and knowledge is a bodily phenomenon. Judgment and sensation are already conjoined in the originary sense of the Greek word *aisthēsis.* We must recall that the original meaning of *aisthēsis* refers not to a rarified discourse on art but rather to "sensation," "perception," and "feeling." In its history, already checkered in the Greek sources, *aisthēsis* refers not only to the senses of sight, smell, hearing, and touch but also to affects such as pleasure, pain, desire, fear, and so forth.[25] *Aisthēsis* refers first and foremost to the effects of the world striking our senses, including the feelings evoked by such stimuli. Aesthetic form, then, is the process by which one makes sense, habitually, of worldly stimuli; it is not a rarefied term referring to a realm that hovers above politics and the crude, primitively material world. Rather, aesthetic form, because it arranges the world into sense, necessarily has its shielding aspect, in the same way that habit does. That is, aesthetic forms allow permeability between the sensing subject and the world, but in this traffic between things and thoughts, perceptions and conceptions, the material and the immaterial, certain elements must be filtered out. The terms under which aesthetic forms perform this kind of shielding and filtering—however inevitable and necessary—are places where politics enters into the business of sensing and making sense of the world.

Attachment and the Past

Figure I.3, a photograph by Samuel Bourne, taken in the 1860s, shows an Englishman contemplating the famous memorial well at Cawnpore, which was, just a few years earlier, the sight of bloodshed. In June 1857, at the height of the Sepoy Revolt and after about a month of constant siege, Nana Sahib, the local Indian leader and rebel, promised the British in Cawnpore safe passage to Allahabad. As they began to make their way onto the boats that would take them down the river and away from Cawnpore, Nana Sahib called out the order for their massacre, and the men, women, and children were attacked. All of the men were killed on the riverbank, which would become known as "the slaughter ghat" or "massacre ghat" in imperial memory, and the remaining one hundred to two hundred women and children (the number varies according to source) were imprisoned in a small empty house. On July 17, Nana Sahib's men dragged out both the living and the dead from the house, stripped them of all possessions including clothing, and pushed them into a nearby well.[26] This is the spot on which Baron Marochetti's monument was erected soon after the Sepoys were defeated in 1858 and upon which the figure in Bourne's photograph casts a melancholy gaze. The scale of the small figure in comparison to the significant pictorial space taken up by the memorial garden and the distant monument accentuates the enormity of the loss that surrounds the living. George Trevelyan, in his 1866 account of the revolt, writes of the monument, "It is the very place itself where the act was accomplished. . . . There, at least, in the November evening, an Englishman may stand with bare head, and, under the canopy of heaven, breathe a silent petition for grace to do in his generation some small thing towards the conciliation of races estranged by a terrible memory."[27] If only it had been simply memory that continued to estrange the Anglo-Indians and the Indians. And yet, in spite of Trevelyan's liberal pleas, which cannot touch on the material causes of the continued enmity between colonizer and colonized, he astutely notes the importance of memory in maintaining such divisions. In fact, the persistence of memory itself (which photography aids) lent an uneasy calm to the Raj after the Sepoy Revolt. The memorial well and garden at Cawnpore quickly became a fixture on tours of India, and the scene circulated in the form of postcards and albumen prints that one could purchase and add to his or her own private photographic collection.

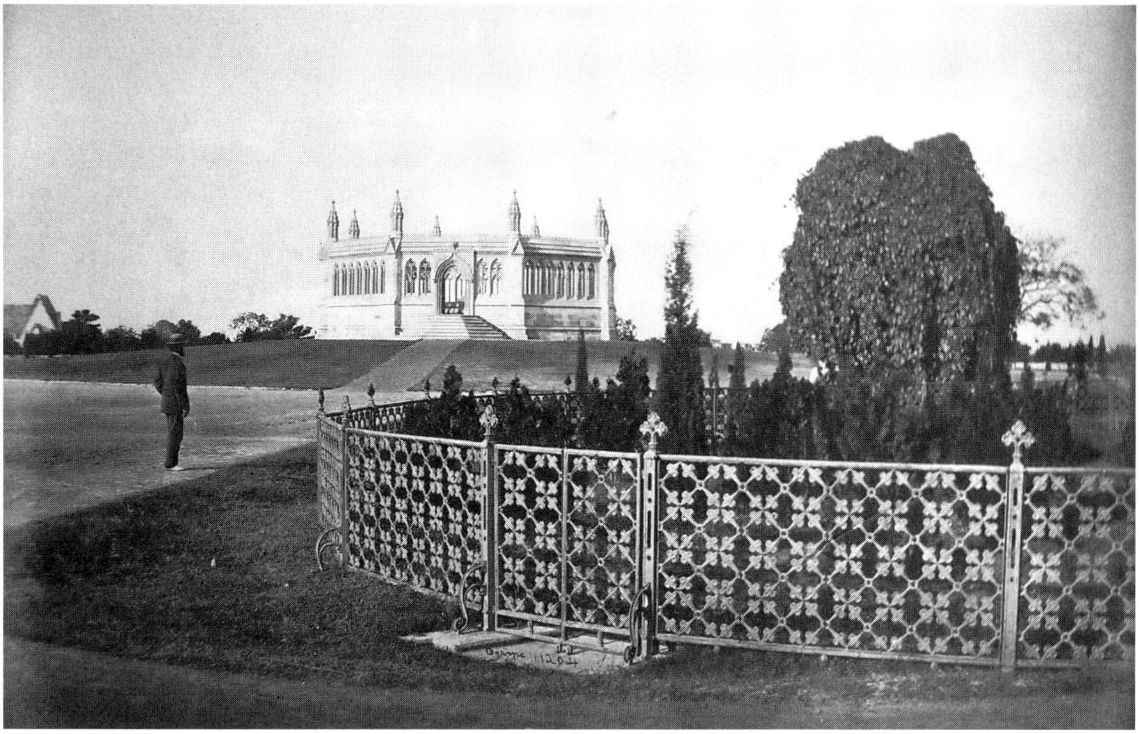

Figure I.3. Samuel Bourne, memorial well at Cawnpore, 1860s. The Alkazi Collection of Photography.

Forty-three years after the Sepoy Revolt, the American photojournalist and entrepreneur James Ricalton published a guidebook to India, titled *India through the Stereoscope: A Journey through Hindustan* (1900), printed in both New York and London and complete with a box of one hundred pairs of stereoscopic photographs taken by Ricalton himself (scope sold separately). These paired stereoscopic views are numbered as one hundred chapters, or "viewing positions," and Ricalton provides touristic historical and architectural details corresponding to each scene. In spite of the intervening forty-three years, the guidebook continues in the vein of post-1857 British tours of India, taking in the major sights of the Sepoy Revolt: the Cawnpore massacre ghat by the river, the memorial well and garden, various memorials in Lucknow, sights associated with particular battles in and around Delhi. Although Ricalton was an outsider to the cultural politics of the Raj, the inclusion of such an abundance of material on "Mutiny memorials" in this American's stereoscopic tour through India is a testament to the enduring and well-known appeal of the pilgrimages to the sites of the Sepoy Revolt, which by 1900 had become standard stops on British tourist circuits through India.[28] These sights of bloody battles—centered around Delhi, Cawnpore, and Lucknow—are interspersed with scenes such as position 79: "Your money's worth of juicy fruit, at a stand on Chandni

Chouk [Silver Street], Delhi," and in between an elegiac entry on the Cawnpore memorial well and the "Bailie Gate from east, torn by mutineers' guns during siege; where rescuers entered Lucknow," we find position 62: "Industrious dhobies [washermen] at work in river, west from Lucknow," complete with caste information on *dhobies* and the kind of soap they used for washing clothes. As a successful entrepreneur (he had previously published *Stereoscopic Tour through China*) who knew that the book would find its largest commercial market in England, Ricalton seamlessly assimilates the peculiar combination of the touristic pleasures that India afforded the English: descriptions of the colonial ethnographic and landscape picturesque side by side with sweet melancholic reflections on Anglo-Indian death. Much of the text in Ricalton's guidebook paraphrases passages from the more famous British guidebook *Handbook for Travellers in India, Burma, and Ceylon,* printed by the firm of John Murray but without the stereoscopic photographs that were Ricalton's specialty. The first edition of Murray's handbook appeared in 1858, soon after the revolt, and it continued to be updated and released into the 1970s. Tourist handbooks dwell on all kinds of traces of the 1857 war: bullet scars in the walls of churches and British cantonment areas, tombstones of English people killed in the war, bedrooms where certain people's blood was spilled, now peaceful and nondescript sites (such as a riverbank) that were once scenes of "native" betrayal. The obsession with sights of the Sepoy Revolt in the Murray guidebooks began to wane only in the 1940s, as the empire itself waned.

Ian Baucom, in an insightful reading of this melancholic imperial obsession with loss and death, which animates so many aesthetic projects in colonial India, notes that Murray's handbook, in its 1924 edition, exhorts the traveler

> [to] think, *thankfully and proudly,* of the events and deeds of that summer of 1857:
> Ever the labour of fifty that had to be done by five
> Ever the marvel among us that one should be left alive,
> Ever the days with its traitorous death from its loopholes around,
> Ever the night with its coffinless corpses to be laid in the ground.
> Heat like the mouth of a Hell, or a deluge of cataract skies,
> Stench of old offal decaying, and infinite torment of flies.[29]

One must remain thankful for coffinless corpses, the torment of flies, and the stench of old offal decaying, because, as Baucom notes, the English traveler is asked to be thankful for the war itself. The war, including its costs, secures the narrative of native betrayal so central to the continuation of the Raj, and the Mutiny memorials—whose postcard images continued to circulate into the twentieth century (see Figures I.4 and I.5, Plates 1–3)—simultaneously comfort the colonizers and become reminders to Indian subjects of the imperial wrath that hovers over peacetime as a threatening potentiality. The Mutiny memorial preserves the threat of what Baron von Clausewitz called "Absolute War" (the disruption of peacetime, the deployment of force) even in the midst of peacetime, which Clausewitz called "Real War," since "peacetime" is simply the ambiguous suspension of the technologies of Absolute War. So the English traveler must be grateful for these enduring reminders of death, because they are the very ground of attachment and entitlement to the subcontinent, the very proof of the gallantry of English victimhood. Baucom's reading of the Mutiny memorial's consecration in the imperial imaginary demonstrates how death was a form of occupation that had to be reproduced and made continuously present, rather than being avoided or its memory properly overcome.[30]

Like the act of judgment as explained by Husserl, the repetition of visits to Mutiny sites and the reproduction of their images provide opportunities to return to one's sedimented habits of judgment and to reinforce the attachment to familiar affects and to the familiarity of one's own self. Rudyard Kipling's tales consistently return to the melancholic theme of dying in India,[31] George Trevelyan's magisterial account of the revolt, *Cawnpore,* is haunted by it, and Flora Annie Steel, whose "mutiny novel," *On the Face of the Waters,* has become a canonical text on the revolt, circles around the scene of Anglo-Indian death. An 1884 *Calcutta Review* article comments comically on such an obsession. In a review of William Trego Webb's poetry, the reviewer writes:

Figure I.4. Postcard of memorial well at Cawnpore, early twentieth century.

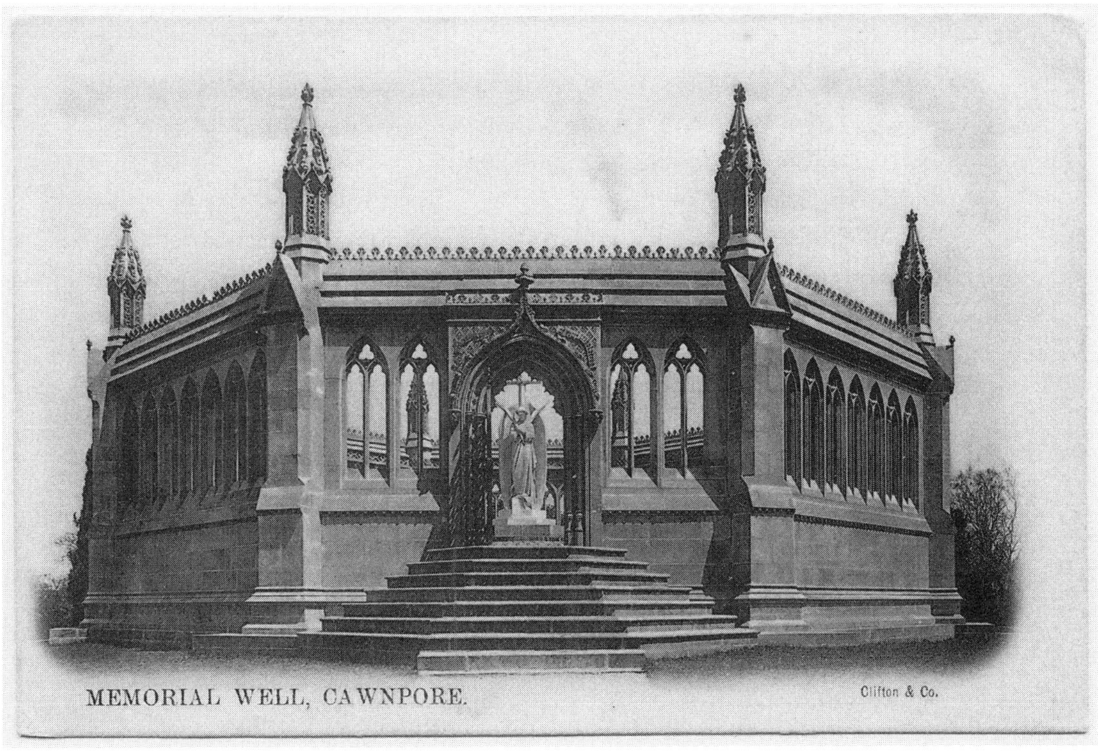

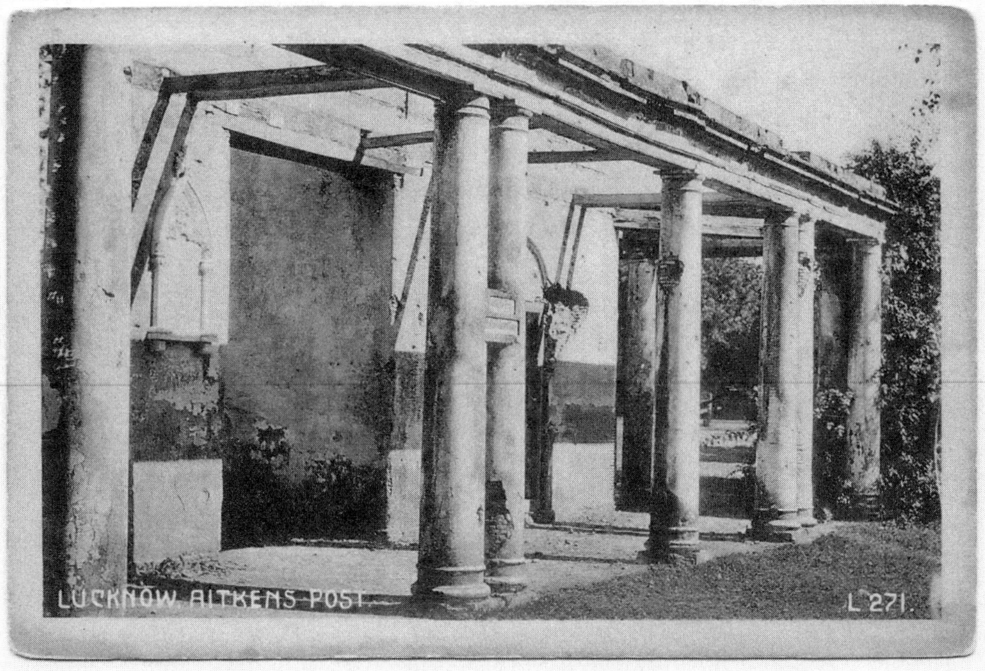

Figure I.5. The residency at Lucknow where the English were under siege. Postcard, early twentieth century.

> As gathered from his verses the career of an Anglo-Indian is a dead round of uninspiring work, carried on under a continual heart-ache for the Homeland, tempered by the fierce excitement of mosquito hunting, and by an endless conflict with indolent punkah-wallahs [fan bearers], and closing dismally in that dreariest of resting places, a Calcutta cemetery. We wish Mr. Webb had been able to keep up his strain of happy banter in treating of the exiled European, instead of falling at once into the dolefullest of "blues." Here are a few of the titles of "Lyrics," relating to European life in India:—"Indian Cemeteries," "The Landslip," "In Memoriam, Lord Mayo," "A Himalayan Cemetery," "The Song of Death," "The Memorial Well and Gardens, Cawnpore," "Baby's Grave," &c. This dismal list will suffice to show how Mr. Webb's gaiety deserts him when he leaves punkah-wallahs, pariah-dogs, and mosquitos, and comes to sing of his own countrymen in India. We should have been grateful to Mr. Webb if he could have done anything to lift from our dull lives the depressing weight of seriousness that is over them.[32]

The reviewer faults the would-be poet for being too true to dull Anglo-Indian lives that already need the depressing weight of seriousness lifted from them. These were lonely wasted lives, in their accounts, often spent recovering from

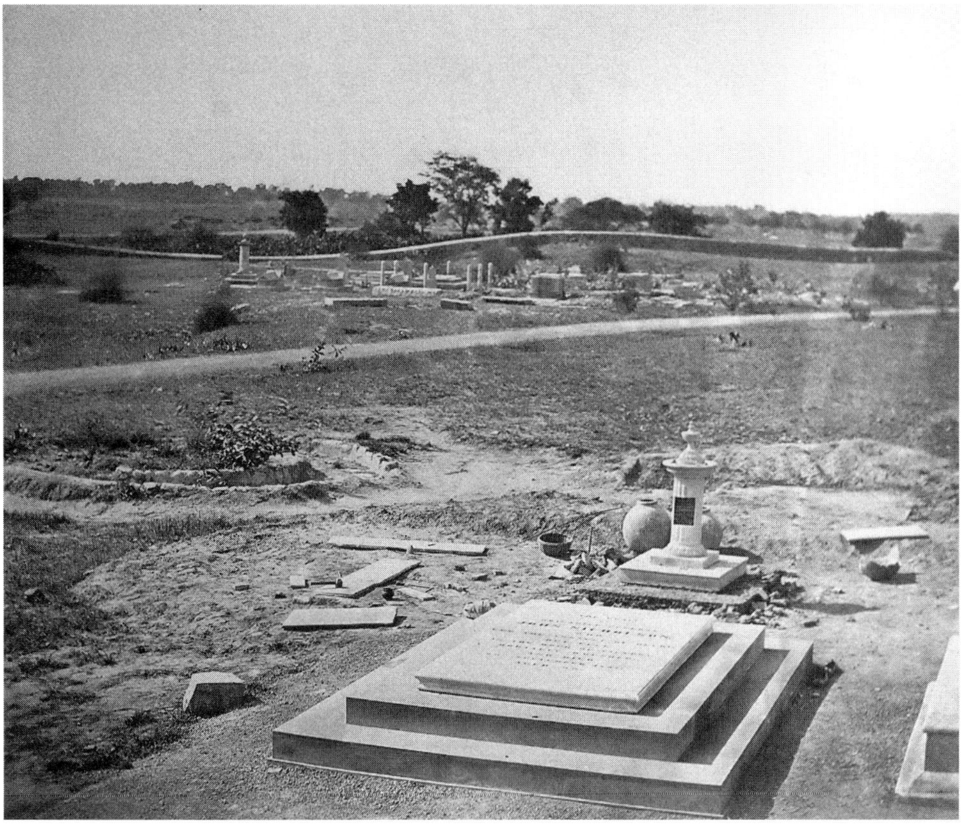

Figure I.6. Felice Beato, *General Nicholson's Tomb, View of Cemetery in Delhi,* 1858. The hydrant-shaped tombstone just behind Nicholson's grave is for a girl named Jessy Eleanor Blewitt (age three years, ten months). The Alkazi Collection of Photography.

ill health in thankless and depressing conditions. If Anglo-Indian death marks loss, then the wasted Anglo-Indian life, too, is a kind of loss. This structure of feeling, which secures attachment to the subcontinent by means of loss and traverses literature, historiography, personal memoirs, parliamentary debates, and newspapers, also sets the tone for Indian colonial photography.

Hence the importance of 1857 for this early period of photography in India, whether produced by Anglo-Indians, English visitors, or local photographers such as Lala Deen Dayal. For the Anglo-Indians, mere presence in India implied nostalgia for home, and yet the losses suffered in India gave rise to an intensely wounded attachment to it. Indians, on the other hand, witnessed the princes of the last Mughal emperor killed by the British general William Hodson and the exile to Burma of the last emperor himself, Bahadur Shah Zafar (Figure I.11). The British were infamously ruthless in taking revenge for the violence of the mutineers, and one of the common forms of execution was

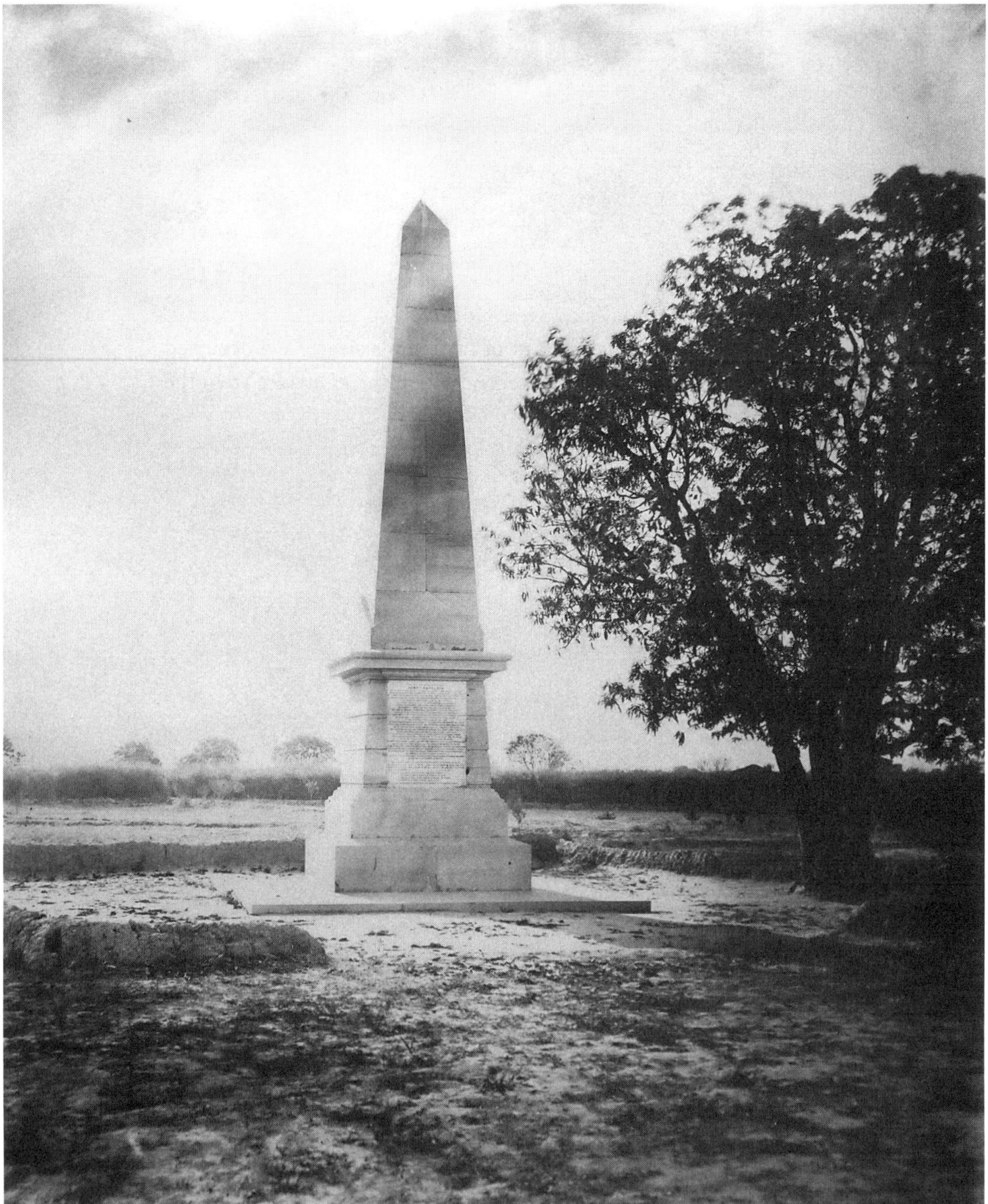

Figure I.7. *General Havelock's Tomb, between Cawnpore and Lucknow,* 1860s. Photographer unknown. The Alkazi Collection of Photography.

to tie the rebels to the mouths of cannons, and fire a cartridge through the bodies, blowing them up in front of their kinsfolk.[33] One soldier reports in his memoir: "[General] Havelock asked me if I 'knew how to blow a man from a gun?' Naturally this had not formed part of our *curriculum* at Woolwich; but I had no hesitation in answering in the affirmative," and the soldier gives a detailed report of singed body parts landing everywhere, of British soldiers covered from head to toe with "minute blackened particles" of Sepoys' flesh.[34] The monuments to British death were matched by the unmarked graves, including mass graves, of Indians. Figure I.9 shows one of the rebel batteries and the ditch where about six hundred bodies were buried. Colonel Francis Maude and John Sherer record, in their account of Lucknow's siege: "We occupied this post . . . [and] as I lay there, on the second night, the effluvium from the festering heap of bodies, though they were covered with earth, was so overpowering that I was totally unable to sleep."[35] The major cities involved in the conflict, including Delhi, were reduced to wastelands, and British officers did very little to curb the mass rapes of local women, believing the rumor (which

Figure I.8. Blowing up a Sepoy rebel with a cannon: "'Naturally This Had Not Formed Part of Our Curriculum at Woolwich.'" From *Memories of the Mutiny* (1894 edition).

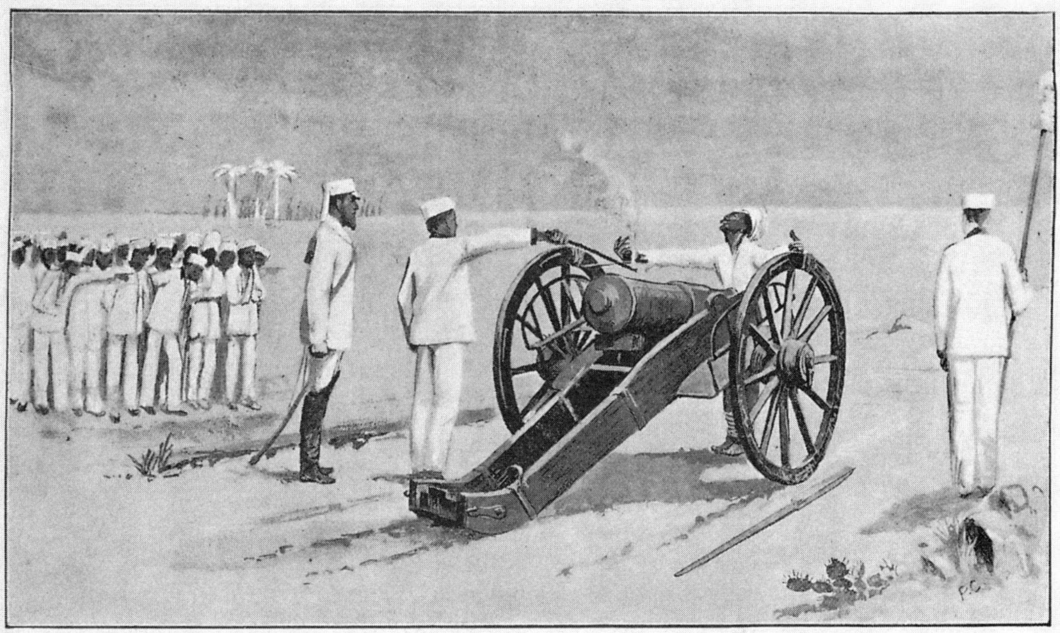

" NATURALLY THIS HAD NOT FORMED PART OF OUR CURRICULUM AT WOOLWICH."

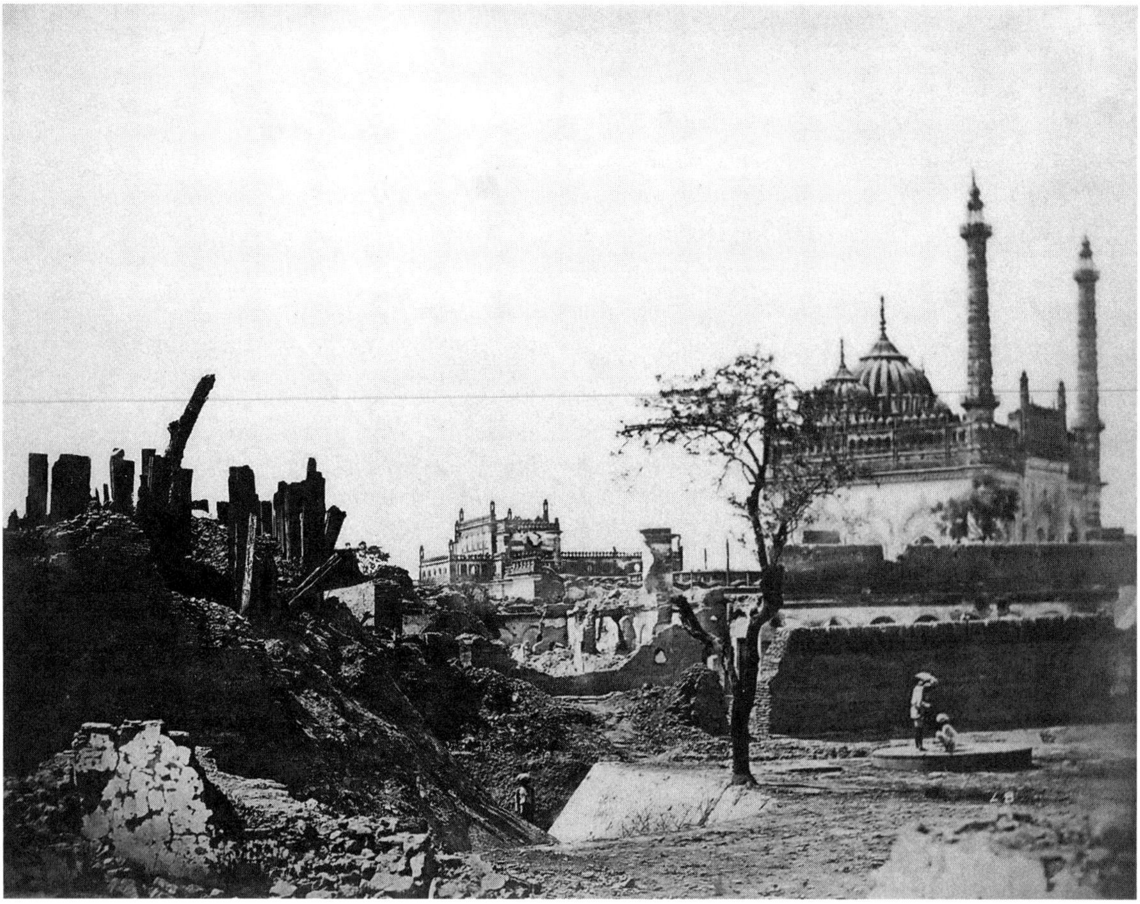

Figure I.9. Felice Beato, battery at Begum Kottee, showing the ditch that was a mass grave, on the left, 1858. The Alkazi Collection of Photography.

proved false) that mutineers had raped British women.[36] As Michael Taussig notes, in any arena in which racial difference plays a part, "it is this very animality that projected onto the racial Other . . . that is desired and mimicked as sadistic ritual, degradation, and ultimately in genocide against that Other."[37] The mimetic relays across this divide between self and other necessarily reproduce oneself in a phantasmatic relationship to the other, and the recognitions of one's own sadistic nature only compound the loss of a self that once was. *Afterimage of Empire* situates photography within a colonial genealogy of mimesis, here understood broadly as a means of bodily engagement with the other, and recognizes it as precondition to building a world. This understanding of mimesis as an originarily bodily phenomenon stems from Adorno and Benjamin's work, as well as Taussig's recent elaboration of it.[38] It emphasizes not only semblance and copying but also the sensory circuit of stimulus and response between the body and the world that is the precondition of all mimetic practices. If aesthetic form is a means of making sense of the world and a kind of habit and habitation, then in the scene of colonial photography in India, loss has necessarily underwritten aesthetic form.

This loss and its attendant nostalgia crystallize in the forms in which photographs have circulated as material objects: private collections composed of individual photographic albums, commercially produced albums, and photographs rendered into line drawings for newspapers. In colonial practice, private albums often included a combination of commissioned portraits and stock reprints of Indian scenes sold by commercial photographic studios, which abounded in Indian capitals such as Bombay, Madras, Calcutta, and Delhi, supplying prints in India as well as to studios in English cities. Some of the most lucrative items for commercial studios were set albums, beautifully bound and produced in multiples, with titles such as *Souvenir: The Viceregal Visit to Indore* and *Souvenirs of Bombay,* showing local architectural and landscape sights (see Plate 4). Such labeling reveals the nature of private photographic albums, themselves souvenirs of India, collections of lost moments in the form of images. The photograph as souvenir encapsulates the longing at the heart of colonial photography; like all souvenirs, the photograph seeks to authenticate experience, not by offering up the lost experience itself, which is lost forever, but by marking the distance from it. As Susan Stewart writes:

> The photograph as souvenir is a logical extension of the pressed flower, the preservation of an instant in time through a reduction of physical dimensions and a corresponding increase in significance supplied by means of narrative. The silence of the photograph, its promise of visual intimacy at the expense of other senses (its glossy surface reflecting us back and refusing us penetration), makes the eruption of that narrative, the telling of its story, all the more poignant. For the narrative of the photograph will itself become an object of nostalgia. Without marking, all ancestors become abstractions, losing their proper names; all family trips become the same trip—the formal garden, the waterfall, the picnic site, and the undifferentiated sea become attributes of every country.[39]

Like all souvenirs, the photograph is a defense against the inundation of the senses experienced by tourists everywhere, and it becomes a material anchor for a narrative about the past. This explains the photographic habits of tourism: if habit secures a certain map of the world, making it manageable and legible to the senses that would be overwhelmed otherwise, then the touristic photographic shots, sometimes snapped obsessively, become a kind of buffer against such an overload of signification and sensory stimulation.

As all photographic albums, including commercial ones, enter private time and the space of the bourgeois interior, the narratives that the owners

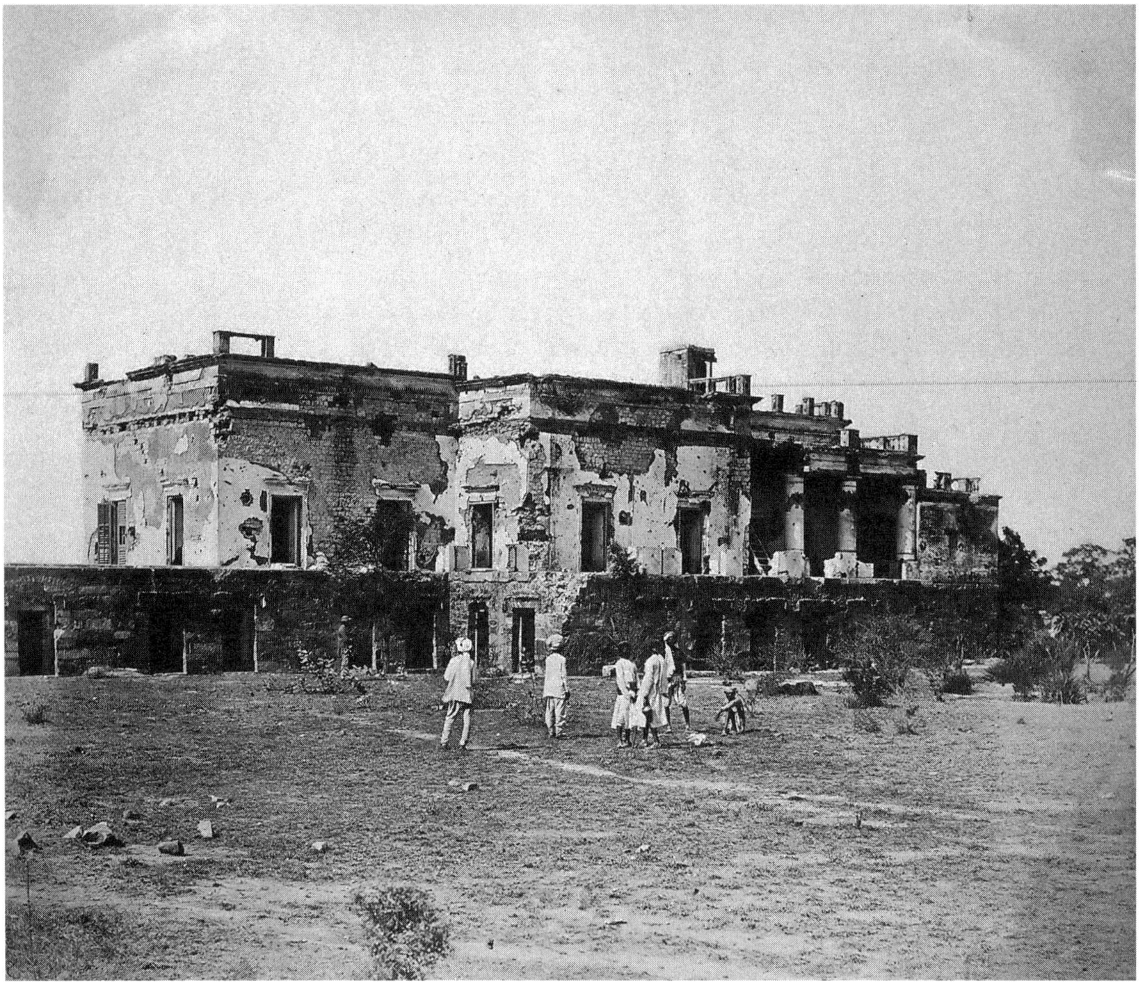

Figure I.10. Felice Beato, *The Ruins of "Hindoo Rao's House"* (a British post on the Delhi Ridge), 1858. Wellcome Library, London.

of these albums construct around the photographs—traces of which can be found in personal marginalia and revised captions—become central to the buttressing of past experience's authenticity. Part scrapbook, part photo album, something about privately owned albums resists reproduction in the same way that scrapbooks have affective charge only when the souvenirs they contain are "original"; the reproduction of a scrapbook is necessarily impoverished in comparison to the original.[40] So the nostalgia at issue in the private photographic collection that is replete with personal notation and assortments of mementos is nostalgia for origins as well as originality, working against the grain of the reproductive technologies that made the photographic collection possible in the first place. Yet without the photographs and their promise of

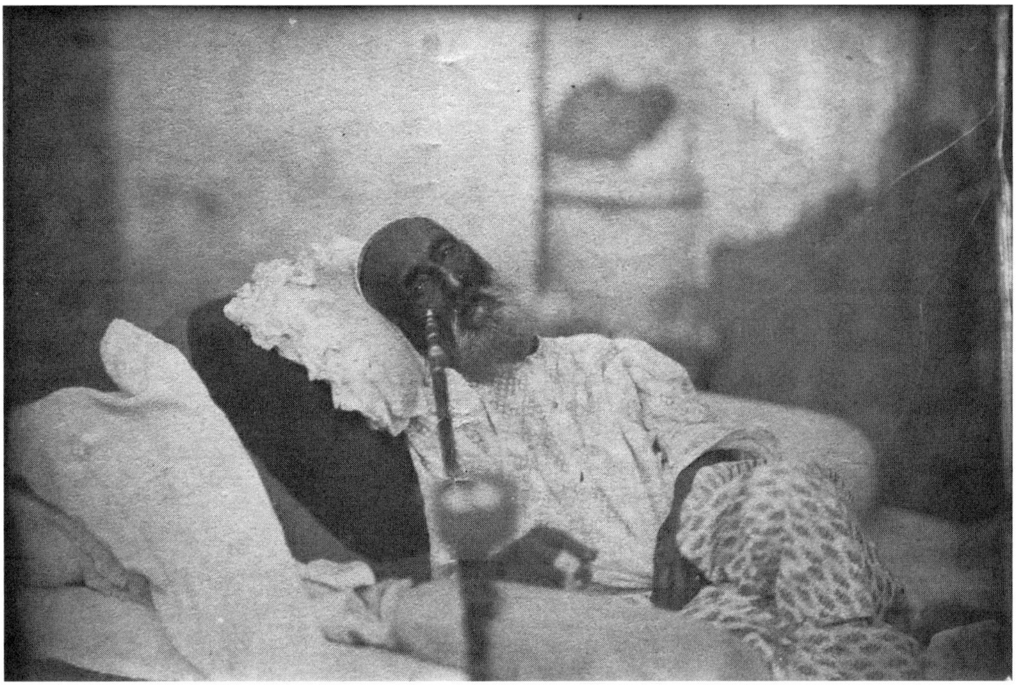

Figure I.11. Robert Tytler or Charles Shepherd [previously attributed to P. M. Egerton], *The Last Moghul Emperor, Bahadur Shah Zafar,* Delhi, May 1858. The Alkazi Collection of Photography.

presence, personal narratives of nostalgia cannot be anchored. At every moment, however, the personal specificity of the photographed threatens to become general; the photograph invokes a lost past and also the disappearing present, which can anchor past signification only temporarily.

As objects of desire, photographs point inevitably toward the past, toward their own origin, which becomes a site of longing and nostalgia, even if the origin is a national or personal wound, as in Felice Beato's photographs of Lucknow and Robert and Harriet Tytler's photographs of 1857 sites. Since at the heart of nostalgia's continuation is the renewal of loss, colonial photographs from India in the nineteenth century, the vast majority of which were produced after 1857, wed colonial melancholia to the structure of loss inherent in souvenirs and photographs in the first place. After the fall of Lucknow, its vibrant courtly culture of dancing courtesans, poets, cockfights, and musicians would become the object of nostalgic longing in India well into the twentieth century, when Bollywood cinema would reinvigorate such nostalgia through films set in courtly times, most notably in *Umrao Jaan,* released in 1981 and then remade in 2006. Plates 5 and 6, from Darogha Abbas Ali's album titled *Beauties of Lucknow* (1874), show the patina of distance that is the true object of nostalgic desire.[41] The truth claim of photography depends on its capture of a trace of an object or person existing in a particular time and place, that is, its indexical nature. It retains a trace of the object simultaneous with the representation of that object.[42] Yet what this index points to is not merely the existence of the lost past but also the distance in time between the privatized moment of the photograph's contemplation and its time of origin. This is the sustaining distance that discredits the present moment and, secondarily, raises alarm at its eventual passing. In the colonies not only is such nostalgia connected to the primary colonial claim to the land, but also the form of private introspection that photographic collections make possible turns nostalgia into the very mode of affective belonging to the colonial space. Regardless of the diverse genres of colonial photography that can be found across a single photographic album—portraiture, landscapes, ethnographic photographs, architectural views, war scenes—this nostalgic turn to the lost past and to the disappearing present subtends all photographic genres.

Such is the work of nostalgia at the level of the photographic medium. In nineteenth-century India, nostalgia also takes the following historically specific forms: a displacement from home, whether caused by moving away from it (as for Anglo-Indians) or caused by epistemic violence (as for Indians); a melancholy attachment to the losses of 1857; and the preservation of the scenes of fading ethnographic purity, as in the photographic examples I discussed earlier. In this book I have sought to analyze those genres of colonial photography in which the historical specificity of loss and nostalgia melds seamlessly with the nostalgia that underwrites photographic practices themselves. The interactions between the nature of the photographic medium and the imprint of history are the primary objects of my study. Hence, two of the following four chapters are devoted to war and memorial photography following the Sepoy Revolt, since this cataclysmic event brings together most forcefully the nature of photographic absence with personal and national loss. The picturesque aesthetic (chapter 3) in the colonies becomes indexical of nostalgia for home, and such nostalgia in turn transforms the nature of this aesthetic itself. Photographs of famine victims, as afterimages of Empire's splendor, register the quotidian violence and the losses sustained as a result of colonial extraction (chapter 4). Given that my genre selection follows from tracking the intersections between historical loss and the loss that subtends the phenomenology of photography, I do not explore topographical and cartographic photography, photography of imperial durbars, or architectural photography, and I touch on portraiture only briefly in chapter 3.[43] It is remarkable how quickly colonial photography sediments into such genres; just years after its invention these generic tendencies became apparent. Mikhail Bakhtin, for whom genres were "organs of memories,"[44] notes, "Always preserved in a genre are undying elements of the *archaic*," and such archaic elements can be preserved in a genre "only thanks to their constant *renewal,* which is to say, their contemporization."[45] This is to say that generic differences are themselves subject to the vicissitudes of history and are not "natural" forms.[46] Since genres exist not only in relation to other genres (which define them) but also in relation to history (which transforms and determines them), the narrative of sensing and meaning making offered by *Afterimage of Empire* is necessarily relevant to other colonial photographic genres. The particular organs of memory at issue in this book crystallize tendencies of perception, affect, and ideation that emerge out of the specificity of colonial arrangements of perception but also partake of the general transformation in perceptual apparatuses that photography makes possible globally.

Prostheses and Instruments

Thus far I have spoken of general transformations in perception and the arrival of photography in India, without considering the phenomenological scene of photographic practice itself. Keeping the foregoing discussion of the affective, historical, and aesthetic place of colonial photography in mind, we should find it worthwhile to analyze the scene of the photographer and camera and their corollary, the spectator and the photograph, in order to arrive at a more textured understanding of how exactly photography transforms the perceptual apparatus. I read the phenomenology of photography as a phenomenology of sense perception. Take, for example, Maurice Merleau-Ponty's famous scene of the blind man making his way through the world with a stick. This method of sensing the world becomes, over time, a habit, and the stick itself forces us to reconsider our commonsensical understanding of the body, the senses, and even habit. The body, which Merleau-Ponty dubbed "our anchorage in a world,"[47] figures as the ground for the traffic between sensing the world and making sense of it. The camera extends human perception, just as the blind man's stick does: "The blind man's stick has ceased to be an object for him, and is no longer perceived for itself; its point has become an area of sensitivity, extending the scope and active radius of touch, and providing a parallel to sight."[48] It is not only an extension of the body, whose materiality proves remarkably supple in its incorporation of objects in the world, but has also become, in effect, a sense organ. It simultaneously points, of course, to the man's blindness and is therefore not a replacement of sight but provides a parallel experience. Merleau-Ponty shows how bodily perception is not bound by the surface of the given body but often overreaches it: "To get used to a hat, a car or a stick is to be transplanted into them, or conversely, to incorporate them into the bulk of our own body. Habit expresses our power of dilating our being-in-the-world, or changing our existence by appropriating fresh instruments."[49] The woman who is aware of the feather on her hat and comports herself in such a way so as not to break it "feels where the feather is just as we feel where our hand is."[50] The nature of our body image is such that it morphs during the course of a day, and historical and technological transformations inevitably make possible new forms of perception and new spaces into which body image and bodily space may extend in unexpected ways. Moreover, not only do we appropriate objects as instruments in order to extend our perception, but also we transplant *ourselves* into such objects. The stick is both a point of sensitivity (a corollary to a sense organ) and an instrument at hand to be appropriated. This movement between transplanting ourselves into objects and making objects instrumental for our perceptions is left unaddressed by Merleau-Ponty, and we are to assume that these two aspects are indissociable. I suggest below that the camera mediates this movement between points of sensation and instruments, and this is the source of the phenomenological specificity of photography itself. For the time being, I would like to emphasize Merleau-Ponty's insight that our capacity to perceive the presence of objects in the world can place those objects in the service of such a capacity. The senses are radically open to the world and can overrun the limits imposed on them.

At first sight, the camera would seem to be another instance of the blind man's cane: it gives us the capacity to see differently, to extend our sight into heretofore unknown spaces, to note the presence of objects in a way unseen before, and so forth. But the camera also radically changes the terms of visibility itself because of the persuasive power of its images. The phenomenology of the photographic image must necessarily account for photography's persuasive power. As André Bazin notes, "In spite of any objections our critical spirit may offer, we are forced to accept as real the existence of the object in time and space. Photography enjoys a certain advantage in virtue of this transference of reality from the thing to its reproduction."[51] This gets to the heart of photography's medium specificity, namely, its reality effect. When looking at a photograph we register both the reality of the photograph being "just" a picture in the same instance in which we recognize the reality of the object photographed having been there and then. The materiality of the paper on which the photograph is printed does not interrupt the materiality that we read into the depicted object. Unlike language, which makes description of objects commutable, in other words, the photograph's reproduction makes the reality of the object itself commutable. To call this effect of photography its "rhetoric" is not to reduce photography to language but to note its power to "bear away our faith," as Bazin succinctly puts it. As a direct reflection of the material world in the form of light and shade, the photograph comes the closest to Henri Bergson's definition of "the image" in *Matter and Memory* (1896): "a certain existence which is more than that which the idealist calls a *representation*, but less than that which the idealist calls a *thing*—an existence placed half-way between the 'thing' and the 'representation.'"[52] This definition highlights the play of (in)visibility at the heart of photography's halfway position between the material world of things and the representations that become forms of knowing in an idealist sense, the sense that photography appeals to in its production of truth.

Recall that Merleau-Ponty refers to habit as the means by which we transplant ourselves into objects (turning them into points of sensation) and appropriate objects as instruments. The same object, in our case, the camera, can be both a sense organ of sorts and an instrument. At the pivot between these two aspects of photography lies its rhetorical power. It is photography's rhetoric, which includes its power to transport us, to lend an aura of truth to the object, to crystallize previously half-known notions, to bear away our faith, that explains the slippage between the two aspects of photography: camera-as-point-of-sensation and camera-as-instrument. The phrase "camera-as-instrument" is meant not to signal the intentions of the photographer, thereby locating the rhetorical power of the medium in a particular person (and, perhaps by extension, in a set of ideologies), but rather to refer to the rhetorical powers of the medium, which is an instrument at hand like the blind man's stick. Rhetoric, in this reading, marks the point where sensation meets intellection, perception becomes concept, and feeling crystallizes. People can obviously harness this rhetoric for their own ends, but its presence is made possible by the medium itself.

In addition, the photographer and the spectator of the photograph have different relationships to the medium and its rhetorical power. When considering the camera-as-point-of-sensation, we are primarily considering photography at the level of production. At this level of perception, movement, motion, and inhabitation of the world take place for the most part below the threshold of language and consciousness. The composition of the shot, however conscious or unconscious, is the result of certain habits, and habit strides the boundary between consciousness and the unconscious. For the photographer, the photograph is created as an extension of the senses and the body, by incorporating the camera into the bodily field. For the spectator of the photograph, however, incorporating the *photograph* into his or her bodily field means to be in thrall to photography's rhetorical effects, which come from the medium itself. Of course both the photographer and the spectator are captivated by photography's rhetoric, even if the point of production emphasizes sense and the point of reception emphasizes making sense.

History's Afterimages

What might this classic scene of phenomenological incorporation have to do with colonial representations? How does colonial history enable us to reconsider the phenomenology of the photographic image? An answer to these questions becomes possible if one takes seriously Walter Benjamin's critique of Henri Bergson, which arises in the course of his own speculations on the changes in the nature of modern experience:

> [Bergson] rejects any historical determination of memory. He thus manages to stay clear of that experience from which his own philosophy evolved, or, rather, in reaction to which it arose. It was the alienating, blinding experience of the age of large-scale industrialism. In shutting out this experience, the eye perceives a complementary experience—in the form of its spontaneous afterimage, as it were. Bergson's philosophy represents an attempt to specify this afterimage and fix it as a permanent record.[53]

Certainly the alienating, blinding experience of large-scale industrialism becomes possible only at the height of colonialism, as the commodity form (itself a play of the visible and invisible, as Marx has shown) becomes the basic unit of global political economy.[54] The play of blindness and insight that is the precondition of Bergson's philosophy reproduces itself in much European thought, including Benjamin's. If restoring an aspect of historical determination to Bergson's account of experience and memory is Benjamin's aim, then traces of such historical determination, however complex or overdetermined, must be borne in mind when considering the transformation of experience under modernity. After all, as Benjamin himself writes in another essay:

> Technology . . . is obviously not a purely scientific development. It is at the same time a historical one. . . . The questions that humanity brings to nature are in part conditioned by the level of production. This is the point at which positivism fails. In the development of technology, it was able to see only the progress of natural science, not the concomitant retrogression of society. Positivism overlooked the fact that this development was decisively conditioned by capitalism. . . . They [positivists] misunderstood the destructive character of this development because they were alienated from the destructive side of dialectics.[55]

Benjamin sounds a warning here, because to forget the historical determination of our phenomenological experiences is to reify our concepts and misunderstand the processes that make our experience possible. The camera, like all technology, is also a historical artifact, and this basic fact is not a mere addition to analysis; rather, this historical aspect is a catalyst whose implications become clear only when one analyzes distinct photographic practices in the context of their material histories. These histories condition the phenomenology of photography itself, not as mere additive facts, but as generative principles that help us to revise our understanding of photography itself.

So the colonial context is not merely incidental in photography's early history: documentary photography is produced, at its outset, as a documenting of imperial interests (photographer Felice Beato worked alongside Roger Fenton in the Crimean War before arriving in India); the picturesque aesthetic has a longer afterlife in the colonies than it does in Europe; memorial photography from the colonies finds tropes of expression unprecedented in its European forms. Early photography in India is marked by the same spirit of experimentation and wonder that it is marked by elsewhere in the nineteenth century, but with the key addition that its circulation in the colonial economy of signs freights it with meanings not entirely captured by photography's theorizing within the European frame. In *Afterimage of Empire* I demonstrate that not only can colonialism be understood through phenomenology and a consideration of perception but also that these categories themselves need to be read in light of colonial history. That photography transformed the nature of aesthetic experience has become a truism at least since Walter Benjamin's 1936 "Work of Art" essay, but what remains relatively underexplored is the potential, even within the work of Benjamin and the Frankfurt School, for rethinking the relation of bodily sensation to the formation of historically specific lifeworlds.

In this book I am primarily concerned with British colonialist photography, with the exception of the work of the Indian photographers Lala Deen Dayal, Darogha Abbas Ali, and Ahmed Ali Khan, all of whom I discuss briefly in chapter 3. Especially when speaking of colonial discourse, one has an understandable tendency to inquire into the possibility of narratives of resistance on the part of the colonized, in order that current discourse does not represent the colonized as wholly subjugated and victimized. While such a move is theoretically laudable, one must keep in mind several things, including the obvious: at certain moments in history, populations are in fact subjugated and victimized. The question of photography also necessarily takes into account that in the early days of the medium only the upper levels of the indigenous bourgeoisie could afford to commission photographs, and even then the forms and conventions of these photographs were often borrowed from the British aesthetic conventions. An identifiable Indian "counter-photography" does not exist in the first few decades of photographic practice. Here, I take my cue from Gayatri Chakravorty Spivak, who writes of a similar problematic in another context, the tradition of the nineteenth-century British novel:

> Attempts to construct "Third World Woman" as a signifier remind us that the hegemonic definition of literature is itself caught within the history of imperialism. A full literary reinscription cannot easily flourish in the imperialist fracture or discontinuity, covered over by an alien legal system masquerading as Law as such, an alien ideology established as only Truth, and a set of human sciences busy establishing the "native" as self-consolidating

> Other. . . . For a later period of imperialism—when the constituted colonial subject has firmly taken hold—straightforward experiments of comparison can be taken, say, between the functionally witless India of *Mrs. Dalloway,* on the one hand, and literary texts produced in India in the 1920s, on the other. But the first half of the nineteenth century resists questioning through literature or literary criticism in the narrow sense, because both are implicated in the project of producing Ariel. To reopen the fracture without succumbing to a nostalgia for lost origins, the literary critic must turn to the archives of imperial governance.[56]

Likewise, *early* photography in India is imbricated in specifically imperialist representational terrain and is in fact less flexible than literature as a system of representation, since its relatively pricey technology during this early period severely restricts its usage by most Indians. There was, however, a vibrant photographic tradition among the elite. In chapter 3 I develop a variegated notion of mimesis through which the colonial difference of nineteenth-century Indian photographers may be read, on the one hand, as successful repetitions-with-a-difference of European aesthetic traditions and, on the other hand, as local differences of aesthetic form that are commensurate with regional aesthetic differences that can also be traced in England and France themselves in the early days of photography. Aesthetic differences of nineteenth-century Indian photographers are marks of both the local and the particular, but they also index global transformations in perception; as such these local differences are not grounds for "contestation" or "resistance" to metropolitan aesthetic forms but rather evidence of an intricate relation between the local and the global, the particular and the universal. Contestation in the realm of photography would not take place until the twentieth century, with the concomitant rise of nationalist movements as well as a cheaper and more mobile photographic technology. In Christopher Pinney's study of Indian photography, it is instructive that his most thorough elaboration of what he calls *Camera Indica* is located in the twentieth century, and Kajri Jain's finely textured notion of the "vernacular" in Indian calendar art depends predominantly on twentieth-century calendar production.[57] If in the study of literature, the representational and epistemological orbit of the novel in the early nineteenth century is bound by imperialism and the literary critic must turn to the archives of imperial governance if she or he is to reopen the fracture of colonialism, then in the study of early photography uses of the camera in India are similarly overdetermined by imperialism, and to reopen the fracture in this instance would require an inquiry into local representational practices outside photography as well as the archives of imperial governance. The arguments presented in chapters 1 and 3 conduct such an inquiry by analyzing, in part, subaltern forms of communication one the one hand and elite Indian photographic practice on the other.

While attention to local forms of representation is necessary so that one does not end up reproducing the dominative aspects of colonial discourse, colonial discourse analysis, for all its insight, often arrives at a repeated set of conclusions that almost come to resemble traumatic repetition. The archive or particular instance may change, but the roles for the cast of characters seem foretold. Of course, history has already demonstrated these roles. Ann Stoler's recent work, which shows that colonial authority does not operate according to a predetermined grand plan but is better understood as a series of ad hoc, haphazard, and reactive policies, is a welcome corrective to some of the predictability of colonial discourse analysis.[58] Still, certain facts remain indisputable: colonialism subjugates, breaks up local forms of affiliation, constitutes epistemic ruptures within the local order of things, pillages raw materials, makes profit for the metropole. In a certain sense, as Benjamin would remind us, the real catastrophe is that the cast of rulers has not stopped winning. Colonial discourse analysis is most valuable when read as a reminder of this historical fact.

The present work is deeply indebted to this line of thinking, as I hope I have made clear. Where it departs from Saidian-derived readings is in its attempt to provide a narrative of colonial representations that is noniconophobic. Iconophobia takes the following form in postcolonial discourse: all colonial representation is to be mistrusted, and the work of analysis reveals the horror that the representation sought to cover up. This book aims to respond, in part, to a question recently posed by Rey Chow in her study of Chinese film: Given one's sympathy with anti-orientalist reading practices and the limits of such practices, "is it at all possible to conceive of a noniconophobic way of handling social and visual relationships?"[59] An iconophobic reading of colonial representations would reveal the import of these representations as revelatory of the cultural labor of domination, a meaning covered over by the representation but simultaneously made possible by the traces of the "real" within it. Syed Ahmed Khan's letter from London, in its paradoxical affirmation and negation of colonial forms of knowing, has already shown that such neat assumptions regarding the dominative aspects of colonial representations, though they may be propelled by theoretical inertia, often do not prove useful when analyzing the fragmentary and contradictory archives of colonialism.

Even in the practice of "reading against the grain," or what Said more poetically called "contrapuntal reading practice," the aim is to make visible, for example, the colonial underpinnings of Austen's and Conrad's "consolidated vision," that is, to pierce the surface of the representation in order to elucidate its depths, to distrust representation in order to provide an account of its supposedly actual underpinnings.[60] This form of critique that seeks to demythify and to present the real behind the representation relies on familiar Platonic notions of mimesis. It also assumes an Archimedean point outside the representation itself, when in fact both the representation at issue and its critique are made possible by the mimetic faculty, the capacity that underwrites worlding itself. The fact is that our categories of analysis by which we seek to apprehend our objects of study necessarily share the same mimetic ground with those objects. Instead of assuming a point outside the illusionistic realm of representation, my noniconophobic reading of colonial photography seeks to work against notions of surface and depth, by reading "surfaces" and "appearances" as themselves constitutive of critique. By analyzing the cultural work done by the photograph itself (at its very surface), we gain insight into the sensory conditions of possibility that render things visible, and these conditions do not preexist the appearance but are commensurate with it. Moreover, in colonial discourse analysis representation is curiously divorced from embodiment and is abstracted as pure conception, when in fact to be confronted with representation already assumes a bodily engagement with it; *Afterimage of Empire* concerns itself with the ways in which images penetrate bodily space and how bodies incorporate themselves into images. Hence, much more can be said about colonial photographs than their imbrication in colonial forms of violence. This is not to minimize that violence, which I take up explicitly in chapters 2 and 4, but to attempt an accounting of the conditions under which it becomes possible.

Since one of the guiding threads in this book is the question of persuasion—of how we can be so consummately persuaded by photographs—chapter 1, "Death and the Rhetoric of Photography: X Marks the Spot" takes up this question directly. From its inception, photography promised that the event depicted by the camera actually took place. That is, the image stood for an indexical trace of the object. Chapter 1 concerns the work of the post–Sepoy Revolt photographers John Dannenberg and Harriet Tytler and analyzes photographs that memorialize the death of important British army officers by showing the literal places where generals and officials were believed to have fallen dead or where British civilians were killed. The chapter also considers photographs taken of allegorical drawings rendered by anonymous artists seeking to memorialize the significant loss of British lives during the conflict. The contemporaneous descriptions of these photographed drawings insist on their photographic quality, thereby investing the drawings with the realist and evidential authority of the photograph. The concern with truth in this subgenre of documentary photography that seeks to make visible the very space of death is an occasion, in chapter 1, for unpacking the notion of the photographic index. Indexical notions of truth haunt memorial photography as well as drawings and sketches that often use photographic backgrounds, as in the work of John

Dannenberg. These photographic practices have to be read alongside two other contemporaneous phenomena: rumor and bodily and religious forms of contamination. Examining the circulation of rumors and notions of contagion on both sides of the colonial divide, I argue that photography as rhetoric has the logic of the circulation of rumor, and in the context of the Sepoy Revolt it secures the certainty of the friend/enemy divide. The photographic index, moreover, needs to be read as a kind of allegorical sign whose truth renews itself in light of the historical and material conditions in which it is read. This is the source of its power as the ground for truth: the photographic index cuts across varying representational registers, since it is simultaneously a material trace, an allegorical sign, and an empty pointer that in itself cannot provide the object that it promises.

In chapter 2, "Anaesthesis and Violence: A Colonial History of Shock," I situate the rhetoric of photography in the context of Benjamin's theory of shock and modern experience. This chapter analyzes documentary photography in the wake of the Sepoy Revolt of 1857 through a reading of the work of photographer Felice Beato, a commercial photographer who produced some of the first documentary photographs during the Crimean War and the aftermath of the Sepoy Revolt. Beato produced a series of photographs documenting the major sites of the Sepoy Revolt, sometimes exhuming corpses of the native dead in order to pose them among architectural ruins, all for the sake of presenting the immediacy of battle. Beato's projects in India seek, belatedly, to recapture time, even if that means restaging it. Such a project is congruent with the aims of much anthropological photography in India, which also strives to capture forms of life that colonialism/modernization gradually makes extinct. Both projects arise out of the epistemic and literal violence that lies at the heart of colonialism and, in a certain sense, are direct and indirect engagements with such violence. This chapter explores the implications of modernity's bodily shock effects in the colonial arena, where reassuring spectacles of the violence done to the other (the colonized in this case) mirror the perverse and numbing enjoyment in imagining one's own destruction. At stake in these early documentary photographs is the management of others through the same strategies that enable domination over one's own sensory existence.

The third chapter, "Armor and Aesthesis: The Picturesque in Difference," continues the concern with sensory management in the context of landscape photography. The chapter analyzes Samuel Bourne's photography alongside the work of the Indian photographers Deen Dayal, Abbas Ali, and Ahmed Ali Khan. All of the photographers, including Bourne, are contending with a shifting representational terrain, and their aesthetic choices have much to teach us about the differential nature of mimesis itself. Abbas Ali and Khan represent transitional aesthetic strategies insofar as they look to local tradition and

Mughal miniatures in their photographic practice, and Dayal is invested in assimilating the conventions of the picturesque. Their varying aesthetic impulses reveal the stress and pressure that signifying systems undergo at times of historical change. In the landscape photographs by Samuel Bourne, mimesis—as a reflection not only of the object but also of the feelings that the object has provoked—is inextricable from visual pleasure. The pleasure of the picturesque, rather than the terror of the sublime, converts difference into the familiar, the experiential into a recognizable image. Because the picturesque aesthetic in the colonies overlays the foreign with the familiar, I read this genre of photography as a subjective engagement with objective structures of colonial extraction. In this chapter I make the case that the picturesque aesthetic marks a modernizing point of view for which the conversion of experience into an image serves a compensatory function; the conversion of the foreign into the familiar takes place at the level of aesthetic form, and this form is at the same time a kind of armor, a second skin that enables and inhibits perception. Such a production of a second skin through aesthetic form occurs both at the level of composition and at the level of reception.

The fourth chapter, "Famine and the Reproduction of Affect: Pleas for Sympathy," focuses on photography in the context of the multiple famines across the Indian subcontinent in the late nineteenth century. Reading Adam Smith's eighteenth-century notion of sympathy in *The Theory of Moral Sentiments* through the nineteenth-century circulation of W. W. Hooper's famous photographs from the Madras famine of 1876–79 in conjunction with the various pleas for sympathy in the popular British and Indian press, I examine how sympathy as an affect enters the domain of technological reproducibility and the slippery nature of the photographic medium with respect to sympathetic feeling. Such pleas for sympathy continue to animate our own contemporary appeals to pity for the other. The sentiments that images of social suffering arouse, if understood through Smith's formulation of sympathy, reveal not only the deeper representational conundrums that all projects of "awareness raising" face with respect to their subjects but also the unpredictable nature of photography's own sympathetic mimesis.

That the formation of the senses is a political matter has been clear at least since Marx's remarks on the education of the senses. This book explores the politics of such formation; in order to do so, it deploys phenomenology itself like the blind man's stick, prodding a nearly invisible colonial terrain. The historical specificities of photography's phenomenology in colonial India are indispensable to my aims in this book. Since we have always lived in history, this project is necessarily historical, but history enters the frame as the set of elements that make meaning and sensation possible, rather than as a (historicist) chain of causes and effects. I am interested in tracking tendencies in colonial photography that reveal its imbrication in the aesthetic and political dimensions of the photographic medium and in examining the nature of sentient experience as constituted through the practice of photography. The readings that follow deliberately shuttle from historical fact to its philosophical implications, from forms of aesthetic expression to the sensory arrangements they presume, rather than offering an overarching historical narrative either of photographic practice in India or of the progression and development of its dominant aesthetic forms.[61] Thus, in a discussion of photography's rhetoric in chapter 1, the historically specific cases of rumors and threats of contagion are central to understanding the photographs that arise from the aftermath of the Sepoy Revolt; chapter 2 dwells on the effects of war and the lessons that photography's engagement with these effects can teach us; in chapter 3, history takes the form of interventions in the colonial landscape that render it picturesque—it is condensed in the picturesque aesthetic itself and in the colonially different reception of that same aesthetic for Indian photographers; chapter 4 ponders the manifestation of photographic affect in light of actually existing famines. These historical aspects—rumor, contagion, the picturesque, war, famine—are, as we will see, necessarily aspects of photography itself, since photographic practice is one process by which some people make sense of these specific historical experiences. Not only does *Afterimage of Empire* concern itself with the practices of making sense, but also it refers to "the composing sense," or the mimetic faculty, the capacity that underwrites the means by which experience becomes commutable, framed, and transmuted.

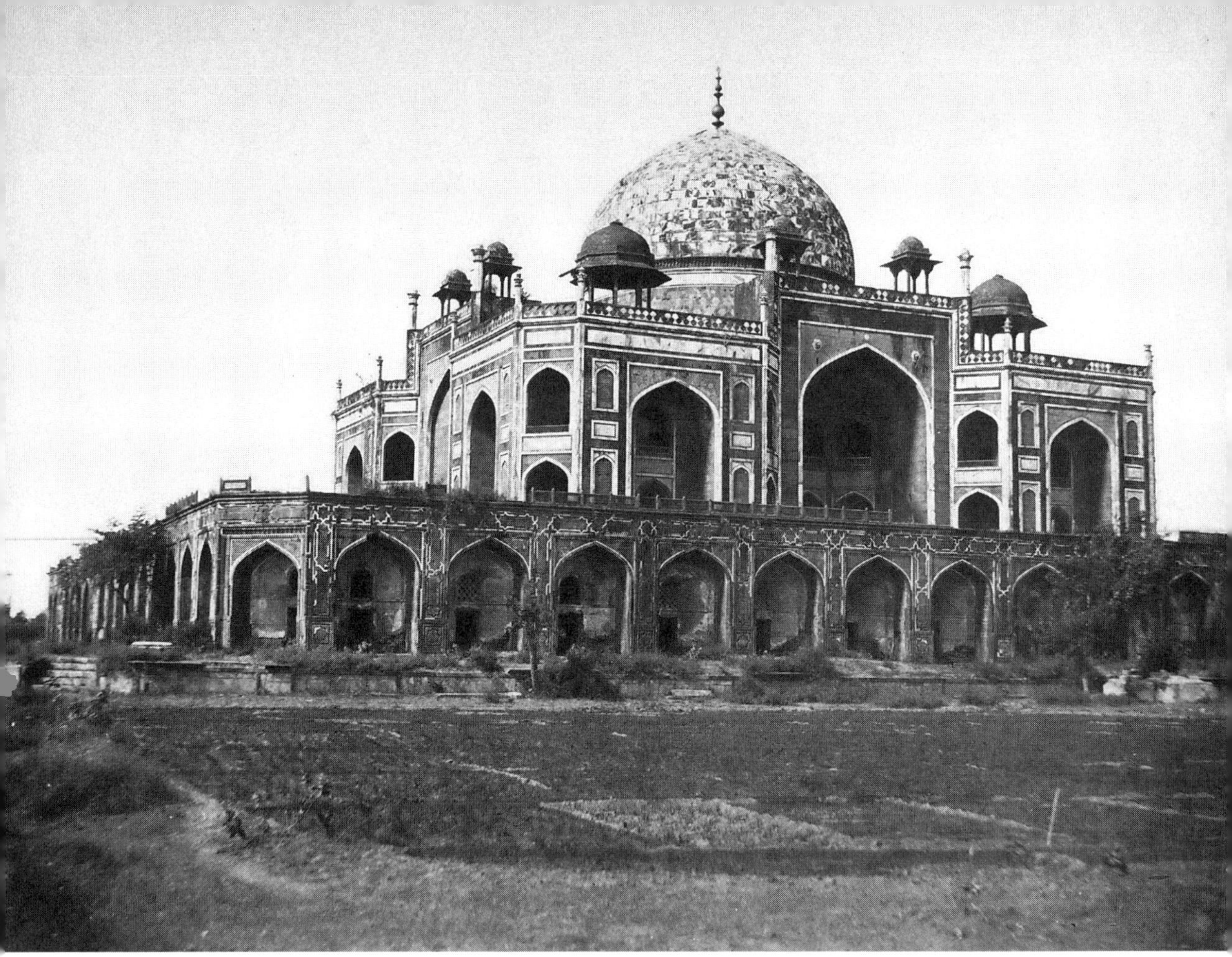

Figure 1.1. Robert and Harriet Tytler, *Huamaion's Tomb, Where the King Was Captured by Hodson,* Delhi, 1858. Copyright British Library Board.

ONE

Death and the Rhetoric of Photography
X Marks the Spot

> Like the photographic image, the playing of an old hit song or the reading of letters written long ago also conjures up anew a disintegrated unity. This ghost-like reality is *unredeemed*. It consists of elements in space whose configuration is so far from necessary that one could just as easily imagine a different organization of these elements. Those things once clung to us like our skin, and this is how property still clings to us today. Nothing of these contain us, and the photograph gathers fragments around a nothing.
>
> —Siegfried Kracauer, "Photography"

X Marks the Spot

Harriet Tytler, who, along with her husband, Robert, photographed many sites of the Sepoy Revolt, was born in India but, like many others, thought of herself as a foreigner to it. Yet as a small child ("a little over two years old"), when her mother was about to depart, leaving her in the care of her aunt and uncle, Tytler exclaimed to her mother, "Hum janta mamma chulla gia, chulla gia! [I know Mamma has gone away, has gone away]." It goes unexplained why this English child, who would grow up to give birth herself to another "foreign" child in 1857, in the thick of the battle at Delhi, would speak in Hindi to her mother. Tytler elaborates, "I recollect that scene [of parting] perfectly; no one could comfort me, till I sobbed and sobbed myself to sleep again. Strange, I have no recollection of their coming back."[1] The memoir was written years later, after more traumatic partings from her mother—once when Tytler is sent off to England for school and again when the mother must leave Tytler in India as she herself quits India for good. It seems Tytler connects the repeated childhood trauma of being abandoned with the spontaneous utterance of a "foreign" tongue. Her own children, incidentally, also take up Hindi as their first language ("Mamma burra durram hai," screams little Edith when the bathwater is too hot), along with a singularly aggressive attachment to their mother. For example, when traveling across war-torn Delhi in a cart during the Sepoy Revolt, Edith keeps fainting. Tytler devises a solution: "At last a bright idea entered into my head. It was a rather unique one, which was to scratch holes in my feet and tell her she must be my doctor and stop their bleeding. This process went on daily and for hours. No sooner did my wounds heal, when she used to make them bleed again for the simple pleasure of stopping the blood with my handkerchief. But it had the desired effect of amusing her for hours."[2] Earlier in the same paragraph, Tytler notes that the flies of Delhi "doubled and trebled from all the carcasses of animals and dead bodies lying about everywhere."[3] The startling passage about amusing her daughter Edith by allowing her repeatedly to make the mother's feet bleed and then stop the bleeding crystallizes the intimate relationship between trauma and play: both function by means of repetition. For Tytler, the deep-seated fear of becoming a cadaver, a carcass like the ones she sees along the road, takes the form of asserting her own body's living, bleeding, healing materiality and in turn the living activity of her own children.[4] The disavowal of the contamination of Englishness with Hindi, which one sees in the colonial insistence on being a *foreigner* to the colony, is of a piece with the repression of death's contamination of the living.

In this vein it is instructive to examine Harriet and Robert Tytler's photographs of post–Sepoy Revolt sites of conflict. For example, the photograph titled *Humaion's Tomb, Where the King Was Captured by Hodson* (Figure 1.1), simply shows the tomb itself, and the photograph of the slaughter ghat in Cawnpore shows an empty space by the river where British civilians lost their lives (Figure 1.2). In Christopher Pinney's reading of Robert and Harriet Tytler's photography, he notes that given the technomaterial limitations of photography in the 1850s, photographers could record events only belatedly: "The stage, long empty, and in many cases metaphorically darkened, refuses to release its evidence of the event."[5] Unlike Felice Beato's theatrical photography, the Tytlers' work asks us to find in these photographs "a living historicity" that would no longer be left to the imagination, according to Pinney, when "an increasingly mobile [photographic] technology would eventually permit this—indexically," which is to say that an increasingly mobile technology would be quicker to capture the traces of the object on film before the object passes on.[6] Pinney points to the promise of the photographic index, but can the brute literalism congealed in the concept of the index—a sign that is simultaneously a (material) trace of its referent—be taken at its face value? Must we be bound to the truth regime that the index-as-evidence constructs in order to be legible?

Put simply, the index refers to that semiotic category for which the relationship between the sign and the referent is physical, and it lends the sign evidence of the referent's existence.[7] Recent scholarship on the persistent conundrum of the index in photographic representation ranges from situating

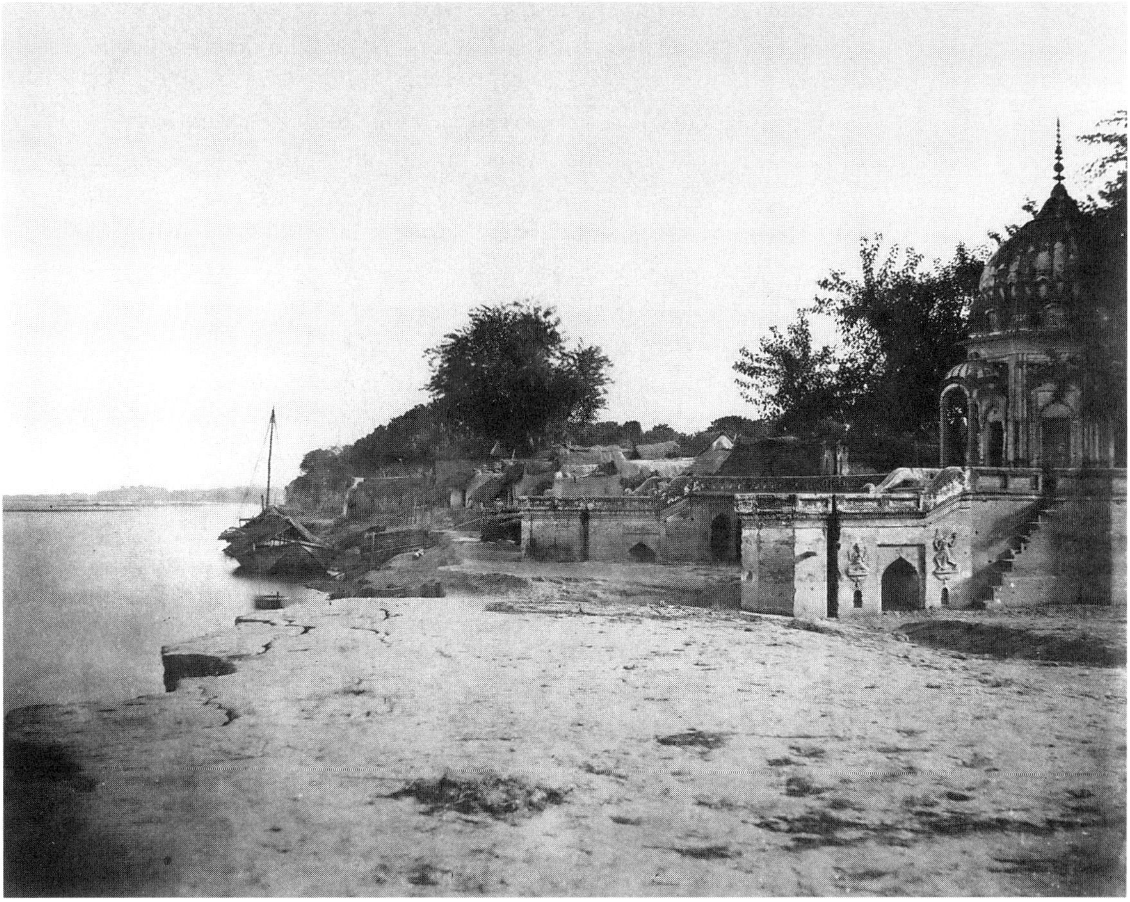

Figure 1.2. Robert and Harriet Tytler, the slaughter ghat in Cawnpore, 1858. The Alkazi Collection of Photography.

it as a deconstructive trace of absence-as-presence, through reading it as an intrusion of seemingly competing sign systems into each other, to debating about whether or not the index is a "false problem" unworthy of further analysis.[8] Revisiting the events following the Sepoy Revolt poses a different sort of dilemma: What does it mean to capture absence indexically? These historical events gave rise to a unique form of photographic practice, in which British visitors documented the empty spaces of the Sepoy Revolt's key battles or the blank spaces where certain loved ones had been killed. In the Tytlers' photograph of Humaion's tomb (Figure 1.1), the mise-en-scène is distorted and eccentric, giving far more space than would be necessary to show only the tomb itself. There is too much foreground, and the tomb is situated too far to the right. We certainly are being asked to imagine the event, as Pinney notes, rather than invited to see the event itself.[9] Hence, the photograph depicts an excessively blank foreground. Moreover, such seemingly "bad" composition practices (at least according to the dictates of the picturesque) are persistent in Sepoy Revolt photography. In the photograph of the slaughter ghat at Cawnpore, most of the image is taken up with a blank space of the ghat. These empty spaces contain their own indexical rhetoric; otherwise what would be the point in recording them? As Ulrich Baer writes in a another context of the photography of traumatic spaces, "Some events attain full meaning only in retrospect—or to use Freud's term, *nachträglich,* or belatedly," and such belated apprehension can either "facilitate or block remembering or forgetting."[10]

These photographs obviously have an X-marks-the-spot feel to them, as the captions make clear. Like a cataphatic mantra ("God is God is God is God . . ."), these photographs solicit our faith by inviting infinite scrutiny of the selfsame hallowed space. The spot itself, in all of its plenitude, is there for us to see. The photographs invite us to imagine the horrors that took place on that very spot. If, in the classically cataphatic utterance "God is God is God . . . ," the recognition that "God" is no more than an utterance I am sounding leads to a corollary doubt about the possibility of capturing God's being in language (or, to apophasis), then in these photographs, the beams of light that emanate from the "very spot itself" to form the photographic image also lead to a recognition of the primal loss of that spot itself. After all, what one can see is only an image of it.

I invoke cataphasis and apophasis because what concerns me in this chapter is the faith that the rhetoric of photography solicits. At the heart of this rhetoric lies the perennial problem of the photographic index. Although these photographs do not depict the violence that they are meant to invoke, they continue to bear an indexical relationship to the scenes of violence for several reasons. At the most straightforward level, these photographers found it necessary to go back to the very literal space of death in order to record the scene. Yet what they record is blankness, the void, or emptiness. In these photographs the object of the frame is absence itself, and so the images strive toward allegory in their depiction of loss, a shift in photographic representation necessitated, I will argue, as a result of the indexical quality of the X that marks the spot.

In the post–Sepoy Revolt photograph titled *The Diving Well, Kootub (Delhi),* for example, the Tytlers have highlighted a void that descends into murky depths (Figure 1.3). Even if the viewer does not know that in 1857 news circulated widely over the subcontinent and in London about the throwing of British women and children into a well in Cawnpore, this image seems ominous, representing threat, downfall, and death all in one frame. It represents, in photographic form, the psychic and historical conditions that led Tytler to digress seamlessly from a discussion of flies and rotting corpses in the Delhi landscape to a discussion of the entertainment she provided for her children. The photograph signals, in other words, the persistent threat of death in the midst

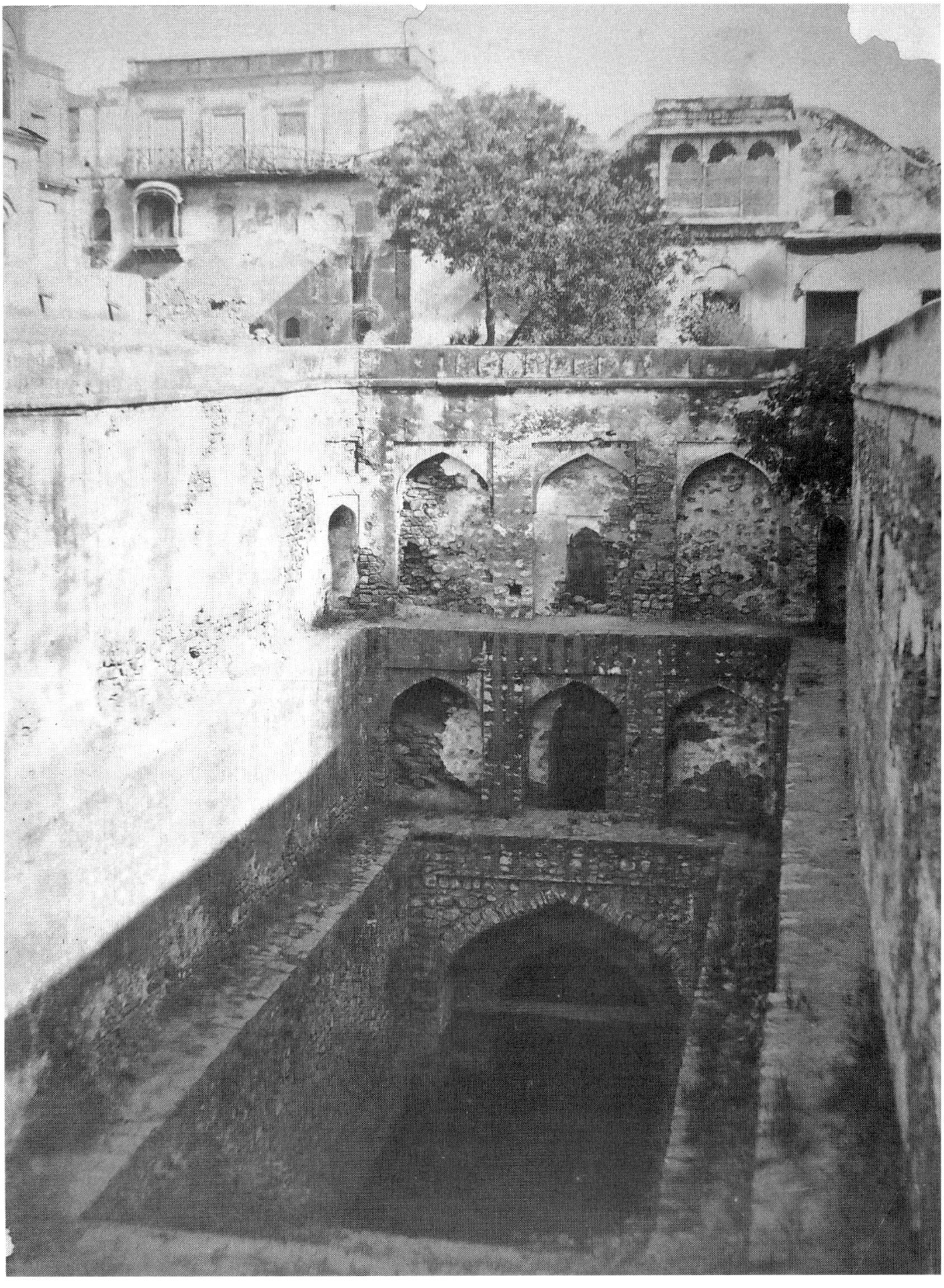

Figure 1.3. Robert and Harriet Tytler, *The Diving Well, Kootub, Delhi,* 1858. Copyright British Library Board, Photo 53/(13).

of living, the unavoidable contamination of life with death, and the anxiety about seeing oneself as a cadaver.[11]

These meanings emerge as much from the rhetorical nature of photography as from the literalism of the empty spaces of absence and loss. I invoke rhetoric here not only in the general sense, as an "art of persuasion," but in the more specific sense stemming from Cicero's designation of the three "offices" of the orator: to please, to move, to teach. These three duties, of course, find a close parallel with the functions of the work of art in the nineteenth century, at least as designated by the traditional discourse on aesthetics. Photographic practices emphasize one or more aspects of these offices, as we will see over the course of this book. The rhetoric of photography, which must rely on photography's indexical qualities, often threatens to undo the very terms on which the index strives to persuade. Through an analysis of a hybrid genre of photography that arose during the Sepoy Revolt—photographs of drawings whose background is taken from famous photographs of the revolt—I will explore in this chapter the unstable nature of photographic rhetoric. Rather than exploring how the index does or does not provide access to a certain truth, I am interested in the function of the photographic index, that kernel of photographic representation that is responsible for what André Bazin calls the photograph's "irrational power to bear away our faith."[12]

This kernel, the photographic index, lies at the heart of the intimacy among faith, irrationality, and objective scientific truth. One has to consider only two of the earliest applications of photography to see such intimacy at work: spirit photography on the one hand, and scientific photography on the other. Since both rely on the photographic index for their truth claims, this index occupies a borderland between reason and faith, certainty and the uncanny. Revealing spirit photography or "false photographs" (as old as photography itself) to be doctored compositions changes nothing about the rhetorical aim of such manipulations. The photographic index, in other words, can be rethought as a figure of rhetoric that serves to contaminate seemingly incommensurable domains: enchantment and disenchantment, faith and reason, certainty and doubt. The Sepoy Revolt, itself in part provoked by the threat of contamination (the famous rifles distributed to Sepoys allegedly greased with pig and cow fat), provides a confluence of historical events and their uncertain narration that sheds light on the porous boundaries between, for example, the photographable and the unknowable, the contagion of dirt and disease and the contagion of slippery signifiers. When photography is enlisted in the national and personal projects of preserving memory of the dead, the permeability of these boundaries comes more readily to the photograph's surface. The long memorializing process that followed the Sepoy Revolt entailed the construction of monuments to the British dead, the reconstruction of British neighborhoods, the photographing of the sites of the conflict, and the circulation of postcard drawings showing such famous sites. Many of the state-sponsored memorials made use of conventional symbolism, as in the memorial erected in Cawnpore marking the site of the well where British women and children were killed. But photography, perhaps better suited to private introspection than public monuments, shows a memorial practice remarkably different from the practices of officialdom.

In what follows, I will analyze the kinship between photographic rhetoric and other forms of signification, specifically allegory and rumor. The aim is to arrive at an understanding of the specificity of photographic meaning, of its unique form of making sense. Instead of turning to older forms such as Mughal miniatures, or even the Anglo-Indian genre of "company paintings" that proliferated in India in the late eighteenth and early nineteenth centuries, I turn to these more archaic forms of signification, because they allow a reading of aesthetic form that is not strictly formalist. That is, rather than tracking continuities and discontinuities of visual motifs and formal elements of composition in colonial photography in India, this chapter tracks the phenomenological makings of a new aesthesis that resituates some of these most archaic forms of representation.[13] Moreover, I turn to allegory and rumor as forms of signification contiguous with photography, because the historical sources and colonial photographic practices themselves point, as we will see, to these forms as critical modes of knowing and sensing in post-1857 India. What Mikhail Bakhtin argues in the case of genre—that archaic elements are renewed and regenerated with each iteration of the genre's repetition—is also true in the case of new forms of media: photography relies on the most archaic of forms, such as allegory and rumor, and contemporizes them by transforming them through the prism of its own rhetoric, which these archaic forms also inflect. So while allegory and rumor are obviously not specific to photographic practice—print culture, complete with its forms of reproducibility, has its own mechanisms for reinvigorating these forms—they nevertheless provide clues about the creation of photographic sense, in the functioning of this new organ of memory, if you will.[14]

Allegory

Listen to the following contribution to an 1892 edition of London's *Morning Post,* describing an album of photographs from the revolt:

> But what, save human sight, in immediate observation of the scenes reflected in the pictures can fully interpret the solemn pathos of the hieroglyphics of the writing on the wall in the room where Sir Hugh Wheeler lay . . . [Figure 1.4] or the ghastliness of the general view of his entrenchments with the human skeleton lying in the foreground and the

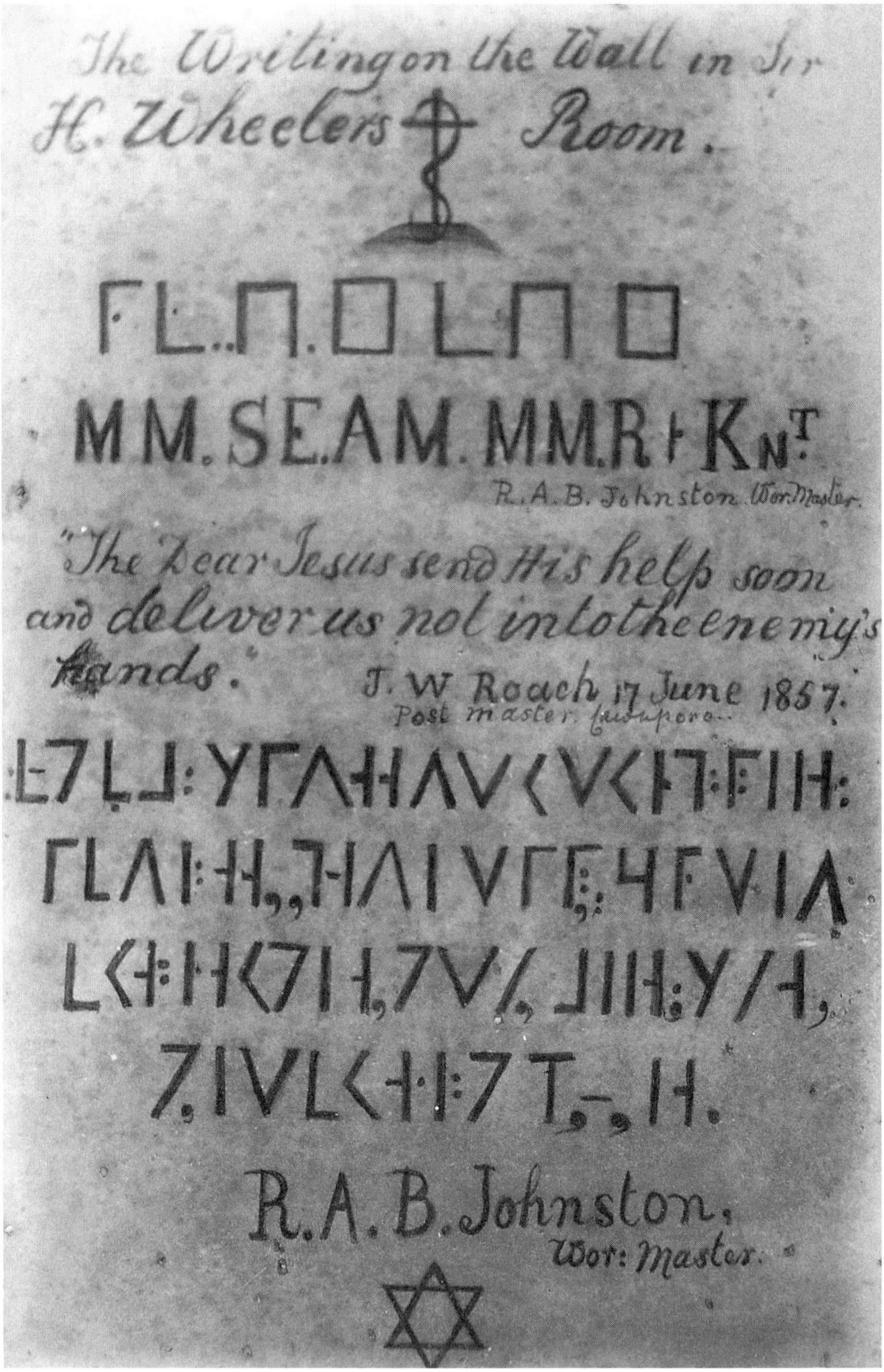

Figure 1.4. *Writing on the Wall of Sir Hugh Wheeler's Room,* Lucknow, 1858. The Alkazi Collection of Photography.

> pensive adjutant contemplating the desolation of the scene from a short distance, where he stands with his long beak and immovable posture as if spell-bound [Figure 1.5]; nor the horror evoked by the marks of human agony in the inner "Chamber of Blood, where the ladies and children were murdered" at Cawnpore [Figure 1.7]. How different the view of the primitive Well, where the women and children were thrown, from the finished structure as it now stands . . . [Figure 1.8]. The intense realism of the pictures defies description when we look at the charred barracks occupied by Sir H. Wheeler where he was mortally wounded, every crevice and hole produced by shot and shell telling of human suffering and despairing anguish in language too eloquent for words [Figure 1.6]. The contrast of the calm of the river-side and the rippling water with the sand almost peering through and the group of natives having a prosaic confabulation over the horrors enacted at that bathing ghat [Figure 1.9], where neither bird nor beast disturbs the solemnity of the scene associated with the memory of the slaughter of our women and children, as if it were all too dreadful even for ordinary natural laws to explain or be attended by.[15]

The hieroglyphic nature of the writing on Wheeler's wall seems to have contaminated the whole series of photographs devoted to the memory of British loss, since each image figures as a cipher whose significance is just out of reach because the loss these images index is incomprehensible. This series of photographs, which included many photographs by Felice Beato, was assembled into an album titled *Mutiny Memoirs* about twenty-five years after the revolt.[16] How many copies of the album sold is in fact unclear, though one writer for the *Pioneer*, an Allahabad-based newspaper, wrote in May 1892 of "a rare curiosity" of a photograph album depicting "rare photographs" of the sites of the revolt in Lucknow and Cawnpore and proceeded with an accurately detailed description of the Dannenberg Album, as it is known in the British Library archives.[17] In fact, some of these photographs cannot be seen as transparent views of the real at all. Three of the images are photographic copies of lithographs from drawings prepared by Charles Wade Crump (see Plates 7 and 8), yet these photographs of Crump's drawings are read as if they were "rare photographs."

The image of the skeletons and the image titled *Chamber of Blood* are photographs of allegorical drawings that were made for circulation immediately after the Sepoy Revolt and were republished as frontispieces in histories of the revolt.[18] Their inclusion in several private albums of photographs highlights the allegorical nature of the "real" photographs of ruins. In the quotation above, the standard appeal to the immediacy of sight afforded by photography as a grounds for knowing is directed at knowing the mysteries that take the form of ruins and hieroglyphs, that is, of knowing the mysteries as mysteries.

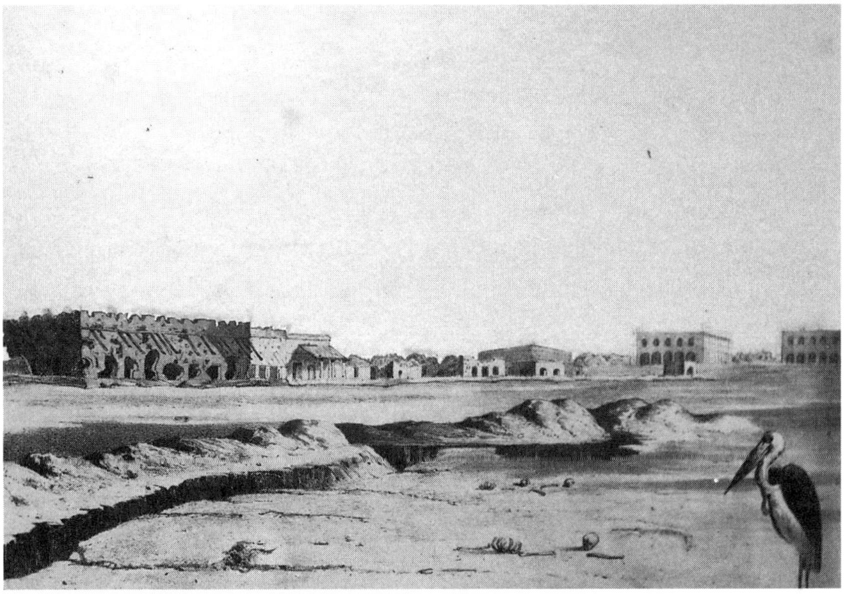

Figure 1.5. *General View of Sir Hugh Wheeler's Entrenchment with barracks in the distance,* Lucknow, 1858. The Alkazi Collection of Photography.

Figure 1.6. Felice Beato, *The Barracks which General Sir Hugh Wheeler occupied, and where he was shot and killed near the broken pillar,* Lucknow, 1858. The barracks shown in Figure 1.5 are based on this photograph. The Alkazi Collection of Photography.

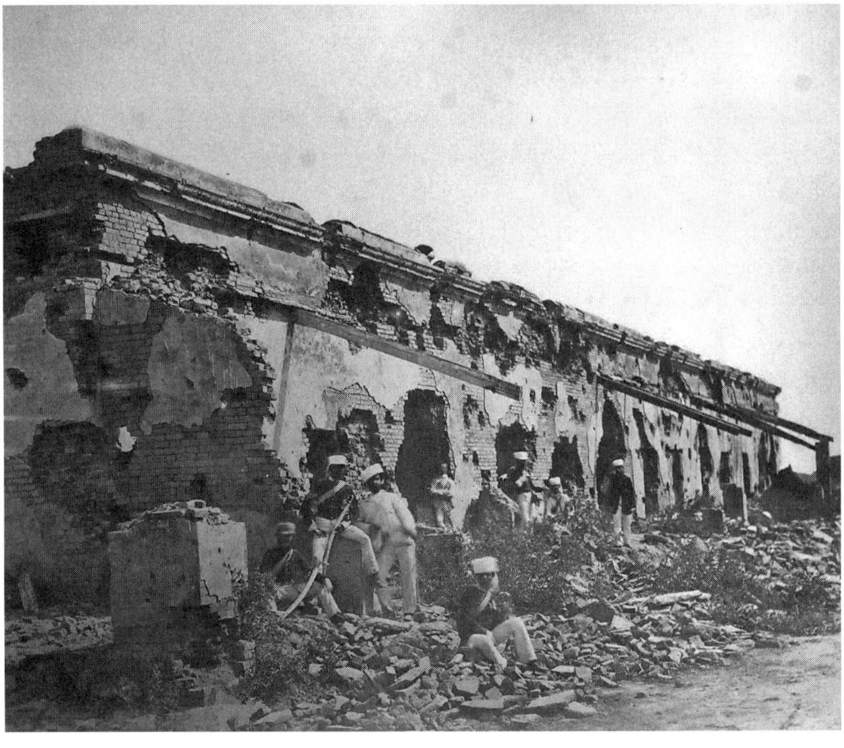

In Figure 1.5, we are to identify with the adjutant (a large Indian stork known for its military gait) and to see the skeletons from its point of view, and we are told that it is spellbound, in thrall to the mystery of violence that it contemplates. The skeletons have become runes whose meaning exceeds mere loss, because their appearance calls out for an explanation of a mystery that is all too dreadful and foreign to natural laws.

If, as in the passage cited above, "every crevice and hole produced by shot and shell [tell] of human suffering and despairing anguish in language too eloquent for words," then it seems that this language also eschews any claims to the sort of realism upon which the authority of photographs has depended. The truth effect of photography has been set aside for the allegorical representation of loss, a representation in which a contemplation of loss is itself a primary subject of the frame. The much-vaunted immediacy of the photographic apparatus has given way to an engagement with another kind of truth, one in which the authoritative status of sight resides not in the mathematical certitude of the camera lens but in the allegorical presentation of historical events.

In Figure 1.5, showing a view of Sir Hugh Wheeler's entrenchment, the bird is attentively fixed (spellbound) upon objects that litter the ground. In the ruined landscape that forms the backdrop for the bird's contemplative stance, there is no sign of life. The trench between the human remains and the architectural ruins in the background, most likely dug for the purposes of warfare, has issued forth skeletons, each in a progressively worse state of decay. Nature is as hollowed out as the skulls of these skeletons, mere objects for a bird's melancholy contemplation and destined to return to the hallowed earth from whence they came. Such images of death and passing time concerned Benjamin in his study on German tragic drama. Of the emblem of the skull, Benjamin writes:

> In allegory the observer is confronted with the *facies hyppocratica* of history as a petrified, primordial landscape. Everything about history, that, from the very beginning, has been untimely, sorrowful, unsuccessful, is expressed in a face—or rather, in a death's head [skull]. . . . This is the form in which man's subjection to nature is most obvious and it significantly gives rise not only to the enigmatic question of the nature of human existence as such, but also of the biographical historicity of the individual. This is the heart of the allegorical way of seeing.[19]

The skull simultaneously registers the particular and the universal, our collective and ultimate fate, as well as the singular story of one's own life and death; such is the polysemic nature of the allegorical emblem. The placement of the skeletons, three in a row, like the nutshells of the con artist hiding the absent object, ensures the anonymity of Sir Hugh Wheeler's skeleton within this image of loss.[20] Because the actual skulls of the British dead were not

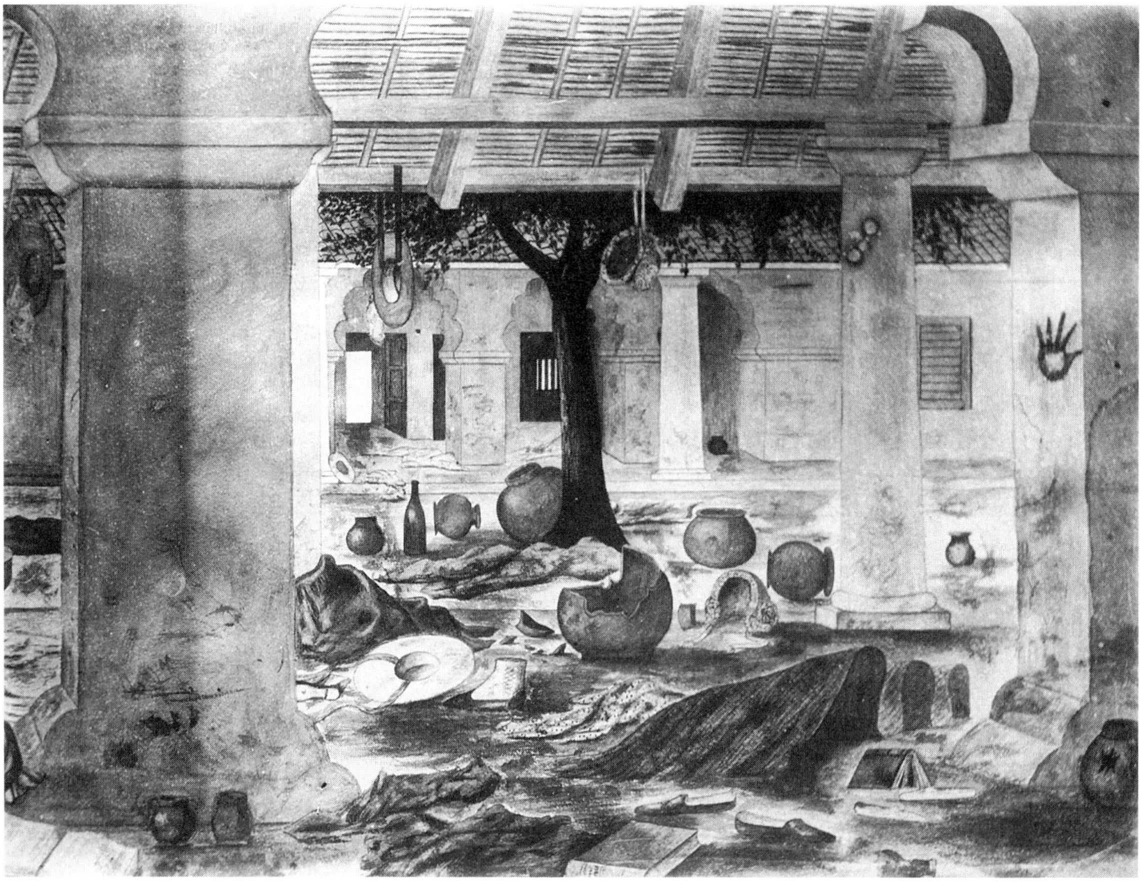

Figure 1.7. *Chamber of Blood, where the ladies and children were murdered,* Cawnpore, 1858. The Alkazi Collection of Photography.

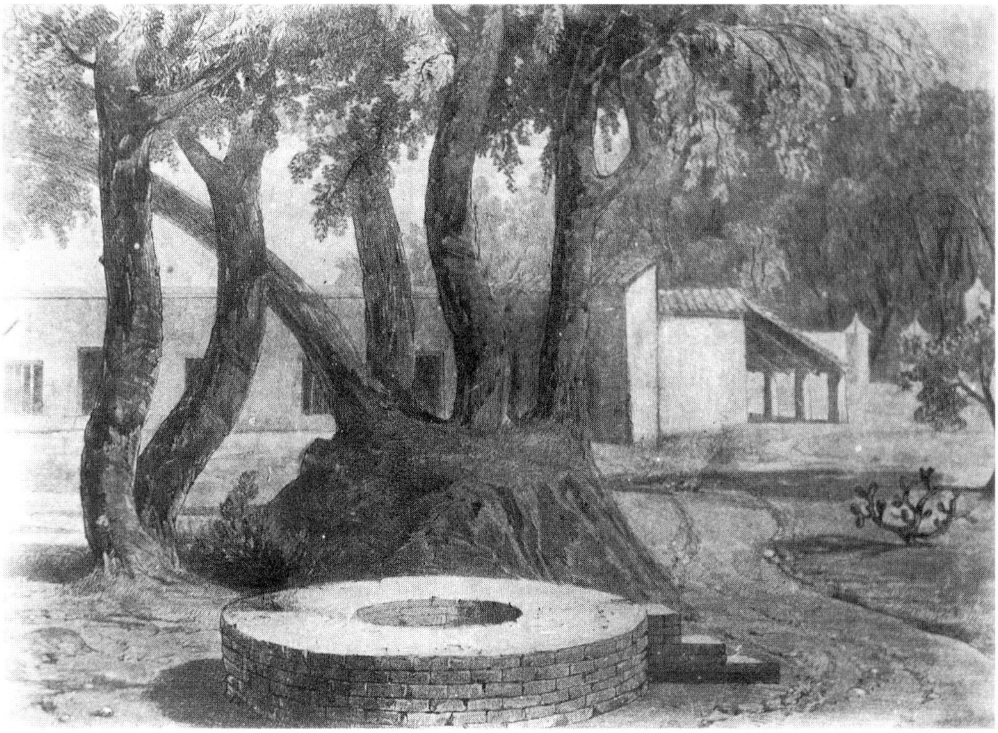

Figure 1.8. *The Cawnpore Well,* 1858. The Alkazi Collection of Photography.

Figure 1.9. *Slaughter Ghat,* 1858. The Alkazi Collection of Photography.

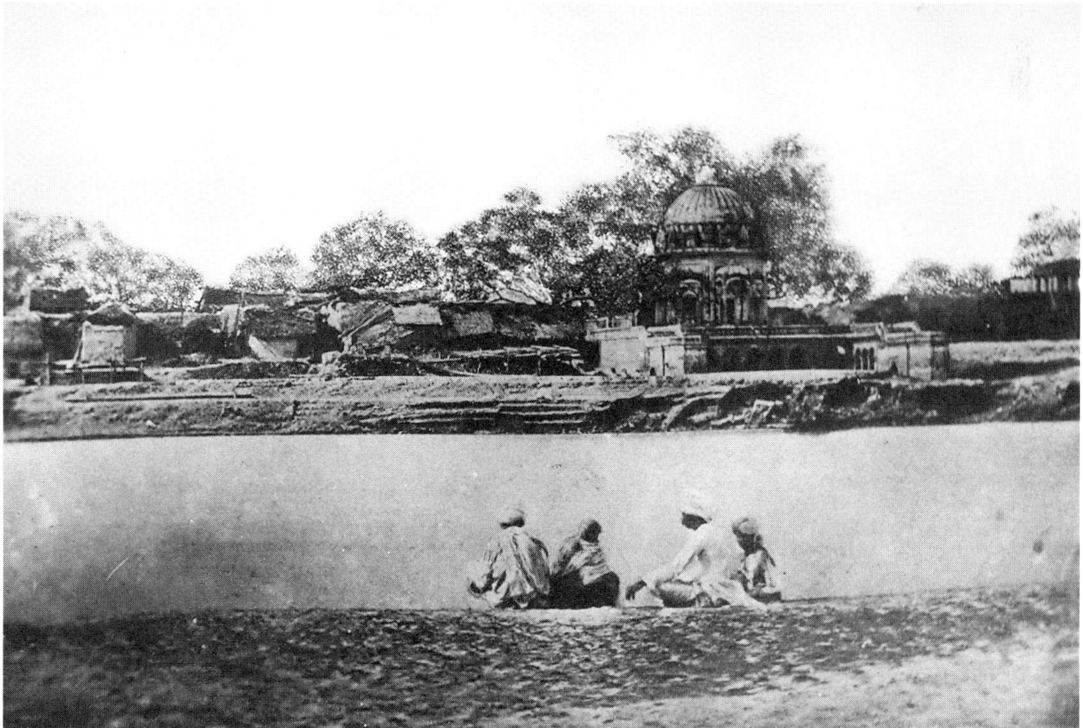

readily at hand for the photographer, this appears to be a radically different photograph from Felice Beato's photographs of Lucknow, which include the human remains of the Indian dead in their frames (more on this in chapter 2), yet fundamentally it relies on a similar structure of truth making. The barracks in the background are rendered directly from Felice Beato's photograph of them (Figure 1.6) and bear the weight of indexical truth. However, because in itself the image of the barracks is without content, the drawing of the adjutant and the skeletons serves as a kind of caption of the barracks, providing us with an allegorical interpretation: the entrenchment is simultaneously a grave, and the loss of bodies, of actually existing life, reveals itself to be the true focus of Beato's photograph of the barracks. Of course, the skeletons are themselves an index, if not photographically so; they are traces of once-animate bodies. The skeletons as an indexical sign are an explanation for the other indexical (and photographic) sign, the photographically based barracks. Yet as allegorical caption, the skeletons and bird also allow different valences of the index to contaminate each other. Although the archival caption, *General View of Sir Hugh Wheeler's Entrenchment with barracks in the distance,* tells us what we are looking at, if one pushes the allegorical reading, this "general view" also shows us the transience of the very foundations of the colonial claim to India—that is, British military prowess itself. Because the figure of the skull, as *vanitas,* carries in its fore-history associations with the transience of human life itself—in particular, the inevitability of death and decay ("man's subjection to nature")—it would seem that the military foundations of British colonialism, of which Wheeler's entrenchment has become an allegory, are just as inevitably destined to crumble with time. The architectural ruins left in the aftermath of the conflict appear as the ruination of the British claim to India. The irony of this "truth" is that the Sepoy Revolt appears, in the light of this knowledge, as a tool of (natural) history, on the side of "natural law," to which colonialism appeals to justify its claim. What is lost here is not just Hugh Wheeler or the abstract notion of Britannia for which he stood but also the naturalized claim to India. Allegorical signification swerves from meaning to meaning, and the unstable play of signification to which it gives rise can often be the source of allegory's power. Given that dying in the colony was itself the grounds of colonial attachment to India for Anglo-Indians, this threat to the naturalized colonial claim to the land keeps alive the ambiguous affects of what Baron von Clausewitz called "Real War," or war in the state of its suspension, as a threat that hovers over peacetime. In this image the indexical and the allegorical bleed into each other, becoming indistinct.

The loss represented in the mutiny memories of the Dannenberg Album is a wound that is cryptic in form and in the face of which representation can only attempt a contingent translation. The image titled *Chamber of Blood* seems to have emerged from a housewife's nightmare—the broken objects of everyday use litter a dirty room, the stage for a violation of pristine domesticity. The objects stand in for the people, and in the image we see them torn and smashed. The absent presence of butchered women pervades the scene, but these objects—broken bottles, wigs, discarded shoes—reveal the investments and principles that women have always been made to stand for ideologically: domesticity, order, knowledge, fashion, sustenance. These objects signal the quotidian symbolic mode in which women themselves are deployed as fetish objects, from the angel in the house to the figure of Britannia. National loss in this image is the violation of ideal domesticity. The broken objects and littered clothes acquire the weight of fetishes. This is clear in the personal accounts of Cawnpore, many of which repeat versions of the following, a description of the scene encountered by the British upon opening up the house of the "chamber of blood," where women and children were killed:

> On a near approach to the building, the mind imperceptibly filled with the most harrowing thoughts, felt as if a strange indescribable *something* hovered round the place which impressed one with awe, and the deepest melancholy. Then, as the horrified beholder entered the court-yard and stood at the threshold, his eyes fell upon the floor inside, covered over with blood. . . . Tresses of women's hair, some nearly a yard long, mats steeped in gore, children's clothes, and articles of female wear, hats, bonnets . . . , leaves of Bibles and other religious books, children's frocks and socks, ladies' boots, broken daguerreotype cases, small earthen pots and pans, bottles and water vessels, broken and unbroken, were to be seen strewn all about the place, dotted thickly with blood. . . . Many little bits of paper carefully folded up were found containing hair of children and men, some had inscribed on them "dear Willy's hair," "Ned's hair with love."[21]

The proliferation of daguerreotype cases found among personal mementos and bloodied clothes illustrates the profoundly cathectic relationship of photography to personal memory. Perhaps there is no better representation of loss than an empty daguerreotype case: the images of absence examined here are no different in spirit from such emptiness. This quotation is from a published narrative that uses the drawing of the *Chamber of Blood* as its frontispiece. The status of the image as a drawing enabled it, ironically, a much wider circulation immediately after the Sepoy Revolt, when the reproduction of photographs was a costly endeavor. In any case, not only do the fetishes enumerated in the passage conflate personal and national loss, but also the presence of the strands of hair and the daguerreotype cases raises fears about the loss of memory itself. In addition, the desecrated Bible leaves, the children's frocks, and ladies' boots stand in for entirely different sets of losses. This chamber of blood, littered with ciphers, is a field in which losses blend, converge, and turn upon themselves as if the grid that would make them legible has been lost. The only certainty in the scene is represented by the handprint on the column, indexing a body no longer alive and animate. Once one recognizes the indexical nature of this handprint, it becomes clear that each of the objects in the frame is also an indexical sign, each one—like the lock of hair and the daguerreotype—is a trace of a person who no longer lives.

When the spectator moves from these photographs of allegorical drawings to the photographs of actual sites of British loss, it becomes clear that the melancholic replication of these stations of mourning, whether as drawings or as "real" photographs, remains within the rhetorical orbit of allegory. The photographs allegorically disclose loss to the spectator and stand in for meanings and correspondences ultimately indeterminate, because they cannot contain the object of loss. These scenes of crimes establish evidence not for a trial but for memory and are diametrically opposed to the most literal understandings of photographic indexes. Put simply, the index signifies differently depending on the affective or instrumental use to which it is put. A lock of hair, for example, could signify a beloved or a possible victim, as Eduardo Cadava and Paola Cortés-Rocca note.[22] In other words, while the photographic index may be defined as a trace of the referent, one must situate the relationship between the trace and the referent in one's own reading practice. Given that the same indexical trace is subject to radically different kinds of meaning, a certain indeterminacy resides at the heart of the photographic index. Rosalind Krauss, in two early essays on the index, reads the index as a "shifter," Roman Jakobson's category for linguistic signs such as pronouns (for instance, the words *this* and *that*), which remain empty until filled in by enunciation.[23] If in Cadava and Cortés-Rocca's reading of the index, it marks the interpretive desires of the reading subject (and not merely, as in its commonsense understanding, the trace of the object itself),[24] Krauss's reading highlights the foundational "emptiness" of the indexical sign that permits a fluctuation of indexical meaning across subjects in the first place. In order to keep both of these subtle readings of the index in play, one might conceive of it as a rhetorical figure that functions, at times, like allegory.

According to Hans-Georg Gadamer, allegory names an aesthetic strategy that seeks to "present in images something that is imageless," sharing with the symbol the limitation that knowledge of the divine cannot be acquired except through the world of the senses: "The symbol is the coincidence of the sensible and the non-sensible; allegory, the meaningful relation of the sensible to the non-sensible."[25] Cadava and Cortés-Rocca's and Krauss's readings of the index remind us that the photographic object does not coincide with its index; rather, the index is merely the sensible trace of an object that already has slipped from sense perception. If allegory names the "meaningful relation" between the sensible and the nonsensible, then this relationship cannot be decided in advance (in the ideological sense, for example, of conceiving photographic indexes as police evidence). As a result, this rhetorical and aesthetic strategy is consistently described as polysemic, mystical, and indeterminate.[26] Paradoxically, allegory is conceived in its medieval iteration as a didactic discourse that seeks to express (divine) truth even as it gives rise to a dizzying and potentially contradictory set of meanings. The lessons of allegory, in other words, cannot be fixed, and yet its didactic thrust, like the persuasive power of photography, remains somehow in force.

In Benjamin's reading, allegory is more than a representational mode: it names a historical experience of fragmentation in which history appears as catastrophe. In *The Origin of German Tragic Drama,* Benjamin notes that the "allegorical way of seeing" comes to fruition at history's "stations of decline," such that the material world seems to be evacuated of meaning and shows up as a sign,[27] perhaps a Jakobsonian "shifter," in the allegorical emblem, awaiting a significance that will be read by future readers. In his reading of Baudelaire as an allegorical poet at the height of the nineteenth-century culture of capitalism, Benjamin seeks to show a similar hollowing out of meaning created by the production process at the height of capitalist material abundance: the rate at which objects reach obsolescence accelerated in the nineteenth century, revealing commodities to be hollowed-out matter in which consumers may insert their own wishes, desires, and meanings.[28] The meaning of the allegorical sign, or the hollowed object trace, is subject to a certain interpretive desire. Photography at the time of the Sepoy Revolt can best be understood as encapsulating allegorical dimensions of history's decaying, fragmented state—but also, dialectically, providing insight into history itself. The power of allegory lies in its capacity to shift meanings depending on the specific historical and material conditions in which the allegorical sign is read; likewise, photography's origin and circulation lie in reproduction, which allows photographs to renew their meanings continually, depending on the historical constellations in which they appear. As Roland Barthes has demonstrated, the photograph gives rise to a unique temporality that combines the "here-now" with the "there-then";[29] in Benjamin's reading of allegory as a mode of perception that lends historical insight, it is precisely the juxtaposition of these temporalities through which the past becomes legible in the present. In other words, the photographic index is a shifter in a much deeper sense than that described by Rosalind Krauss: its meaning shifts not only as the spectator changes (and such a change in the subject is necessarily a shift of the object as well, since the object is resituated) but also as historical conditions shift.

In the context of post–Sepoy Revolt photography, the shifting of the specific historical and personal loss—of this fallen British soldier here and that felled soldier there—into an allegorical rendering depends on the shifting and paradoxical nature of the index. Even as a trace, the index was always a pointer, a shifter. Hence the necessity of captions, particularly if the scene depicted is one of violence. For example, despite the accelerating mobility of photographic technology and its alleged power to capture history indexically, contemporary news photographs depicting violence require captions in order that we may "properly" situate our feelings of loss at the carnage before us (a dead Israeli citizen? Palestinian? Iraqi? American soldier?). Should visual markers of race or other objects in the frame, such as military uniforms, signal to us the "meaning" of the photograph, making captions redundant, such indexical signs, in substituting for the caption, also carry with them a trace of the whole baggage that attends language, alongside their (expected) traces of the referent. In short, such traces link photography to narrative. And the caption need not be rendered in language, as we have seen above in the example of the photograph of Wheeler's barracks, for which the allegorical drawing of the bird and skeletons serves as a caption. There is something deeply directive, in other words, about certain juxtapositions of images.[30] In these images from the Sepoy Revolt, the fixation on sites of loss manifests itself in the circulation of these same images as postcards, by means of which mechanical reproduction comes to the aid of traumatic repetition.

In the rest of this chapter I would like to explore other rhetorical dimensions of the index, since allegory names only one dimension of photography's rhetoric. To this end, the colonial history of nineteenth-century India proves instructive, particularly with respect to two interrelated types of phenomena that proliferate after the Sepoy Revolt: the rumor and one of its specific manifestations, the effigy. These, too, I argue, are rhetorical practices, and their surfacing at the time of the Sepoy Revolt has much to teach us about the rhetoric of post–Sepoy Revolt photography.

Rumor

The binary relationship of colonizer/colonized, like the political dyad friend/enemy, is not merely given but must be reproduced constantly. The contestation over meaning that occurred as part and parcel of such reproduction during the time of the Sepoy Revolt took a singularly intriguing form. George Trevelyan, in *Cawnpore,* written decades later, notes:

> During the spring of 1857 the native society of Hindostan presented those remarkable phenomena which, in an Asiatic community, are the infallible symptoms of an approaching convulsion. The atmosphere was alive with rumors, of the nature peculiar to India;—strange and inconsequent fragments of warning or prediction, which, with irreverent credulity, are passed from mouth to mouth throughout a million homesteads. No one can tell whence the dim whisper first arose, or what it may portend; it is received as a voice from heaven, and sent forward on its course without

FACSIMILE OF THE NANA'S PROCLAMATION

Picked up by GENERAL FRED A. WILLIS, at Cawnpore, and lent to COLONEL MAUDE for the purposes of this book.

اشتہار

ایک مسافر وارد حال شہر کانپور جو کہ کلکتہ سی آیا تہا سنا گیا کہ کارتوسون کی بٹنی سی پہلی واسطی لینی دین اور مذہب ہندستانیونکی
کونسل ہوئی صاحبان کونسل کی یہہ رای ٹہری کہ چونکہ یہہ مقدمہ دین کا ہی اسمین سات آٹہہ ہزار گورہ انگریز کام آویگا اور پچاس
ہزار ہندستانی قتل ہونگا تب کل ہندستانی کرستان ہو جاویگا اسمضمون کی عرضی ملکہ وکٹوریہ کی خدمت مین بہیجی گئی وہان سی
منظور ہی آئی پہر دوبارہ کونسل ہوی اور انگریزی سوداگر ہی شریک کونسل کی کئی گئی یہہ تجویز ہوا کہ واسطی مدد کی سیاہ گورہ اسقدر
مرحمت ہو کہ جسقدر فوج ہندستانی ہی کہ مبادا بروقت فتنہ بلند ہونے کی ہار نجاوین جب یہہ عرضی ولایت مین پڑہی گئی
وہان سی ۳۵ ہزار گورہ بہت جلدی جہازون پر سوار ہو کر روانہ ہندستان ہوی اور اونکی روانگی کی خبر کلکتہ مین آئی
صاحبان کلکتہ نی واسطی باٹنی کارتوسون کی حکم جاری کیا کہ اصل مطلب اوس سی کرستان کرنا فوج ہندستانی کا تہا کہ
جب فوج کرستان ہو جاویگی تب رعایا کی کرستان کرنی مین دیر نہوگی اور کارتوسون پر سور اور گائی کی چربی ملی ہوئی تہی
یہہ حال بابت بنگالیون کی جو کارتوس بنانی پر متعین تہی معلوم ہوا چنانچہ اسبات کی ظاہر کرنیوالون سی ایک شخص جان سی
مار ڈالا گیا اور باقی سب قید ہوئی یہان یہہ اپنی تدبیرین کرتی تہی وہان یہہ خبر وکیل سلطان روم نی لندن سی اپنی سلطان
پاس بہیجی کہ یہان سی ۳۵ ہزار گورہ واسطی کرستان کرنی ہندستانیونکی روانہ ہندستان کی ہوئی سلطان روم خلد اللہ ملکہ نی
پادشاہ مصر کی نام فرمان جاری کیا خلاصہ اوسکا یہہ ہی کہ تم ملکہ وکٹوریہ سی سازش کرتی ہو یہہ وقت صلح کا نہین ہے کیونکہ ہماری وکیل
کی لکہنی سی معلوم ہوا کہ ۳۵ ہزار فوج گورہ واسطی کرستان کرنی رعایا اور فوج ہندستانکی روانہ ہندستان کو ہوئی ہے پس اسصورت
مین اوسکا تدارک ممکن ہے اگر ہم غفلت کرینگی تو خدا کو کیا منہہ دکہاوینگی اور یہہ دن ایکروز ہماری بہی آگی آنیوالا ہی کیونکہ اگر انگریز
ہندستانیون کو کرستان کر لینگی تو ہماری ملک کا بہی قصد کرینگی جب یہہ فرمان سلطان روم مصر کی پادشاہ پاس پہونچا والی مصر نی
قبل پہونچنی فوج گورہ کی انتظام و اجتماع اپنی فوج شہر اسکندریہ مین کیا کیونکہ وہی راہ آمد ہندستان کی ہی بمجرد پہونچنی فوج گورون
کی فوج پاشا مصر نی چارون طرف سی توپین مارنا شروع کین اور جہازونکو توڑ تاڑ کر ڈبو دیا کہ ایک گورہ بہی اون مین سے
باقی نرہا انگریزان کلکتہ بعد جاری کرنی حکم کاٹنی کارتوس کی اور بلند ہونی اس فتنہ و فساد کی منتظر مدد فوج لندن کی
تہی کہ حق تعالی نی اپنی قدرت کاملہ سی وہین پہلی ہی اونکا کام تمام کیا جب خبر قتل ہونی فوج لندن کی معلوم ہوئی تب
گورنر جنرل نی بہت رنج و غم کیا اور اپنا سر پیٹا ٭ بر سر شب سر قتل و تاراج داشت ٭ سحرگہ نہ تن سر نہ سر تاج داشت ٭
بیک گردش چرخ نیلوفری ٭ نہ نادر بجا ماند و نی نادری ٭ حسب الحکم پیشوا بہادر طبع شد ذیقعدہ سنہ ۱۲۷۳

Figure 1.10. Rumor and Proclamation, 1857. From *Memories of the Mutiny* (1894 edition). See Appendix for translation.

> comment or delay; for the Hindu people, like the Greeks of ancient time, hold Rumour to be divine.[31]

Only in retrospect, of course, can these rumors be read as "symptoms" of a convulsion. As rumors, they ranged from warnings about the new cartridges for the Enfield rifle, allegedly smeared with the fat of pigs and cows, stories of flour mixed with the ground bones of these unclean and sacred animals, and as Trevelyan writes, "other treacherous devices by which the demon who swayed the scepter of Hindostan, the impalpable but omnipotent Kumpani, aimed at the destruction of sect and caste, and the universal establishment of Christianity."[32] For all the local embellishments, the rumors circulated widely and consistently across the subcontinent, framing the British as carriers of contamination and the East India Company as an agent of conversion, chaos, and defilement. The rumors also told of a prophecy that the British rule in India would end one hundred years after the battle at Plassey, and in 1857 that time was quickly approaching.

While an intrinsically oral form, the hearsay that preceded the Sepoy Revolt has been documented copiously in "mutiny memoirs" and historical accounts, and the consistency across the sources is remarkable. One memoir includes the "proclamation" allegedly written by Nana Sahib, the local aristocrat of Cawnpore, who was detested by generations of the English for his role in the famous massacres there. Written in Urdu, the announcement details British plans to convert all of India, starting with the Sepoys. It also explains that the sultan of Turkey and the pasha of Egypt, when they heard of British plans, became so horrified that they decided to assist Indians and had already attacked British ships bound for India (see Figure 1.10 and the Appendix). All of this is related, of course, by a traveler *(musafir)* who has arrived from Calcutta. Anonymous passing travelers, mendicants, and barbers are the classic figures of Fama, the Roman goddess of rumor, who is simultaneously ever-present and yet elusive. Rumors are collective, subjectless discourses, citations of citations whose origins are always just over the horizon.[33] They are not necessarily true or false but derive their force from collective and repeated circulation. The standard of truth, in fact, is irrelevant to the rumor's effects. As a form of rhetoric, the rumor proved itself to be the most incendiary form during the Sepoy Revolt.

Moreover, rumors circulated on both sides of the colonial divide. Jenny Sharpe has discussed the tenacity of rumors of the rape of British women by Indian men during the Sepoy Revolt,[34] and indeed such rumors are explicitly invoked in former soldiers' accounts as a way to explain their thirst for revenge. The newspapers published sensational rumors about Sepoys throwing English babies into the air to impale them on the ends of their muskets. The fact is, after the hostilities began in Meerut, the reading of signs became a preoccupation of gravest consequences. One Captain Mowbray Thomson writes of the fateful summer of 1857, "On the return of the Queen's birthday, no salute was fired, lest the natives should construe it into the signal for rising."[35] In light of rumors and heightened tensions, "any accidental spark may set the whole of the regiments of infantry, and one of cavalry, in a blaze of mutiny."[36] In these uncertain times, when every event appeared as a signal and every communication was overdetermined with meaning, the capacity to deduce the right meaning could mean the difference between life and death. For the British populations under siege, such as the ones in Cawnpore and Lucknow, who in their cantonments were cut off from outside communications, the figure of the visitor or traveler who came bearing news was simultaneously a figure of disrepute (especially if he or she was a "native") and authority. Figures of Fama always have given rise to such paradoxical reactions.

The very symmetry of the circulating accusations aligned on both sides—threat of defilement and contamination on one, of rape and descent into barbarism on the other—suggests that rumors bear a relationship to the basic unit of the political as analyzed by Carl Schmitt: rumors come to define the two sides of the friend/enemy dyad. In a time in which things cannot be taken at face value, rumor, paradoxically, provides the political certainty and assurance of one's place in the socius.[37] It has a part to play, however subterranean, in the violence that is made possible once the friend and the enemy have been defined. The British discourse around the Sepoy Revolt admits no indeterminacy or free play during the time of the conflict itself; muskets and cannons attempted to solder the signifier and signified by blowing apart the bodies of the enemy.[38] The newspaper reports from the time are infamously sensational;[39] the published letters and testimonials assume a fundamental difference between "natives" and the British;[40] the memoirs of the British soldiers recall the rush experienced in taking revenge on the "natives." Harriet Tytler, upon the sight of a dead Sepoy, remarks, "Serve you right for killing our poor women and children who had never injured you."[41] Novelist Flora Annie Steel writes in her autobiography of the effigies of Nana Sahib (the man responsible for the death of British women and children in Cawnpore) being hanged, "drawn, and quartered by children hundreds of times."[42]

Rumor secures certainty in the face of a shifting political landscape. Captain Thomson relates stories of locals who were lynched or shot by the British because of "rumours having reached the authorities."[43] On the other hand, the threat of defilement, conversion, and contamination that allegedly caused the Sepoys to revolt and raised the ire of the British soldiers who believed British women had been defiled may yet hold a key to understanding the force of rumor. If fears of contagion on the part of the British meant regulating the racial and civilizational boundaries between the English and the "native," it also required that one ignore actually existing intercourse across these boundaries. For example, Sir Henry Lawrence's wife, newly arrived in India in 1837, writes, "I was surprised to find among Europeans the prejudices of caste, and that many of them object to a low-caste native (simply on that ground) as much as a Hindoo would."[44] Lieutenant Mowbray Thomson reports that the memsahibs and children held captive at Cawnpore "were fed with only one meal a day of dhal and chupatties [flat breads], and these of the meanest sort; they had to eat out of earthen pans, and the food was served by menials of the lowest caste (mehter), which in itself was the greatest indignity that easterns could cast upon them."[45] According to Philip Mason's history of the Raj, a hundred years after Honoria Lawrence's observation, her remarks remained true, and the British continued to be "contaminated" by local class and caste prejudices;[46] if this is true, then it is unclear if "the greatest indignity" that could be cast upon the captive memsahibs was only a result of "Eastern prejudice." The cross-contamination of cultural and epistemic systems that gives rise to what Bhabha has famously called the "not-white-not-quite" subject works both ways across the colonial divide, and yet during the Sepoy Revolt, in spite of such Bhabian hybridity, the dyad of friend and enemy was hardly undermined on either side: the captive memsahibs had to be dealt indignity even as they were fed. If the memsahibs and their captors shared the same set of meaning conventions, then their indignity was assured all the more.

Moreover, contamination is a risky business and can itself provide the basis for punishments as ancient as the Homeric epics. George Trevelyan, in his account, quotes a letter from General Neill, one of the British saviors at the siege of Cawnpore:

> Whenever a rebel is caught he is immediately tried, and, unless he can prove a defence, he is sentenced to be hanged at once: but the chief rebels or ringleaders I make first to clean up a certain portion of the pool of blood, still two inches deep, in the shed where the fearful murder and mutilation of the women and children took place [the chamber of blood]. To touch blood is most abhorrent to the high-caste natives. They think, by doing so, they doom their souls to perdition. Let them think so. My object is to instill a fearful punishment for a revolting, cowardly, barbarous deed, and to strike terror into these rebels. The first I caught was . . . a high-caste Brahmin, who tried to resist my order to clean up the very blood he had helped to shed: but I made the provost-marshal do his duty, and a few lashes soon made the miscreant accomplish his task. When done, he was taken out and immediately hanged, and, after death, buried in a ditch at the roadside.[47]

Upon this extract, Trevelyan remarks, "The ablest among our officers had forgotten . . . the age in which he lived, and the religion he professed."[48] Trevelyan goes on to cite an incident from Homer's *Odyssey* in which the maids in the palace of Ithaca were forced by Ulysses to carry the dead bodies of their lovers and clean the area of blood and all signs of violence before themselves being hanged:

> It is curious that an act, which the Pagan poet allows an old moss-trooper and his son to perpetrate in the flush of revenge and victory, should have been revived by a Christian warrior after the lapse of twenty-five centuries. And it must be owned that Neill surpassed his model: for apparently the primary object of Ulysses was to sweep away the traces of the butchery, and make his refectory clean and habitable: . . . whereas the Englishman desired only to wound the sentiments of the doomed men, and prolong their prospect of death with a vista of eternal misery. And this, when the rallying-cry of the insurrection was the preservation of caste:—when in the wide-spread confidence that our faith did not seek to extend itself by carnal weapons lay the salvation of the British supremacy![49]

This is a rare moment in the discourse on the mutiny: a direct criticism of British soldiers' excesses. According to Trevelyan, such excesses posed the biggest threats to colonial authority, not least because in forcing the rebels to act against the dictates of their caste, Neill in effect became precisely the cruel colonizer bent on violating local customs, that is, precisely the foreigner against whom the rallying cry of the insurrection was aimed. This insight does not flower into a full-blown critical consciousness in which Trevelyan may begin to shake off his confidence that their faith did not seek to extend itself by carnal weapons and recognize that carnal weapons were not new to the functioning of British supremacy. In fact, such carnality was being replicated at home by British children, who would hang, draw, and quarter effigies of Nana Sahib, a prominent Indian rebel. Trevelyan's slight criticism does not last for long. The next paragraph immediately brings relief from these thorny issues: "But there was a spectacle to be witnessed which might excuse much."[50] He follows this statement with a description of the bloodied dresses, broken daguerreotype cases, and the rest of the horrors of the chamber of blood—images meant to instill in the reader precisely the feelings of revenge that motivated General Neill's excesses.

Flora Annie Steel's own account of having participated in the ritual killing of Nana Sahib's effigies is instructive: "Nevertheless, I burnt and hanged and tortured the Nana Sahib in effigy form many times. In truth he really was a scoundrel; and as my eldest brother was going out to the Civil Service in 1858, it was only natural that the personal element prevailed over soft-heartedness. For none of us, as a family, were cruel; we didn't kill flies, or torture, or even tease animals."[51] This personal element, a personal investment in the colonial enterprise, is both the precondition and the result of the friend/enemy distinction. The effigy, like the iconic aspect of the photograph, gives the perception of presence through resemblance, even in its grotesque and exaggerated resemblance; it crystallizes rumor in its most primal mimetic form and reproduces the friend/enemy distinction. When rumor's persuasive power has its hold over us, we abuse effigies, and as such, the burning, hanging, and torturing of effigies releases the pent-up affective charge that rumors accumulate. Also, unlike the torture of humans, which must take place in secluded spaces, effigies have to be tortured in public view. (To torture them in private reveals more starkly the occult nature from which they draw their energies.) If they mark the persuasive power of rumor, they also help to make a spectacle of the power of one's feelings and the force of the faith in one's beliefs. Yet unlike effigies, rumors themselves can be circulated without firm belief in their veracity. The circulation of rumor is a test of rumor's veracity and power, not the result of its persuasive power; the sharing of an uncertain rumor inevitably leads to a reading of the listener's reaction, some sign that might tell us if we, too, should reject or adopt the rumor's claim. This certitude is not a search for truth, or "reality" testing as such, but serves as an anchor for our conscious and unconscious feelings about the subject of rumor. This is why rumors circulate so easily and so widely, since their transmission, at every point, is a kind of testing whose standard of certitude is purely subjective and leads to a mirroring of the recipient's feeling that is part and parcel of the reproduction of belief/disbelief. Rumors also provide the frisson of being in the know, securing a sense of belonging in a group, and every moment of passing on the rumor affirms this sense. This is, in part, why the "testing" of rumor does not come to an end with the first inclinations of belief or disbelief. Rumors endure because of the delight in such repeated testing, of the consolation of an imaginary social belonging, and of the possibility of experiencing certainty (of one's own feelings if not the truth of the rumor) in a flash. A similar emotional charge attaches to the practice of photography, as we will see.

From the scene of Flora Annie Steel torturing the effigy of Nana Sahib as a young girl, we switch to the scene of subaltern forms of symbolic and imaginary figuration, which also function by means of reproduction and circulation as their basis: in the winter of 1856 in the North-West Frontier Province of India, a few months before the outbreak in Meerut that initiated the Sepoy Revolt, British collectors, magistrates, and political agents reported a strange occurrence:

> A chowkeedar [village watchman] appears in the village adjoining his own with two small chupattees, which he delivers to his brother chowkeedar, with an injunction to make six others—to be then delivered by him, two and two, to the chowkeedars of the adjacent villages with instructions to act in a similar manner: each chowkeedar was to keep two for presentation to the hakim or "when called for."[52]

William Kaye, in his *History of the Indian Mutiny* (1898), reports that "the most experienced men [were] incompetent to explain" this practice, which coursed throughout the region and, with dramatic speed, encompassed a large swath of northern India within a week.[53] Although at the time no British administrator could determine what the traveling *chapattis* could mean, in many analyses, personal narratives, and official histories written after the suppression of the Sepoy Revolt, writers interpreted this phenomenon as a signal and as evidence of conspiracy on the part of the "natives."[54] It was the British who suddenly could not read the signs, who were in the position of the foreigners, for whom to speak in the local language meant not just to speak with a broken tongue but to have no access to meaning at all. Such loss of comprehension can be perceived only as a threat to the very foundations of colonial governance.

The traveling *chapattis* were loosely read in retrospective accounts as a sign alarming Indians about alleged British plans to subvert local religious and cultural practices. The fact that the *chapattis* have remained largely illegible as a sign—their meaning never fully determined by British or Indian historians—not only points to the incommensurability of official grids of history writing vis-à-vis subaltern agency but also indicates the foreign, uncanny element within all sign systems. Guha cites J. W. Sherer's influential memoir of the Sepoy Revolt: "If the transmission of these cakes was only intended to create a mysterious uneasiness, that object was gained."[55] Not only is this mysterious uneasiness the sign of what Homi Bhabha, in his analysis of the *chapatti* incident, has called "the politics of indeterminacy,"[56] the semiotic unsettling that hybridizes the colonial system of signs, but also this uneasiness is a marker of the uncanniness that subtends British authority.[57]

It is telling that in Ranajit Guha's seminal work on peasant insurgency, almost every single mode of transmission—that is, the means of communication and the means of fomenting revolts—of subaltern agency resides in particular objects that become symbolically invested with meanings relevant to the particular struggle at hand. These objects include anklet bells worn by traveling dancers, drums and horns, *lathis* and *polos,* buffalo horns, flutes, arrows, and, of course, the *chapattis.* Even branches of particular trees are appropriated and made to function as meaningful signs, as objects that reveal a concept.[58] These subaltern practices can appear only otherworldly in written British accounts. And perhaps this is so because what they reveal is often not a purely political order sanitized of supernatural presences but precisely the political order seen from the point of view of magical, otherworldy nature.[59] Kaye himself cites a certain Captain Keatinge, who read the passing of *chapattis* in the context of local religious practices (and therefore saw the *chapattis* as wholly unrelated to the Sepoy rebellion): "This habit of passing on holy and unholy things is not unknown at Nimár. When smallpox breaks out in a village, a goat is procured, a cocoa-nut tied to its neck, and it is taken by the chowkeedar to the first village on the road to Mandáta; it is not allowed to enter the town, but is taken by a villager to the next hamlet, and so passed on without rest to its destination."[60] Its fitting destination, of course, can only be death. Such scapegoating practices are known as *chalawa* in Hindi–Urdu, meaning "passing on [the disease],"[61] but also a "going forth." *Chalawa* comes from the root *chal,* meaning to walk, to flow, to go, or to continue.

Guha draws on William Crooke's discussion of the practice of *chalawa* to indicate that a variety of "transmitters" may be used to pass on the same illness, "irrespective of whether its victims were people or cattle," and the same transmitter may, in turn, be used to pass on a variety of illnesses: "Thus, if we consider the region as a whole, the range of instruments for the transfer of cholera could include images of the cholera goddess, doles of rice collected from local residents, filth and sweepings picked up from the affected villages, domestic animals such as goats, buffaloes and fowl."[62] *Chalawa* always risks an overload of "meaning" to the extent that in the interplay of exchangeable transmitters and myriad illnesses, what is passed on (or goes forth) may be subject to a certain pathological indeterminacy. In any case, such techniques were meant to ensure the end of an affliction, and in 1856 the *chapatti* acquired the characteristics of such a transmitter. Having done so, it shifted the realm of *chalawa* from "pathology to politics: a carrier of one kind of catastrophe it came now to symbolize, by a semantic slide, a catastrophe of an altogether different kind."[63] But if the realm shifts here from pathology to politics, a translation also occurs in this semantic slide between magical, enchanted nature and secular, disenchanted nature, the field of modern politics. This becomes starkly clear in Colonel Vibart's account of the revolt, in which he describes a "native" who repeatedly asks, "Khoon kub chullega?" Vibart translates this as "When will the blood be spilt?" but the verb */challna/* shares the same root *(chal)* as *chalawa,* so the question may be translated as "When will the blood start to flow?"[64] The slide between magical violence and political violence is secured by the friend/enemy distinction that *chalawa* presupposes even as it produces that distinction.

The practice of *chalawa* in whose service the *chapattis* become legible enframes British colonizers as signs of an affliction—both the symptoms and the source—that need to be dispatched, expunged, passed on, and killed (since death is the proper end for the malady carried by *chalawa*), in order to restore a sense of (religious, political, psychological, economic) security. The mimetic faculty links the magical and the political, and the circulating *chapattis* are themselves an index of this traffic between sensible and nonsensible realms, not least because their own ultimate meaning, as a form of subaltern figuration, remains obscure in all historical accounts. As symptoms of a strange malady, the British in 1857 would become targets for an assault that enlisted magic and prophecy as well as guns and knives in its pharmaceutical arsenal.

Analogy

Circulating rumors and circulating *chapattis* both reproduce the friend/enemy distinction, a distinction that in no way undermines the actually existing contaminations (cultural, epistemic, historical, semiotic) in both directions across the dyad. The relationship between rumors and the body politic is made abundantly clear in many accounts of the Sepoy Revolt, in which the language of infection, disease, and contagion finds a natural home in the description of rumors' circulation. In one narrative, the writer opines, "This unjust report, once having been freely spread, like a flame urged to vehemence by the breeze, took possession of the minds of all; and it was found impossible, by sensible reasoning, by appealing to common sense, or, latterly, by more stringent measures, to eradicate the infection."[65] The slippage among sensible reasoning, common sense, and more stringent measures, or violence, signals the intimacy between consent and coercion, the twin poles of modern governance. Moreover, the metaphor of bodily infection is particularly apt in a context in which political contestation takes place across the rituals and rules regarding the body's consumption, sanctity, and integrity (Sepoys rebelling against the forced consumption of forbidden foods, etc.). In the case of rumor, "consumption" is synonymous with circulation; that is, a rumor merely heard and not passed on expires. Likewise, the traveling *chapattis* described above are meant to be not eaten but consumed in an entirely different order of signification, by being passed on.

Photography's technological specificity, at this historical juncture, resides in its capacity for reproduction, and as Hubert Damisch notes, its phenomenological contributions must be assessed at the level of *consumption* rather than at the level of *production.*[66] This intimacy between photography and rumor takes on particular significance if one rereads anthropological photography, and perhaps the whole genre of "manners and customs," as a form of rumor about the states of "civilization" and "barbarism." Such photographic rumors reinforce the persuasion of the friend/enemy distinction in spite of the contaminations across these two groups, hence Sir Syed Ahmed's account of the unease caused by an Indian's reception of a volume like *The People of India,* as discussed in the Introduction. Certainly the enlistment of photography as a technology of propaganda (not only by the state) is an extreme instance of photography's work as rumor, a dimension of photographic meaning that points to its mass consumption.

Even at the level of "mere" analogy, rumor has much to teach us about photographic practice. Analogical comparisons are of value, according to Immanuel Kant, because they allow us to sense the coincidence of relations across dissimilar objects. In *Prolegomena to Any Future Metaphysics,* Kant writes, analogy "does not signify (as is commonly understood) an imperfect similarity of two things, but a perfect similarity of relations between two quite dissimilar things."[67] Kant reminds us of both the value and the limits of analogical deductions: they can show us the patterns of relation across dissimilar things and provide insight into each object of comparison, but at the same time the dissimilarity of the objects compared is not overcome by analogical deduction. Rather, dissimilarity is the condition of analogical comparison, the supplement that makes analogy itself valuable, since it is only by apprehending the similar patterns of relation across *dissimilar* objects that we have access to a truth otherwise ignored.[68] Rumor is, as I mentioned at the outset, as archaic as allegory, and certainly photography does not exhaust the patterns of relation we find either in the circulation of rumors or in the ways that allegory signifies.[69] But rumor and allegory do name tendencies of photography, which relies on these archaic forms of making sense and regenerates them.

Recall the discussion in the Introduction of the photograph as a souvenir: it serves to make sense of an experience that signifies too much and necessarily points to the distance between the present disappearing moment and the authentic but lost past. All photographs are, to some extent, souvenirs insofar as they give shape and signification in the midst of the uncertainties of the present at the moment the aperture is set to work, and the resulting photograph invokes the distance from the past, which is now handed down as a framed scene in the midst of the disappearing present's uncertainties. The nature of rumor and allegory overlap in this process: like the rumor, the photograph anchors conscious and unconscious feelings; like allegory, its signification is polysemic and renews across time; and like both, it *promises* the pleasure of certainty in a flash. Here, narrative, a form of making sense older than allegory, rumor, and photography put together, shows the similarity of the patterns of relations across these modes. Take, for example, the parable (a subset of allegory, complete with its didactic intent), which necessarily begins with a set of narrative givens: the thirsty bird who comes across a vessel of water that it cannot reach initially with its beak, the watchdog punished for barking in the night and waking up its master, the boy who thought crying wolf was a good idea. These givens are not questioned by us but are entered into on faith; there is a theological aspect to this primary narrative function. Narratives must begin, as it were, from nothing, and we are well trained to accept these opening terms, since they are the basis of a story to follow. We enter into these terms because the pleasures of narrative cannot be had without them, and what attends such pleasure is the delight in the certitude of these givens, even if we discard that certitude later. The photograph sets this primal delight in the first principles of narrative—a delight that is central to the circulation of rumor and the grounds for allegory's truths—in an entirely novel economy of rhetoric and truth. What it presents to the eye is always and necessarily the opening terms, the founding principles of narrative, even if the construction of narrative based on those terms is determined differently from narratives written in language. In photography, the narrative that might emerge from the set of givens in the frame is the work of any number of factors: captions, context, history, memory, propaganda, art historical canons, and so on. The photograph in itself does not provide a narrative but rather provides only its opening terms. As an "organ of memory" (both memory of older forms of signification and memories depicted in its frame), it renews and regenerates archaic elements such as allegory, rumor, and narrative itself, through a new ground for certitude, a new anchor of aesthetic effect: the photographic index.

In a flash, the photograph creates a meaningful relation between the sensible and the nonsensible, as allegory does in its telling, and as rumor's circulation strives to do in its asymptotic movement that keeps it alive. When speaking of photography's economy of truth in a phenomenological sense, we are speaking of the sphere of photographic consumption, as Hubert Damisch advises. The rhetorical promise of the photographic index is conditioned by an originary contamination between the sensible and the nonsensible realms, for which allegory is a figure (as Gadamer reminds us). The photograph, in a manner similar though not at all identical to the conception of sacred script, signifies the mark of the nonsensible within the phenomenological world. The transactions across the realms of the sensible/visible and nonsensible/invisible give rise to a strange kind of rhetoric specific to the photographic image, and in defining the force of this rhetoric we must necessarily turn away from photography to see how photography itself is figured in the discourse around the Sepoy Revolt.

The Index

The nineteenth-century investment in the photographic image becomes clear in the rhetoric that Flora Annie Steel deploys in the preface to her novel about the Sepoy Revolt, *On the Face of the Waters* (1896):

> And now a word for my title. I have chosen it because when you ask an uneducated native of India why the Great Rebellion came to pass, he will, in nine cases out of ten, reply, "God knows! He sent a Breath into the World." From this to a Spirit moving on the face of the waters is not far. For the rest I have tried to give a photograph—that is, a picture in which the differentiation caused by colour is left out—of a time which neither the fair race nor

> the dark one is likely to forget or to forgive. So that they may come nearer to the latter is the object with which this book has been written.[70]

Invoking the monochromatic objectivity of the photograph in the same instance in which Steel disavows her own racism (the differentiation normally read into the fair and dark races is allegedly not at work in her novel), she asks us to read her novel in the same way as we would view photographs. Steel wishes to appropriate the contemporaneous discourse about photography's indexical truth to lend her own representation a patina of disinterested objectivity. Certainly the painstaking research with which Steel constructs her fictional account is well-documented,[71] and she intends her novel to be a corrective of the "bloodthirsty tone" of the public discourse and of the sensationalism of much "mutiny fiction" from the nineteenth century.[72] What I would like to foreground here are some of the concerns raised by Steel in the brief passage cited above. Steel seems to align the "native" explanation with all that is fictional in her account, and for the rest she has tried to "give a photograph" of a historical moment. The photograph in Steel's account is the smallest unit of secular, objective thought. The flash of the camera allegedly evaporates all that arises from superstition, imagination, and heterogeneous affiliations outside the domain of disenchanted objectivity.

The title, *On the Face of the Waters,* translates, as Jenny Sharpe has noted, "the religious discourse of peasant insurgency into a Christian allegory for the righteousness of British rule," and in this move, Steel "delegitimates the native voice in the act of invoking it as an authoritative text."[73] So the novel is written as an allegory invoking the great mystery of creation itself, and it structures the causality of the events of "the great rebellion" as similarly deeply mysterious. As Captain Morecombe remarks at the conclusion of the novel, "Truly the whole thing was a mystery from beginning to end. I asked a native yesterday if he could explain it, but he only shook his head and said the Lord had sent a 'breath into the land.'"[74] The bloody events of 1857 are allegedly like ciphers whose comprehension exceeds both native and British faculty.[75]

While Steel's narrative in *On the Face of the Waters* does not fundamentally depart from an imperialist view of colonialism as white man's burden or minimize the uses of colonialist tropes in its representation of Indians (the sensual harlots, the treacherous and patriarchal Eastern men), her objective is to help bring the dark and the fair races closer to forgiveness, as stated in the last sentence quoted above. She imagines such forgiveness, moreover, beneath the comforting Christian allegorical understanding of God brooding upon the face of the waters in the story of Genesis, protecting Its "brood" by covering them with a wing—a sort of primal nesting under the wing of the Spirit. Earthly violence appears to be a short-lived affair in the face of such Mystery. The implication of Steel's title seems to be that the ruins (architectural, bodily, psychological, social) of war and the violence enacted by the dark and fair races alike have a mysterious source that itself can be subsumed under the greater mystery of God. Theology serves a compensatory function, disabling inquiry into the historical and material conditions of the Sepoy Revolt itself. Earthly violence is translated into a theological idiom on both sides of the colonial divide, and written narrative calls out to be read as a photograph.

Steel's fictional account of the Sepoy Revolt begins by foregrounding mystery and ends by affirming it. The conclusion is asserted as a premise, and under scrutiny the premise, that the causes of the revolt are a mystery, itself is without content and provides little explanatory force as a conclusion. While novels can hardly be read like photographs, Steel's exhortation to read her novel as a word-photograph emphasizes the fact that the referential rhetoric of this particular novel does approximate the rhetoric of photography. If photography necessarily has an allegorical aspect, then we must remember, following Gadamer, that "allegory originally belonged to the sphere of talk, of the logos, and is therefore a rhetorical or hermeneutical figure."[76] How might we then conceive of the rhetoric of photography?

Roland Barthes, in his classic essay "Rhetoric of the Image," very deliberately highlights this hermeneutical aspect of the photograph. Emphasizing the iconic element of photographic referentiality, in which the referent is presented to the spectator through nonsymbolic, sheer mimeticism, Barthes concludes, "The sign of this message is not drawn from an institutional stock, is not coded, and we are brought up against the paradox . . . of a *message without a code*."[77] And so results the seeming immediacy of photographic representation, as well as the promises of the photographic index. In Peirce's original triad of icon, symbol, and index, the index is among the slipperiest of categories. It is a sign that has a tangible connection to its referent "by being really and in its individual existence connected with the individual object."[78] Peirce lists the footprint, the weathervane, the hand of a clock, the bullet hole, the sundial, and photographs as examples of indexes, as each has a direct connection to its referent: foot, wind, time, bullet, sun's movement, and light bouncing off objects. In the example of photography, the index is simultaneously iconic if the image resembles the referent (assuming the referent has not moved faster than the shutter speed). But Peirce also associates the index with deixis, since "the index asserts nothing; it only says 'There!'"[79] The shifters discussed earlier, such as *this, that,* and other pronouns, also are examples of indexes, so the index also figures as a symbolic rather than an iconic phenomenon. Mary Anne Doane notes that the two critical aspects of the index are the symbolic (akin to language) and the iconic (akin to the image). In the photographic image, the index promises plenitude; it promises the object itself even when that object is absent. And yet, its symbolic aspect remains that of a shifter, a deixis, that merely points to a plenitude elsewhere but in itself remains empty. The uncanniness of the photographic index results from this oscillation between emptiness and plenitude, an oscillation that is not shared by other kinds of signs.[80]

The fact that Peirce, in his original formulation of the index, leaves these paradoxical aspects of the index unexplained only shows that the symbol, icon, and index were not meant to be consistently opposed to one another. Peirce's complex semiotics instead aim to explore their overlaps as well as their diversions across the semiotic continuum. After all, the photographic index as a shifting trace serves a deixic function as allegorical emblem insofar as its "truth" transforms and emerges anew as the photograph passes through time. That is, the iconic aspect of photography, its promise of plenitude in its picture-like qualities that have "captured" a real scene, cannot be dissociated from its deixic aspect. The photograph promises the object itself, and this irrational promise is what bears away our faith, and yet what it delivers is an empty trace, a "mere" shifter, a "mere" pointer. The pleasures of photography, it seems, must rely on this rhetoric of desire, of fulfillment promised and almost obtained.

Thus far I have isolated allegory, rumor, and, to a certain extent, the effigy as representational practices that shed light on the nature of photography itself. Each one of these examples is enmeshed in a paradox: allegory promises truth and yet provides an unstable set of meanings; rumor provides (political) certainty of the friend/enemy distinction, and yet its standard of truth remains suspect; the effigy gives the semblance of presence through the magic of mimesis and yet is necessary only as a result of the referent's absence. The image in the photograph is, as Bazin noted years ago, "the object itself, the object freed from the conditions of time and space that govern it,"[81] and simultaneously, it is merely an index that "points" to the object. It would seem that, like allegory and rumor, photography's rhetorical power lies in its promise to provide certainty, to offer up the referent itself. The referent, moreover, may literally be the object—much as the photographic index is read in police discourse—or it may be the object indissociably inflected with affect, as in the strange genre of memorial photography following the Sepoy Revolt, which records empty spaces. The "referent" as an (empty) indexical trace that serves a deixic function in no way detracts from the power of photography's rhetoric. This rhetoric may be characterized as having elements of allegoresis, apophasis, and cataphasis.

As rhetoric, photography appears to be the opposite of apophasis. If in apophatic propositions something is affirmed by explicitly denying its proposition ("Today we will not mention x, y, and z"), then in photography something is explicitly claimed as in cataphatic utterances ("Behold the scene/object/person," or rather "X marks the spot"). Yet photography cannot be said to be cataphatic, since that would mean that it does in fact deliver on its promise to provide us with the referent itself. While such a claim proves to be inadequate to its promise, the force of the promise carries the mystical aura of cataphatic utterances ("God is God is God is God," for example, as the classically cataphatic utterance). However, when Barthes notes that in the photographic image "the relation between signified and signifier is quasi-tautological," it is precisely *quasi*-tautological because the referent can hardly be captured fully in its image. Meanwhile, the image, like the allegorical signifier, turns out to signify something other than itself, not only at the time of its production, but also as it is subject to time's vicissitudes.

These abstract remarks might be more concrete if we consider the discourse surrounding the origins of the Sepoy Revolt. Flora Annie Steel ascribes the causes of the revolt to a "great mystery," in part agreeing with what she calls the "native explanation" for the revolt, and she is not alone; many of her contemporaries also resort to "mystery" as an explanation.[82] Rumors start from nowhere, effigies are burned, bread changes hands across neighboring villages, and the atmosphere is rife with illegible signs. Certainly the protocols of a certain reading practice would read all of these discursive hesitations regarding mystery as ideological hocus-pocus that conceals actual material conflicts over land, resources, and self-governance. Such a reading would have much to offer, and though its conclusions would be predetermined, they would be no less true for being so. If we resist such a model of reading and its attendant iconophobic assumptions of surface and depth, symptom and cause, how might we understand the profound befuddlement of nineteenth-century novelists, historians, and photographers in the face of the violence of the Sepoy Revolt?

Working within the terms of the "surface" explanation, that is, with "mystery," we find rhetorical moves complementary to the rhetorical work that post–Sepoy Revolt memorial photography performs. On the one hand, labeling the origin a mystery is a cataphatic statement that assigns a grammatical object (mystery) to the first cause. At the same time, as Michael Sells has demonstrated in his study of apophasis, mystery as the object of a cataphatic utterance immediately signals the twin of cataphasis, apophasis, since mystery marks the refusal of all explanations, a kind of "unsaying" that recoils from conceptual capturing of first causes.[83] Much of the nineteenth-century discourse on the Sepoy Revolt is characterized by a certain apophatic impulse that crystallizes in the preponderance of a language of mystery, unknowability, and illegible signs. These unknowns and mysteries can be replaced, in retrospect, with any number of critical explanations: contradictions between labor and capital, slippages across sign systems, symptoms of primary repressions. But to do so would risk explaining away this rhetoric itself. What interests me is this apophatic impulse at the heart of colonial photography that precisely cannot be explained away. Such a play of exposure and concealment, naming and unsaying, may well lie at the heart of all photography.

My claim here is not simply that the photograph does not provide the "real" that it claims, is subject to social construction, or is "simply" a sign. Such claims are not novel, and no amount of argumentation seeking to demystify photographic representation can account for the powerful rhetoric of photography, both its promise and the betrayal of its promise. Hermeneutically, a fundamental contamination lies at the heart of photography's rhetoric, between the index-as-plenitude (cataphasis) and the index-as-empty-shifter (apophasis/allegoresis). If cataphasis names the commonsensical understanding of the photographic index as the actual trace of an actual object ("look, it really was there at this time and place!"), then in photography this trace takes an iconic rather than a symbolic form. But all iconic signs have the potential to function symbolically, and cataphasis, as mentioned earlier, necessarily invokes apophasis, which is a metaphysical withholding of explanation. If cataphasis and apophasis of necessity imply each other, then allegoresis names the afterlife of photographic meaning, which shifts with changing historical conditions. My argument is that this contamination between index-as-plenitude and index-as-empty-shifter is the reason that photographs have, again in Bazin's words, an "irrational power to bear away our faith."[84] The images of the Sepoy Revolt examined here are enveloped in a cataphatic logic that is belied by pressing photography into the service of such faith.

Faith

In order to memorialize the death of the British, Trevelyan foregrounds his faith in the necessity of the index. He is critical of the monuments of officialdom: "A truce thenceforward to that mistaken reverence which loves to express sorrow and admiration in guineas, and rupees, and the net product of fancy bazaars!"[85] Rather, an economy of private mourning is in order, one in which the ruins may circulate as already monumental:

> Not urn, nor monolith, nor broken column is so fit a monument for brave men as the crumbling breastwork and the battered wall. And in like manner the dire agony of Cawnpore needs not to be figured in marble, or cut into granite, or cast of bronze. There is no fear lest we should forget the story of our people. The whole place is their tomb, and the name thereof their epitaph. When the traveler . . . , rousing himself to learn at what stage of his journey he may have arrived, is aware of a voice proclaiming through the darkness of the city of melancholy fame,—then those accents, heard for the first time on the very spot itself which they designate, recall, more vividly than written or engraven eloquence, the memory of fruitless valour and unutterable woe.[86]

In a gesture of respect, Trevelyan allows these voices of the dead to resonate without speculating on what they, proclaiming through the darkness, might have to say. The ruins—crumbling breastwork and the battered wall—will speak for themselves, and photography, often showing the very spot itself of the loss, steps in to allow these voices to proclaim their truth as widely as possible. As transmitters of a strange sort of *chalawa,* post–Sepoy Revolt photographs participate in a transaction between the supernatural and the material. No wonder that Thomas Evans, who writes of the Dannenberg Album in the *Pioneer* in 1892, notes that if "places have the adumbrations of human souls still inhabiting their precincts as a sort of delicious spiritual aroma of self-sacrifice pervading the localities where noble life and beautiful human love were shed in profusion for a nation's cause, then this album of Mutiny memorials will remain a sort of incense to the heroic deed in pictorial form."[87] Faith is indeed at stake. Both photographic projects as disparate (and desperate) as capturing the aura of the spaces of death and the topography of spaces designated for capitalist extraction find a home in the rhetoric of photography, that strange sign image that delivers more, less, and other than its promise.

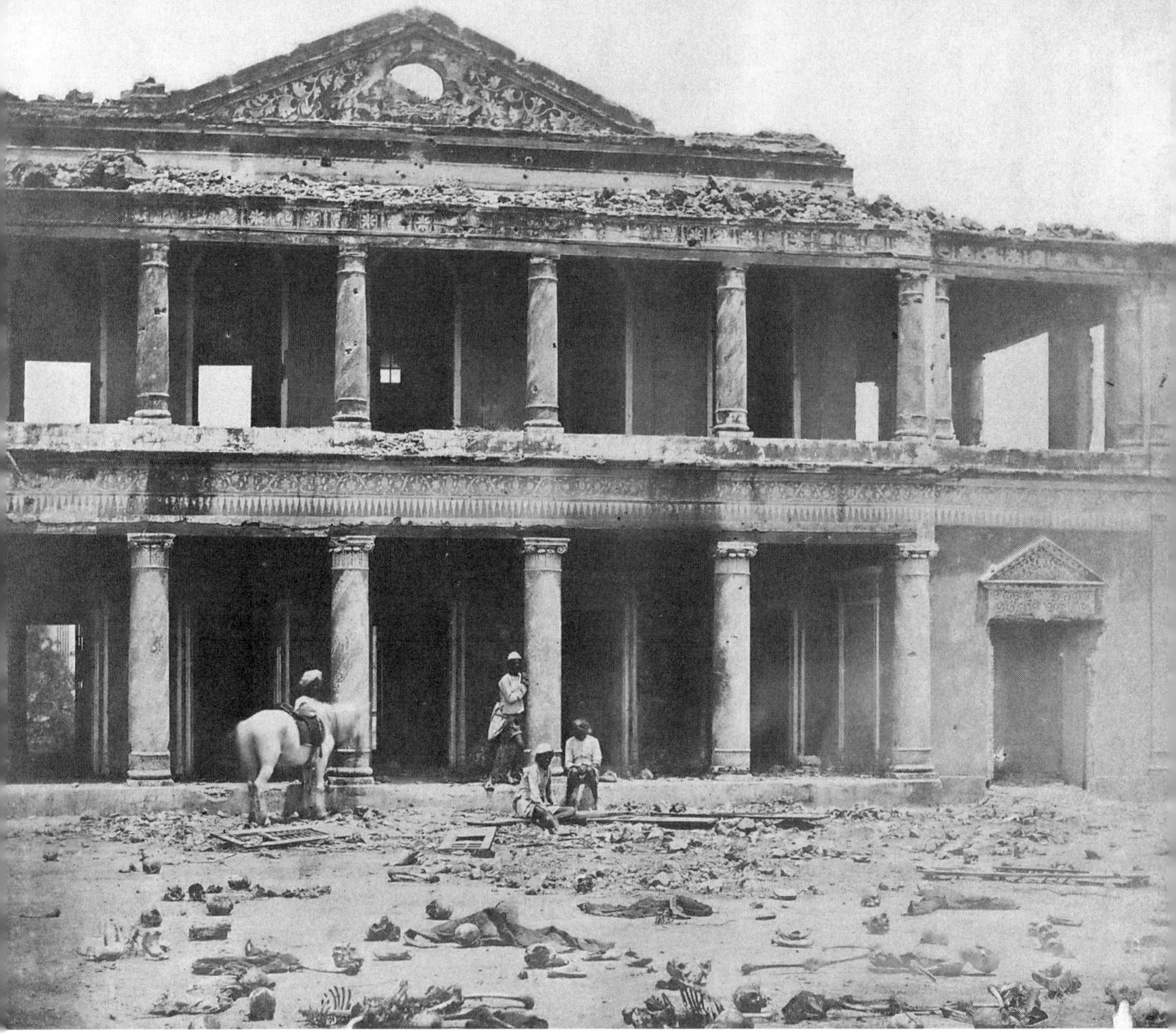

Figure 2.1. Felice Beato, *Interior of the Sikanderbagh after the Slaughter of 2,000 Rebels,* by the 93rd Highlanders and 4th Punjab Regiment. First Attack of Sir Colin Campbell in November 1857, Lucknow, March or April 1858. Copyright British Library Board, Photo 27/(2).

TWO

Anaesthesis and Violence
A Colonial History of Shock

> The constantly encountered assertion that savages, blacks, Japanese are like animals, monkeys for example, is the key to the pogrom. The possibility of pogroms is decided in the moment when the gaze of a fatally-wounded animal falls on a human being. The defiance with which he repels this gaze—"after all, it's only an animal"—reappears irresistibly in cruelties done to human beings, the perpetrators having again and again to reassure themselves that it is "only an animal," because they could never fully believe this even of animals.
>
> —Theodor Adorno, *Minima Moralia*

"A Glorious Sight"

YOU ARE LOOKING AT ANOTHER PHOTOGRAPH from the Sepoy Revolt of 1857–58 (Figure 2.1). The massive building confronting us and extending off-frame to the left is still imposing in its ruin, and it takes a blink of the eye to discern the litter of shattered skulls, decomposing bodies, and skeletons—only one complete—that extends into the space where a camera and now we stand. The faces of the remaining native onlookers are virtually indistinguishable, the focus of their gaze ultimately indiscernible, though some appear to stare directly back at the lens of camera and eye. Only the horse, its face turned away from us, has moved and blurred. This photograph's most common archival caption, *The Interior of the Sikanderbagh after the Slaughter of 2,000 Rebels,* describes what it shows; it is an image from Lucknow, taken not long after the Sepoy Revolt. In Figure 2.2 we see another image taken by the same camera, captioned in one collection *The Ruins of Sammy House Surrounded by Scattered Bones of Sepoys Killed in Action.*[1] Again, the eye adjusts to see the traces of material and human destruction that survived the suppression of the Sepoy Revolt. These massacres were milestones in the British victory. To "see" the full extent and implications of this imaged event, we need to turn, as we tend to do, from the visual to the written, but only in order to return to

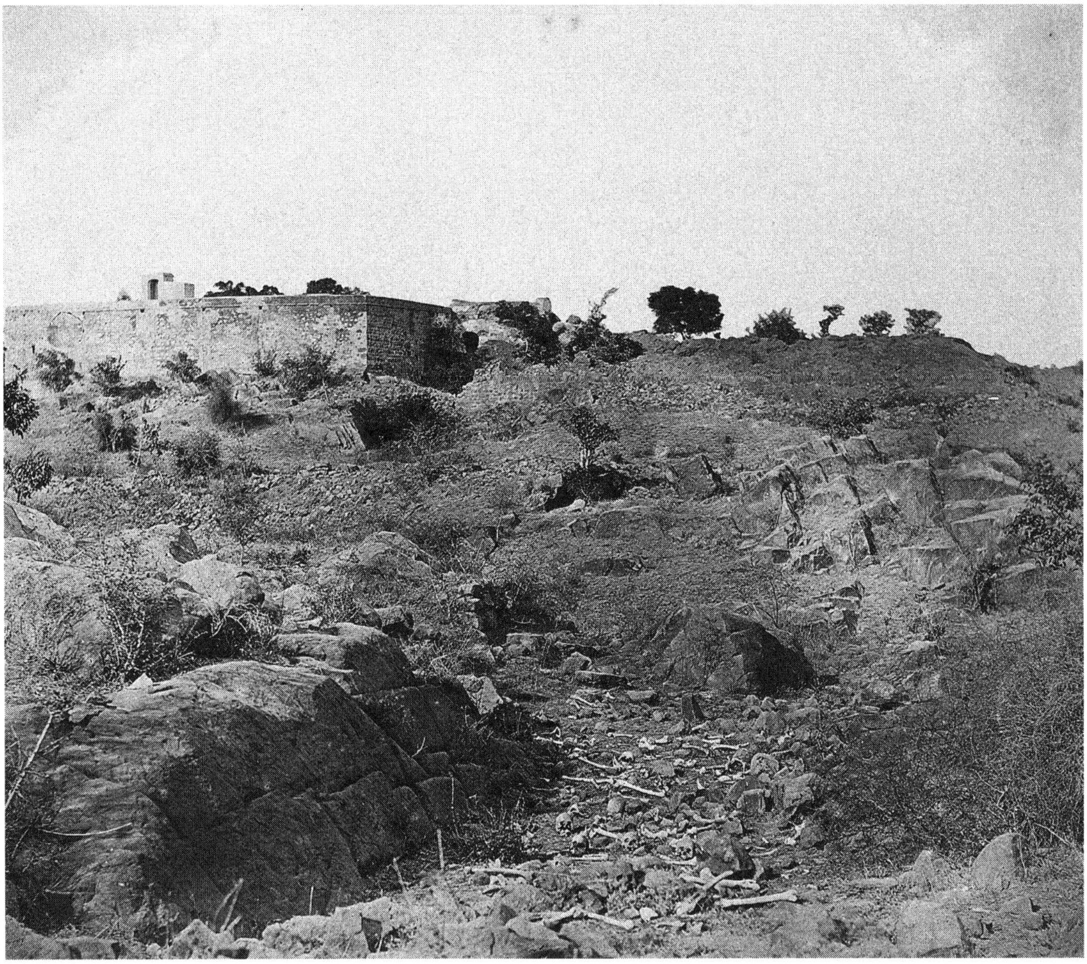

Figure 2.2. Felice Beato, *The Ruins of Sammy House Surrounded by Scattered Bones of Sepoys Killed in Action,* 1858. Wellcome Library, London.

the photographs in a new light and discern the nature of the (in)visibility of violence laid out before us.

At the start of the revolt, Karl Marx, in his London exile, interrupted work on *The Grundrisse* to write for the *New-York Daily Tribune* on September 4, 1857:

> The outrages committed by the revolted Sepoys in India [are] only the reflex, in a concentrated form, of England's own conduct in India, not only during the epoch of the foundation of her Eastern Empire, but even during the last ten years of a long-seated rule. To characterize that rule, it suffices to say that torture formed an organic institution of its financial policy. There is something in human history like retribution; and it is a rule of

> historical retribution that its instrument be forged not by the offended, but by the offender himself.[2]

Marx refers here to the revolt (or "mutiny," as the British were pleased to call it) that had started that May in Meerut. Its overdetermined causes included the discontent of some Indian landowners at losing estates to the British under the policies of Governor-General Dalhousie, the hyperexploitation of peasants through taxation and land "reforms," and the unequal treatment and abuse of Sepoys (Indian recruits in the British Army) by British officers and enlisted men. One particular incident consistently cited in nineteenth-century sources as the spark for the hostilities was the issuance of the new, faster-firing Enfield .303 rifle to all Sepoy regiments. In the course of their nomadic wanderings, fakirs and sadhus apparently spread the rumor that the new cartridges were greased with the fat of pigs and cows, thus defiling Hindu and Muslim Sepoys alike.[3] Refusing to use the new cartridges, the Sepoys took up the older discarded arms and aimed them at their British superiors. The major centers of resistance quickly spread throughout the north, from Bengal to Haryana, with Meerut, Cawnpore, Delhi, and Lucknow being the regional centers of the most sustained battles, which were initially won by the insurgents.[4]

In his writings on what he called the "War of Independence in India," Marx clearly saw the revolt—which was not only fought by the Sepoys but also, to a large extent, supported by an unprecedented "historical bloc" of peasants, urban proletariat, and former property owners—as a step toward the unfolding of a revolution proper. Four years prior to the manifest disturbance among the Sepoys, Marx had already sensed that the conjuncture was opportune, insofar as India was not merely in a position to benefit from the modern industry (and nascent proletariat) brought to it by the British but also poised to overthrow the concomitant yoke of inequality, exploitation, and torture. Sooner or later, he thought, Indians would overcome the oppressive forms of their own social organization as well: "Modern industry, resulting from the railway system, will dissolve the hereditary divisions of labour, upon which rest the Indian castes, those decisive impediments to Indian progress and Indian power."[5] So it was for Marx that the colonized Indian was also aligned with the English proletariat:

> The Indians will not reap the fruits of the new elements of society scattered among them by the British bourgeoisie, till in Great Britain itself the now ruling classes shall have been supplanted by the industrial proletariat, or till the Hindus themselves shall have grown strong enough to throw off the English yoke altogether.[6]

Marx was being optimistic, and in his idealist teleology indigenous Indian forms of social organization in tandem with modern industrialism and colonialism would inevitably lead to the new future grasped as an *Aufhebung* of tightly intertwined economic, political, social, and increasingly military developments.

Unfortunately for this teleology, and for the "natives" themselves, by the end of 1858 the revolt had been effectively smashed by a combination of brute force and lack of organization on the part of the resistance, though not without considerable costs to the other side as well. From the throwing of British bodies, living and dead (including women and children), into a well in Cawnpore to the more or less spontaneous British destruction of neighborhoods believed to be the revolt's centers, the confrontation was arguably the single most violent armed one in the history of the Raj. Although ill fated, its sheer violence left the formerly rather cheery confidence of the British considerably shaken.[7] Virtually all the mechanisms of the colonial apparatus were mobilized, from the repressive to the ideological, from an initial deployment of thousands of new troops to India to revitalized programs for greater hegemonic control—economic, political, and cultural, as well as epistemic—over the Indian population.

But let us return to Sikanderbagh. On November 16, 1857, Sir Colin Campbell, hero–savior of the British under siege in Lucknow, marched on Sikanderbagh with brutal consequence. A member of the British garrison, Edward Hilton, coolly reported: "In the space of a short time, . . . two heavy guns (18-pounders) effected a breach in the south-east corner of the wall surrounding Sikander Bagh," resulting in what Hilton dubbed "a magnificent sight, never to be forgotten—that glorious struggle to be the first to enter the deadly breach, the prize to the winner of the race being certain death."[8] It should go without saying that he meant British death only. Another eyewitness recounted in a letter home to England:

> The main gate gave way and in streamed the rest of the attackers, driving back the enemy into a house behind which was a compound. The door of this the mutineers had bricked up as they had expected an attack from the north; they could not, therefore, get out, and now ensued a scene of carnage, for there was no thought of surrender, and Cawnpore and many another massacres [of the British] were remembered.[9]

And so, too, Lieutenant Arthur Moffat Lang reported:

> The effect was electrical, down we dropped the ropes and rushed along too . . . shouting "Revenge for Cawnpore" as we went . . . and then! Didn't we get revenge! The first good revenge I have seen. . . . The air was alive with bullets, I never heard such distracting row. . . . at the house in the middle of the rear wall and in the semicircular court beyond, it was a glorious sight to see the mass of bodies, dead and wounded, when we did get in: they shut the many thin doors and *thousands* of bullets were poured into the masses. The Mass were set fire to, and you may fancy how the wounded cried out to be shot.[10]

In effect, these references to Cawnpore justified the carnage and propelled the soldiers forward without mercy in collective retaliation for the throwing of British military and civilian bodies earlier that year into that aforementioned well. So it was, then, at Sikanderbagh that native bodies were hastily buried (so to speak) just outside the walls of the courtyard, while others were left to decompose in a sealed chamber within the building. A certain Francis Collins remarked on that spectacle: "The stench here of decaying bodies is beyond description, but somewhat lessened by the burial of some of the corpses, and the covering, as far as possible, of the remainder with earth."[11] Fortunately, at least for history—or rather what Hegel famously called "the slaughter bench of history"—what is beyond description is not necessarily beyond photography. Photography steps in where language fails; it promises to make visible those parts of a story that slip from the grasp of language.

War by Other Means

It was five months after Sikanderbagh that photographer Felice Beato arrived in Lucknow, intending to document history in its making.[12] He had come directly from the Crimean War, where he had worked alongside Roger Fenton to photograph the vicious battles of Sebastopol, which had so shocked the European consciousness (if not conscience) in a way that the events in India precisely did not. Beato had arrived in Lucknow too late, however, and the official "history of the mutiny" had already entered its memorializing stage. Not content with mere architectural ruins and in search of the immediacy and truth of battle as well as the very instants of death, Beato ordered full exhumation of the half-buried corpses and posed them in the courtyard of Sikanderbagh.[13] The resulting photograph was (mis)captioned in London, advertising the image as taken later the very day of the assault on Sikanderbagh.[14] Our archives contain less information about Figure 2.2, but the overly "naturalized" path of human skulls and bones again suggests manipulation of the dead. After Beato's photographs were exhibited at London's Victoria and Albert Museum,[15] reproductions of them began to appear in private albums of the British whose connection to Lucknow ranged from having actually fought there in 1857–58 to having some family member or acquaintance who did. These albums often intersperse Beato's brutal "mutiny" photographs (Figures 2.1–2.7, 2.14) with those of loved ones decked with military regalia or those of equally generic subjects, such as landscapes of the colonial subcontinent.[16]

In Figures 2.1 and 2.2, what, precisely, is the aesthetic desire that dictates the arrangement of human remains, as if they were a column or drapery, mere props for the photographer's staging? Within the context of British imperialism, these photographs sit uneasily next to generic images of the Raj: the British

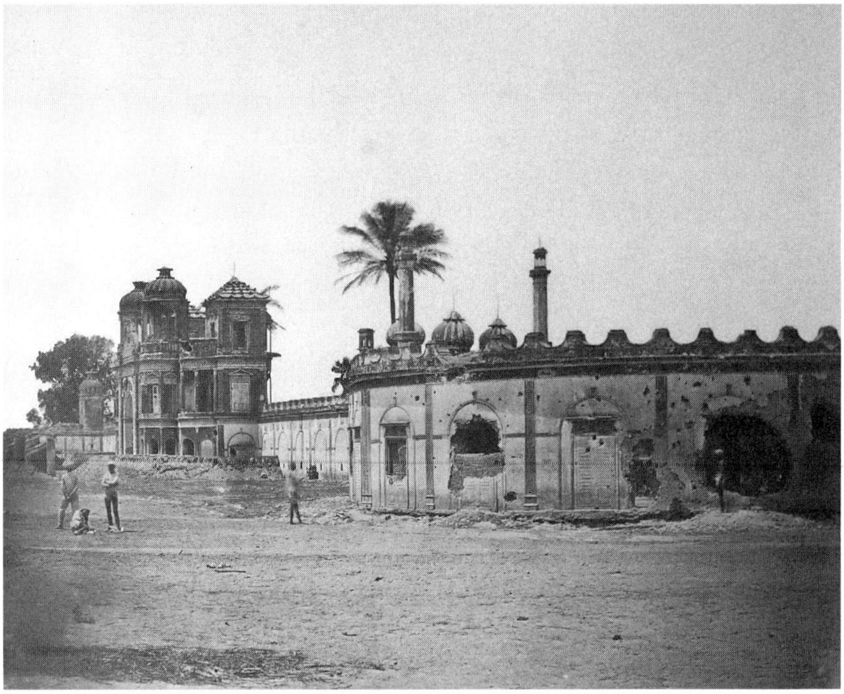

Figure 2.3. Felice Beato, *The Sikanderbagh, Showing the Gateway, and the Breech Made by Sir Colin Campbell's Troops,* Lucknow, 1858. Figure on far right stands at the breach. The Alkazi Collection of Photography.

Figure 2.4. Felice Beato, *The Mine in the Chutter Munzil,* Lucknow, 1858. The Alkazi Collection of Photography.

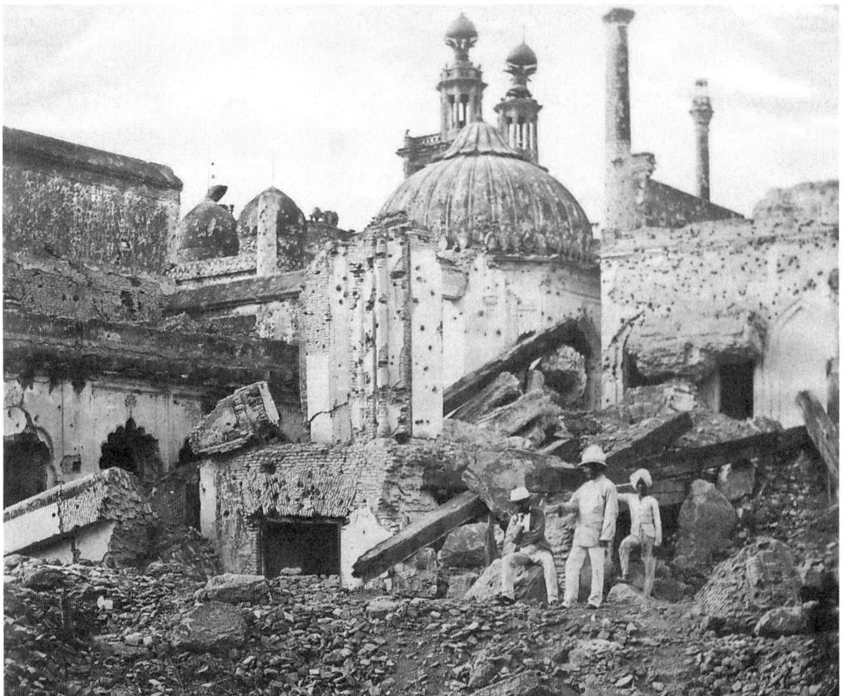

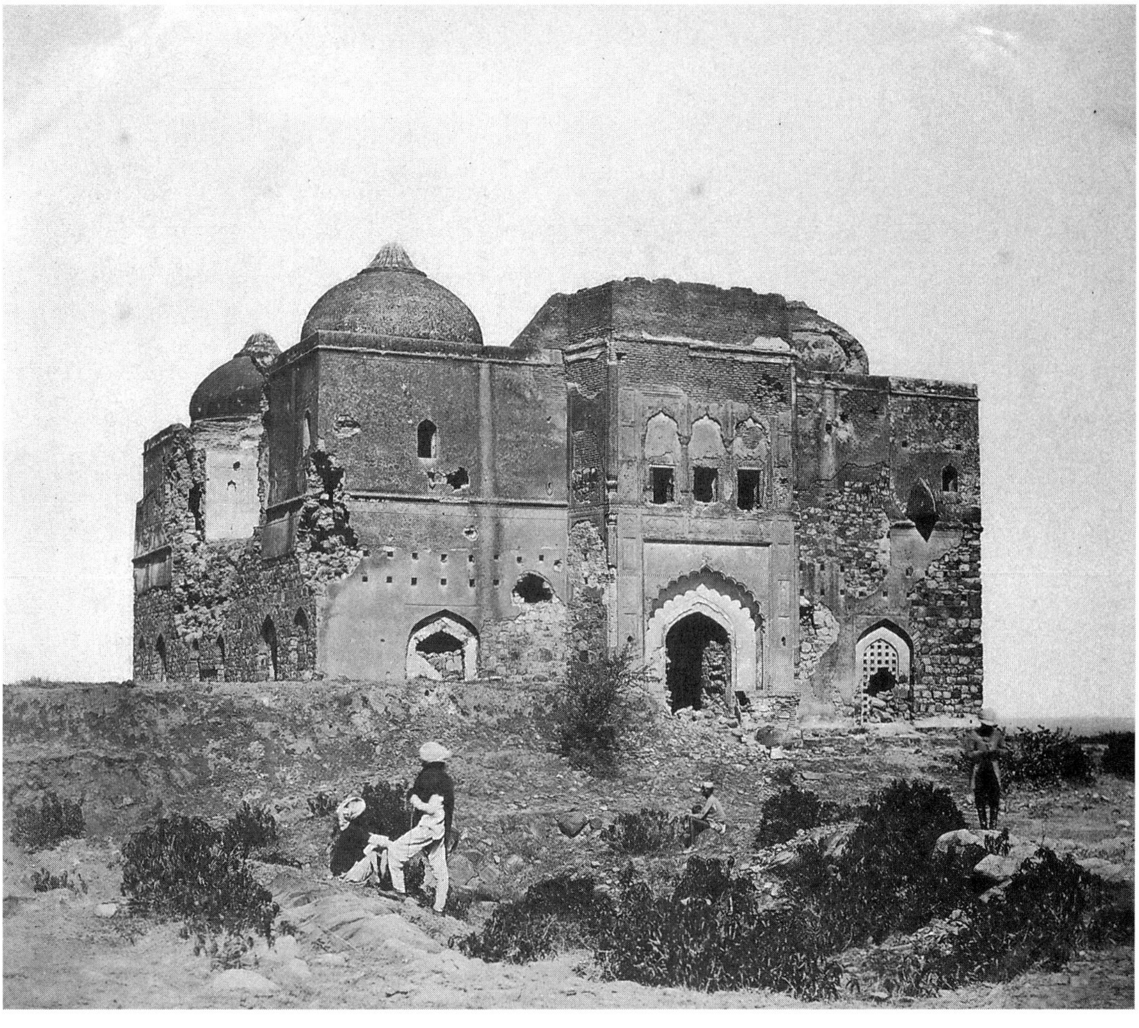

Figure 2.5. Felice Beato, *A Ruined Mosque,* 1858.
Wellcome Library, London.

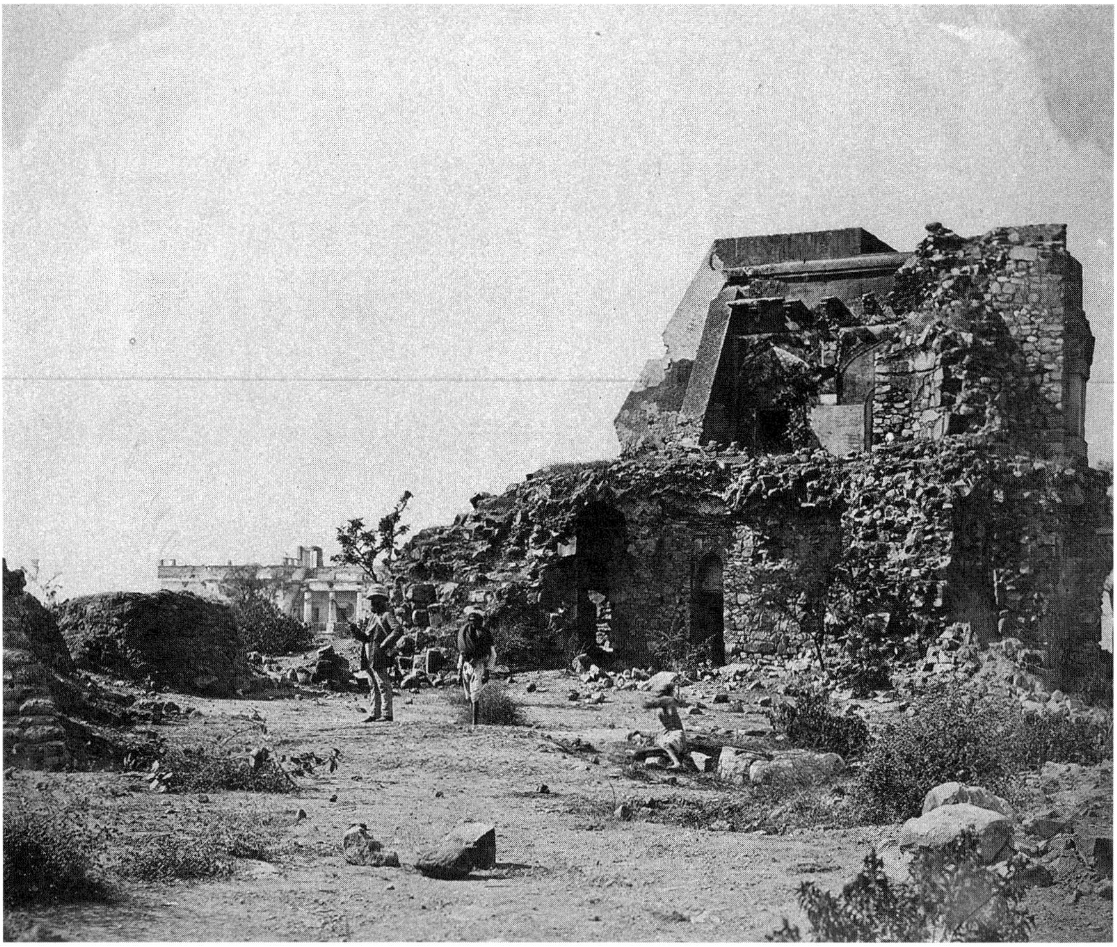

Figure 2.6. Felice Beato, *A Ruined Observatory and Battery with Distant View of "Hindoo Rao's House"* (a post on the Delhi Ridge occupied by the British), 1858. Wellcome Library, London.

dressed in Victorian garb, enjoying tea on the terrace, or posing in full military regalia. The construction of these photographs' aesthetic effect depends, nevertheless, on the same structures of perception as do all other genres of colonial photography. Arguably among the first documentary photographs in their tradition (a tradition that still brings us images of carnage into the security of our domestic spaces), they at once record and reproduce the brutality of history.

Beato's photographs are symptomatic of what I call the "phantasmagoric aesthetic." This aesthetic is among the results of the technological mediation of vision, the penetration of reality with apparatus that in turn transforms our understanding of what counts as reality. Walter Benjamin uses the phrase "deepening of apperception" to refer to these and other aspects of experience in modernity. Such apperception includes an alienation from one's own social and physical embodiment that becomes the ground from which otherwise invisible violence toward others as well as oneself may be witnessed with comparative ease.[17] This chapter develops this concept of the phantasmagoric aesthetic, which, in British India, helps perform the cultural–political labor of the colonial management of "natives." I argue that photography makes its most widespread and effective impact in India during a precise shift in the ordering of colonial power and that the phantasmagoric aesthetic marks the point at which this power begins to extend its scope into the lifeworlds of colonial subjects. This aesthetic renders invisible the violence of colonial relations of production, just as after the Sepoy Revolt this violence intensifies its epistemic and material intrusion into the everyday life of colonial subjects.[18] The genre of "manners and customs" images, for example, though not unique to the colonies (or to photography), highlights the social spaces, habits, and ways of being

Figure 2.7. Felice Beato, *Clock Tower, Lucknow,* 1858. The Alkazi Collection of Photography.

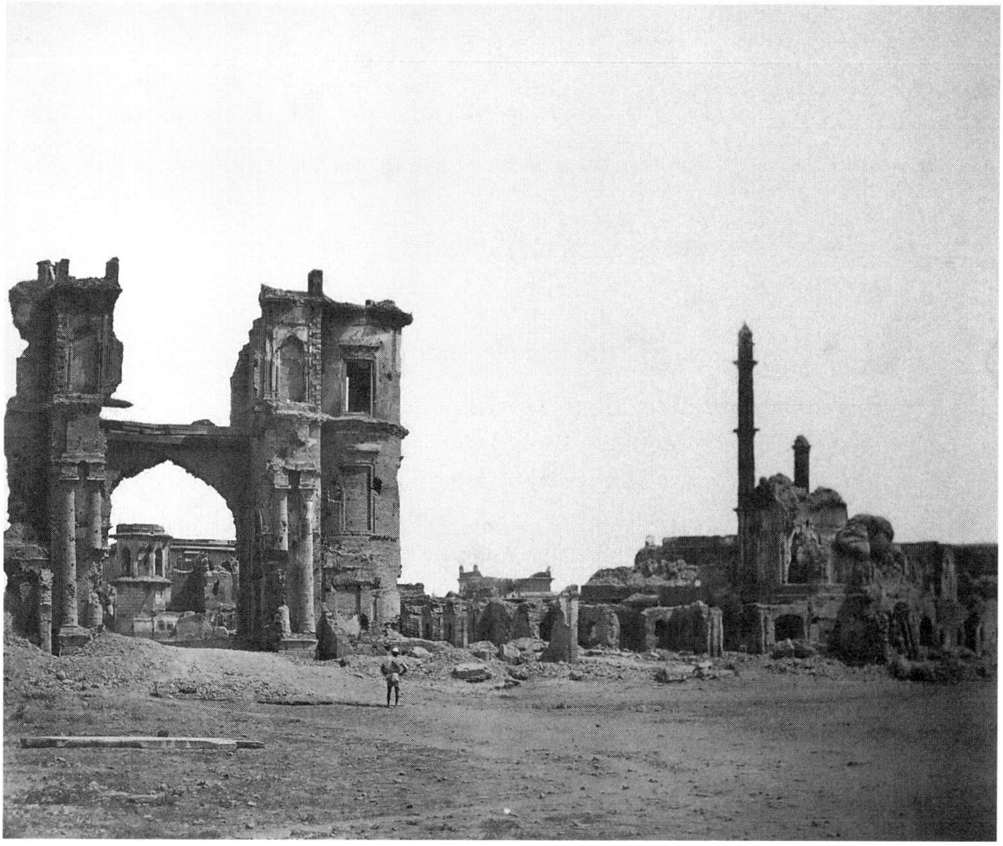

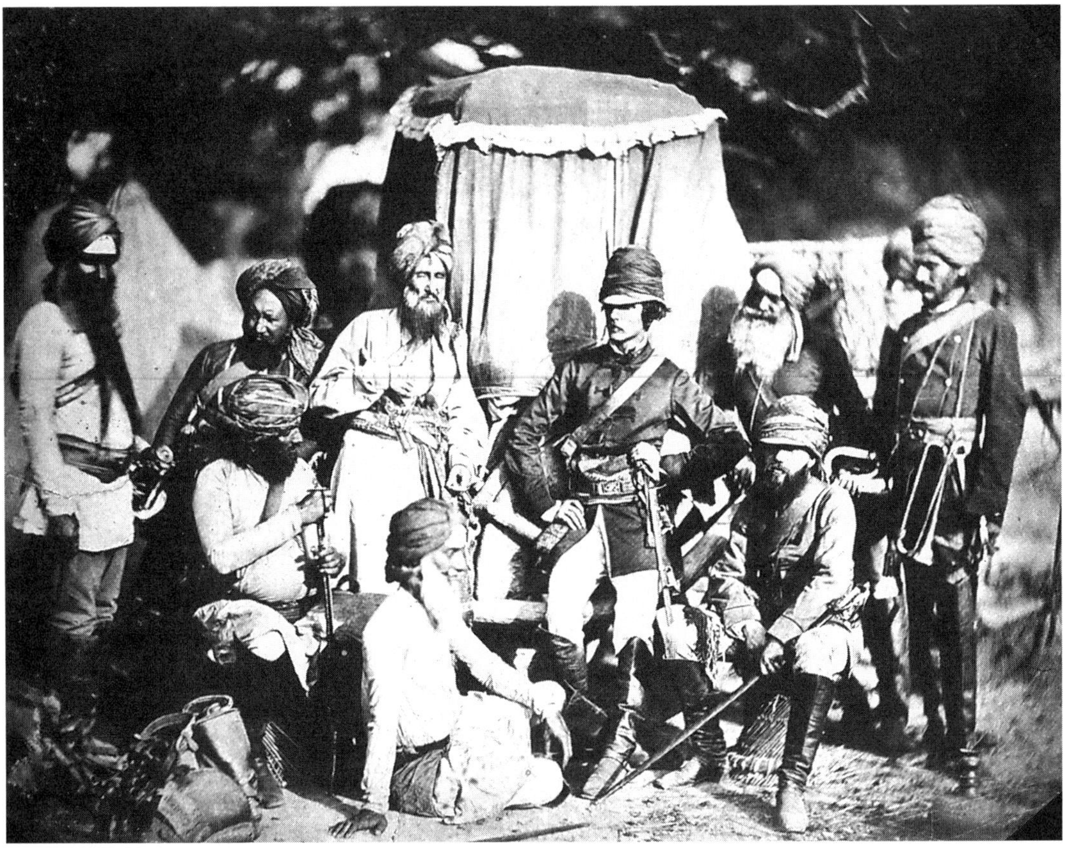

Figure 2.8. Felice Beato, *Hodson's Horse* (the name of the cavalry regiment raised by William Hodson), 1858 or 1859. Digital image courtesy of the Digital Content Library, University of Minnesota.

that now come under the purview of colonial governmentality.[19] I borrow the term *governmentality* from Michel Foucault, who notes that in the modern era the foundations of governmental sovereignty shift from being based almost exclusively on territory and property to being based on a "complex composed of men and things."[20] By "men and things," Foucault is referring to the whole network of social relations that constitute a principality:

> The things with which in this sense government is to be concerned are in fact men, but men in their relations, their links, their imbrication with those other things which are wealth, resources, means of subsistence, the territory with its specific qualities, climate, irrigation, fertility, etc.; men in their relation to that other kind of things, customs, habits, ways of acting and thinking, etc.; lastly, men in their relation to that other kind of things, accidents and misfortunes such as famine, epidemics, death, etc.[21]

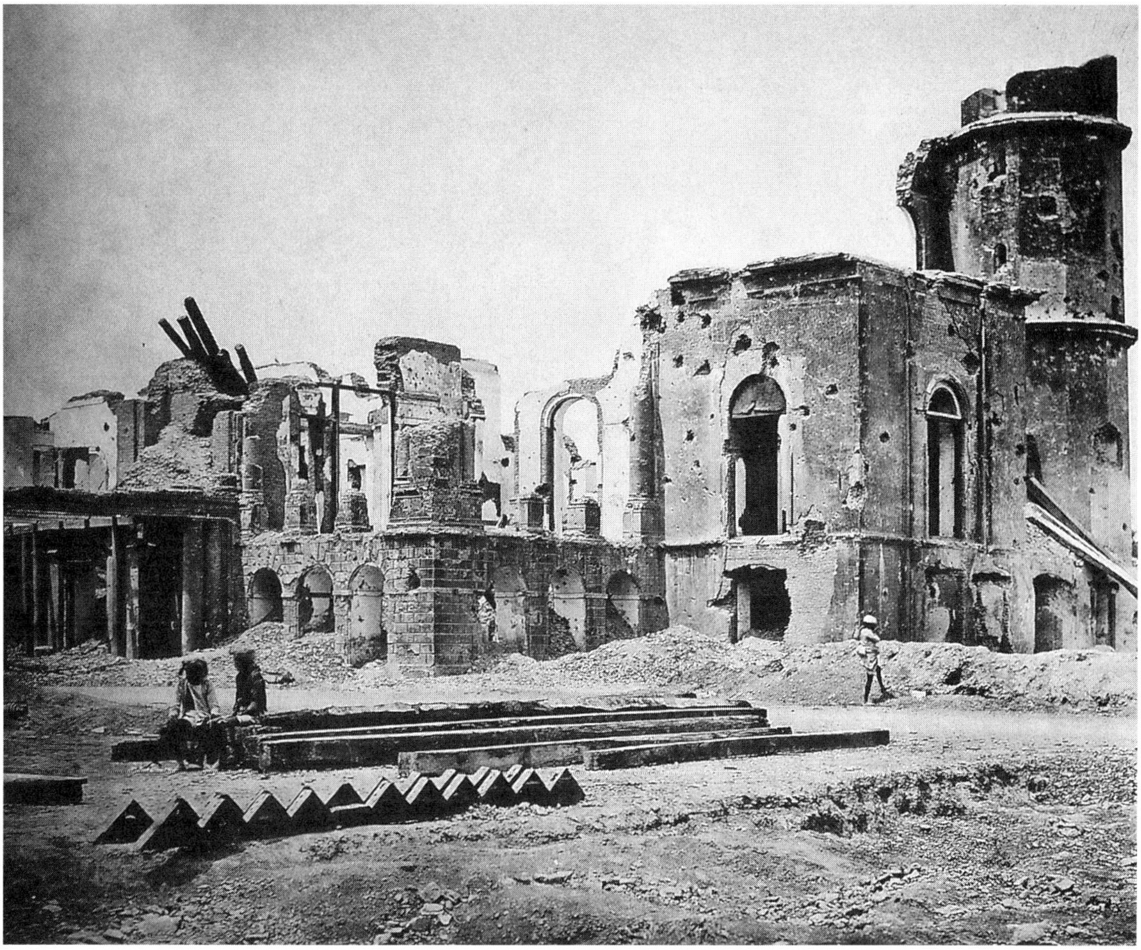

Figure 2.9. Felice Beato, *The Residency Taken in Front, and Showing the Room in Which Sir Henry Lawrence Was Killed,* Lucknow, March or April 1858. Digital image courtesy of the Digital Content Library, University of Minnesota.

This new field of governance can roughly be defined as having "the population" (or the "mass"), complete with its social relations and political–economic structures, as its object. But in addition to population, governmentality includes within its scope "things" as well as "men," that is, "wealth, resources, means of subsistence, the territory with its specific qualities, climate, irrigation, fertility"—in short, all of those material things that constitute social relations. Foucault points out that this power does not overlap with state power as such, so modern governmentality as a concept is not simply interchangeable with governance, administration, or general dominance: "Maybe what is really important for our modernity—that is, for our present—is not so much the *étatisation* of society, as the 'governmentalization' of the state."[22] In other words, governmentality exceeds mere state governance/administration; it is a process employed as much by private capital as it is by the state.[23] In this modern form of governmentality, statistics become "a major technical factor" through which the regularities of population can be ascertained: "its own rate of deaths and diseases, its cycles of scarcity, . . . ascending spirals of labour and wealth," all of which come to bear, among other things, on "specific *economic* effects."[24]

Statistics became a science of its own by the end of the nineteenth century, and its methods quickly adapted to colonial administration in India, especially after the Sepoy Revolt.[25] Through the development of statistics and other technologies of management, the violence of modern governmentality effectively penetrates into the social pores of society. Moreover, this shift is both discursive and material; it is as implicated in the production of official and unofficial knowledge as it is in the regulation of the means of extracting surplus value from increasingly alienated colonized bodies. I use the term *phantasmagoric aesthetics* to underscore this material—*bodily*—dimension of colonial governmentality, both a dimension that exceeds the discursive sphere of colonial knowledge production and also one upon which colonial governmentality comes to depend. We will return to the question of the body and statistics, and their importance to both material and discursive aspects of colonial photography, later in this chapter. The phantasmagoric aesthetic, at the juncture of discursive and material dimensions of colonial relations of production, mystifies violence even as that violence becomes more present and diffused into the management of the very "manners and customs" of colonial subjects; like the commodity form, this aesthetic obscures actually existing social relations in the partial service of their perpetuation.

Photography comes to play a crucial role in this process. Widely seen to be an immediate emanation of reality, a transparent window onto the real, photography allegedly gave us access to scientifically certifiable truth. Even in the late nineteenth century, according to Allan Sekula, "the lingering prestige of optical empiricism was sufficiently strong to ensure that the terrain of the photographable was still regarded as roughly congruent with that of knowledge in general."[26] This powerful truth effect of photography was singularly important for photography's functions in the nineteenth century, placing it in a different realm altogether from other visual mediums and rendering it instrumental for the purposes of governmentality.

Since photographic projects were commissioned on an unprecedented scale in India only after the Sepoy Revolt of 1857, the terms in which photography was discussed in India are revealing. The extraordinary proliferation of photographs of "the native" in the Raj immediately after the Sepoy Revolt suggests both the wider availability of photographic apparatuses and materials and a more complex network of representation, misrepresentation, and colonial anxiety, which this violent uprising intensified and which had to be "subjected" in all senses. Listen to anthropologist E. F. Thurn, lecturing to the Royal Anthropological Society of Great Britain and Ireland in 1893:

> My special concern, tonight . . . is as to the use of the camera for the accurate record, not of the mere bodies of primitive folk—which might indeed be more accurately measured and photographed for such purposes dead than alive, could they be conveniently obtained when in that state—but of these folk regarded as living beings.[27]

After the military suppression of the Sepoy Revolt, a revolt that haunted the London administration for decades to come, the image of the dead native perhaps came too readily to Thurn's mind. Earlier in the lecture, Thurn states that the true aim of anthropological photography is to capture the living "primitive phases of life" that are "fast fading from the world."[28] Yet later, Thurn modifies this initial position by asserting the equal importance of what he calls "physiological photographs." These would be "taken in accordance to a fixed scale" and accompanied by the "exact measurements of" the subject photographed (see Figures 2.10 and 2.11).[29] The longer statement (when not overly read against its intended grain) tacitly proposes to kill the observed primitive, if it weren't so "inconvenient," in the service of a desire for "scientific" documentation. If the accuracy of the measurement of "mere bodies" is a function of the death of those bodies, what does the corollary "measurement" of the body's living daily rituals (the genre of "manners and customs") imply?

The recurrence of the language of violence in discussions on photography suggests more than a merely metaphorical affinity in the following excerpt from Samuel Bourne, an illustrious figure in Indian landscape photography:

> As there is now scarcely a nook or corner, a glen, a valley, or mountain, much less a country, on the face of the globe which the penetrating eye of the camera has not searched, or where the perfumes of poor Archer's collodion have not risen through the hot or freezing atmosphere, photography in India is, least of all, a new thing. From the earliest days of the calotype, the curious tripod, with its mysterious chamber and mouth of brass, taught the natives of this country that their conquerors were the inventors of other instruments beside the formidable guns of their artillery, which, though as suspicious perhaps in appearance, attained their object with less noise and smoke.[30]

In short, the camera could replace the gun, at least under certain conditions. Now, my claim here is not simply that the visual is related to the knowable but also that a double shadow of fear and displaced violence accompanied colonial photographic practice generally and specifically. After the revolt was

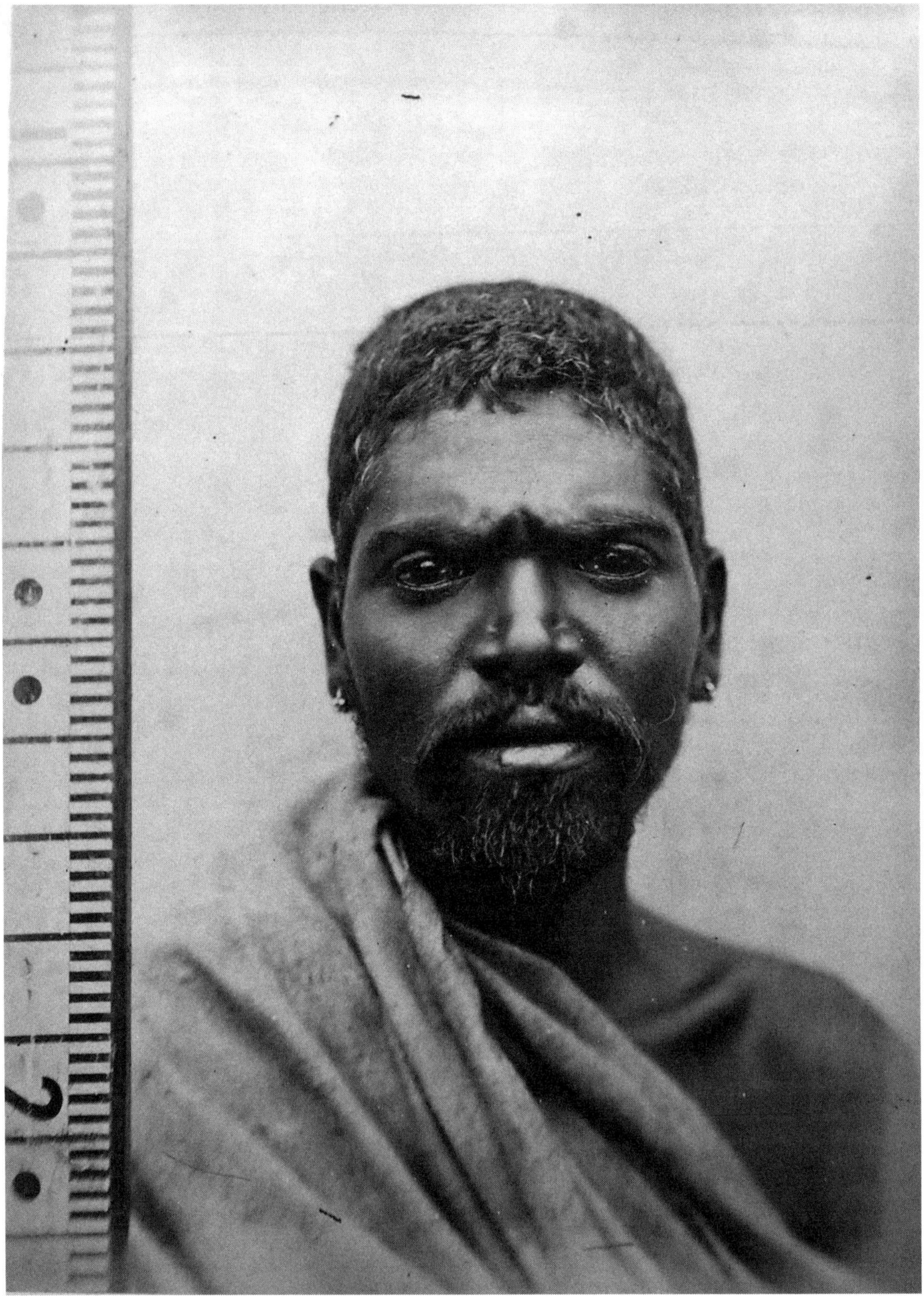

Figure 2.10. Kota Man. From J. W. Breeks, *An Account of the Primitive Tribes and Monuments of the Nilgiris,* 1873. The Alkazi Collection of Photography.

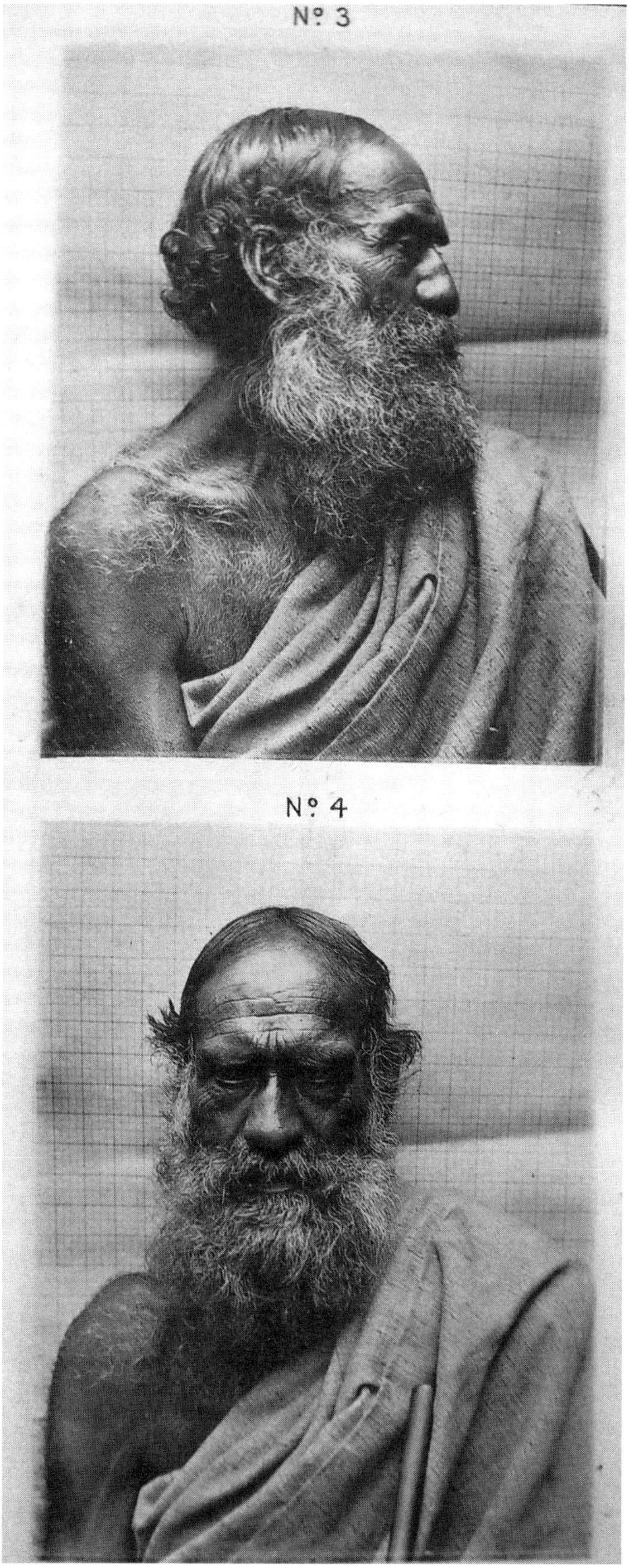

Figure 2.11. Toda Man. From W. E. Marshall, *A Phrenologist amongst the Todas,* 1873. The Alkazi Collection of Photography.

"pacified," close scrutiny of the Indian population—as a remarkably direct extension of "pacification"—became a necessity in the new mode of governance; that is, it became war by other means.[31] I mean this quite literally. If, as Baron von Clausewitz stated in his posthumously published *On War* (1832), "war is nothing but the continuation of political activity with the admixture of other means," then, less than a century later British photographs of India had become the scientific and artistic shock troops of those very means.[32]

On the Visible

The colonial violence that took military form in the suppression of the Sepoy Revolt was simply one crystallized instance of a violence that governs colonial relations. The colonial context, arguably a constant state of war and occupation, exemplifies Walter Benjamin's reading of history as a series of catastrophes, the violence of which the progressive narratives of history mystify. The invisibility of violence, so necessary for the perpetuation of modernity's truths (progress, universal freedom), structures the self-definition of (British) imperialism. I would like to develop this claim via a diversion through Benjamin's critique of modernity in order to situate the epistemic and historical force of Beato's photographs.

In *The Arcades Project,* Benjamin elaborates on the ways in which capitalist modernity wraps itself in mists of various stripes, from the phantasmagoria of the glittering marketplace to the one of the private bourgeois interior. One of Benjamin's concerns, congruent with Marx's *Capital,* is to show the social bases of things, the unequal circulation of power that often invisibly structures what appears to us as immediate and free of violence. Criticizing newspapers for presenting to the public a vision of the world that amounts to nothing more than an "endless series of facts congealed in the form of things" that have no connection to one another, Benjamin writes, "The riches thus amassed in the aerarium of civilization henceforth appear as though identified for all time. This conception of history minimizes the fact that such riches owe not only their existence but also their transmission to a constant effort of society—an effort, moreover, by which these riches are strangely altered."[33] This constant effort, at the height of industrialism, was not restricted to the bounds of Europe but extended outside it, following the contours of the reach of imperialism. So to the collapse of the Second Empire and the Commune of Paris must be added hundreds of struggles, not only daily struggles, but also the climactic struggles of other social movements, other victories and failures.[34]

The centerpiece of Benjamin's *Arcades Project* (much as in Marx's *Capital*) is the commodity itself. Since the arcades were "temples of commodity capital," the commodity figured as central to the concerns of writing what Benjamin called the "ur-history" of the nineteenth century, and simultaneously it was central to the awakening from phantasmagoria. Examining social relations that are the basis of the commodity, we inevitably bring to the fore the presence of the colonies, both literally and formally. At the literal level, the arcades housed shops selling, among other specialties, exotic artifacts from the colonies that would make their way directly into the bourgeois interior, where Benjamin locates the bourgeois subject who "brings together remote locales and memories of the past."[35] It is a site that telescopes the external world into its space and serves as a shrine for memory. The domestic interior of the bourgeois subject does not exist outside a global political economy but is conditioned by it: "His [or her] living room is a box in the theatre of the world."[36] In this theater—and here we come to the more fundamental and formal relationship between metropolitan centers and the colonies—capital produces a surplus through mass colonial labor (as a powerful supplement to local labor).

In addition to appearing in the domestic interior and the arcade shops, the colony made a visible appearance as an exotic setting for panoramas. World exhibitions, with their massive displays of machine technologies, attractions, curiosities, and reproductions of foreign spaces (for example, the Cairo street scene in the Paris Exposition of 1889) also frequently brought the material of the colonies into the metropole.[37] At the world exhibitions, the masses were trained by the large-scale displays of commodities: "Barred from consuming, [they] learned empathy with exchange value. 'Look at everything; touch nothing.'"[38] These exhibitions displayed the latest in the wares of progress, and, as Buck-Morss writes in her reading of *The Arcades Project,* "proletarians were encouraged by the authorities to make the 'pilgrimage' to these shrines of industry, to view on display the wonders that their own class had produced but could not afford to own, or to marvel at machines that would displace them."[39] And this laboring class extended outside Europe and into the plantations, sweatshops, barracks, and factories of the European colonies, stretching around the globe.

At issue in discussions of the commodity form is not only its global reach but also what Marx formulates in *Capital,* volume 1, as the dialectic of (in)visibility that regulates this form. Crystal Bartolovich locates this dialectic in the network of relations between metropolitan (imperial) centers and the colonies: "The everyday experience of imperial relations by African peoples was (is) often invisible in the metropole as such—either completely so, because unspoken, or because diverted by fantastical displacements."[40] This sort of invisibility is, as Bartolovich implies, the transposition of the logic of the commodity into global political economy. Marx analyzes the commodity form as that which contains an element of the imperceptible: when the table becomes a commodity, it exceeds the materiality of the wood and "changes into a thing which transcends sensuousness."[41]

> The commodity-form, and the value relation of the products of labour within which it appears, have absolutely no connection with the physical nature of the commodity and the material relations arising out of this. It is nothing but a definite social relation between men, which assumes, for them, the phantasmagoric form of a relation between things.[42]

What the commodity mystifies is the network of social relations that come to bear upon its very existence; Marx's aim is to illustrate precisely the social nature of commodities, which mystify even as they present themselves as immediate and wholly visible. This dialectic of (in)visibility—which manifests itself at both global and local levels—is what I explore in this chapter.

The nineteenth century reveled in the world of images, inventing visual technologies that arguably changed the very order of modernity and that are the basis of our contemporary televisual world.[43] Technology produces an aggregation of the visual that is the signature of modernity, and therefore critical knowledge of the present moment must necessarily turn to these visual forms and work through them. When the images of the past are brought into constellation with the present moment, the "lightening flash" of truth is born, according to Benjamin,[44] and this critical knowledge begins the task of seeing through the phantasmagorias of modernity. The inspiration for this knowledge does not come from official histories, which are always written by the victors, but rather from the scraps, the "garbage heap," of modern history, from the failures and aborted processes, the ruins of the commodity world. The wreckage remaining after the catastrophes of history, the debris littering the path of global progress, forms the material for Benjamin's historical materialist hermeneutics.[45] The discarded and outdated image fragments of the past become legible in the present so that we may gain critical knowledge befitting the present moment.

Anaesthesis

Felice Beato's photographs, taken in the aftermath of a failed historic revolt and picturing ruins left in the wake of progress, are themselves outdated, almost forgotten images in the current pyrotechnics of serial war imagery. As noted earlier, these photographs bespeak an aesthetic distance that runs counter to the claims of photography's immediacy. One assumption of this new aesthetic mode is that the world and its objects are always at hand, always at the mercy of the aesthetic imagination. Scenes of destruction are overdetermined by their social reality and transformed into glittering, aesthetically coherent assemblages of a reality placed at a distance and on display, and this distancing is the precondition for an aesthetic that manages to convert brutality into beauty. What accounts for such strategies of distancing that simultaneously proclaim the immediacy of the real and their transformation of it?

An answer is suggested in the final section of Benjamin's "Work of Art" essay, which, while celebrating the emancipation of art brought about by its technological reproducibility, closes with a note of warning:

> *"Fiat ars—pereat mundus"* [create art—destroy the world], says Fascism, and expects war to supply, just as Marinetti confesses that it does, the artistic gratification of a sense perception that has been altered by technology. This is the obvious perfection of *"l'art pour l'art."* Humanity that, according to Homer, was an object of spectacle *[Schauobjekt]* for the Olympian gods, now is one for itself. Its self-alienation has reached such a degree that it is capable of experiencing *[erleben]* its own destruction as an aesthetic enjoyment *[Genuss]* of the highest order. So it is with the aestheticization of politics, which is being managed by fascism. Communism responds with the politicization of art.[46]

Buck-Morss, in an extended reading of this passage, explores the conditions of possibility for this modern self-alienation. She argues that the alienation referenced in this passage refers to a crisis in cognitive experience: "Benjamin is saying that sensory alienation lies at the source of the aestheticization of politics, which fascism does not create, but merely 'manages.' We are to assume that both alienation and aestheticized politics as the sensual conditions of modernity outlive fascism—and thus so does the enjoyment taken in viewing our own destruction."[47] From this problematic, Buck-Morss begins her account of a history of the transformation in perception that becomes the ground for fascism and, most crucially, *outlives* it. She reminds us that its etymological origin, *Aisthitikos,* meaning "that which is perceptive by feeling," foregrounds the human sensorium. As a form of cognition spanning all of the senses, aesthetics foregrounds the surface of the body, "the mediating boundary between inner and outer," upon which the sensory receptors for touch, taste, smell, sight, and hearing are located. Buck-Morss calls these the "synaesthetic system."[48]

Buck-Morss provides a noncartesian account of perception, whereby the synaesthetic system of human perception is not contained within the body but operates in and through the world.[49] Experiences of shock under modernity eventually block the openness of this system and reverse its role, numbing the organism instead of enabling perception. Consciousness then becomes a numbing shield against excessive stimuli, and this marks the impoverishment of experience under modernity, destroying the person's ability to respond politically even when self-preservation is at stake. In the nineteenth century, in addition to the body's self-anesthetizing defenses, methods for intentional manipulation of the synaesthetic system proliferated, including a plethora of new intoxicating substances and therapeutic practices. Most crucially, "a narcotic was made out of reality itself" through phantasmagoric spectacles.[50]

The word *phantasmagoria* comes from England and was coined in 1802 to refer to a spectacle of optical illusions that move and change in size, blending into one another, through the manipulation of magic lanterns.[51] In Benjamin's work this came to designate all manner of mass distractions, from the consumer's experience of the shopping arcades in Paris, dazzling with their display of commodities from around the globe, to the panoramas and dioramas that would engulf the observer and encapsulate a world.[52] The phantasmagoric floods the senses and strives to construct patterns of wholeness, unity, and surface harmony in order to numb the body to reality. Incidentally, I would note that the colony, in addition to being structurally present in the very commodity form in the nineteenth century, is literally present in many forms of nineteenth-century phantasmagoria: in the panorama (there was a "Siege of Lucknow" panorama in London in the 1860s);[53] the arcade (in the sale of exotic artifacts); the world exhibitions (the Cairo street scene, for example, in the Paris Exposition Universelle, of 1889); and in the phantasmagoria of the bourgeois interior, with its overfull orientalia (Figure 2.12).[54] If Europeans imported exotica from the colonies to display in their interiors, such traffic in commodities worked both ways for Indian elites, such as Mehboob Ali Khan, the sixth nizam of Hydrabad, whose taste in European furnishings is artfully captured in a photograph of the nizam's drawing room, taken by his court photographer Lala Deen Dayal (Figure 2.13).[55] Unlike the use of individual drugs, phantasmagorias are experienced collectively, and therefore they "assume the position of objective fact."[56]

The factory figures in the nineteenth century as a counterphantasmagoria based as it is on principles of fragmentation rather than visions of wholeness. It is also a total environment, as Marx reminds us, since all the senses are injured equally. In this atmosphere, the surgeon emerges as a new socially prominent figure, responsible for piecing back together the casualties caused by industrialism, which can now be predicted with statistical certitude (a crucial factor, the reader will recall, in the production of what Foucault calls the "population," the unit that is the modern object of governmentality). The development of anesthesia allowed the surgeon to treat the body as raw material to be shaped, whereas before he had to desensitize himself from the experience of seeing another person in pain. In short, the body could be seen as insensate inert material; it becomes the subject of statistics, its behavior can be measured against a "norm," and it develops a new virtuality, able to "endure the shocks of modernity without pain."[57] Buck-Morss argues that this perception of another's body as inert matter eventually extended to the social body (population) itself:

> [Now] any number of operations could be performed upon the social body without needing to concern oneself lest the patient—society itself—"utter

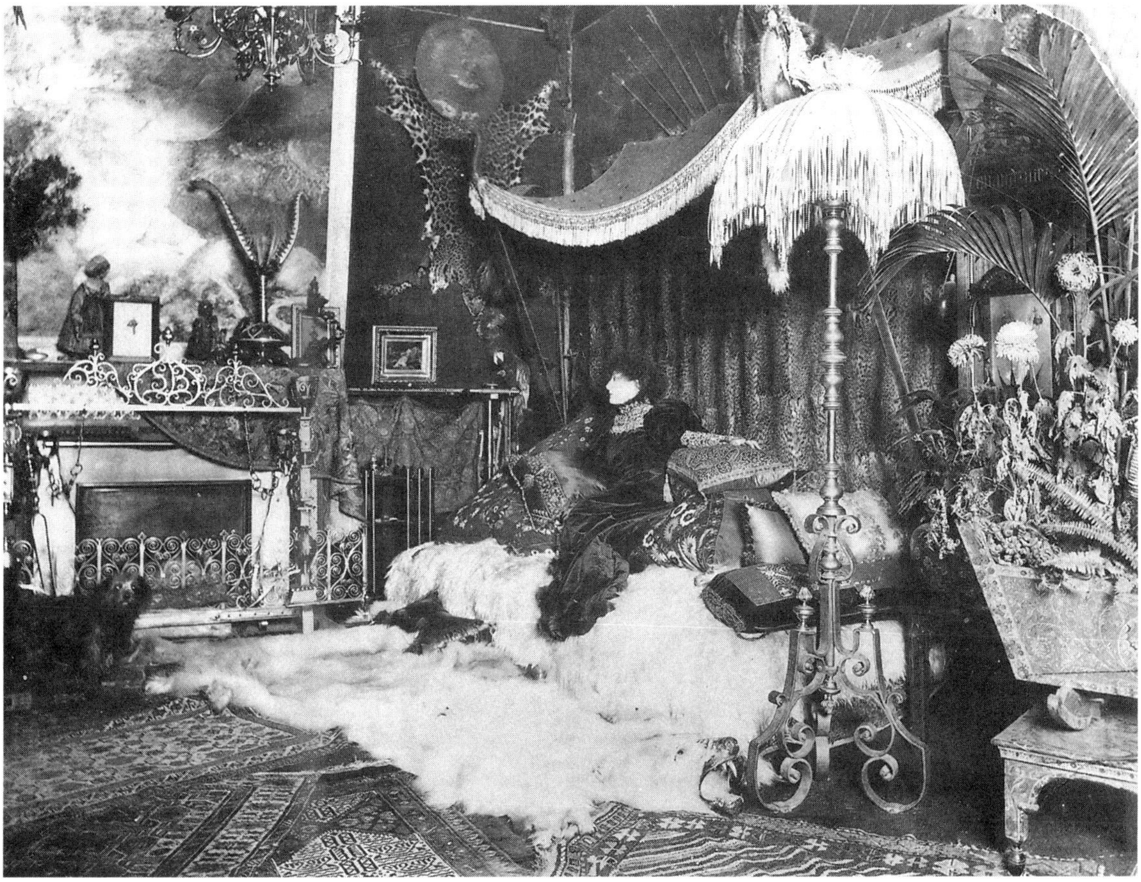

Figure 2.12. Nineteenth-century interior (Sarah Bernhardt at home), date unknown, from John Russell, *Paris.*

> piteous cries and moans." What happened to perception under these circumstances was a tripartite splitting of experience into agency (the operating surgeon), the object as hyle (the docile body of the patient), and the observer (who perceives and acknowledges the accomplished result).[58]

Hence the main features of the synaesthetic experience become separated, as is evident in what Husserl writes: "If I cut my finger with a knife, then a physical body is split by driving into it a wedge, the fluid contained in it trickles out, etc."[59] Here, "the bodily experience is split from the cognitive one, and the experience of agency is, again, split from both of these. An uncanny sense of self-alienation results from such perceptual splitting."[60] Phantasmagorias, in this context, become necessary for survival. They depend upon surface unity for their effects, hiding fragmentation just as the commodity conceals the traces of its own production.[61]

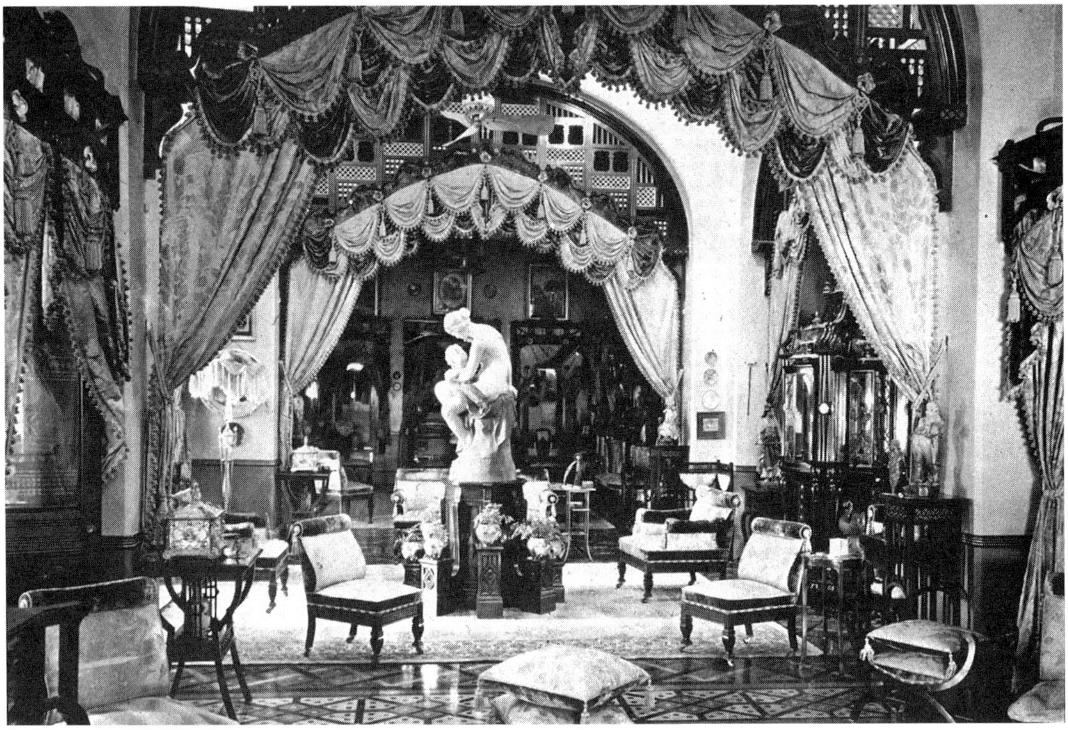

Figure 2.13. Lala Deen Dayal, *The Drawing Room of Mehboob Ali Khan* (sixth nizam of Hydrabad), 1888. Digital image courtesy of the Digital Content Library, University of Minnesota.

Colonial Techno-Aesthetics

What passes for "mystification" in the Marxian sense correlates with the very arrangement of perception under the shock effects of modernity. The phantasmagoria's compensatory role against the shock experience of modernity serves to protect not only the human sensorium of the modern individual but also the relations of domination. Treating the masses as inert matter to be formed and worked upon has its ur-form in the phenomenon of the civilizing mission, a system that strived to create the colonized masses in the colonizer's image through educational, governmental, and religious institutions. In India, the civilizing mission coincided with the consolidation of the East India Company's territorial control in the early nineteenth century: "It slowly shed its character as a body of traders whose eyes were on quick and ill-gotten profits, and settled down to fashion a despotism aimed at developing and exploiting the territory's resources efficiently and systematically."[62] This entailed a revision of educational policies and disciplinary policies and aimed at molding the colonized mass into civilized form.

The disciplinary mechanisms of modernity, according to Foucault, have as their aim the education of "docile bodies," or an obedient populace, ideally self-governing. The statistical body is synonymous with the body politic, and its behavior is calculable, its contours shaped by the "norm." While Foucault is not concerned with perception as such, it is clear that this body politic that the modern state attempts to mold is the same body politic whose perceptual organization interests Benjamin and Buck-Morss. On the other hand, the political dangers of the splitting of perception remind us that discourse is itself produced out of specific material and historical conditions. Statistics produce patterns out of the seemingly chaotic world of material life, which is the realm of the "aesthetic" in its root sense, according to Eagleton, not conceptual reason, but the "dense, swarming territory [that is] the whole of our sensate life together—the business of affections and aversion, of how the world strikes the body on its sensory surfaces, of that which takes root in the gaze and the guts and all that arises from our most banal, biological insertion into the world."[63] This sensory material world is the object of statistical knowledge: what results from our most banal, biological insertion into the world are the regularities of birth and death rates, patterns of famine, and the rhythms of normality itself. Recall that phantasmagorias produce reality as a series of surface patterns; statistics are symptomatic of a widespread rationalization of the material world, a kind of mirror that returns the image of the rational body politic stripped of its capacity for pain.

Statistics reveal the symbiosis of the material and the discursive in the service of political–economic interest.[64] Industrial labor produces its own rhythm of casualties—"a list of those killed and wounded in the industrial battle"—because of the ceaseless capitalist necessities of efficiency: the regulation of labor-time into increasingly productive (because smaller and more intense) segments of time, and the constant use of machinery that injures every sense organ "by the artificially high temperatures [amid] machines which are so closely crowded together."[65] The aim is to produce as much value out of labor-power as possible, and to this end the factory clock figures as the ruling disciplinarian, giving orders to the management that demands work at given times and at a certain pace. The clock breaks up labor-time into a pattern of shifts and breaks these into a pattern of measured mechanical bodily movements. Time is the measure of labor, and as a result it is fundamental to the production of value; it determines the rhythm of the snapping, switching, and jolting of machines and bodies. Benjamin writes, "The article being assembled comes within the worker's range of action independently of his volition, and moves away from him just as arbitrarily."[66] Reduced to automatic movements determined by the pace of the conveyer belt, the worker inhabits the temporality of hell—in Benjamin's view, "the province of those who are not allowed to complete anything they have started."[67] The factory clock, often accompanied by an alarm mechanism, is the emblem of the temporality of shock, the inescapable experience that pervades modernity and serves to numb the synaesthetic system. The tempo of the material practices of value production is set by a fundamentally dematerialized "reality" represented by the movement of hands on the clock face, an empty movement that measures the gradual degradation of the worker, even as it measures the value secreted by labor-power.[68]

By measuring, both statistics and the clock produce the regularities and patterns of material existence, presuming the fundamental given-ness of the mass of the social body that comes under the purview of statistical knowledge and the temporality of shock. Statistics are the (phantasmagoric) equivalent of the factory clock at the level of the social body. Colonial photography has an affinity with these technologies: while it produces rational patterns out of the diversity of individual lifeworlds, it also records, in a double movement, the material and epistemic changes wrought upon the foreign landscape through the colonial encounter.[69] The impoverishment of modern experience, the sectioning of time into moments of shock, and the closing of the synaesthetic system that becomes necessary for survival, all bear upon the nature of colonial measurements of foreign space and primitive bodies, as the phantasmagoric becomes the dominant mode of modern experience and therefore the grounds of knowledge.

The process of molding foreign subjects into familiar form under colonialism is mediated by the civilizing mission. At the level of sense perception, the clinical molding of inert matter assumes a radical disconnect between the self and the matter being formed. This disconnect, founded upon self-alienation, renders the world foreign and defamiliarized. Such a view of the world was the starting point of the civilizing mission, which saw the undifferentiated material world as raw material to be molded into a recognizably civilized image. This project came with its own contradictions. For example, as Homi Bhabha argues, the process of making available Christianity and other accoutrements of a civilizing mission is meant to assert the authority of (for example) British culture and texts and to presuppose a fundamental and insurmountable gap between the colonizers and the colonized. However, the investment in converting the natives also assumes that the natives can be transformed, trained, and taught, and this difference, or gap, can be bridged.[70] Although the civilizing mission treats the colonized as inert matter that is radically other, it also simultaneously assumes the agency of the individual members of the colonized mass (or, more specifically in this case, their initiative to learn), insofar as conversion is seen to be a personal "choice" to find salvation.[71] Under colonial management, then, as opposed to fascism, the ones in charge of shaping the population to their will retain a double role for themselves: rather than allowing the mass to approve its own manipulation, the colonizers occupy the role of the agent as well as the observer, roles represented as much by the whip as by the Bible.[72]

The fundamental sense of foreignness that is produced from the colonial encounter and is apparent in binaries such as barbarism/civilization, black/white, primitive/developed brings with it all of the notions of impurity, error, and impropriety that are congealed within the concept of the foreign in the first place.[73] What I call the phantasmagoric aesthetic is, in effect, a management of perception produced from the experience of a sensory self-alienation, and this experience renders the world defamiliarized. Under colonialism, this defamiliarization of the world is an everyday experience, hence the necessity of the quotidian reproducibility of the familiar markers of "civilization," either in the form of advertisements for colonial commodities,[74] or in the form of recently familiarized sites of colonial imaginings: refurbished local archaeological treasures, series of disappearing indigenous cultural practices, and so on.[75] Phantasmagoric aesthetics emerge out of a sensory engagement with this experience of the foreign and unfamiliar. In colonial photography, this engagement takes the form of practices that seek to measure, order, and break into patterns the foreign realm of affiliated races and tribes—or that, in the case of Beato's photographs, formalize the chaos of war.

Colonial photographic practice was an attempt to bridge the gap of foreignness by making sense of it, by creating rational grids of legibility in much the same way that the civilizing mission aimed to create civilized subjects from an undifferentiated mass of "primitive barbarism." This aesthetic serves a dual purpose: on the one hand, it assumes a sensory disconnect from the world, which then appears to be radically other, and on the other hand, it mystifies this disconnect and presents the spectacle of the world as an immediate reality. So the self-alienation that enables violence toward another is itself mystified through the very immediacy of phantasmagoric forms. This immediacy is, of course, conditioned by the patterns and regularities imposed upon the sensory material world. The temporality of shock, represented by the factory clock, produces the need for an aesthetic experience that presents the world (and the self) as whole, even as it meets that need by setting down the principle by which that wholeness is to be achieved: an imposition of pattern, familiarity, and reason upon the sudden foreignness of the world. The phantasmagoric aesthetic fulfills this need. Foucault writes, "I studied madness not in terms of the criteria of the formal sciences but to show how a type of management of individuals inside and outside of asylums was made possible by this strange discourse. This contact between the technologies of domination of others and those of the self I call governmentality."[76] This contact is the locus of phantasmagoric aesthetics, which depends on the numbing of the self that results from the shock experiences of modernity and which mystifies this primary alienation. The sort of self-alienation represented by Husserl's cutting his finger is a modern form of dominance over the self, and this form is the precondition for the domination of others. Phantasmagoric aesthetics is the name of the process that mystifies the linkage between self-domination/self-alienation and the domination of others.

Appearance Is Truth, Truth Appearance

Returning to the photographs that opened this chapter, we recall that Felice Beato ordered the arrangement of the skeletons himself, in order to capture the immediacy of a historical event; the human remains (inert matter) are the stuff of Beato's compositions. These particular photographs occupy a space somewhere between the phantasmagoric and the counterphantasmagoric, between a total environment and one in which fragmentation is the ruling principle. This latter principle is evident in the very appearance of the shattered architectural and human ruins. Yet the human remains, in a grotesque staging of Kant's mathematical sublime, threaten to extend infinitely beyond the frame in both photographs. In regard to the Sikanderbagh photo (Figure 2.1), Ben Lifson points out that the broken skeletons in the courtyard, "seen in low relief against the hard and flat earth," are "a frieze in the making, echoed by the Secunderbagh's broken frieze above them."[77] The aesthetic rendering of decay in Beato's photograph of Sikanderbagh enables the cognizing spectator to skim its surface, as is typical in the experience of the phantasmagoric. A recurring motif in the original phantasmagorias, the magic lantern shows, was the projection of the face of a known deceased figure (Benjamin Franklin, Marat), which, through rapid changes of magic lantern slides, turned into a skull.[78] The imbrication of the phantasmagoric with death and the unearthly, that which (like the commodity) "transcends sensuousness," is consistent throughout its history.

The composition of Beato's Sikanderbagh photograph suggests an endless circular relation: from the live Indians set in the background, through the almost whole skeleton in the right foreground and then the skeletal ruins to its left, echoing the ruined frieze above, and finally back to the live natives. The grand aesthetic motif of the cycle of life and death and the beginning and end of civilizations finds articulation in the meaningfully arranged bones of the slaughtered "natives." The universalism of this gesture places the photograph outside lived history and therefore makes the image independent of the social relations that come to bear upon its history. These fragments of architectural and bodily remains are reveries upon form itself. As an occasion for reverie, the scene presupposes a denial of the artificial nature of the photograph, directed as it is at producing a certain mood in the spectator. A subtle surrender of any responsibility for the ruins placed on display is also evident.[79] The frequent reproductions of these photographs in private and public spaces in Britain present a sutured self-definition of imperialism as a rational social structure that has to resort to violence in the pursuit of a greater common good.

In showing a path littered with skulls and bones, the photograph of Sammy House (Figure 2.2) evokes universal images of war as well as the stock "paths of destruction" used to refer to the seriality of violence throughout history. Nevertheless, this photograph differs from the photograph of Sikanderbagh in one crucial detail: it deploys phantasmagoric aesthetics in the service of a more critical and reflexive engagement with itself. Though at first sight we do not see the scattered skulls and bones within this landscape, the momentary blink of the eye, after which we realize that the path presumably leading to the building on the hill is littered with human remains, coincides with the knowledge that, as spectators, we are "walking" this path. The human remains and the path extend into the foreground and out of the bottom edge of the frame. We do not know how many skulls we may have trampled before we arrived at our current vantage point. Without the caption, the skulls and bones are unidentifiable as British or Indian. Situating the spectator in the middle of this deathly path, the photograph seems to invite the spectator's recognition of his or her possible complicity in the violence that has taken place. Even if this photograph is seen with the caption—and many photographs in "mutiny memorial" albums are accompanied by captions—it is difficult to sustain a reading of the image as a triumphal representation of the end of the Sepoy conflict. On the surface it appears to represent an otherwise unremarkable landscape, but the path of human remains denaturalizes the naturalizing impulses of the picturesquely placed trees, scattered rocks, architecture: the path of bones reveals that what may appear natural and unified is in fact the result of a violence upon which that unity rests. The self-estrangement necessary for the artful arrangement of the human remains itself enters into the subject of this photograph.

Unlike the Sikanderbagh photograph, which, by placing live "natives" between a ruined building and shattered skeletons, represents these "natives" as disciplined and docile, the photograph of Sammy House does not include anyone in its view. The scattered bones form a path *within* the landscape, belonging to it as its "spontaneous afterimage," and have somehow become trapped in the world of the visible as a result of war. The path is a catastrophe that can render visible the violence that preserves daily social relations. The British, like the Romans, prided themselves on building great roads and bridges and, surpassing Roman technology, train tracks.[80] This photograph is a glimpse into the other side of such production. In the absence of more "natives" to kill within this frame, the image gives back to the colonialist the picture-perfect "end" of colonialism, the essential destiny of a civilizing mission stripped of its benevolent disguise. Phantasmagoric aesthetics in colonial photography, then, do not necessarily indicate the strictly ideological aspect of colonial relations. Colonial photographs carry within them, in a material sense, traces of historical potential that have been failed by history itself.

Seen in light of phantasmagoric aesthetics, the line demarcating the end of anthropology and the beginning of documentary photography is obscure at best, as both the anthropological and documentary photographs taken by the British in India frequently represent their scenes in phantasmagoric terms. The projected primitive fantasy of the preserving anthropologist is akin to the "phantasm" of the harem explored by Malek Alloula in his analysis of the *carte-de-visite* from Algeria.[81] Yet the word *phantasm,* when referring to an unreal spectral form, does not contain the movement inherent in the referent of *phantasmagoric.* In the phantasmagorias of the early nineteenth century, shapes would blend and form at a rapid rate. To use the word *phantasmagoria* rather than *phantasm* to refer to the genre of colonial photography is to accentuate the possibility of the given phantasm to refigure itself immediately into new forms with the next click of the camera, even if the image remains static in function—hence the almost hypnotic and pleasurable experience of flipping through "exotic scenes" in books such as *The Colonial Harem,* among others on colonial photography.

But what does the overlay of the phantasmagoric and the epistemological yield? That is, what does it mean to know through phantasmagoric forms? Nineteenth-century phantasmagorias were collective experiences, and as such their force stemmed from appearing as a collectively agreed upon reality, as objective fact. While a photograph may not easily lend itself to collective viewing (even in a museum exhibit, the photograph is viewed individually), as a medium its rhetoric commands the place of truth or, rather, faith.[82] When the phantasmagoric transmutes into the photographable, its effects under colonialism render the gleaned knowledge to be knowledge of the surface, and this surface may itself contain the flash of critical knowledge that goes beyond the idealist circuit of seeing and knowing. This idealist structure is the basis of photography's claim to truth: since the photographable was seen to be congruent with the knowable, photography granted "unmediated" access to the object of the spectacle. In photography, then, the phantasmagoric grounds itself in the truth production of the medium, generating universal truths even as it produces the concrete abstractions that are colonial types, bedecked with characteristic manners and customs.

"Exterminate All the Brutes"

The civilizing mission (changing its form from a mission of conversion to one of education, but on the whole retaining a constant presence through the shifts in colonial governmentality) has been built on universalisms that are often antinomies, poised precariously between notions of universal freedom and a corrupt understanding of what constitutes the universal subject worthy of this freedom. These antinomies find their material form in the spatial organization of the colony, so central to colonial governance, in which fragmentation, rather than projections of wholeness, is the order of the day. The colonizers export the accoutrements of their phantasmagoric interiors to far-flung corners of the world where, perhaps, there is a greater need to sustain one's illusions. This function of the bourgeois interior becomes increasingly important to regulation of space in the colony, to the point where the illusions fostered in the interior inevitably require regulation outside it, so that colonial space is often fragmented: divided into the imperial quarter and the native quarter, in the service of the dialectic of (in)visibility. Frantz Fanon refers to these quarters as mutually exclusive zones:

> The colonial world is a world cut in two. . . . The zone where the natives live is not complementary to the zone inhabited by the settlers. The two zones are opposed, but not in the service of a higher unity. Obedient to the rules of pure Aristotelean logic, they both follow the principle of reciprocal exclusivity.[83]

The settler's quarter, a "strong-built town," enjoys all the amenities of sanitation and asphalt roads; it is an area for well-fed "white people."[84] The native quarter—"the Negro village, the medina, the reservation"—is "peopled by men of evil repute"; cramped, dirty, and stifling, "the native town is a hungry town," starved of the basics of life. This town is "a town of niggers and dirty arabs," writes Fanon.[85] In the colony, racism checks the ideals of universal human freedom, ideals often espoused by the civilizing mission itself. Central to defining the limits of freedom and of the category of the human itself is the persistent tendency of colonial practice to reduce the "native" to a type.[86] Perhaps one of the clearest instances of this reduction emerges in the context of the (occidental) century's fascination with phrenology. In W. E. Marshall's *A Phrenologist amongst the Todas* (1873), the head of one member of the Toda tribe (Figure 2.11) is used to diagnose the characteristic of the entire tribe, in direct contradiction to the practice of phrenology in the European context, where it was a means for detecting individual dispositions and tendencies.[87] The question of race conditions an understanding of class:

> The cause is the consequence; you are rich because you are white, you are white because you are rich. This is why Marxist analysis should always be slightly stretched every time we have to do with the colonial problem. . . .
> It is neither the act of owning the factories, nor estates, nor a bank balance which distinguishes the governing classes. The governing race is first and foremost those who come from elsewhere, those who are unlike the original inhabitants, "the others."[88]

Thus, while colonialism does not exist outside the history of capital as such, race necessarily enters into colonial political economy. While the exploitation of wage labor in the imperial metropole relies on numerous ideological supports and helpers (Fanon lists the educational system and "the structures of moral reflexes handed down") that minimize the need for overt and repressive policing, in the colony "it is obvious that the agents of government speak the language of pure force," which often takes the form of bodily punishment,[89] especially since "barracks and police stations" mark the frontiers between the two zones. This is the result of what Partha Chatterjee has called the "rule of colonial difference," under which the colonized are represented as wholly other, and race serves as a convenient marker for this rule.[90]

Colonial violence requires management at the cultural and political levels, and photography partly fulfills this need. The uncanny connections between photography and violence, drawn by Bourne when he likens the camera to a gun, implied by Thurn between measurement (gathering of knowledge, the production of patterns) and death, and implicit in the actual practice of anthropological photography, link with a history of sensory alienation that enabled (and was produced by) the practices of the civilizing mission, the phenomenon that came to define colonial governmentality. The discourse on photography has often located a certain violence of the photograph already in the camera mechanisms producing the image, as in the Benjaminian thesis that the cold gaze of the lens can always elicit only a dead gaze from its subject, human as well as inhuman, and that the fatal click of the camera fixes the subject in its own image.[91] In other words, if God created humans in his image, then the camera kills them in its. The modern sensory alienation discussed at the close of Benjamin's "Work of Art" essay has its genealogy in Europe as well as in Europe's colonies. If the ur-form of the sensory splitting that allows one to treat a mass of people as inert matter is, as I have suggested, the colonial civilizing mission, then it is also in the colonies that the issue of self-defense is most sensitized. The reader may recall that Benjamin blames humanity's self-alienation for the aestheticization of politics and also for the suspect enjoyment taken in viewing one's own destruction. The spectacle of one's own destruction was, for colonialism, an afterimage of the pleasurable spectacle (recorded in its variant forms, by photography) of the native's denigration. An inevitable synergy can occur between the technologies of the self and the domination of others, and this linkage is what the phantasmagoric aesthetics of colonial photography often mystifies.

We can discern the power of this link through Beato's Sikanderbagh photograph, by examining the photograph's social–historical patina. In one album in which Felice Beato's photograph of Sikanderbagh appears, the private caption given to the photo by a past owner of the album is "Dead Pandies Grouped—!!!"[92] As an echo of Joseph Conrad's *Heart of Darkness,* in which Kurtz scrawls "Exterminate all the brutes!" at the end of his report calling for a benevolent colonialism, this exclamation articulates what Albert Memmi has called the "Nero complex," named after the Roman emperor Nero, who allegedly provided his own musical accompaniment to the spectacle of Rome burning. The Nero complex is a sort of colonial death wish that exists alongside all of the investment and exploitation of colonialism:

> The more the usurped is downtrodden, the more the usurper triumphs and, thereafter, confirms his guilt and establishes his self-condemnation. . . . This self-defeating process pushes the usurper to go one step further; to wish the disappearance of the usurped, whose very existence causes him to take the role of usurper, and whose heavier and heavier oppression makes him more and more an oppressor himself. Nero, the typical model of a usurper, is thus brought to persecute Britannicus savagely and to pursue him. But the more he hurts him, the more he coincides with the atrocious role he has chosen for himself.[93]

Figure 2.14. Felice Beato, *The Hanging of Two Rebels*, 1858 or 1859. The Alkazi Collection of Photography.

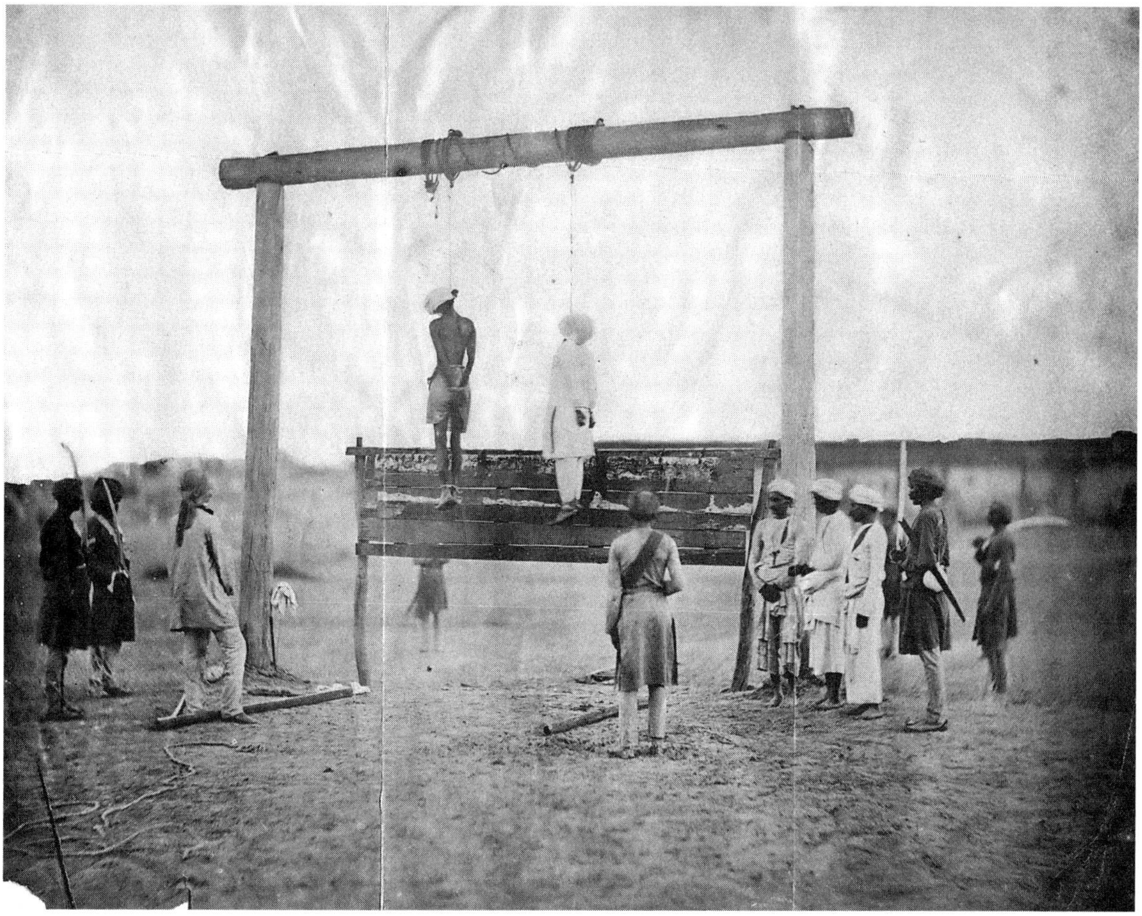

Memmi proposes that the logical end point of colonialism, of the denigration of the colonized, is the desire for the extermination of the colonized, but this would jeopardize the colonizer and colonialism itself, since both require colonial labor, which the initial denigration was meant to secure cheaply. So,

> the system wills spontaneously the death and multiplication of its victims. . . . Whether the colonized are assimilated or massacred, the cost of labor will rise. The onerous engine suspends between life and death, and always closer to death, those who are compelled to drive it. . . . The impossible dehumanization of the oppressed, on the other side of the coin, becomes the alienation of the oppressor. . . . The colonizer must assume the opaque rigidity and imperviousness of stone.[94]

Practicing such rigidity is the work of civilization. The civilizing mission comes to the colony as a corrective to "barbarism": all the benevolence of education and bridge building proves as thin as the veneer of "civilization" itself, revealing neither a barbaric nor a civilized self but the ideally impervious though not actually insensate self that desires the death of the colonized ("Exterminate all the brutes!" / "Dead Pandies Grouped—!!!"), a desire that inevitably and reciprocally reveals the pleasure in witnessing one's own death. If the civilizing mission is intended to train and manipulate the colonized mass, in turn it provides training in the latest methods of self-alienation to the metropole. An alienation from one's own pain is the minimum condition for being insensate to the pain of another. This enables the mass manipulation and decimation of a whole people, but such self-alienation turns upon itself, because the destruction of the other requires a destruction of oneself. To find aesthetic enjoyment in this destruction means that the phantasmagoric under colonialism finds fertile ground in the management of colonized populations and also, through photography, in the production of civilization's truths.

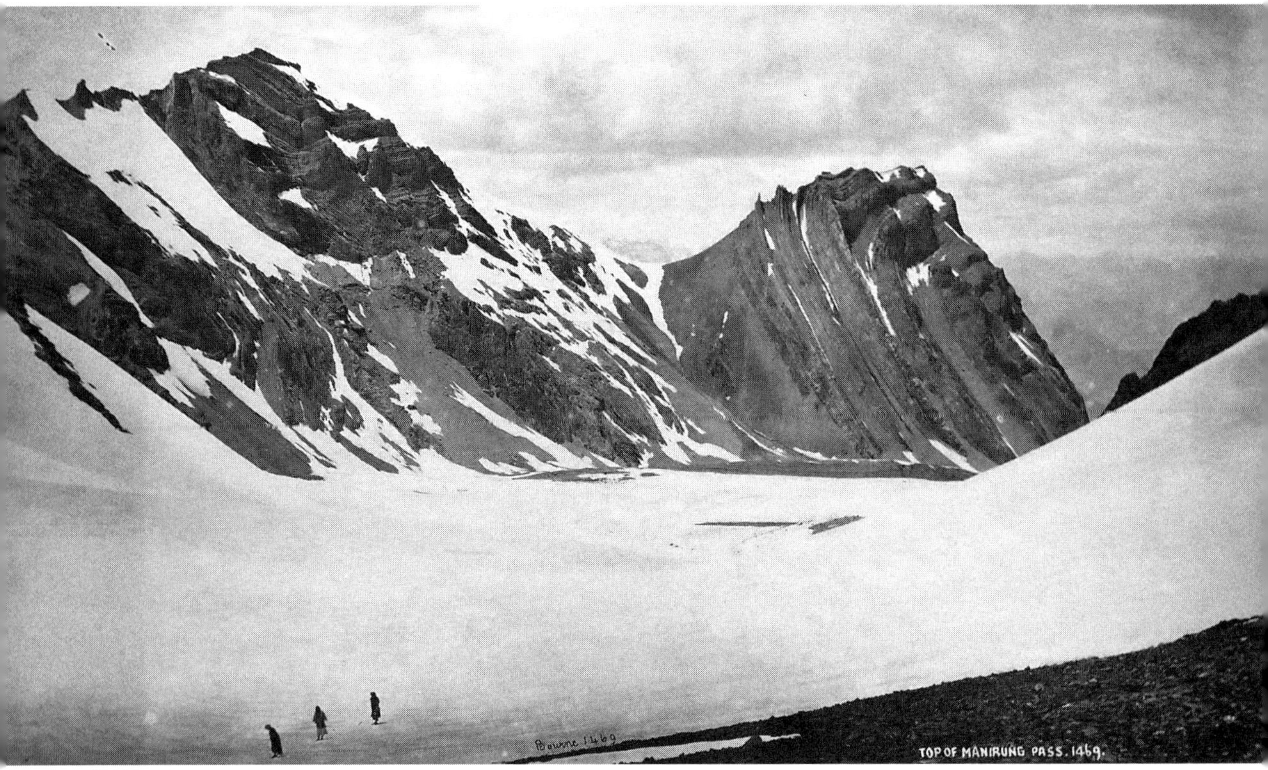

Figure 3.1. Samuel Bourne, top of Manirung Pass (with Bourne's coolies in view), 1860s. The Alkazi Collection of Photography.

THREE

Armor and Aesthesis

The Picturesque in Difference

> Psychoanalysis does not make freedom impossible; it teaches us to think of this freedom concretely, as a creative repetition of ourselves, always, in retrospect, faithful to ourselves.
>
> —Maurice Merleau-Ponty, "Cézanne's Doubt"

Picture Almost Perfect

We are leaving the scenes of 1857–58, and in this chapter I extend the discussion of anaesthesis in the context of the entirely different genre of landscape photography. Because the Sepoy Revolt continued to resonate in British India into the twentieth century, the arrangements of perception and meaning making explored in the previous chapters on the photography of the revolt will continue to haunt the discussions of aesthetics in this chapter and the next. From scenes of violence and ruins we turn to scenes of picturesque vistas of nature. In the 1860s Samuel Bourne undertook several treks into the far reaches of the Himalayas, and in the course of photographing the sublime peaks he saw there he confronted a singularly difficult challenge: how to represent, within a photographic frame, the sheer scale of the immensity that surrounded him. This challenge was both epistemological and practical:

> In some places the precipitous walls are so stupendous as to stagger both the sense and imagination. . . . With scenery like this it is very difficult to deal with the camera: it is altogether too gigantic and stupendous to be brought within the limits imposed on photography. Even the much-vaunted "globe lens" would find itself unequal to extend its great divergence over these mighty subjects, and compress their rays on the few square inches of a collodion plate. . . . The grand difficulty I had to contend with was to find a standing place for tent and camera.[1]

Encapsulating the rational laws of perspective in its very function, the camera, of necessity, must be located in a definite space: What to do when the best vista is to be seen from midair or halfway down a fall? Where is the foothold, or standing place, from which Bourne may capture the infinite images unfolding before him? As Merleau-Ponty writes in his discussion of Paul Cézanne, "Expressing what *exists* is an endless task."[2] How might such infinity—itself found in our experience of all objects but accentuated by mountain vistas—make its way into the photographic frame? For Bourne, God becomes a solace more powerful than his faith in the globe lens or in the rationality of the photographic image and more appropriate to the landscape than the meager understandings of the human mind, here linked to the limits of the camera. God provides the possibility of meaning as well as the knowledge that that meaning is outside mortal grasp:

> What a mighty upbearing of mountains! What an endless vista of gigantic ranges and valleys, untold and unknown! Peak rose above peak, . . . range above and beyond range, innumerable and boundless, until the mind refused to follow the eye in its attempt to comprehend the whole in one grand conception. . . . It was impossible to gaze upon this tumultuous sea of mountains without being deeply affected, . . . without an elevation of the soul's capacities, and without a silent uplifting of the heart to Him who formed such stupendous works, whose eye alone has scanned the dread depths of their sunless recesses, and whose presence only has rested on their mysterious and sublime elevations.[3]

Capturing the totality of the seemingly infinite prospect and his own experience of it is, quite literally, outside the scope of Bourne's lens. What is photography's role in understanding the kind of sublimity that can be knowable in just one glance by God? Bourne continues:

> And it must be put down to the credit of photography that it teaches the mind to see the beauty and power of such scenes as these, and renders it more susceptible of their sweet and elevating impressions. For my own part, I may say that before I commenced photography I did not see half the beauties in nature that I do now, and the glory and power of a precious landscape has often passed before me and left but a feeble impression on my untutored mind; but it will never be so again.[4]

If God is the creator of such extraordinary vistas, then the camera is the tutor that trains us to see them, to be sensitized to their sweet and elevating impressions. Bourne quite explicitly highlights here the idea that photography can educate human vision. The lens of the camera falls short of divine vision, but it teaches us to see "beauty," which inevitably takes the form of a picture. That is, it trains us to see the world as a possible representation. Interestingly enough, if photography does teach the mind to see the beauty and power of spectacular scenes, as Bourne attests, then it must also point to its own limitations, since it cannot fully capture such scenes by itself. Bourne is, of course, heavily influenced by the conventions of the picturesque, an aesthetic unsuited for representing the sublime. Hence Bourne's confrontation with the sublime renders it, as he explains, into a pale version of itself, because that confrontation translates the terror and unfamiliarity of the sublime into picturesque forms. The picturesque is an aesthetic of the pretty view rather than of sublime terror, of the anecdote rather than of the grand historical narrative. Bourne's dissatisfaction with the limitations of photography is necessarily also an expression of dissatisfaction with the picturesque aesthetic itself, which, while it had waned by the 1860s in most European art, had a much longer half-life in photographic practice.

Samuel Bourne's landscape photography was the most celebrated of its kind in the nineteenth century and continues to be highly regarded in histories of colonial photography; it has become paradigmatic of landscape photography on the subcontinent. Not only did Bourne produce the largest volume of landscape photographs in India, but also he was widely recognized as a master of the new magical–rational medium of photography. His photographic oeuvre, while showing a clear preference for landscape, contains extensive architectural studies as well as a few examples of ethnographic and natural history photographs. He was one of the first British photographers in India to establish his own photography firm, Bourne and Shepherd, with his partner, Charles Shepherd, in 1863. The firm, with branches in Simla, Calcutta, Bombay, and London, was primarily responsible for the wide international dissemination of Bourne's photography. Bourne and Shepherd made available extensive catalogues containing thousands of images—including those made by other photographers in addition to Bourne's—showing every aspect of the Raj in its most idealized dreams of itself.[5]

The pedagogical training that goes into seeing land as landscape has a history that coincides with political domination. This case has been convincingly and cogently argued in recent criticism and has become associated more specifically with the picturesque aesthetic. Noting the concurrence of the "practice" of landscape—that is, of seeing nature as an image, of reading patterns into nature even before the sketch is begun or the shutter snapped—and the political practices of imperialism, W. J. T. Mitchell concludes, "Landscape might be seen more profitably as something like the 'dreamwork' of imperialism, unfolding its own movement in time and space from a central point of origin and folding back on itself to disclose both utopian fantasies of the perfected imperial prospect and fractured images of unresolved ambivalence and unsuppressed resistance."[6] This dreamwork aims to unify the disparate parts of natural scenes—rivers, trees, paths, rocks, forests, mountains—into a coherent visual assemblage, which naturalizes the practice of landscape in the same gesture that makes nature transparent to representation and excludes what cannot, or should not, be represented. Emerson notes that one cannot "*freely* admire a noble landscape, if laborers are digging in the field" nearby; Raymond Williams famously states that "a working country is hardly a landscape"; John Barrell's analysis shows how laborers are relegated to the "dark" side of the landscape in order to present natural beauty in its purest form.[7]

This chapter takes the imperialist underpinning of the landscape tradition in general and the picturesque aesthetic in particular as a given. Rather than exploring how the picturesque tradition is based on a certain epistemological violence and will to power—an argument that has been rigorously elaborated in the scholarship on landscapes[8]—I will examine how referentiality functions in the colonial picturesque. That is, if the conventions of the picturesque were, as we will see, set down rather rigidly by its practitioners well before the advent of photography, how do such conventional framings change the meaning of the photographic referent? While studies on landscapes have set the tradition within discursive contexts such as cartography, military campaigns, and property laws, the location of subjectivity is often theorized as that of the dominating painter–photographer–subject who, while converting the world into a picture to be displayed, records his or her own imperialist comportment. These accounts are convincing, and my argument here does not seek to contradict them but to explore a related set of issues surrounding the referential meanings of landscapes and the changing relationship that the picturesque aesthetic marks between bodies and images. I read the picturesque as the symptomatic nineteenth-century fruit of a certain modernizing habitus, which is to say not that it is necessarily colonial but rather that it is a habitus that bespeaks of the historically shifting relationship between bodily perception and the image world. The practice of converting the world into a picture in order to experience it—a practice that the picturesque aesthetic formalizes—is part and parcel of the changing perceptual arrangements of modernity, including colonial modernity.

As an aesthetic mode, the picturesque shapes painting and literature as well as travel memoirs. The grandfather of the picturesque aesthetic, William Gilpin, popularized it in the late eighteenth century by publishing detailed accounts of his "tours" throughout the northern English countryside. These accounts, along with those of Uvedale Price and Richard Payne Knight, have a very conscious pedagogical dimension. If Romantic poetry is, in Wordsworth's words, "the spontaneous overflow of powerful emotions," the picturesque claims to be a spontaneous look at the incidental view of nature's beauty.[9] Such "spontaneous" observations require painfully deliberate actions that are interventionist not only in a literal sense (the manipulation of objects in the view) but also in a subtle and psychic sense, by which the viewing subject comes to imagine the field of the visual as an image that conforms to his or her standards of taste. This is a common enough observation. However, what remains less obvious in the case of the picturesque aesthetic is how the training in seeing picturesque forms is historically and epistemologically isomorphic with the rise of technological reproducibility.

William Gilpin was a parson and schoolmaster in Surrey, and his publications, most significantly his *Essay upon Prints* (1768), encourage the reader to go on rambles, observe the picturelike qualities of the countryside, and sketch scenes from it. Gilpin writes, "He is the true artist, who copies nature; but where he finds her mean, elevates her from his own ideas of beauty."[10] Coming upon Tintern Abbey, Gilpin found it to be void of distinctively picturesque features but suggested that "a mallet judiciously used . . . might be of service in fracturing some of [the gable ends]; particularly those of the cross isles, which are not only disagreeable in themselves, but confound the perspective."[11] The dictates of the idealized image pass judgment upon the lived reality and consistently find it lacking. So Gilpin's essays set out to standardize the elements of the picturesque and lend the act of seeing a certain reproducibility. In this way, certain isolable features of the landscape can be abstracted and given the status of fundamental forms of bourgeois taste against which the beauty of sketches, paintings, and landscape schemes can be gauged. Gilpin's books were enormously popular (*Essay upon Prints* went into five editions by 1802), but they were not uncontroversial; he once defined the picturesque as "that peculiar kind of beauty, which is agreeable in a picture."[12] Though he relied inconsistently on Edmund Burke's *A Philosophical Inquiry into the Origins of Our Ideas of the Sublime and Beautiful,* Gilpin was no theoretician, and his attempts at theorizing the picturesque in *Three Essays* (1792) were deemed incoherent and contradictory by his contemporaries.[13] This systematic theorizing would be accomplished later by Uvedale Price and Richard Payne Knight, respectively, in *An Essay on the Picturesque: As compared with the sublime and the beautiful; and, on the use of studying pictures for the purpose of improving real landscape* (1794) and *An Analytical Inquiry into the Principles of Taste* (1805). The history of the contemporary discourse on the picturesque, its populist bent, its lasting impact on English landscapes and gardens, its engagement with the French Revolution, and its impact on music is all well documented.[14] I would like to invoke these histories briefly in order to show how this aesthetic evidences a transforming perceptual apparatus.

The meanings of the word *picturesque* became so multiple and contradictory in the nineteenth century that by the time of the advent of photography the term retained its self-conscious connection to Gilpin, Price, and Knight only in the practice of the most orthodox landscape painters and gardeners. However, the impact of the picturesque is difficult to underestimate, as many urban and country gentlemen eagerly expanded, elaborated, and transformed its basic categories. Nathaniel Kent, Henry Twining, and Humphry Repton all elaborated on Gilpin's ideas, with or without direct reference to him. One might say that while self-conscious theorizing about the picturesque dwindled into incoherence and eventual nonexistence, the *practice* of seeing landscape as a picture and altering the landscape to make it more "picturelike" was, on the whole, naturalized by the end of the nineteenth century. Combinations of classic figures from the picturesque, such as stillness, roughness, mountainous terrain, shades of strong light and deep shadow, gleams of water, and foreground features (often rocks or fallen trees) framing the view, all became stock paraphernalia of the ideal landscape. By the time landscape photography made an appearance, the conventions of the picturesque were readily available to photographic vision. So in 1863 Samuel Bourne, the most illustrious name in the histories of nineteenth-century Indian landscapes, could list without hesitation the features of the picturesque: lakes, rivers, streams, "rustic bridges," "ivy-clad ruins, trees, and mountains." He continues in a missive to the *British Journal of Photography,* "I have no doubt that in some parts of the Himalayas grand and striking views are to be found, as I hope ere long to verify; but they would consist chiefly of ravines, passes, and mountain ranges—without verdure, without foliage, and without water; and a photograph minus these three elements must possess very striking compensation indeed to render it a pleasing and enjoyable picture."[15] In a subtle shift from the language of Gilpin, in which the picturesque was that which was picturelike, Bourne defined a successful photograph, already and necessarily composed as a picture within a frame, as one that contains elements of the picturesque aesthetic. Landscape photography and the picturesque aesthetic became one and the same.

That is, for Bourne aesthetic form was inseparable from the medium of representation. Something about composing a scene in a camera's viewfinder domesticates the scene itself. As Arthur Ollman writes of Samuel Bourne's project:

> The rectangle that forms a photograph is an abstraction, a shape not necessarily found in nature; a window from behind which one may safely view a potentially threatening world, one that allows a rational organization of the randomness of nature. If this frame is imposed on rugged mountains, they become mere lines to compose; glaciers become areas of light and shade; buildings become objects to balance; a Bengali porter is but an artful counterpoint.[16]

The scientific and rational gaze tames the sublime into digestible, picturesque beauty. Bourne's initial problem with finding the right vantage point for a photograph in the Himalayas relates to an implicit question about form under colonial conditions. He expresses tremendous anxiety about the limits of representation when it confronts certain prospects in all of their vast, awe-inspiring greatness: "How often have I lamented that the camera was powerless to cope with these almost ideal scenes, and that with all its truthfulness it can give no

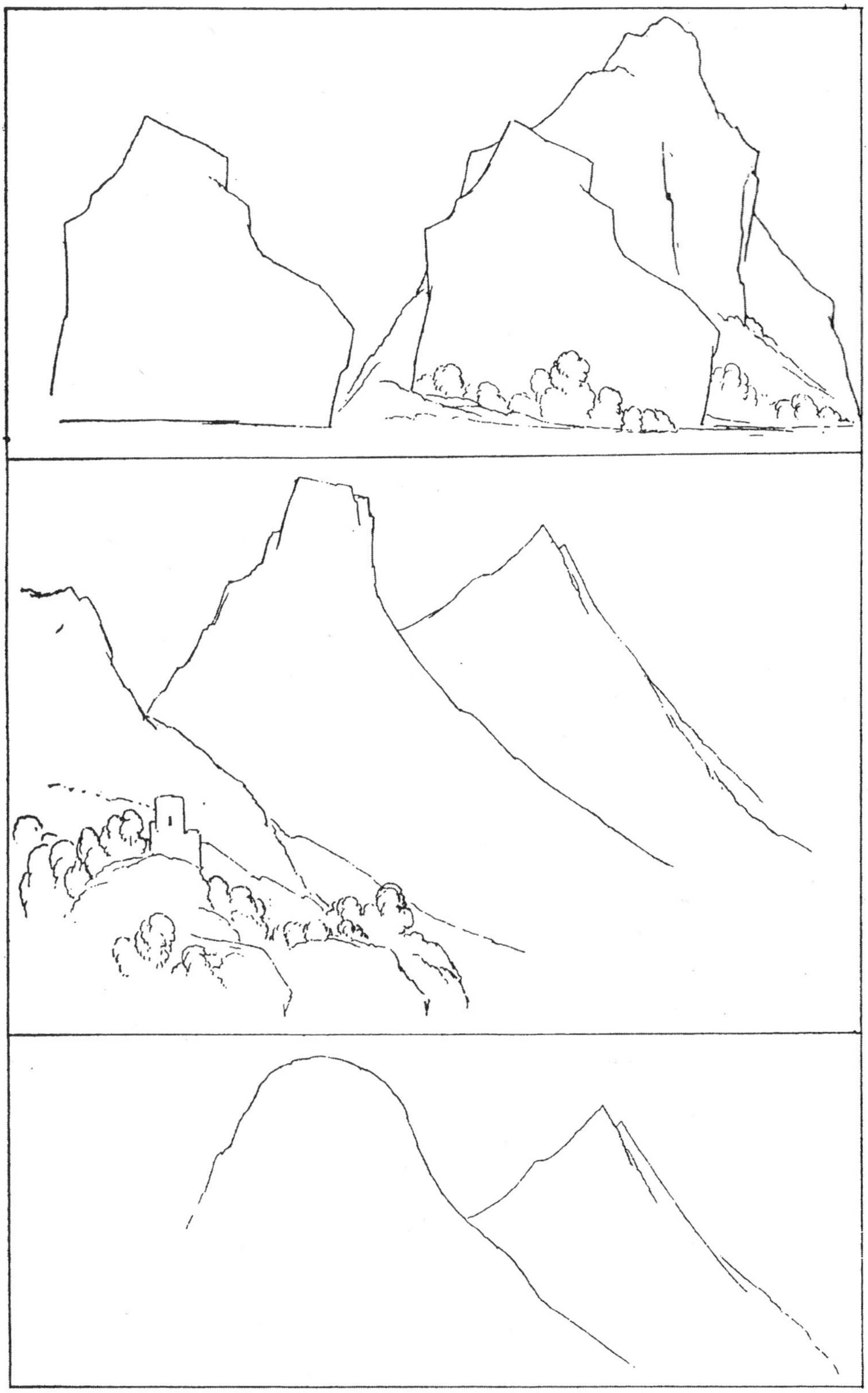

Figure 3.2. Diagrams of picturesque mountain forms: the upper two panels show picturesque forms, and the lower panel shows unpicturesque forms. From Henry Twining, *On the Elements of Picturesque Scenery, Considered with Reference to Landscape Painting* (London: George Barclay, 1846).

idea of the solemnity and grandeur which twilight in a vast mountainous region reveals partly to the *sense* and partly to the *imagination*."[17] The rationality of the camera—its mechanized perspective, its machinelike and decisive snap—is, it turns out, its most unfortunate limit. When the camera's allegedly inherent truthfulness is the source of its epistemological authority, how does one capture the solemnity and grandeur that are the effects of imagination? It seems that in the realm of fantasy, or in the development of an acutely picturesque vision, the camera is insufficient: the confrontation with the timeless renders it obsolete. And yet it was Bourne's glee at the prospect of taking the first photographs of the timeless landscapes and highest elevations on earth that led him to India in the first place. In a tangential acknowledgment of the myth-producing aspect of his landscape photographs, Bourne admits reaching the far limits of photography's claims to absolute truth. He elaborates:

> The photographer can only deal successfully with "bits" and comparatively short distances; but the artist, who has colour as well as outline to convey the idea of distance, might here find something worth coming for.[18] [Artists could] furnish to people at home some idea of what the Himalayas are really like, which we of the camera can hardly do. . . .
>
> In fact, it is in the dim and solemn twilight only that the *true* grandeur of the Himalayas can be felt. . . . It is when the monarch of day is retiring behind one of their frowning, shadowy masses, with a halo of crimson light around him, gilding their summits with his level rays, and leaving the valleys in gloom, that the poetry and sublimity of this sublimest part of the earth are learnt and felt. The haze of the day has then given place to that bewitching purple indinstinctness which seems at once to fill with silence and sublimity every open valley and every deep recess, rendering obscurity more obscure, and impressing a majestic awe upon the hills. Then every outline stands out bold and clear . . . , though the forests are sunk in gloom, and every object of detail has vanished in the blue shadows of the lessening light. If the immensity and impressiveness of such scenes could be transferred to canvas, what would such a picture not be worth![19]

In a rare moment of ambivalence, Bourne relocates pictorial truth in painting rather than in photography. He echoes his contemporary Auguste Rodin, who famously claimed, "It is the artist who is truthful, while the photograph lies; for, in reality time never stops."[20] Bourne's own account of the sunset emphasizes the passage of time, and photographic vision cannot match up with our lived experience of duration.[21] The camera really has come to the edge of the world in its aim to capture fantasy, and it can only return us to the painted landscape. Bourne wishes to capture something of the contemplative Romantic spirit so masterfully rendered in a painting like Caspar David Friedrich's *Wanderer above a Sea of Fog* (see Plate 9). The crucial insight of this moment is an admission on Bourne's part that the camera, for all its claims to truth, is both more and less than a truthfully documenting device. And in this moment, the world appears to Bourne not simply as a static reality to be captured but as something that resides within the subject:

> The effects which I have sometimes witnessed in the evening, just before sunset, have been such as will remain impressed on my *memory* for ever—effects which must be *seen* to be felt, for no description can conjure up to the reader the *magic* and almost *dreamlike visions* which the writer has *witnessed.*[22]

The realms of imagination and magic, of dreamlike visions and memory, figure here as the locations of the real experience of the world. It is this subjective and, according to Bourne, fundamentally *visual* experience that he strives to capture in his frame. If the mantle of truth covers the landscape only when the monarch of day is retiring behind a summit, then why does this knowledge appear as a form of magic and a dreamlike vision?

Certainly one answer to this question would point to the obdurate limitations of photographic technology that Bourne was forced to use in the 1860s: the heavy glass plates, the enormous and cumbersome camera, the necessity of the right amount of light, the lack of color. Bourne invokes each of these technomaterial limits over the course of his accounts of photographing the Himalayas. Christopher Pinney, in discussing these limitations, notes, "Behind the remarkable beauty and technical perfection of Bourne's images we continually feel this trudge, the movement of feet, the straining of packages held by leather straps, of large boxes of negatives suspended on poles and carried by several coolies, none of whom, as he writes, like being 'puckeroed' in these expeditions."[23] Given these constraints, it would make sense that truth and sublimity, as the two are intertwined in Bourne's account, are located on the far side of what is possible to represent. This is one definition of both truth and sublimity, as that which lies beyond the technomaterial horizon of any given form of representation; so what Bourne calls "the mantle of truth" can exist only in the form of magic and dreamlike visions.[24] Such experiences can be felt but not represented, at least not by photography in the 1860s. Only a return to older forms, like painting, holds for Bourne the hope of approaching such experiences in the face of photography's severe limitations. And to that end, the indexical power of photographic representation must be sacrificed for the sake of an image truer to the "imagination" and to the heights of feeling elicited by sublime scenes.

But surely more than a technomaterial limit is at work in the impossibility that confronts Bourne. If that which is picturelike (i.e., picturesque) is that which is properly photographable, then it would seem that aesthetic form and technomaterial limitations work in tandem. If picturesque conventions keep the terror of sublimity at bay, then such aesthetic forms are a kind of armor against precisely the feelings and experiences that Bourne witnesses at dusk as he faces the mountains. That is, if aesthetic forms enable one to sense and know the world in a certain way, then these forms also regulate the permeability of body and world, sense and sensation. These boundaries are, of course, highly policed in the colonial context, in particular after the Sepoy Revolt in India, when it became paramount to keep the traffic between the body and the world as sanitized as possible. In between the lines of Bourne's lament about photography is a lament about the failure of the picturesque aesthetic itself. Yet this subtext is, paradoxically, part celebration: on the one hand, real experience (or truth) calls out for a supersession of one's current frame, and on the other hand, such an overreaching risks giving up altogether on the project of making sense of the world. To compose sense means to don an aesthetic armor against such overreaching, such lapses into unintelligibility, however sublime. Hence the picturesque aesthetic is not, and possibly cannot be, an aesthetic of the sublime. In the rest of this chapter I would like to explore how the domain of the visual comes to be so intimately tied to sensing the world and to the regulation of the viewing subject's body space. The picturesque aesthetic in India may well provide insights into how such regulation, the play of armor and aesthesis, mutated as the global age of mechanical reproduction got under way. Felice Beato was himself influenced by this aesthetic; in albums, his macabre photograph of Sikanderbagh sits side by side with more palatable and familiar scenes of the picturesque (Figures 3.3 and 3.4).

Curious Familiarity

Bourne was a late arrival to the scene of the picturesque in India. About a hundred years earlier, in 1780–83, under Warren Hastings's patronage, William Hodges published a series of aquatints titled *Select Views of India, Drawn on the Spot.* Ten years after the release of *Select Views,* Thomas and William Daniell set out to "correct" what they found to be Hodges's overly idealized eye, and with the use of the camera obscura they redrew many of the same scenes that Hodges had published. Although they sought scientific certitude in their paintings, like Hodges they, too, employed the conventions of the picturesque (see Plate 10), making their aesthetic commitments clear in *A Picturesque Voyage to India* (1810) and even anticipating the investment in scientific truth that would later become a cornerstone of nineteenth-century discourse on photography:

> Delineation is the only medium by which a faithful description can be given of sensible images: the pencil is narrative to the eye; and however minute in its relations, can scarcely become tedious; its representations are not liable to the omissions of memory, or the misconceptions of fancy; whatever it communicates is a transcript of nature.[25]

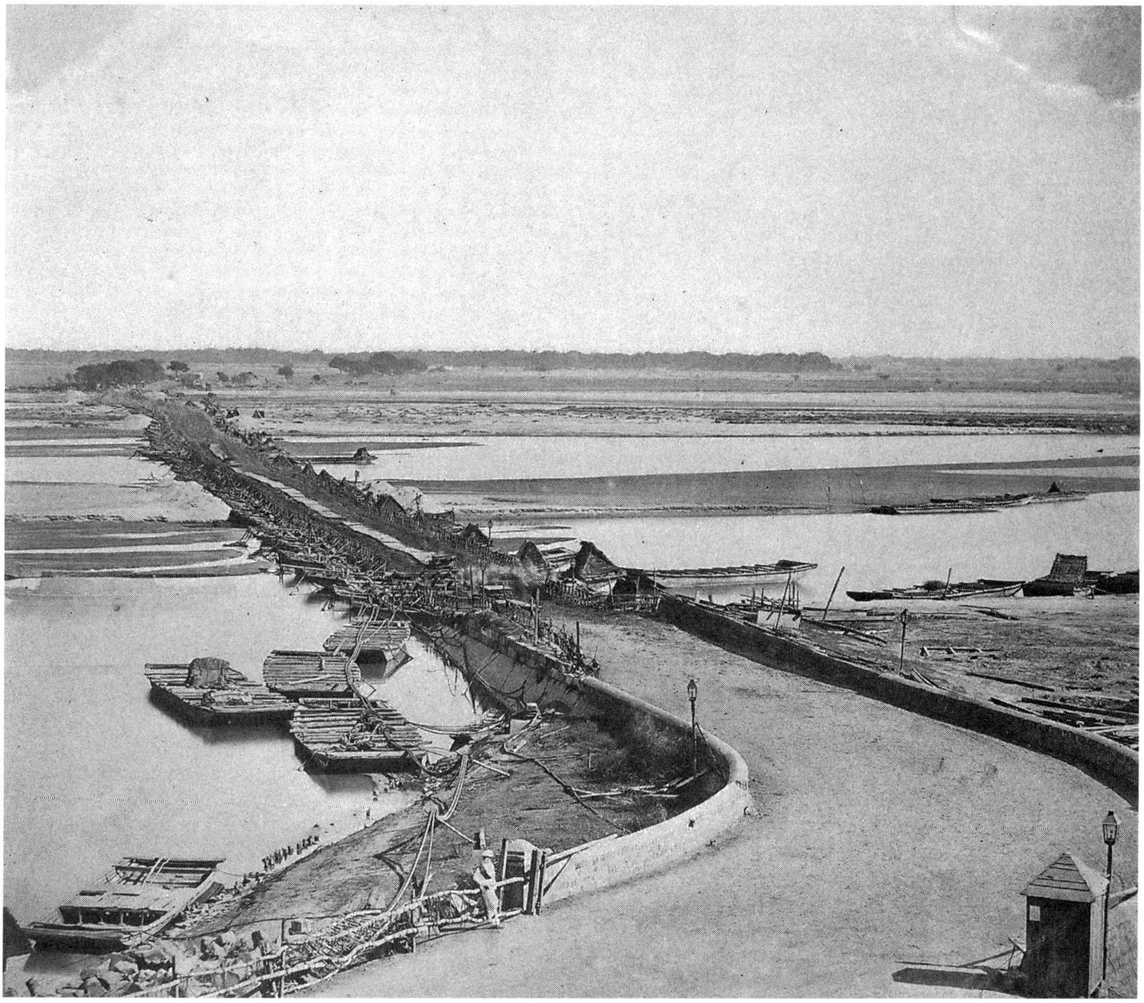

Figure 3.3. Felice Beato, *A Bridge of Boats over the Jumna River*, 1858. Wellcome Library, London.

Because the camera obscura was seen to evacuate subjective tendencies from the image, it bolstered the Daniells' claims to transparency and truth. In fact, buoyed by such transparency, the aesthetic realm could free itself from the mire of colonial commerce and war for this reason:

> The passion for discovery, originally kindled by the thirst for gold, [is now] exalted to higher and nobler aims than commercial speculation. Since this new era of civilization, a liberal spirit of curiosity has prompted undertakings to which avarice lent no incentive, and fortune annexed no reward: associations have been formed not for piracy, but humanity: science has had her adventures, and philanthropy her achievements: the shores of Asia have been invaded by a race of students with no rapacity but for lettered

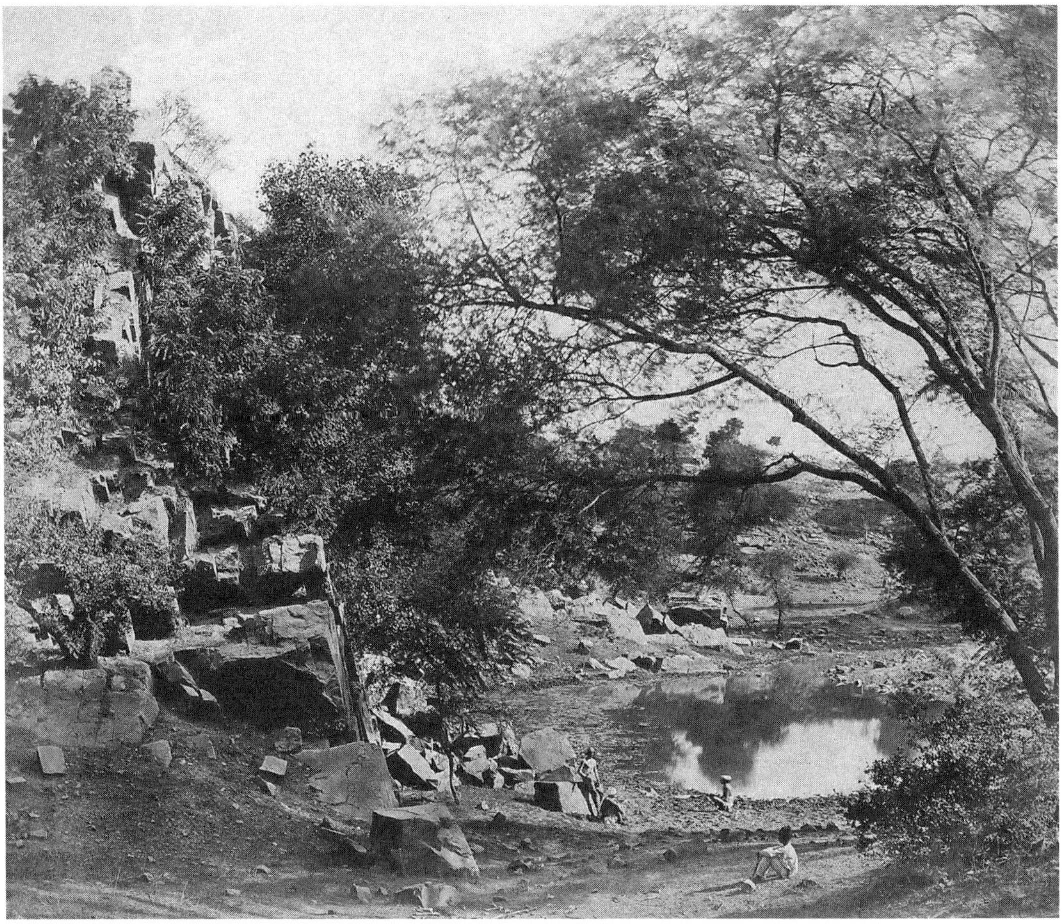

Figure 3.4. Felice Beato, *The "Crow's Nest" Battery beside a Small Pond,* 1858. Wellcome Library, London.

> relics; by naturalists whose cruelty extends not to one human inhabitant; by philosophers, ambitious only for the extirpation of error and the diffusion of truth. It remains for the artist to claim his part in these guiltless spoliations, and to transport them to Europe the picturesque beauties of these favored regions.[26]

Though on the surface this is another ideologically banal expression of the "disinterested" nature of colonial knowledge, on closer examination the theory of truth in art that emerges in this colonial encounter is distinct and subtle. The aesthetic realm does not transcend the material world, but a liberal spirit of curiosity ties it to the material world, which is its only source of truth. However, because the camera obscura secures an understanding of vision as decorporealized, producing for the artist a transcript of nature, the images produced by this mechanism come to stand in for the human subject. A subjectless discourse on aesthetics, in other words, replaces the untrustworthy subject—complete with his or her omissions of memory, impaired vision, and misconceptions of fancy—with a picture that is a transcript of nature. The subtlety with which the image "replaces" the embodied subject points to the subtlety with which the space of the body merges with the space of the image, because the body, of course, can hardly be usurped. An *embodied* artist must, after all, claim his part in these guiltless spoliations. A transformed, disembodied vision secures the merging of body and image space, a merging that would become the condition for all kinds of aesthetic practices by the end of the nineteenth century.[27]

If, as the Daniells claim, the spoliations of the artist are guiltless because artists are simply motivated by a liberal spirit of curiosity, it turns out that curiosity is the initial incentive for the picturesque aesthetic as well. In his 1794 *Essay on the Picturesque,* Uvedale Price comments, "The effect of the picturesque is curiosity; an effect which, though less splendid and powerful [than the sublime], has more general influence; it neither relaxes nor violently stretches the fibers, but by its active agency keeps them in full tone . . . correct[ing] the languor of beauty, or the horror of sublimity."[28] Reminiscent of Burkean aesthetics, in which physiological phenomena become the ground of aesthetic experience, the discourse of the picturesque is, at its inception, a theory of the means by which images penetrate and affect the body, the means by which the body reaches out to images. So the picturesque is that which produces the effect of curiosity, a feeling one may understand as a desire for or an attraction to the unfamiliar. As noted earlier, the picturesque also seeks to represent a spontaneous view, an incidental detail, or, in the words of Samuel Bourne, "peeps" along a journey through a landscape. Yet such curiosity, such an attraction to the unfamiliar, is mediated in India by the familiar—by reference, for example, to images of Britain or to British idealizations of the classical world. The paintings of Hodges and the Daniells, for example, often render Indian scenes with a veneer of classical Greece and Rome.[29] For Bourne's part, his scenes of the Indian picturesque derive their power from their correspondence with the English countryside, a correspondence he often searched for in vain:

> The sensations which a devoted disciple of our art, who has only followed his hobby in England, feels when . . . he emerges into a tropical climate, must be experienced to be understood. . . . If he could only transport English scenery under these exquisite skies, what pictures he would not produce! For I am perfectly convinced that no scenery in the world is better or so well adapted for photography, on the whole, as that of Great Britain. Its mountain streams and lovely fertile valleys—its rustic cottages, overhung with thickly-foliaged

> trees—its cascades and waterfalls—its lakes, rivers, and verdure—are especially suited for and often so combined as to meet the peculiar requirements of the camera.[30]

The camera's lens is, of course, inseparable from the habits of picturesque viewing. The nostalgia for Britain (or rather for images of Britain) pervades Bourne's accounts of his photographic tours and is a recurring motif of contemporaneous travel writing.

The mediation of curiosity through the familiar permeates colonial discourse, showing up in realms far removed from art and aesthetics. For example, in the *Imperial Gazetteer of India* one comes across the following comment, surprising for a publication dedicated to objective and scientific knowledge, about the Andaman and Nicobar islands, long considered by British administrators to be the very edge of civilization in South Asia: "The harbors have been compared to Killarny, and no doubt they do recall the British Lakes. One view of Port Blair Harbour is strongly reminiscent of Derwetwater as seen from the Keswick end."[31] If, as Wolfgang Kemp writes, "in a sense, the picturesque is everywhere since it is not a matter of an objective condition, but of camera position, of the right moment, of framing,"[32] then this aesthetic specificity in the gazetteer attests not only to the depth of the colonial longing for the familiar (itself a kind of armor) but also to the modern comportment for which image making and knowing have become inseparable. Just as Marlowe intones at the opening of Joseph Conrad's *Heart of Darkness* that the Thames "too has been a place of darkness," the *Imperial Gazetteer* anticipates a future in which the superimposition of the civilized image of Derwetwater as seen from the Keswick end onto the Andaman and Nicobar islands overlays the actual anticolonial struggles of the "bellicose" Jarawas, an Andaman tribe, whose "belligerent" nature this gazetteer also documents. The mimetic claim works in two directions at once: on the one hand, for both Bourne and the writers of the gazetteer, the reference to England is simultaneously an indication of the colonial land's lack and a reminder that the current darkness (Andaman Islands, the tropics) may yet be converted into an image of light (view from Keswick, the Lake District). Crucially, this complex mimetic relay requires as a precondition that the world be grasped as an image, and this apprehension of the world is not a specifically colonial way of seeing, even if colonialism has traditionally benefited from the aesthetic, political, and philosophical ramifications of such forms of apprehension. A case for continuity can be made, for example, from the Kantian separation of subject and object, through Heidegger's diagnosis of the "age of the world picture," to the colonial figures of authority who require a certain distance from the "native quarters" in order to convert scenes into images, as analyzed by Timothy Mitchell.[33] But Pierre Bourdieu's work on the habitus implicitly demonstrates that grasping the world as image does not leave the grasping subject unchanged; moreover the supposed separation between the subject and the image proves to be an illusion.

The habitus, in Bourdieu's account, names embodied practices and dispositions: "The habitus could be considered as a subjective but not individual system of internalized structures, schemes of perception, conception, and action."[34] In other words, it encapsulates the body (perception), the imagination (conception), and everyday practice (action). It is similar to taste, another category defined by Bourdieu as "social necessity made second nature, turned into muscular patterns and bodily automatisms."[35] What I would like to foreground here is the bodily (which is to say, the aesthetic and perceptual) dimension of the habitus as a naturalized set of practices through which the subject receives a sense of its place in the world. The habitus itself is historically contingent, but its operations disavow such historical determination: the habitus is "history turned into nature."[36] Yet it retains an "endless capacity to engender products—thoughts, perception, expressions, actions—whose limits are set by the historically and socially situated conditions of its production."[37] The habitus can be read as theory of perception, one that underscores the subjection of the senses to history's vicissitudes.

In fact, in a later essay titled "Making the Economic Habitus," Bourdieu explains that the habitus becomes most easily recognizable as such during periods of change, when societies are undergoing seismic shifts in the very structures of recognition and exchange, shifts that occur, for example, as a result of colonization.[38] Bourdieu's case study is of the Kabylia region in Algeria, where there is a "mismatch between economic dispositions fashioned in a precapitalist economy and the economic cosmos imported and imposed, oftentimes in the most brutal way, by colonization."[39] Local socioeconomic practices (gifts, honor, debt, etc.) transmute or disappear in order to assimilate to newly arrived practices (wage labor, etc.). There is no way to opt out, of course, even if assimilation may take temporary or permanent local forms. The colonized must learn to act in a world that operates through codes and transactions that are discrepant with their own economic dispositions (which are, of course, tied to larger social and political codes that incorporate kinship, interpersonal relations, and exchange of all kinds). At these moments of historical change, Bourdieu implies, the shifting habitus becomes most readily visible. While Bourdieu's case study examines what he calls the "economic habitus," his findings regarding the legibility of the habitus at times of radical political and economic change provide a critical perspective from which to examine the aesthetic and political shifts that the picturesque represented in the nineteenth century.

One reading of Bourne and the habitus is provided by Christopher Pinney, who describes Bourne's photographic practice as an instance of the colonizer's habitus. Since Bourne's photographic apparatus required a train of coolies to carry the heavy plates, chemicals, and provisions, Pinney argues that such realities provide a "guarantee of the physiognomy of [the] colonial environment." He continues, "Photography's technomaterial base finds echoes and affirmations in a bureaucratic disposition that affords easements which subtly mould and constrain the possibilities of photography."[40] Pinney's point is indisputable, especially given the repeated descriptions in Bourne's letters to the *British Journal of Photography* of the beatings he gave to coolies who refused to carry him and his strange and unwieldy apparatus over glaciers and mountains. The technomaterial aspect of photography and the colonial habitus do find a mutually generative and yet mutually constraining relation here.[41] However, technomaterial realities clearly do not exhaust the scope of colonial dispositions as such a strongly technomaterial reading unwittingly suggests. While the modern habitus converts the world into a picture and must negotiate the weighty limitations of the photographic apparatus, it is aesthetic comportment—the a priori grasping of the world as picture—rather than technomaterialism that is symptomatic of this flexible habitus, a habitus for which photography is simply one medium among others and colonialism simply one mode of social arrangement among others. The project of the picturesque aesthetic, which Bourne explicitly takes up, is itself not reducible to the colonial scene, as I have mentioned earlier. But if changing historical conditions are the moments in which a habitus becomes most easily perceptible, then perhaps the picturesque, that obsolete and much maligned aesthetic form, may shed light on the transformations effected by modernity in the everyday dispositions—bodily, imaginary, practical—of the modern subject.

Forms of Difference

Such historical shifts, while occurring "unevenly" across the globe or within the same country, nevertheless, do transform the socius. This is not to say that everyone across the globe is suddenly equipped with identical forms of seeing and knowing but, rather, that colonialism forces its subjects to adopt some form of engagement with the traffic it makes possible across the globe. Take, for example, the case of Indian photographer Lala Deen Dayal. If the specificity of the colonizer's habitus can be located in the desire for familiarity, for images of an English "home" in an unfamiliar land, then what does one make of the nineteenth-century use of the picturesque aesthetic by Lala Deen Dayal? Surely curiosity and familiarity do not have the same relationship to each other in Dayal's work, growing up as he did in Uttar Pradesh, with a varied career first as a draftsman and then as a successful photographer with studios in Secunderabad, Bombay, Indore, and Hyderabad. While initially helped by the patronage of Sir Lepel Griffin of the Bengal Civil Service, Dayal eventually settled into a comfortable position as the court photographer for the sixth nizam of Hyderabad (Mehboob Ali Khan), photographing tea parties, maharajahs' portraits, hunts, and durbars. He simultaneously maintained his commercial studios with the help of his sons and held the Royal Warrant as official photographer from both Queen Victoria and King Edward VII. In awe of Dayal's skills, the nizam even penned a couplet in Urdu in his honor:

> Ajab yeh karte hain tasvir mein kamaal kamaal
> Ustaadon ke hain ustaad Raja Deen Dayal.
> [In the art of photography, surpassing all,
> A master of masters is Raja Deen Dayal.]

The word *Ajab,* however, connotes strangeness and magic, in keeping with the wonderment that early photography evoked. Like that of most commercial photographers, Deen Dayal's work ranged from studio portraiture, landscapes, and official events to architectural and tourist scenes. The visitor's book from his studio in Bombay, opened in 1894, contains a comment from Slade Jones of Spicer Bros Ltd., London, noting, "The studio compares more favourably with the best in London and Paris," and Dayal's staff member Antonio Xavier Trindade, who expertly tinted photographs as per the reigning fashion of the 1880s, was known as the "Rembrandt of the East."[42]

These comparisons to London, Paris, and Rembrandt, with their subtle insinuations of the age-old colonial categories of civilization and barbarism, aim to elevate the "native" studio. They are also recognitions of the skill with which Dayal's work had assimilated European aesthetic conventions. Certainly a strand of postcolonial theory would find in Dayal traces of local difference and would possibly construct a genealogy of his image making extending as far back as Mughal miniatures.[43] Several facts would have to be overlooked for the sake of this sort of reading, however: Dayal, like many Indian photographers, relied upon British largesse as well as British aesthetic conventions in his photographic oeuvre; he remained to the end a commercial photographer, like Bourne, and served the same market that Bourne served in India and England; his primary objective was to be legible in the regnant aesthetic conventions brought to India's shores; his work makes excellent use of these conventions. Nevertheless, the element of "curiosity" so central to the colonial rendering of the Indian picturesque takes a different form in Dayal's work; this difference is not grounds for "resistance" or "contestation" at the level of aesthetic form, but at the same time it is also not a simple mimetic replication of the European picturesque tradition. Instead, his picturesque views attest to the subtle processes of assimilation and molding that give insight into the differential relationship that (elite) colonized subjects have to the modern habitus that converts the world into a picture. The picturesque aesthetic, in Dayal's work, is not an overlaying of the familiar onto the foreign but rather an attempt to mold oneself through the terms of the other.

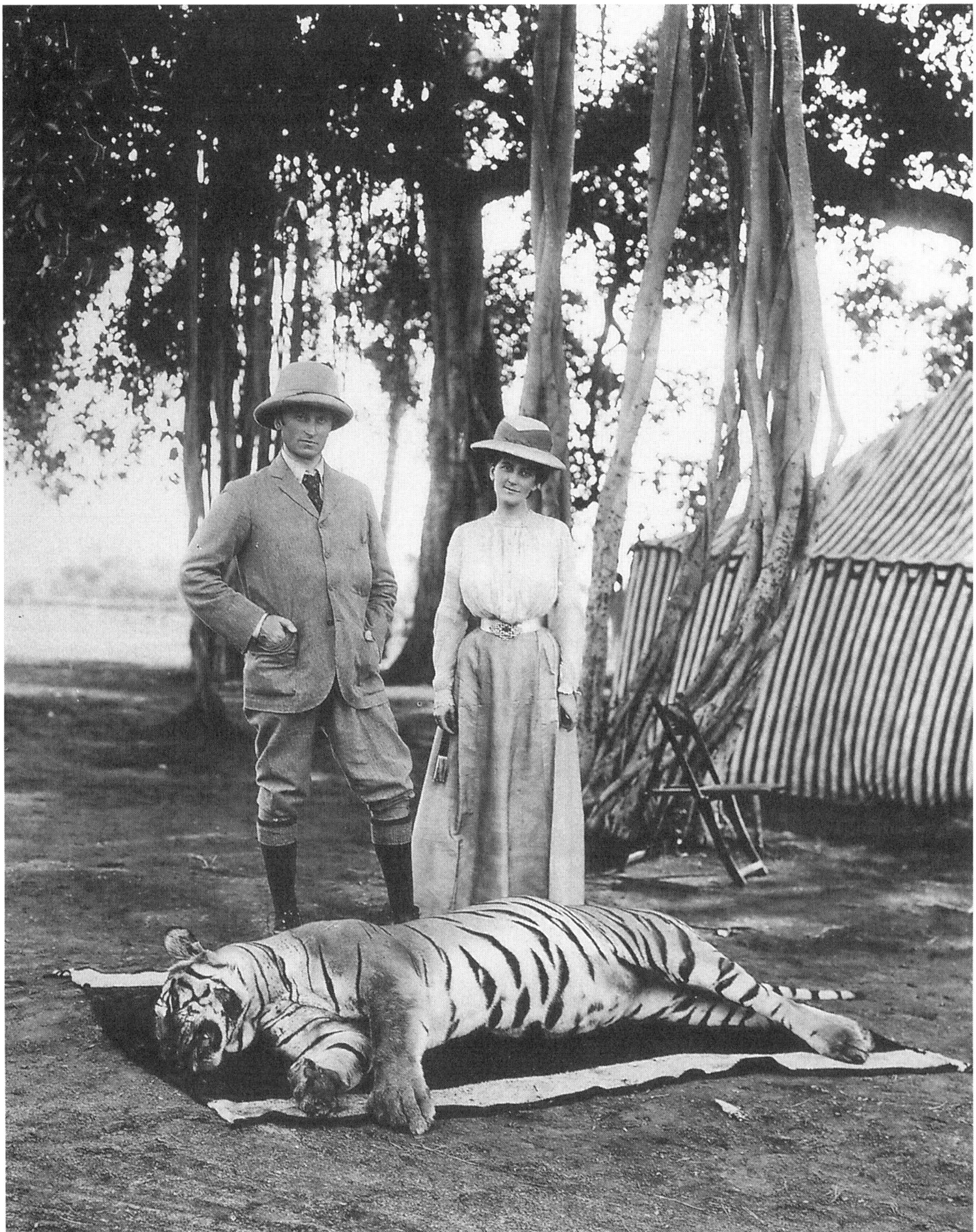

Figure 3.5. Lala Deen Dayal, *Lord and Lady Curzon with First Day's Bag in Camp near Nekonda, Warangal District, Hyderabad,* April 2–12, 1902. Digital image courtesy of the Digital Content Library, University of Minnesota.

A juxtaposition of Samuel Bourne's view of the reversing station at the Bhore Ghat incline with Deen Dayal's late nineteenth-century photograph of it, as well as his photograph of Mount Elphinstone, shows the continuity of the picturesque aesthetic in Dayal's work most starkly (Figures 3.6–3.8). Dayal's landscape photographs clearly evidence a vision imbued with the stock components of picturesque scenes. Figure 3.8, for example, employs the same mise-en-scène as Bourne's famous photograph of the Bhore Ghat incline (Figure 3.6), itself a picturesque spot that Dayal also photographed (Figure 3.7). The aim in Dayal's work is to overlay the familiar with the familiar; that is to say, for his aesthetic project the scenes of the English countryside and the protocols of picturesque seeing are already iconic and known. The foreign is not converted into the familiar by means of aesthetic form (as in Bourne), but rather the familiar is molded, through a subtle reorientation of vision, into a new kind of familiarity. Here, Theodor Adorno's formulation of mimesis proves instructive. By "mimesis" Adorno refers to three simultaneous moments: the comportment toward another that seeks to resemble the other; a kind of assimilation, molding, and "nestling against" the other *(sich-anschmiegen ans andere)*; gesturing, expressing through actions and behavior a kind of imitation of the other.[44] It is this second moment, for which Adorno prefers the term *anschmiegen* rather than *Nachahmung* (imitation), that is particularly useful for understanding Deen Dayal's form of colonial mimicry. Recall that in Bourdieu's account of the Kabylia region of Algeria, he notes that the habitus of the colonized is most legible to the anthropologist when it is in the process of being transformed. The locals must assimilate and mold themselves to the new order, and such processes happen unevenly and can have unexpected results. Rather than a blind copying of the picturesque aesthetic, in Dayal's work we witness a "nestling against" new aesthetic forms that are inseparable, at this historical juncture, from new representational media. Adorno's aim in using the word *anschmiegen* was twofold: on the one hand, it abolishes the myth of subjective agency in the act of mimetic replication, and on the other hand, it highlights the sensuous, bodily, sensate aspect of mimetic experience.[45]

My assertion of the variegated nature of colonial mimesis cannot be proven through a formal analysis of the image itself. Not only would such a move be contrary to Adorno's subtle account of mimesis as *anschmiegen,* but also scrutiny of Dayal's photographic details as compared with Samuel Bourne's photographs will only confirm the sameness of Dayal's pictorial forms with picturesque conventions. Our analytical desires for colonial difference may well turn up a detail here and there that we could hold on to to satisfy our own cravings for evidence of the colonized photographer's expression, but such details would really be evidence of our own desires for Deen Dayal's authenticity as an Indian photographer, a misguided search for his "voice."[46]

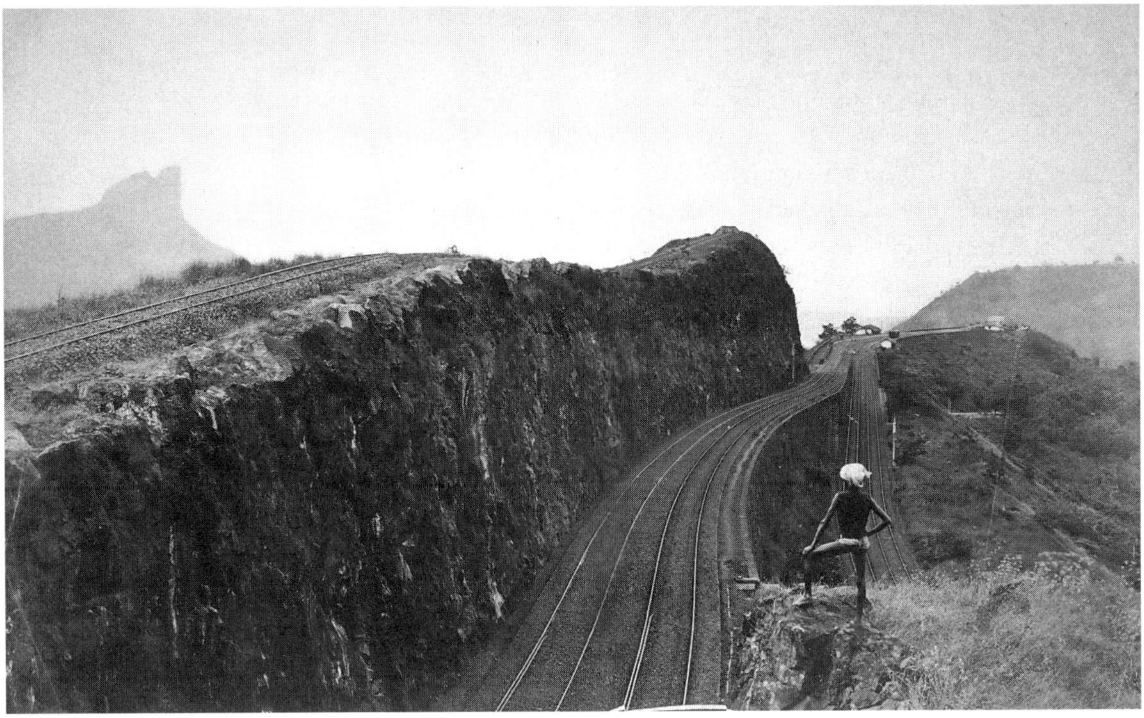

Figure 3.6. Samuel Bourne, *Reversing Station at Bhore Ghat Incline,* Puna, ca. 1870. Copyright British Library Board, Photo 460/(68).

Figure 3.7. Lala Deen Dayal, *Reversing Station at Bhore Ghat Incline,* Puna, 1880 or 1881. Copyright British Library Board, Photo 752/1(33)

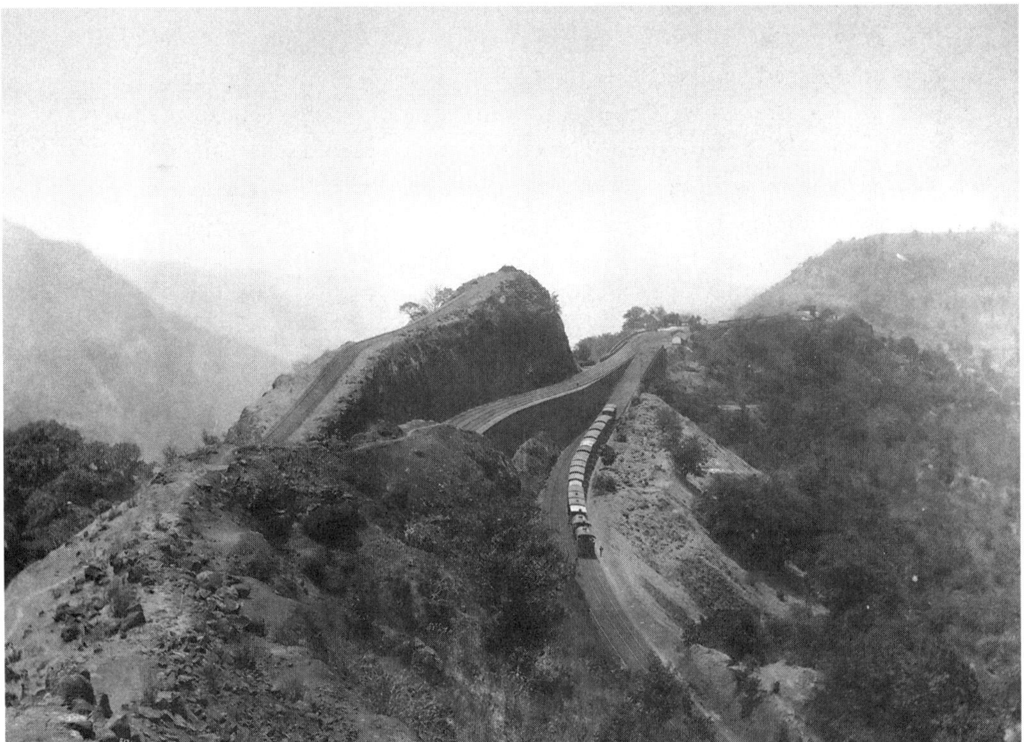

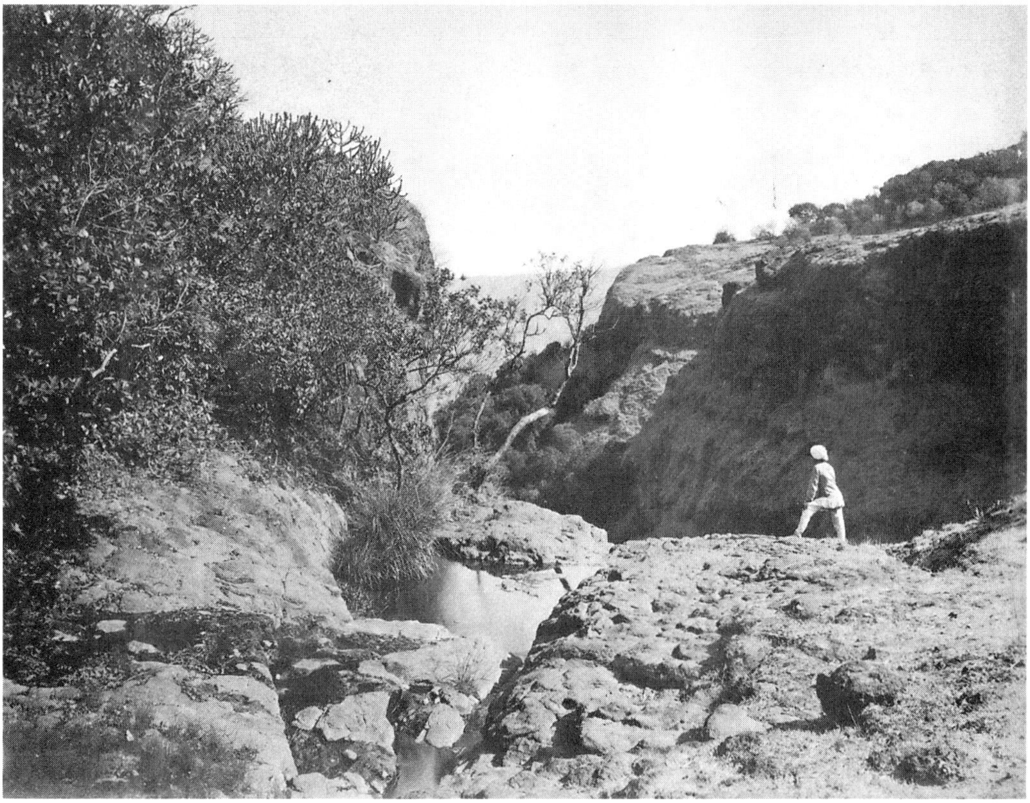

Figure 3.8. Lala Deen Dayal, *Mount Elphinstone,* Mahabaleshwar, 1887. Courtesy of Clark Worswick.

The fact is that the differential nature of mimesis requires that we consider formal elements of the image as one among other registers of mimetic practice. To assume that the visible contours of aesthetic form are both the ultimate arbiter of forms' difference (and the grounds for forms' comparison) and that such manifestation exhausts the notion of form itself is to adopt a naïve view of mimetic referentiality. Adorno's conception is not a return to Platonic iconophobic assumptions of surface/depth, illusion/truth, in which both surface and illusion are inferior to depth and truth. Rather, no such hierarchical binarisms are at work: the "surface," if you will, of the aesthetic form already points to multiple registers of mimetic practice *simultaneous* with the "surface," or appearance, and not preexisting it as determining causes.[47] Aesthetic forms contain rhetorical contents at their very surface, and in Dayal's case, this rhetorical content is the aesthetic aspiration—successfully realized—to the picturesque aesthetic; the stock motifs of the picturesque convert the familiar into a new form of legibility and ensure the continuation of English and elite local patronage. It is an impulse to become similar, in the sense in

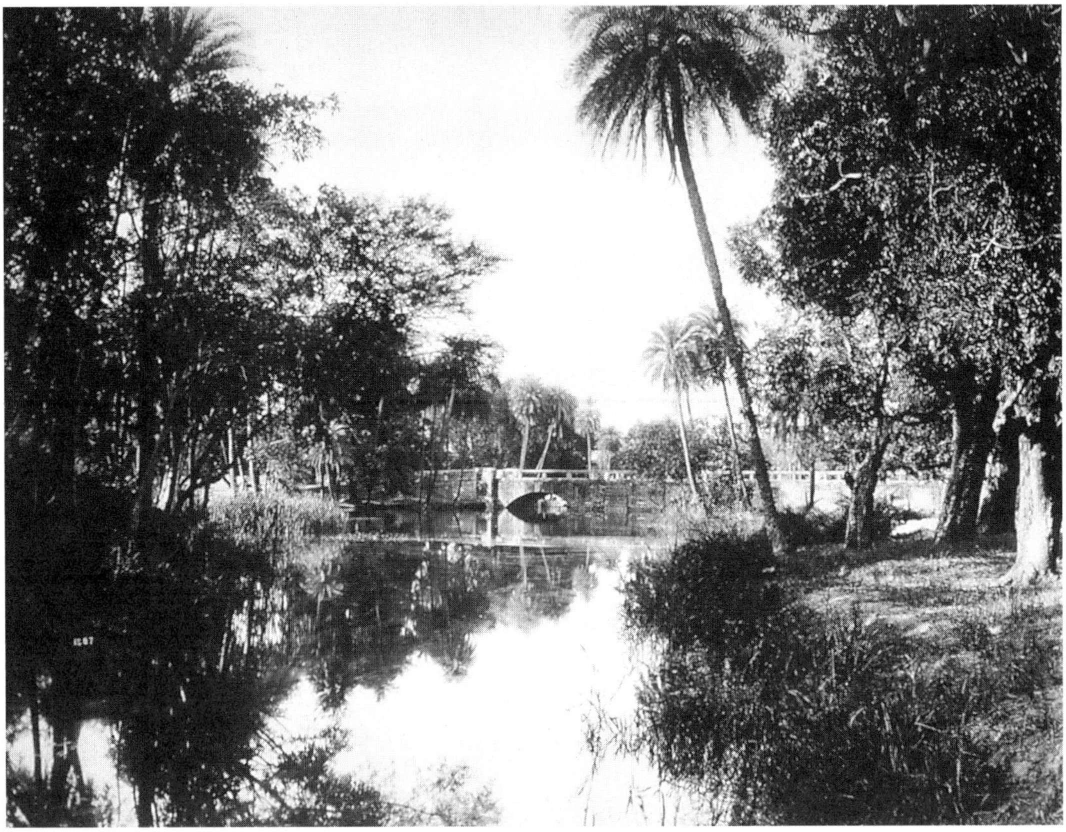

Figure 3.9. Lala Deen Dayal, *The Residency Bridge at Indore*, 1882. Digital image courtesy of the Digital Content Library, University of Minnesota.

which Benjamin speaks in his essay on the mimetic faculty, so influential on Adorno's own theories of mimesis: "[The human] gift for seeing similarity is nothing but a rudiment of the once powerful compulsion to become similar and to behave mimetically."[48] Precisely *what* one is compelled (note the diminished notion of agency at work here) to become similar to determines the lineaments of the aesthetic–political meaning of the mimetic impulse. For Bourne's images of India rendered in the idiom of British picturesque landscapes, the compulsion to become similar is akin to the psychic process of transference in aesthetic form, complete with its impulse to repeat the familiar, but necessarily to repeat it differently each time, because the objects of transference are never identical. Such aesthetic repetitions, or what Merleau-Ponty calls "a creative repetition of ourselves" in the epigraph of this chapter,[49] have a political import when previous habits of looking, by enframing colonial space as versions of metropolitan spaces, become part and parcel of a colonial will to power and of its missions of improvement

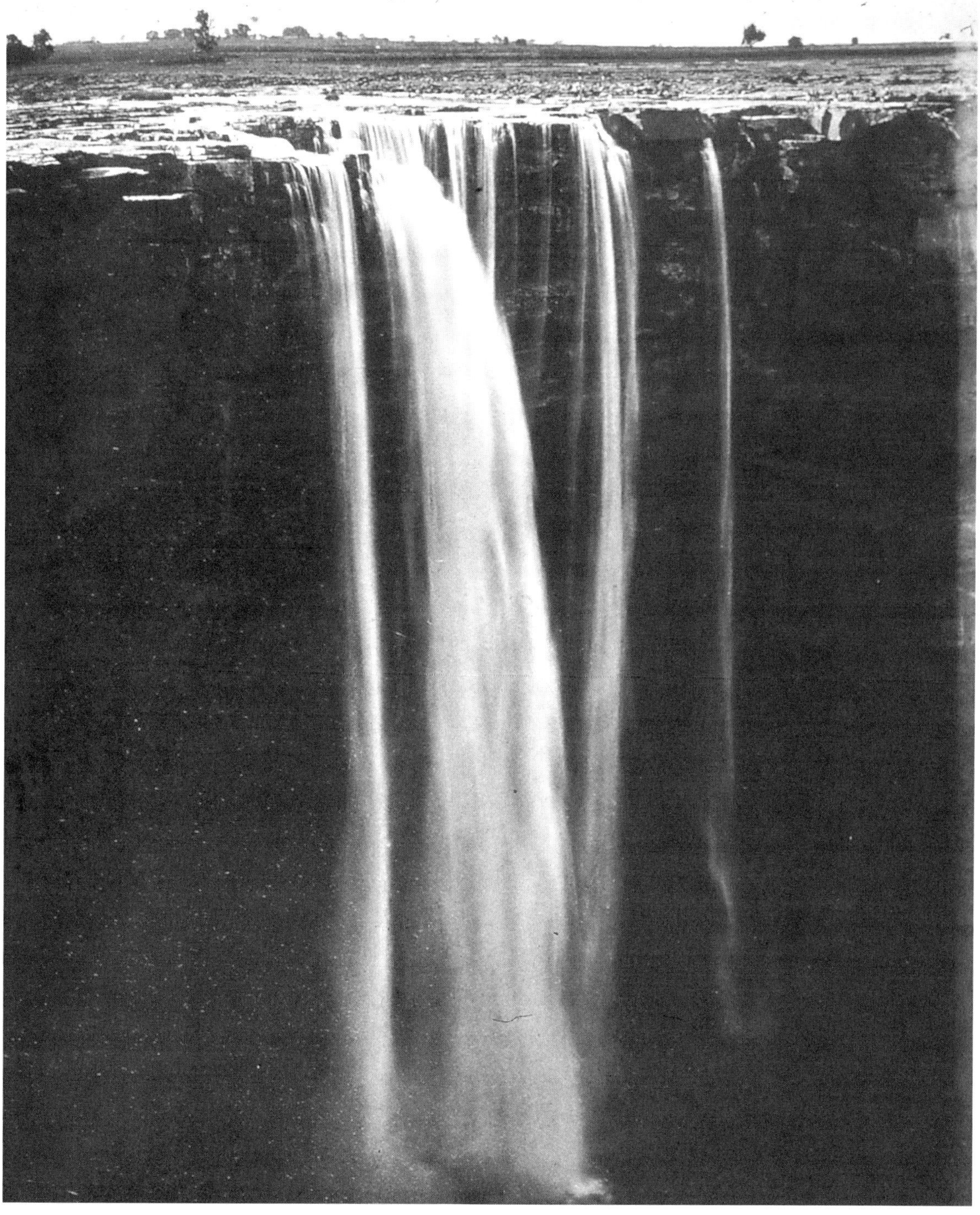

Figure 3.10. Lala Deen Dayal, *Chicha Waterfall near Rewa,* 1882. Digital image courtesy of the Digital Content Library, University of Minnesota.

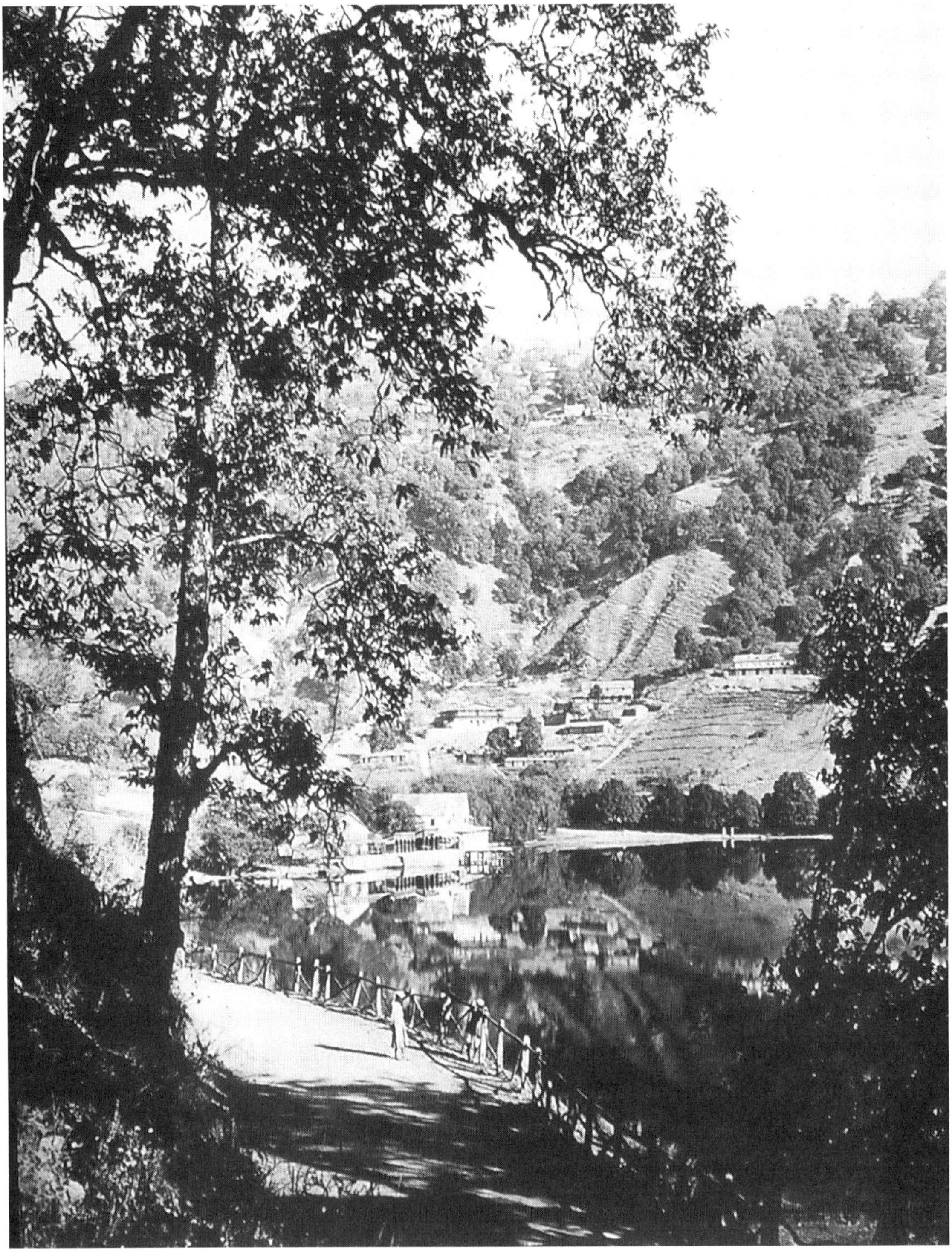

Figure 3.11. Samuel Bourne, *Nainital,* 1860s. Digital image courtesy of the Digital Content Library, University of Minnesota.

that render the colony in the metropole's image. For Deen Dayal, the compulsion to become similar indicates an impulse to be legible in the emerging circuits of aesthetic forms, to render the familiar landscape of home in a new visual idiom.

However, in the early days of photography in India some Indian photographers did invoke local aesthetic traditions in their finished works. Two notable examples are Darogha Abbas Ali and Ahmed Ali Khan. In 1855, Ahmed Ali Khan, a well-known Lucknow-based photographer who regularly took photographic portraits of the British as well as of local Nawabi aristocrats, was commissioned by Wajid Ali Shah, the last ruler of the province of Avadh, in which Lucknow is located, to photograph him and the court at Lucknow. Plate 11, showing Wajid Ali Shah, and Plate 12, a photograph of the courtly Begum Sahibah, are two examples of Khan's efforts. He has placed a nimbus around the head of Wajid Ali Shah (who would be deposed by the British and sent into exile less than two years after this photograph was taken) and framed the portrait with an elaborate colorful border complete with an inscription in Farsi, the favored courtly language, which describes the sitter in words of praise.

In 1880, Darogha Abbas Ali published an extensive collection titled *An Illustrated Historical Album of the Rajas and Taaluqdars of Oudh* in a joint Urdu and English edition.[50] The book contains 344 albumen prints of the rajas and *taaluqdars,* or rulers and landlords, of the province and celebrates the allegiance that landlords demonstrated to British rule during the Sepoy Revolt. The landlords photographed in the book were the primary audience of this album. Out of the 344 portraits, 37 simply give the name of the sitter, and instead of a photographic portrait, we see a medallion with the word *pardanashin* inscribed in Urdu as well as transliterated into English (Figures 3.12–3.14). *Pardanashin,* or "maintaining the veil" (or more literally, "hidden behind the veil"), marks the female presence in deference to the Muslim tradition of women screening themselves or being screened from the public eye, so the only portraits we can see are those of males. The *pardanashin* medallion tucks both Hindu and Muslim females out of sight in this volume. This mimetic choice, which refers to a cultural tradition favoring the blankness of the female presence in the public eye, melds indigenous investment in the visibility of gender difference seamlessly with the practice of photography.

The elaborate colorful border of Ahmed Ali Khan's work and his use of the nimbus around the head of Wajid Ali Shah's portrait hearken back to aesthetic traditions of Mughal miniatures. The inscriptions below the images are exaggerated and conventional encomiums, derived from Mughal portraiture tradition. The wording gives details about the sitters' clothes, rendering the photographs into script but also adding to them senses that the camera cannot capture. For example, the inscription for Plate 12 informs us that the diadem-shaped hair ribbon that the begum wears is made of wood with gold-work,

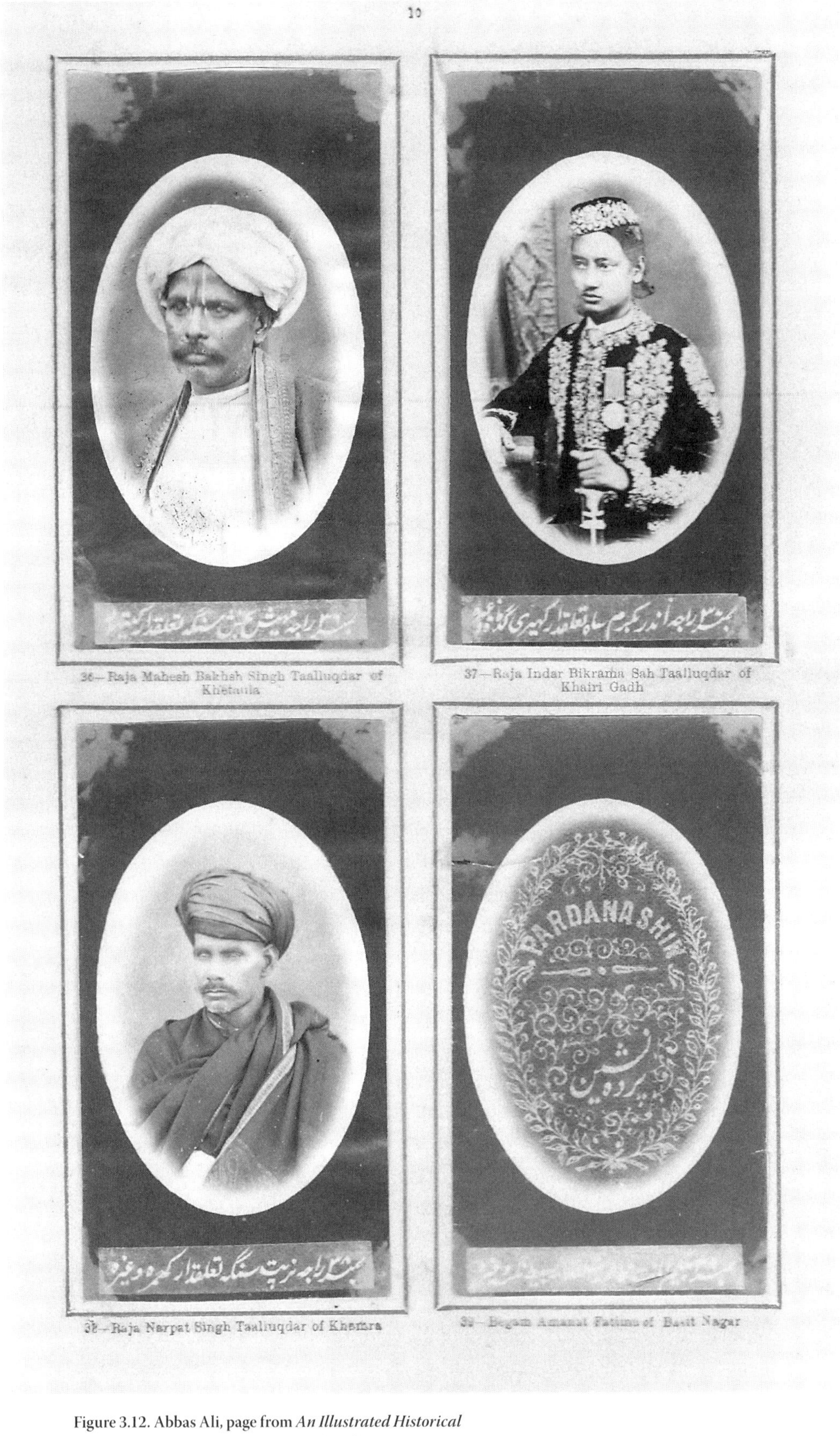

Figure 3.12. Abbas Ali, page from *An Illustrated Historical Album of the Rajas and Taaluqdars of Oudh,* 1880.

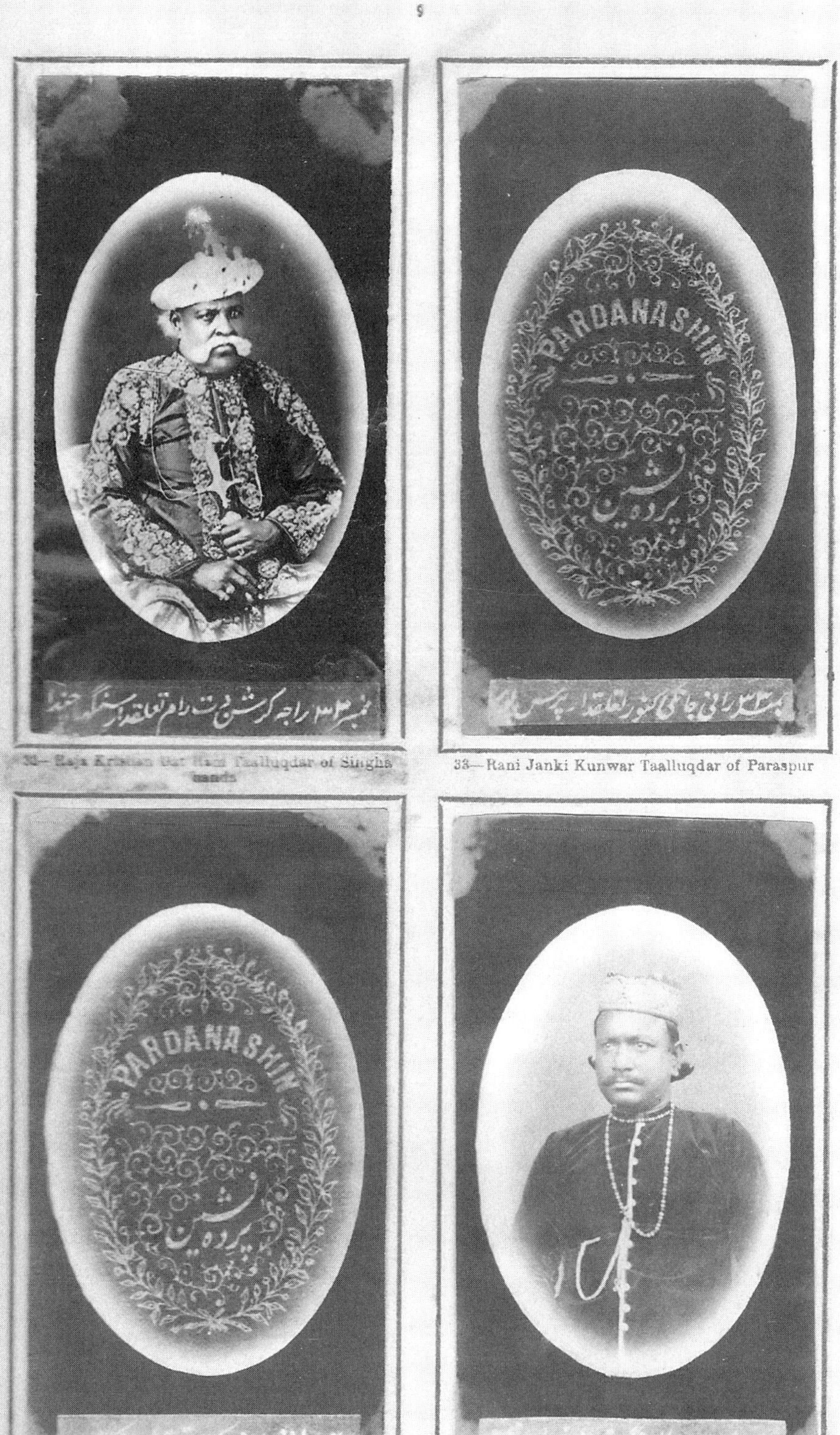

Figure 3.13. Abbas Ali, page from *An Illustrated Historical Album of the Rajas and Taaluqdars of Oudh*, 1880.

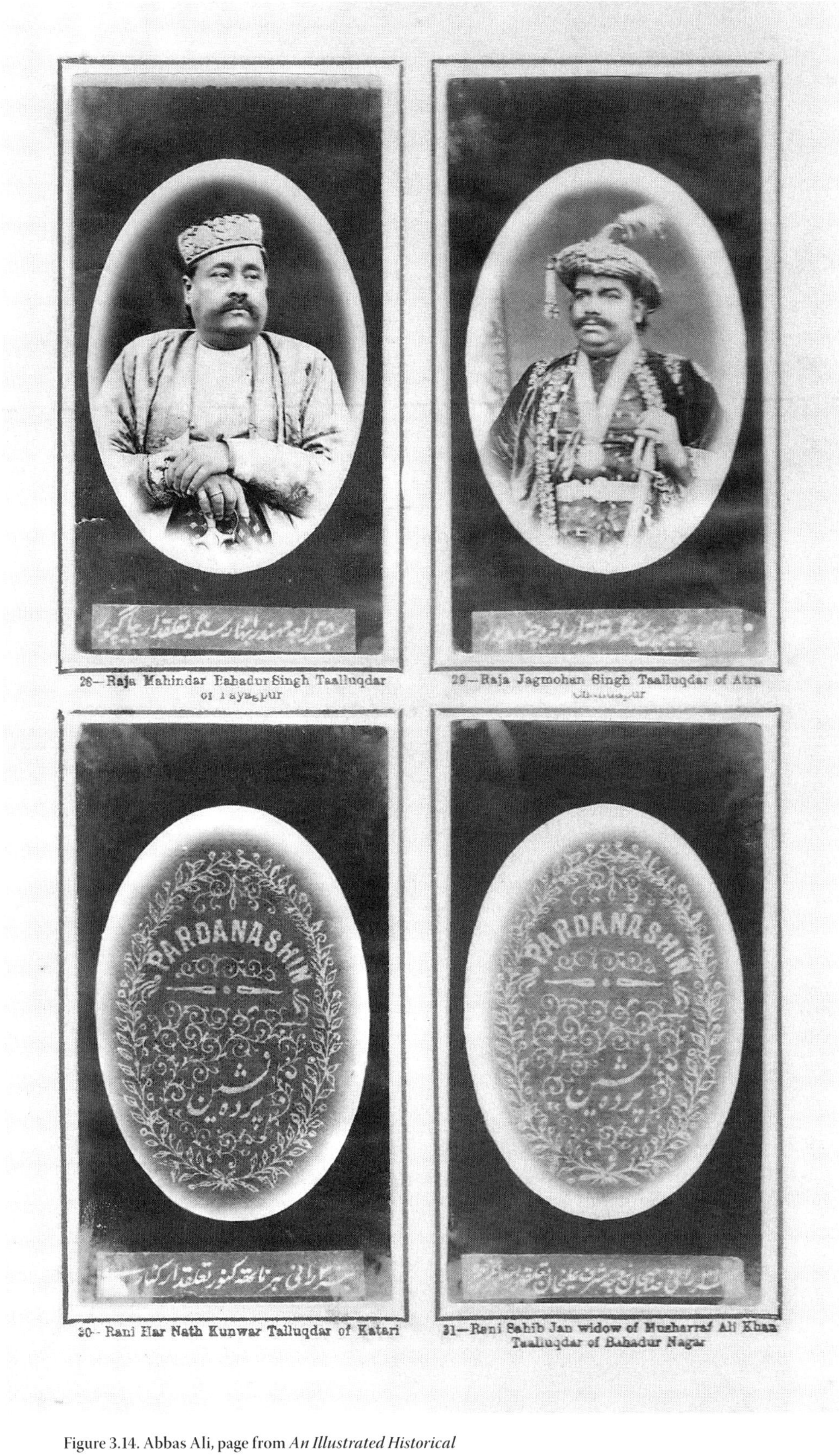

Figure 3.14. Abbas Ali, page from *An Illustrated Historical Album of the Rajas and Taaluqdars of Oudh,* 1880.

directs our attention to the beautiful Indian clothes *(pûshâk-i Hindî)* and jewels that adorn her body, and tells us that she sits on a silver seat as if in a meeting with "Lord Sultan of the World *[Sultân-i 'Âlam]*" (i.e., Wajid Ali Shah), having come out of the women's quarters, from behind the veil, and into this world of "boil-and-turmoil *[dar 'âlam-i jûsh-ô walwala],*" for the purpose of being "pictured *[tasawwur].*" On the one hand, this inscription presumes that photography is inadequate and needs to be supplemented with script, and yet without the photograph these words would be meaningless, so in spite of its inadequacy the photograph still serves as an anchor for the encomiums.

Abbas Ali's album of landlords, in censoring the female presence, shows his deference to the sensibilities of the elite rural rulers to whom the album was addressed. But this practice of blanking out the female presence is a curiosity in the colonial photographic record. It is an exception rather than the rule, even in the oeuvre of nineteenth-century Indian Muslim photographers; Darogha Abbas Ali himself had produced an album just six years earlier, titled *Beauties of Lucknow,* showing the splendor of the Avadh court in female form (see Plates 5 and 6 and Figures 3.15 and 3.16). As aesthetic choices about form, these signs of colonial difference—the photographic portrait in line with the Indian tradition of miniature painting, and the representation of the veil's blankness in a photographic album—written on the very surface of the images, overlay the reality effects of photography with more familiar aesthetic tools. These aesthetic impulses are no different in spirit from the 1859 suggestion of Adolphe-Eugene Disderi, who was so instrumental in introducing mass-manufacturing techniques to portrait photography in France:

> Could not the photographer who was a master of all the effects of lighting, who had at his disposal a large and perfectly equipped studio with blinders and reflectors, who was provided with backdrops of all kinds, with settings, properties, costumes—could he not, given intelligent and skillfully dressed models, compose *tableaux de genre,* historical scenes? . . . Could he not treat of history, like Paul Delarouche in his painting *The Death of the Duc de Guise*?[51]

In *The Arcades Project,* Walter Benjamin cites Disderi as a part of his constellation of ideas surrounding a theory of aesthetic–technological change. He notes that in the emerging forms of the new technological nature, the mimicry of organic "old nature" kept the new in the realm of the mythic, impeding its potential from being realized: early photography invoked a painterly style, electric bulbs were shaped like gas flames, the true potential of iron was overlooked in place of its use as ornamentation. Eventually new technologies come to be based on principles that arise from their technomaterial natures, but the early epoch of technological invention is paradoxically characterized by a giddy experimentation powered by the utopian promises of the new, and yet the potential of the new technologies is also held in check, because these promises (themselves ur-historical) can be rendered only by means of recently known aesthetic forms, the horizon of the imagination of the present, and these aesthetic forms are not up to the task of realizing the potentials of the new technology.[52]

Experimentation and testing are processes that eventually transform aesthetic forms and perceptual apparatuses and discover heretofore unknown uses for emerging technologies.[53] But early experimentation also risks trapping the new in the guise of the old. Hence, Disderi's suggestion that *tableaux de genre* might be a fruitful use of photographic technology. The nineteenth-century photographic tradition of the still life—a literal photographic translation of a painterly tradition—is a version of this same impulse, and this heady phase of technological and aesthetic experimentation can lead to confusion about the relation between old and new media. Benjamin notes, in his reflections on photography, "Symptoms, it would seem, of a profound displacement: painting must submit to being measured by the standard of photography: 'We will be in agreement with the public in admiring . . . the fine artist . . . who has appeared this year with a painting capable of holding its own, in point of delicacy, with daguerrian prints.'"[54] This sentiment, from a review of the Paris salon of 1849, is at odds with Samuel Bourne's ruminations sixteen years later in India, when he would find photography inadequate to represent the views he witnessed in the Himalayas. Such confusions, of which the nineteenth-century debates about photography itself being an art at all, are symptoms of technological–aesthetic shifts that are already in place. The local differences in aesthetic form during this early moment of photographic experimentation, whether in the photographic studios in London and Paris or in Lucknow and Bombay, are symptoms of the historical inertia of familiar aesthetic forms.

Bringing Abbas Ali's and Ahmed Ali Khan's photographic practice into this world-historical narrative about aesthetic and technological change reveals the surface pictorial differences of their photographic practices to be exemplars of changing aesthetic habits.[55] The differences of their particular photographic practices are not, in the end, functional differences insofar as they do not fundamentally alter the phenomenological meanings of photographic practice: the blankness of Abbas Ali's photographs of *pardanashin* begums reinforces the indexical rhetoric of the photograph, since, in the context of an album of photographic portraits, the indexical photographic trace is precisely what threatens the seclusion of the female presence. In Ahmed Ali Khan's case, his photographic embellishments serve to highlight the reality effect of the photograph itself, not detract from it or transform its nature; the nimbus around the head of Wajid Ali Shah is an attempt to secure the rhetorical force of the photograph for an older aesthetic, and the same goes for his painted borders. The changes in perceptual apparatus that these two examples of colonially different photographic practices

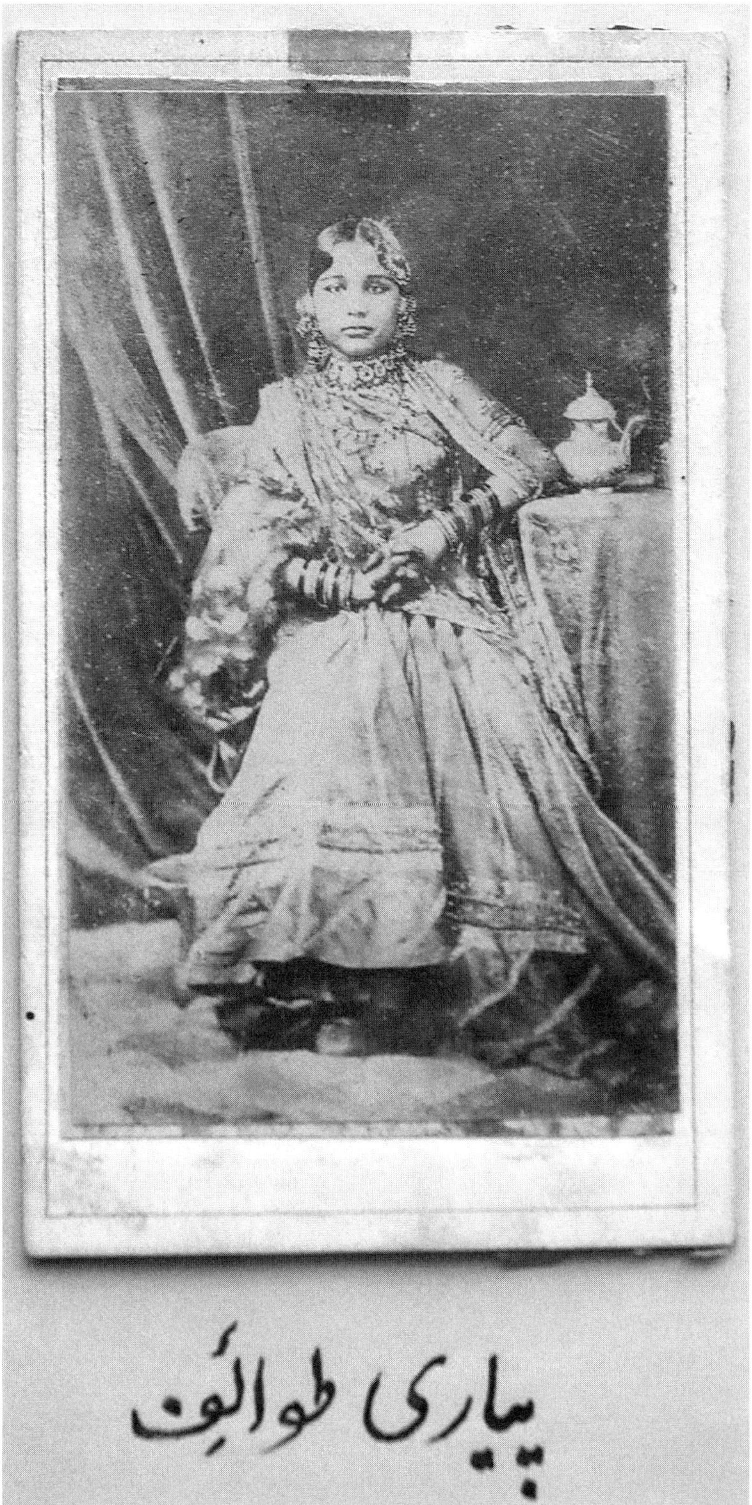

Figure 3.15.
"Pyari," Courtesan.
From Abbas Ali,
The Beauties of Lucknow, 1872.
"Pyari" means "pretty." The Alkazi Collection of Photography.

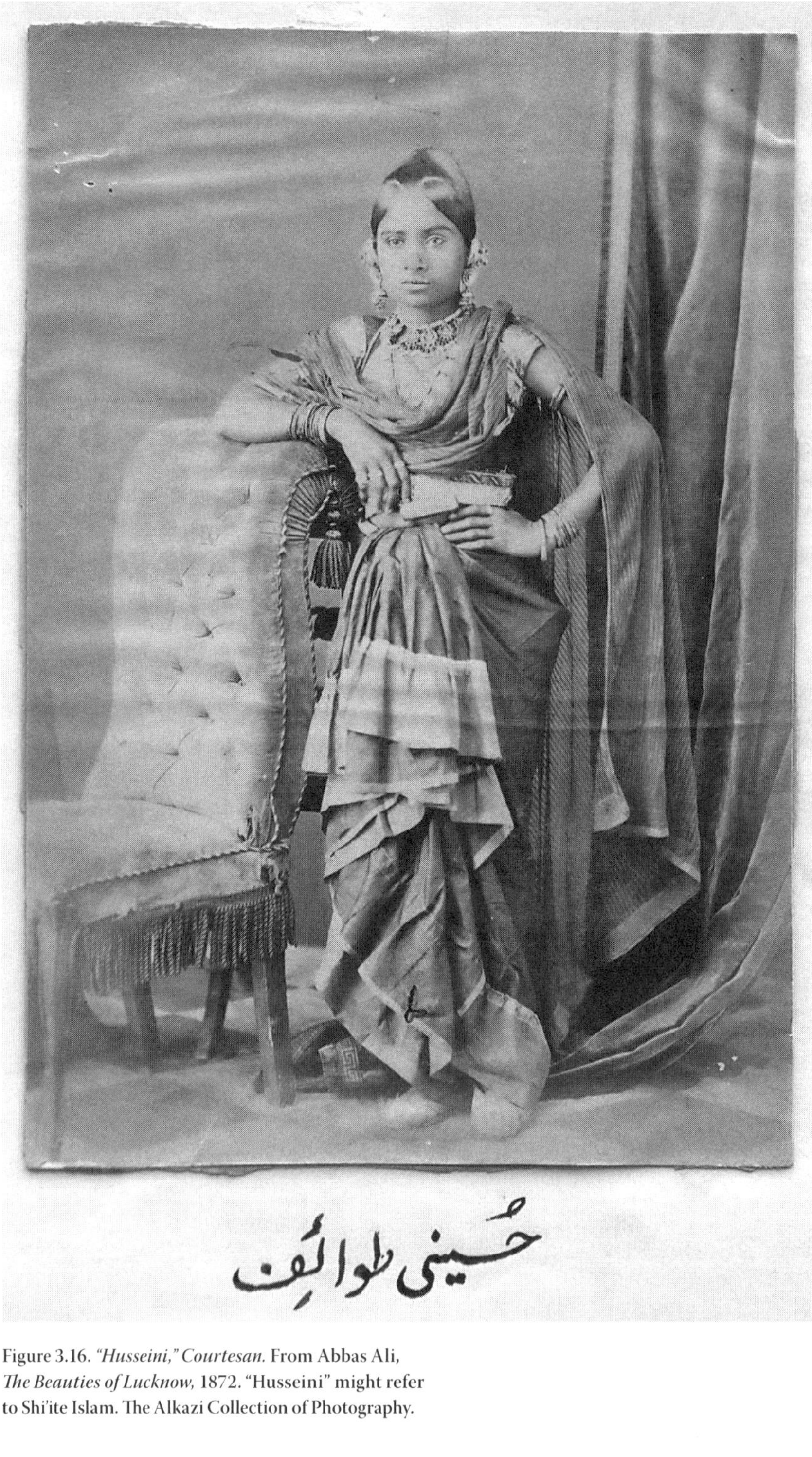

Figure 3.16. *"Husseini," Courtesan.* From Abbas Ali, *The Beauties of Lucknow,* 1872. "Husseini" might refer to Shi'ite Islam. The Alkazi Collection of Photography.

reveal are local versions of a transformation that was happening globally. The local becomes "similar" to the global here, and the supplementary trappings of local flavor that enter into these photographs quickly disappear from the surface of the image over the course of Indian photographic practice in the nineteenth century, but forms of difference do not thereby disappear from the mimetic realm altogether, as Deen Dayal's example shows. If it seems that photographic aesthetics becomes increasingly homogenous over the course of the nineteenth century, then this homogeneity occurs at one level of mimetic practice, and it can be accounted for by historical and material reasons (including but not limited to the technomaterial limits of the photographic apparatus and the aspirant aesthetics of colonial photographers). As photography has become increasingly mobile with the manufacture of smaller cameras, faster shutter speeds, and lowered costs, it has been gradually emancipated from the trappings of other media and older aesthetic imaginings, and differential forms of inhabiting photographic aesthetics made their appearance, by the early twentieth century, at all levels of mimetic practice: the surface of the photographic image, the nature of the photographic collection, the culturally specific uses of the photograph (in secular and nonsecular rituals) that can transform the nature of photographic meaning, and so on.[56] In regard to the nineteenth century, however, in order to apprehend the aesthetic form of difference of Indian photographers, one must recognize that difference at the level of pictorial form is one among multiple coordinates of aesthetic practice.

Certainly Deen Dayal's photographs also do not transform the nature of photographic meaning making, and yet his form of the picturesque, identical to the form inherited from Europe, bespeaks a mimetic replication that is not simple repetition. Dayal's photographic practice alerts us that forms of the picturesque are not themselves equivalent in spite of their sameness. With respect to notions of colonial mimicry, Dayal's work is testament to the fact that seeing the familiar anew and molding the self on the other's terms need not necessarily be an act either of consolidation or subversion of received norms but rather be an indication of a changing perceptual apparatus. While the shifts in landownership and the control of resources that mark the colonial order subtend all cultural politics in the colony, there is a corresponding shift in the aesthetic and perceptual sphere in which both the colonizer and colonized are involved. Moreover, while Dayal represents the edge of this shift in India, this does not imply that Indians are destined to inhabit the picturesque aesthetic in a fashion identical to that of the British.[57]

Body and Image Space

Let us examine more closely the kind of epistemological work done by rendering the world into picturesque forms or by traveling in search of picturesque views. Sir Richard Temple, who held various positions in the British administration in his thirty years in India, including finance minister and lieutenant-governor of Bengal, was a prolific memoirist and published two extensive books on his Indian experience: *Men and Events of My Time in India* (1882) and *A Bird's-Eye View of Picturesque India* (1898).[58] Consider the following passage describing Delhi in Temple's post–Sepoy Revolt memoir:

> I visited the spot where Nicholson fell shortly after the city gate had been stormed. The street was narrow, with houses on both sides, from which musketry *was being poured* into the advancing column; he *was standing forward* to guide his men, and dropped mortally wounded.[59]

Of course Temple has seen no such action taking place; presumably what he sees is an empty place where Nicholson fell, but the sight of the empty space gives rise to an associated narrative that can only be described as filmic, from our vantage point, and photographic, from Temple's vantage point. It is a mise-en-scène complete with the concluding dramatic fall of Nicholson. Elsewhere, Temple praises William Howard Russell, who was a special correspondent for the *London Times* and, in an early example of the embedded journalist, traveled with the army during the Sepoy Revolt: "The Anglo-Indian community were delighted by his power of noting mentally all that passed before him and of depicting it graphically. His word-paintings of the scenes inside Lucknow after the storming hold a high place in the picture-gallery of Indian history."[60] At the start of his "Grand Tour" of India, Temple writes, "When entering upon the field of Indian picturesqueness I feel like one who looks on some vast collection of beautiful objects, say the National Gallery or Kew Gardens, and knows not where to begin his survey."[61] Temple's account, which is representative of the proliferating genre of army and government men's memoirs of India, is rife with statements that convert experience into a picture and then proceed to comment on that composition. While the tendency to see the world as a picture is not the same as the picturesque aesthetic, it does draw attention to the larger habitus that included the picturesque and intensified by the end of the nineteenth century. Regarding the "native representatives" from India who were brought to London to celebrate Queen Victoria's diamond jubilee, Temple notes, "Many of them were Princes, others were nobles; and many were soldiers. . . . They suggested by their presence the thought that the birthplace of such picturesque figures must in itself be replete with pictorial effect."[62] The imputation of pictorial qualities to the world and its people seem perfectly natural to this habitus, for which curiosity and the foreign become assimilable through conversion into images.

To a certain extent, then, photography seamlessly melds with the preexisting habitus that is practiced in seeing the world as a picture. By overlaying scenes of the English countryside in order to compose scenes of the Indian picturesque, Bourne produces aesthetically composite images. But this longing for an image of home (and the trope is consistently visual, not only for photographers, but also for memoirists and travel writers) carries with it a yearning for form, a need to make sense that is amply served by the picturesque aesthetic. Perhaps the ur-form of this recourse to familiar images of home in the midst of the colonial encounter is contained in the seventeenth-century narrative of Mary Rowlandson, who was captured by Algonquin and Narragansett warriors:

> What through faintness and soreness of body, it was a grievous day of travel to me. As we went along, I saw a place where *English* cattle had been, that was a comfort to me, such as it was: Quickly after that we came to an *English* path, which so took me, that I thought I could there have freely lien down and died. That day, a little after noon, we came to a *Squaheag*, where the *Indians* quickly spread themselves over the deserted *English* field, gleaning what they could.[63]

At the height of fear and in the midst of the foreign, images of cattle, path, and fields take on new significance as "English cattle," "an English path," and "English fields." In the colonial context, the habitus that converts the world into a picture consistently converts it into a picture of home. The cattle, path, and fields are associative triggers that allow Rowlandson to see more than what is apparent to the eye.

Uvedale Price focused on curiosity as a hallmark of the picturesque aesthetic, whereas Richard Payne Knight, in his 1808 theory of the picturesque, *An Analytical Inquiry into the Principles of Taste,* found in the associative aspect of the picturesque the grounds for the aesthetic's longevity:

> For when the novelty of the first impression is over, and the interest of curiosity and surprise has subsided, mere imitation of common objects begins to appear trifling and insipid; and men look for, in imitative art, something of character and expression, which may awaken sympathy, excite new ideas, or expand and elevate those already formed. To produce this requires a knowledge of mind, as well as of body; and of the interior, as well as exterior construction of the human frame, or of whatever else be the object of imitation.[64]

Association, according to Knight, becomes a "habitual" and "involuntary" mode of aesthetic experience: "The habit of associating our ideas having commenced with our earliest perceptions, the process of it . . . has become so spontaneous and rapid in adult persons, that it seems to be a mechanical operation of the mind, which we cannot directly influence or control."[65] The ideal picturesque image is, then, a trigger for the involuntary and habitual proliferation of associated images in the subject's mind. The contemporaneous Scottish philosopher Archibald Alison describes the process thus:

> When any object either of sublimity or beauty, is presented to the mind, I believe every man is conscious of a train of thought being immediately awakened in his imagination, analogous to the character or expression of the original object. The simple perception of the object, we frequently find, is insufficient to excite these emotions, unless it is accompanied with this operation of mind. Thus, when we feel either the beauty or sublimity of natural scenery . . . we are conscious of a variety of images in our minds, very different from those which the objects themselves can present to the eye?[66]

As it did for Richard Temple at the site of Nicholson's death, for Mary Rowlandson in the wilderness surrounding the Connecticut River, and for Samuel Bourne contemplating the Himalayas, the scene before the naked eye stands for more than the sum of its parts. Pivoting around a set of interrelated paradoxes—curiosity and familiarity, interiority and exteriority, spontaneity and deliberation—the picturesque aesthetic unsettles the boundaries between the perceiving subject and the object perceived. What initially appears to be a distancing and aloof mode of seeing turns out to be an aesthetic that embeds the subject within the world and the object within the subject so deeply that both the subject and the object have to be seen as parts of a dynamic perceptual environment.[67]

Recall that for Bourdieu, the habitus is "a subjective but not individual system of internalized structures, schemes of perception, conception, and action," which is to say that it refers to a collective arrangement of perception, conception, and action.[68] Walter Benjamin, whose concern with "subjective but not individual" structures of consciousness was criticized by Theodor Adorno,[69] sought to understand how mass technological changes have corresponded to transforming perceptual arrangements in modernity. Relating the discrete individual subjective experience to collective transformations of perception was an aim of Benjamin's philosophy, and he found no better example to articulate this link than the logic of reproducibility in media. If, as Benjamin writes in *One-Way Street,* "the most real, mercantile gaze into the heart of things is the advertisement," it is in part because the advertisement occupies that dialectical space between the individual subject (its immediate addressee) and the collective body (its ultimate addressee). But if what "makes advertisements so superior to criticism [is] not what the moving red neon sign says—but the fiery pool reflecting it in the asphalt," then the significance of the advertisement lies not in its content but in its reproducible nature that trespasses the boundaries of the material sensorial world.[70] The space of the body—the physical environment of the individual—is interpenetrated with images that have saturated the collective image space. But this image space still remains at the same time a body space, since it is inhabited by the body politic. Moreover, the "interior furnishing" of this collective body, that is, the perceptual training that occurs through the apprehension of the world converted into reproducible images, can become increasingly consistent. In Benjamin's oeuvre, film represents the most intensified form of this interpenetration of body and image.[71] Constellating Benjamin's reflections on the interpenetration of body and image space with Bourdieu's formulation of the habitus allows us to think the subjective alongside the collective, as we consider the role of the individual subject in the formation of the picturesque aesthetic.

In considering this diminished role, one cannot presume ideological content of the picturesque forms only on the basis of the personal histories and allegiances of the photographers and travel writers. Such allegiances matter, of course, but my aim here is to locate how a certain individualizing aesthetic (the personal aspect of curiosity, the individually viewed "peep" along a path) comes to have a remarkably consistent form across individuals. (The products of the picturesque aesthetic seem formed by the pedagogical imperatives detailed above.) Ultimately what interests me in the picturesque is the mimetic disposition that comes to ratify certain arrangements as properly picturelike.

In regard to Knight's account of association in the picturesque image, his spectator is hardly a subject of self-mastery: the image leads to an involuntary and habitual chain of association. In the colonial form of the picturesque, such involuntary associations consistently take on the form of "home." If the reflection of the red neon in Benjamin's reading of the advertisement points not to the content of the advert but to its phenomenal and structural location in the world of material things, then in the colonial picturesque the superimposition of images of England, for example, is the superimposition not merely of a new content but also of an arrangement of perception, of what one can crudely call structuration but may also, more accurately, call form. The nostalgia for home is at the same time a longing for form, for a specific mode of perception, a longing at the heart of the picturesque that reveals itself most fully when the aesthetic travels to the colonies. For the colonial picturesque, the English countryside remains the ur-image, the invisible reference point for all aesthetic experience, and also the means by which curiosity can be engaged and simultaneously sated. This is the case for Bourne as well as for Deen Dayal, and it carries with it something more than its referent (the English countryside); it carries a whole way of seeing.

On Longing and Form

Bourne's representational challenges in the Himalayas, then, are not only technomaterial (the weight of the glass plates, the cumbersome nature of photographic apparatuses in the 1860s); they also concern the very form his vision takes, a form that must convert the foreign into digestible and familiar

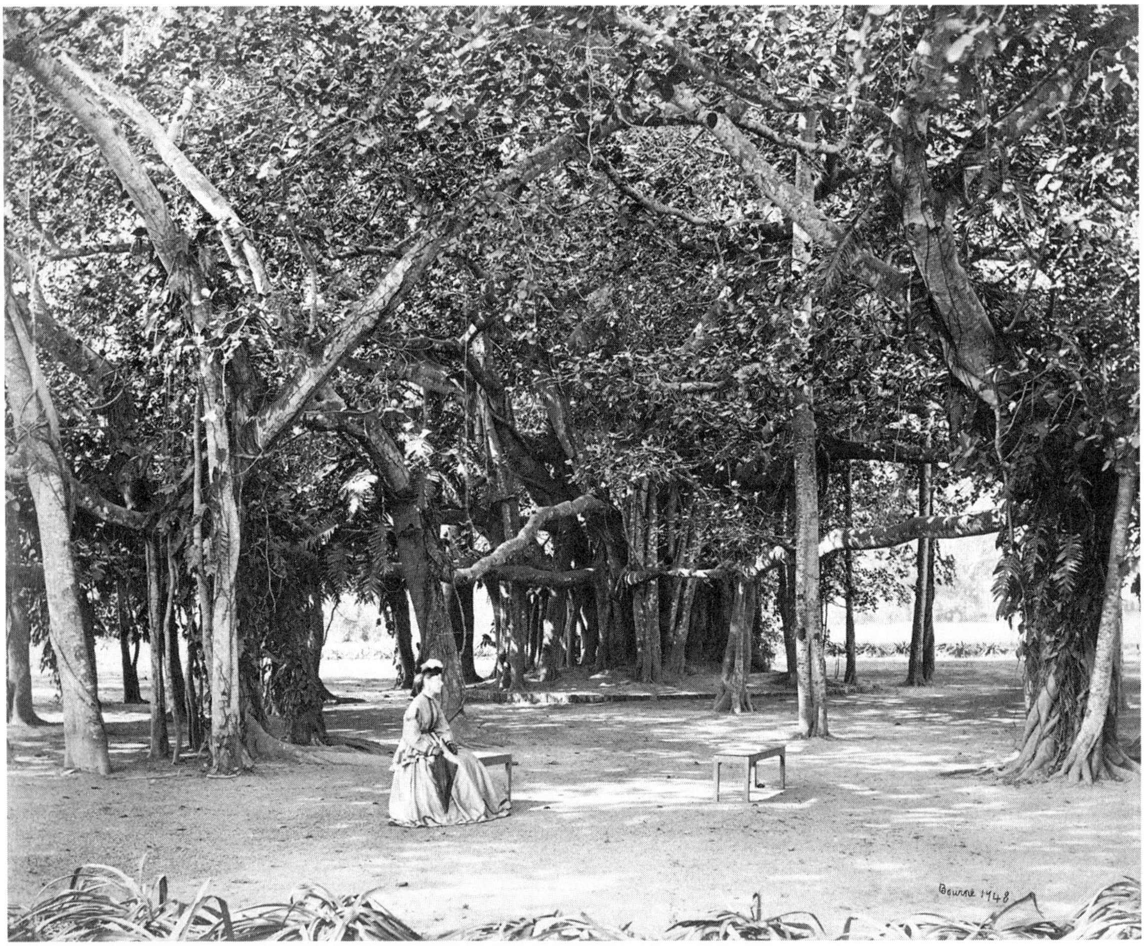

Figure 3.17. Samuel Bourne, *Mary Bourne under the Banyan Tree at Barrackpore Park,* 1866. Copyright British Library Board, Photo 29/(51).

molds. This larger aesthetic challenge repeatedly arises and must be repeatedly overcome, even when Bourne is not faced with the difficulties of photographing mountainous terrain. Take, for example, Bourne's 1866 photograph of his wife, Mary Bourne, seated beneath the banyan tree at Barrackpore Park (Figure 3.17).[72] Without the figure beneath the tree, the image would approach incoherence. In fact, the colonial image of the banyan tree has an extensive forehistory; in the early days of British adventurism in India, the tree was associated with a certain paradisiacal mythos, since it provided shelter for complexly interdependent animals and plants. This was the attitude of Thomas Daniell, who composed the image in Plate 10 at the high point of orientalist scholarship and collaboration in the early days of East India Company's consolidation in India. By the late nineteenth century, however, the unruly canopy of roots, branches, leaves, and trunks, in whose darkness all manner of unpredictable beasts resided, came to serve as a metaphor for racial degeneracy.[73] Bourne took a whole series of photographs at Barrackpore Park, including one from the exterior of the tree (Figure 3.18). This exterior shot, as well as another shot by Bourne (Figure 3.19), allegorizes what India had come to mean after the Sepoy Revolt: a dark void into which one treads at one's own risk. As Gary Sampson notes, placing an Englishwoman—the quintessential nineteenth-century figure of home—in the midst of the banyan tree serves to emphasize civility and virtue in the midst of the wilderness.[74] This motif is repeated in Figure 3.20, also taken in Barrackpore Park, where the seated figure of Mary Bourne mediates between the wild palms on the left and the gothic ruin on the right. The picturesque aesthetic seems particularly suited to the domestication of the unfamiliar and the foreign. Yet at the same time, such aesthetic strategies and longings for form index the actual uncertainty of seemingly stable colonial categories.

To consider Barrackpore Park alone, listen to Lord Dalhousie's impressions of this area about eighteen years prior to Bourne's photograph:

> It is charming, and reconciles me to a residence in Bengal more than anything else has yet done . . . a pretty pleasure ground, beautiful garden, an aviary, a menagerie, and all situated on the bank of the river, and surrounded by a park quite home-like in its character, and *as English as anything can be,* where you have banians and cocoanuts, and palms and mangoes, for oaks and helms, larch and beech.[75]

As long as the landscaping obeyed the imperatives of English gardening—which was among the most literal influences on the early discourse on the picturesque—banyans could take the place of oaks, and palms the place of larches. The form, however, had to be recognizably "English." But Dalhousie's homelike vision of England is already a retrospective fantasy, in which the referent *England* has become mythos. It can only have the fantastically sutured form of nostalgic visions.

In an earlier narrative, Fanny Parks's aptly titled *Wanderings of a Pilgrim in Search of the Picturesque,* the imaginary nature of the image of Britain is even clearer. When discussing a journey toward Darjeeling, Parks writes, "We have still some four hundred miles to march; but the country is to improve daily, and when we arrive at the hills, I hear we are to be carried back, in imagination, to the highlands of Scotland. I have never been there; *n'importe,* I can fancy as well as others."[76] Parks, in an ironic and self-mocking tone, grasps the nature of such longing and the flights of imagination to which it gives rise. Scotland, of course, had already become picturesque, even as its countryside was being subjected to clearance and its people forcibly displaced. Moreover, it need not matter that one has never been to the highlands, since images of

Britain are, as Parks astutely notes, the production of "fancy" in any case. The picturesque aesthetic, by invoking the familiar image of the past, produces that image in the same instance. The colonial picturesque, then, is constantly longing for a form that is itself impossible without the (colonial) opportunity for retrospection and the colonial trigger of association.

Returning to Barrackpore Park, we see it here described by Charlotte Canning, who lovingly tended parts of the park herself while avoiding the dull business of being the wife of Governer-General Charles Canning (Dalhousie's successor). She writes to Queen Victoria:

> The Park is carefully planted with round headed trees to look as English as possible—more so than I approve, and I am glad when Bamboos and Cocoanuts have crept in. All the apparent chestnut, elms, and ash prove

Figure 3.18. Samuel Bourne, *Banyan Tree in Barrackpore Park, General View,* 1860s. Copyright British Library Board, Photo 29/(52).

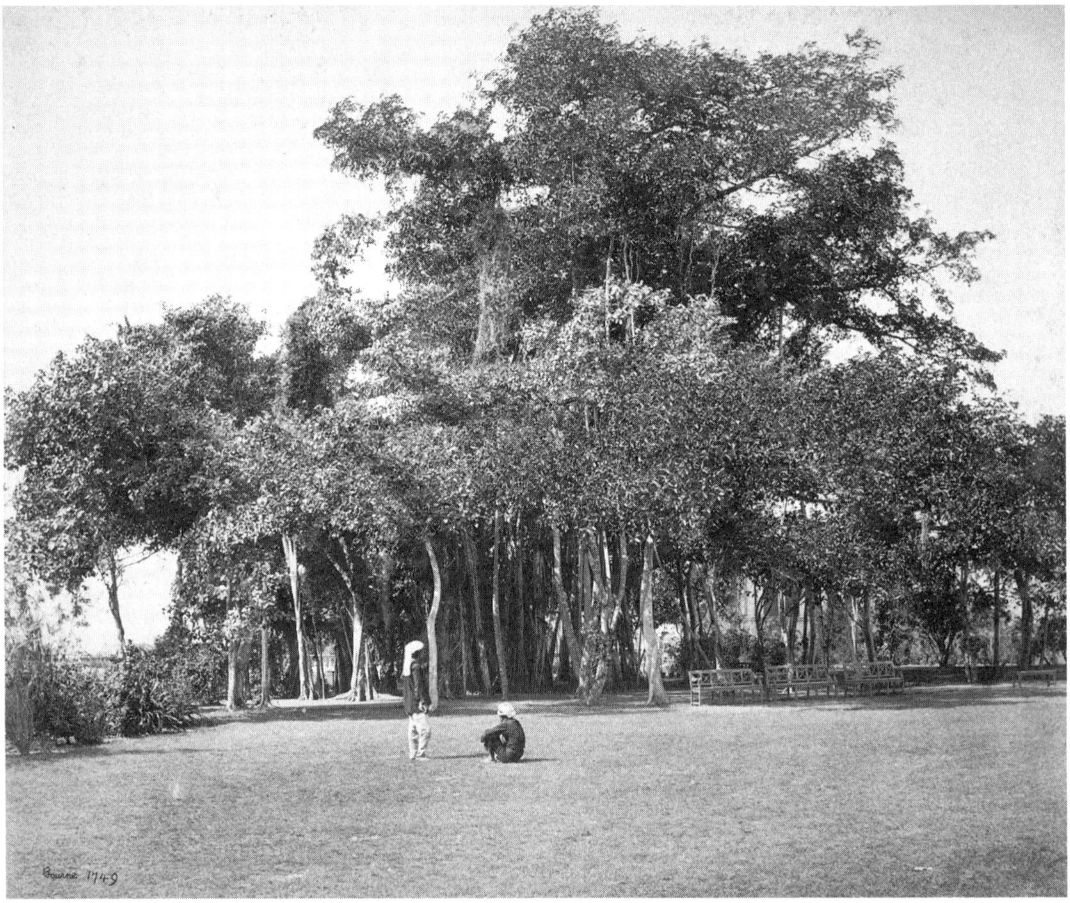

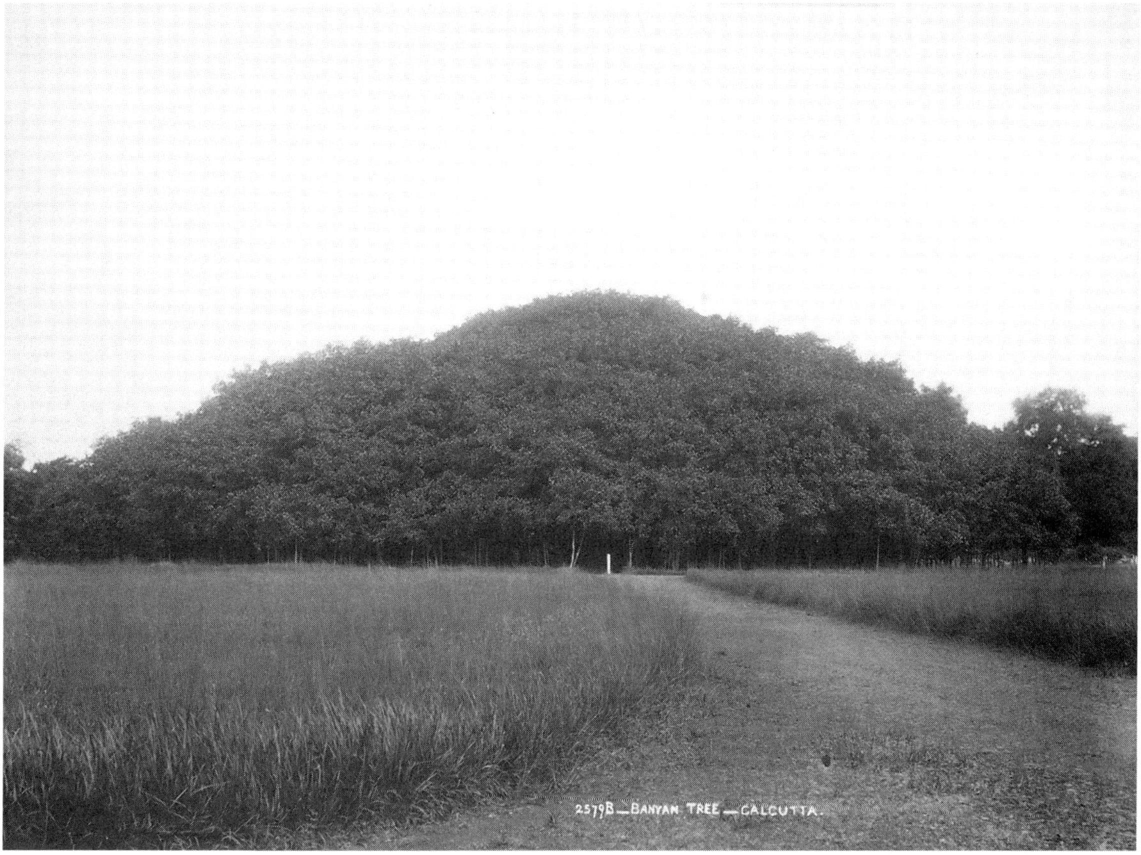

Figure 3.19. Bourne and Shepherd Studio, *Great Banyan Tree in the Botanical Gardens*, Calcutta, 1890. Princeton University Art Museum. Gift of Mrs. George Packer Berry in honor of her husband, Class of 1921, and Charter Trustee of Princeton University, 1956–69 (ui.2011.198).

> quite unknown on nearer view. The luxuriant growth in the jungly ground outside, of dazzling green during the Rains, is more beautiful than I can describe and I always think of the Palm House at Kew which gives a faint idea of it.[77]

Phrases such as "quite unknown," "on nearer view," "more beautiful than I can describe," and "faint idea" signal that Lady Canning is grasping for a description of a scene that is in fact on the far horizon of the aesthetic language and terms of English landscaping that are available to her. Initially Canning appears to object to the picturesque landscaping of the park, but the interlopers upon the scene of the English picturesque—"Bamboos and Cocoanuts"—only remind her of Kew Gardens and its Palm House, a synecdoche of colonial ownership and knowledge.[78] In reaching for a new aesthetic language, she

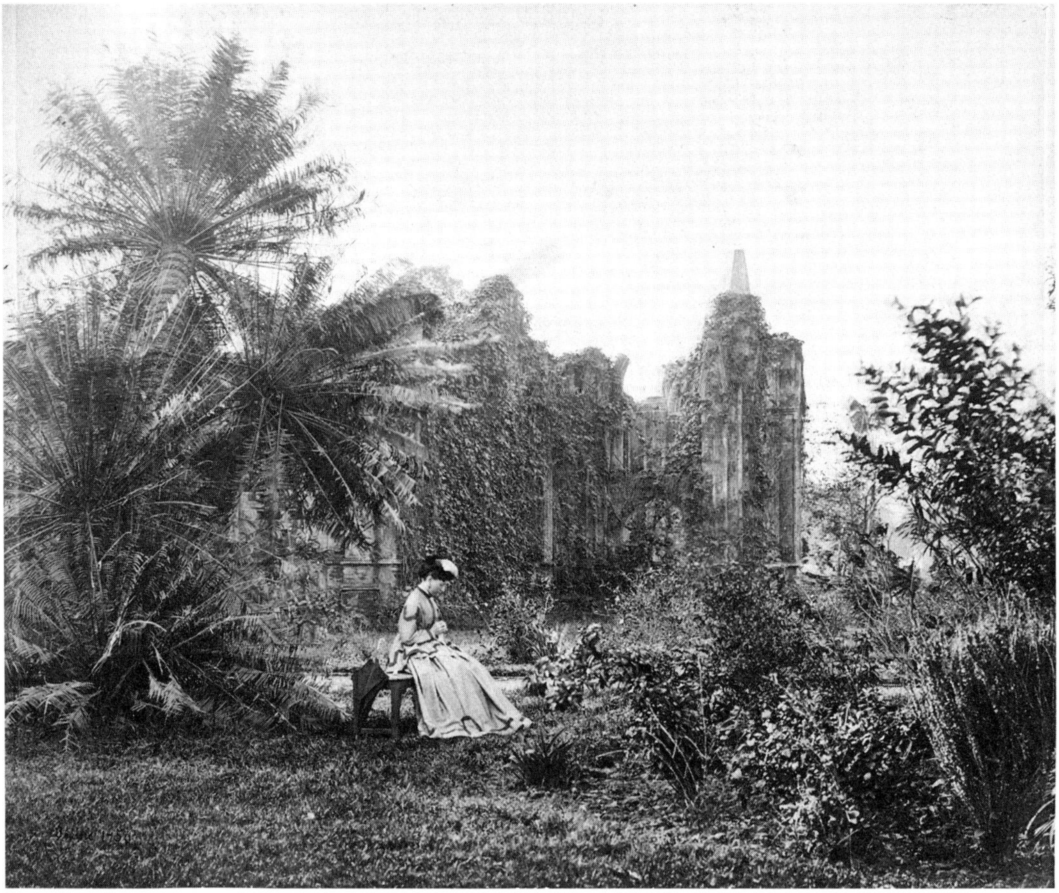

Figure 3.20. Samuel Bourne, *Gothic Ruin with Creepers in Barrackpore Park,* 1860s. Copyright British Library Board, Photo 29/(53).

must necessarily refer to a space other than the landscape before her very eyes; this landscape can, in turn, only refer to an England that has already contained, and yet remains contaminated by, the signs of colonial difference. In this mimetic shuttling back and forth between India and England, an imagined England-in-India (Barrackpore Park landscaped to English protocols) and an imagined India-in-England (Kew Gardens), the referent turns out to have been a reproducible image all along, an image through which one practices the "creative repetition" of oneself.

We can see a similar dynamic at work within the very frame of Bourne's photograph *Mary Bourne under the Banyan Tree at Barrackpore Park* (Figure 3.17). If, as Gary Sampson astutely notes, the female figure signals the entrance of English domesticity and English hearth in the midst of the threatening wilderness,[79] she also at the same time marks the fragility of the colonial order. The solitariness of this figure seems particularly acute, given that the photograph was taken after the Sepoy Revolt. After all, the rallying cry for British troops and the mass hysteria of the English back home were both based on rumors of the rape of British women.[80] If the picturesque aesthetic employs Mary Bourne as an artful counterpoint in the photographic composition and serves to reassure an English spectator, it equally invokes a threat in the form of the banyan tree, which seems to extend infinitely beyond both sides of the frame. Moreover, the camera is positioned on this side of a line of tropical shrubs, from which it peeks over at the solitary woman sitting under the tree. This accentuates the signal claim of the picturesque aesthetic, to bring into view an incidental scene, as if we had just glanced over the shrubs and noticed the woman on our way. The sense of direction and mapping are provided by the stock components of the picturesque: shrubs, the figure of scale, a play of light and shade in the background, an overhanging branch. This highly orchestrated aesthetic claim for an incidental, even anecdotal, significance makes the mapping provided by these stock components feel just as provisional and incidental. As spectators we may pass this scene and then be lost, and should this figure of scale walk out of the frame or we turn in any direction, we may no longer know what we are looking at. The success of the picturesque's claims, in other words, also points to the repeated failure of those claims. Bourne knew this well as he lamented the shortcomings of his pictures and repeatedly took new ones.

But the picturesque shares such successes and failures with nineteenth-century realism, since it lends itself, like realism, to anecdotal claims. No matter how "historical" such anecdotal scenes may be or how cumbersome the nineteenth-century photographic apparatus, the picturesque aesthetic claims to present the unvarnished truth, everyday scenes of ordinary people, a spontaneous look at ordinary reality. This goes hand in hand, of course, with the seemingly contradictory picturesque impulse to dress reality up to its best advantage. In his reading of realism, George Levine notes the preponderance of passages in realist fiction that self-consciously explain, at the start of the narrative, that what the reader is about to experience in the novel is a plain tale told about ordinary people. According to Levine, realist writers of the nineteenth century, wrote "as though the enterprise of the ordinary in fiction were new and difficult, and that in 1860 as well as 1804, the audience had to be warned and cajoled about it."[81] Moreover, the aim of representing the ordinary and the incidental was to "reveal a comprehensible world" at a time when, within a generation, technological and social change had rendered the world unrecognizable:

> We need to shift the balance in our appraisal of realism. It was not a solidly self-satisfied vision based in a misguided objectivity and faith in representation, but a highly self-conscious attempt to explore or create a new reality. Its massive self-confidence implied a radical doubt, its strate-

> gies of truth telling, a profound self-consciousness. . . . As we explore the most conservative of the classic novels of the nineteenth century, we find continuing experiments with forms, styles, modes of valuing. Those experiments are not aberrations from some realistic norm, but intrinsic to its [realism's] nature. Resisting forms, it explores reality to find them; denying excess, it deserts the commonplace self-consciously asserted as its subjects. Positing the reality of an external world, it self-consciously examines its own fictionality.[82]

The claim to represent reality conceals an anxiety that reality may forever be slipping out of reach in an increasingly disorienting world. In the colonial context such realism is also a bulwark against the impoverishment of colonial claims to foreign lands—a claim that in India was challenged around the same time as the rise of the picturesque aesthetic.

In the nineteenth century, photography held out the mimetic promises of realism. For one, the rhetoric of photography then claimed to deliver the real thing itself in the form of the object's photographic index—its "having been there and then." For another, the "spark of contingency" that has long been noted in photography often disrupts the flow of singular meaning in any given photograph.[83] The incidental scenes of the picturesque serve up history in the form of the anecdote and the index. To take the example of Bourne's photograph *Mary Bourne under the Banyan Tree at Barrackpore Park,* the actually existing tree under which Mary Bourne sits (its indexical trace) marks a spot close to the tree in the cantonment area of Barrackpore, where the famous rebel Mangal Pandey was hanged.[84] The image of hanged rebels (Figure 2.14) is the inverse of the image of Mary Bourne under the banyan tree, and the conditions that led to the image of Mary Bourne under the banyan tree made the hangings necessary in the first place. Such a spark and such an indexical trace turn out, after all, to have multivalent and polysemic significances; they approach, in fact, the interpretive excess of allegory rather than the settled claims of realism. So while photography appears to bolster the picturesque aesthetic, its indexical nature calls out to the endlessly experimenting and self-defeating play with form that is the hallmark of nineteenth-century realism. While the picturesque aesthetic predates realism, being associated with the late eighteenth century and early nineteenth century, the colonial photographic picturesque stands at an aesthetic crossroads: it claims to represent indexical truth (Bourne notes the pleasures of photographing the highest peaks in India) and yet signals the forms of "home." It represents the stress and pressure that signifying systems undergo at times of historical change and is of a piece with the shifts in the modern habitus.

A habitus accustomed to converting the world into image—given all of the bodily, psychological, and phenomenological operations implied by

Bourdieu's term—is of a piece, then, with a realism that relates history through images, whether literary, photographic, or painterly. Referentiality, under such conditions, is located in the interplay between aesthetic form and material and historical conditions. The picturesque aesthetic is one experiment with form, among others, in the history of realism. The colonial picturesque is the mark of an aesthetic armor that regulates, however unsuccessfully, the boundaries between subject and object, self and other, and "civilization" and "barbarism." If such aesthetic experimentation is a mark of changing historical, political, and economic conditions and, as a result, a transformation in aesthetic idioms, then it is also an attempt to engage the paradox of aesthetic forms themselves, in that these forms serve as armor and aesthesis, blocking out stimuli as much as they make the world accessible.

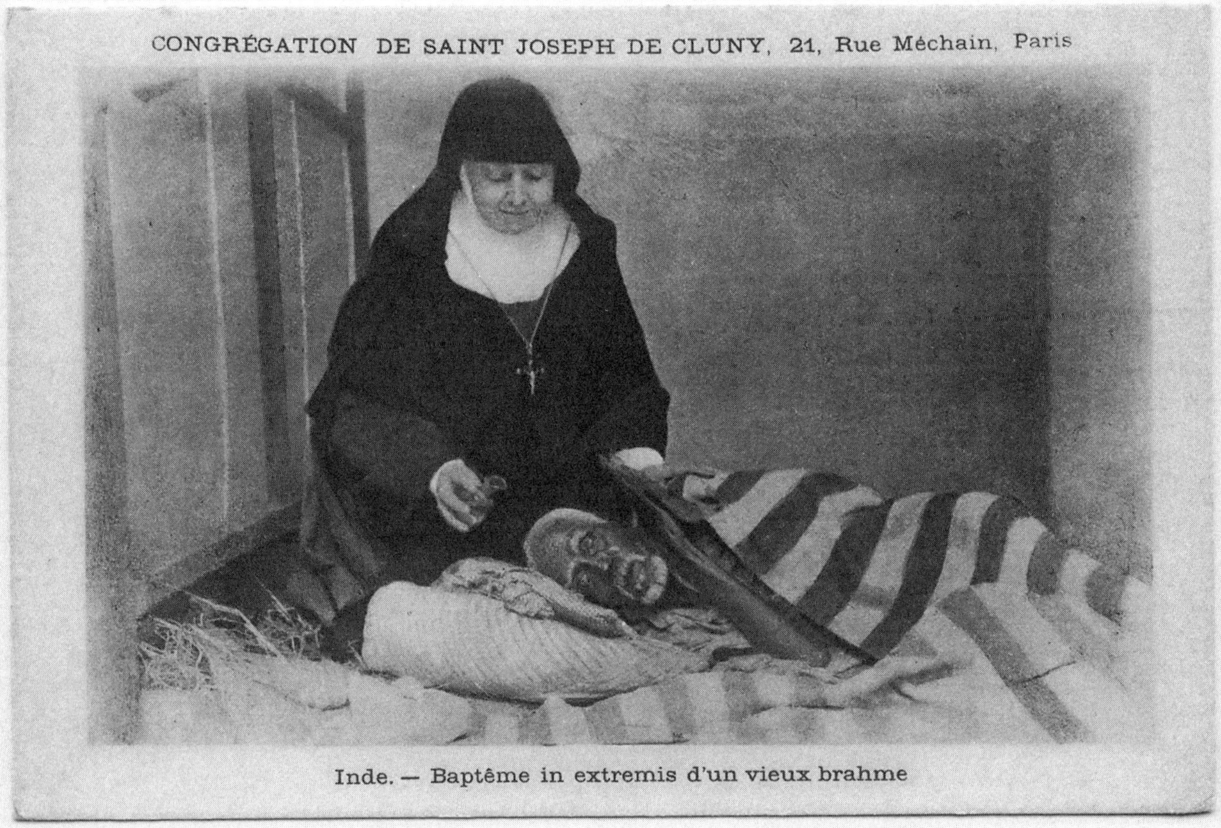

Figure 4.1. Postcard, late nineteenth or early twentieth century. Private collection.

FOUR

Famine and the Reproduction of Affect

Pleas for Sympathy

> The pain we feel, prompts us to relieve ourselves in relieving those who suffer; and all this antecedent to any reasoning, by an instinct that works us to its own purposes, without our concurrence.
>
> —Edmund Burke, *A Philosophical Enquiry into the Origin of Our Ideas of the Sublime and Beautiful*

> The images of things are the very affections of the human body.
>
> —Baruch Spinoza, *The Ethics*

Scenes of Sympathy

In my account thus far, the question of faith keeps returning in various forms: our faith in the indexical truth of the photograph, in rumor, in aesthetic form, and in Felice Beato's case, in the veracity of historical violence. Of course, the punishment that General Neill meted out to Brahmins, by making them clean up the blood of their co-conspirators before executing them, must violate faith in order to condemn people to a fate worse than death. Yet this violation, relying as it does on a finely grained understanding of the other's faith, also marks a certain intimacy shared by all victims and perpetrators.[1] *Intimacy* is a neutral term, even if, in our times, the "substance" of our ethics, the part of us that we subject to constant analysis, according to Michel Foucault, is "feelings."[2] That is to say, intimacy, if understood as the free exchange of feelings, has shifted from a neutral term to a one that has the aura of a positive experience (all of us striving toward intimacy, etc.).[3] When I refer to the intimacy between victim and perpetrator, I am referring to the root meaning of *intimus:* that which is the innermost, the most secret, most profound. Faith, understood not simply as a set of precepts but as an arrangement of phenomenological and affective comportments toward the world, is among the most intimate, but not necessarily "private," forms of subjective experience. The faith that photography solicits and religious faith intersect at this phenomenological level: both presume, on the one hand, that the perceptible is overdetermined by causes beyond immediate perception, and yet, on the other hand, such overdetermination invests the realm of the perceptible with unique significance.

To understand the terms of another person's attachment to his or her faith requires extending oneself imaginatively to the other's position. All intimacy between people presumes this self-extension, but in this chapter I am concerned with a particular form of intimacy, not a form in which one simply extends oneself to another, but a form in which this extension causes one to feel as the other feels, or at least to feel what one *imagines* the other feels. This is the sentiment of sympathy, or "fellow feeling," which receives its most extensive philosophical treatment in the eighteenth century in the works of David Hume and Adam Smith and has clear affinities with Sigmund Freud's nineteenth-century conception of identification. Like identification, sympathy names a process or a technology of relation and is not entirely under the control of subjective agency. In this chapter, in which I analyze photographic and eyewitness accounts of famines in India, sympathy annexes faith as the ground for its own functioning. Even General Neill's punishment of the Brahmins appears in a new light when one considers how sympathy regulates the division of the world into friends and enemies, a point initially noted by Baruch Spinoza in *The Ethics* but then deduced by the French physician Guillaume-Benjamin-Amand Duchenne de Boulogne during the nineteenth century in his experiments on human emotions.

We begin with four scenes of sympathy: The first is an account from Harriet Tytler's memoirs. She recounts the following famine episode from her childhood in India:

> This time on our way to Calcutta we came across a terribly sad sight. We saw numbers of famine-stricken people, never to be forgotten. When my father saw them, he gave orders to the boatmen to draw near to the shore to enable him to speak to these poor people. It appears these unhappy Hindu peasants had left their village to die on the banks of the Ganges, so that when the holy river rose, as it was sure to do, either through the melting of the snow in the Himalayas or the deluges of rain caused by the monsoon, their bones might be carried away into the stream and so ensure for their souls the blessing of reincarnation. My father offered the living food, but one and all made the same reply, "Sir if you will give me food cooked by a Brahmin I will eat, if not I must die!" My dear father was grieved beyond measure for he had no Brahmins on board. He told them so, but they only replied, "Well sir, then we must die."[4]

Though Tytler was about six years old at this time, she recalls saying to herself, "When I grow up to be a woman I will save all the little starving children and bring them up as Christians." And she claims, "[This aspiration] never left me until thirty-three years later, when God permitted me in his goodness to carry out my heart's desire." Tytler refers here to the founding of her Himalayal Christian Orphanage in Simla. The story continues: When her father returned to the boat after having failed to persuade "the poor dying creatures" to eat (they were too weak to cook for themselves), a young Brahmin man came to the boat and said, "Sir I will eat, give me to eat." As the food was ordered for him, "the poor boy went close to the water's edge and, putting up his hands in prayer, took off the Brahminical cord from his neck, muttering something, and threw it into the holy Ganges, which meant renouncing his faith." He ate "voraciously" and died a half hour later: "My dear father, in his desire to help the helpless, never thought of the serious consequences of giving the lad food, which in his weak state he could not digest."[5]

Scene two: Figure 4.1 shows a postcard, undated but most likely from the late nineteenth or early twentieth century, of a baptism conducted by Les Soeurs de Saint Joseph de Cluny, a Paris-based congregation that still runs a Christian high school (Cluny Convent High School) in Mallaswaram, Karnataka, to the present day. This postcard, one of a series showing scenes from the organization's overseas missions, depicts a dying Brahmin who is baptized by a sympathetic nun just before he enters the afterlife. It is Tytler's conversion fantasy made manifest. If for Tytler conversion would secure an end to self-denying folly in this life, for Les Soeurs de Saint Joseph de Cluny, conversion in extremis secures the good afterlife.

Scene three: Figure 4.2 shows a photograph, taken by Willoughby Wallace Hooper, of a group of famine victims from the Madras famine of 1876–79. Such photographs (Figures 4.2, 4.4, 4.6–4.9, and Plate 13), sold commercially by Hooper and others, circulated in private photograph collections, commercially produced albums, and as postcards into the early twentieth century. (Plate 13 shows an early twentieth-century postcard of famine victims from Allahabad.) Showing skeletal groups of people in various arrangements, these photographs are enmeshed in a representational paradox: on the one hand, a series of photographs of famine victims, whether in groups or shown singly, have a remarkable consistency and return to the self-same subject. On the other hand, if we allow ourselves to enter the indexical truth of these photographs, then each person depicted represents a distinctive life history and a tale of suffering that do not become interchangeable with the histories and tales of others' simply because photography is reproducible or because the theme of suffering in famines is explored by the same stock motifs. These photographs, too, have their part to play in a narrative about faith, albeit a kind of faith different from religion but one that also winds magically through sympathy.

Scene four: A cartoon printed in London in 1810, that is, from the days

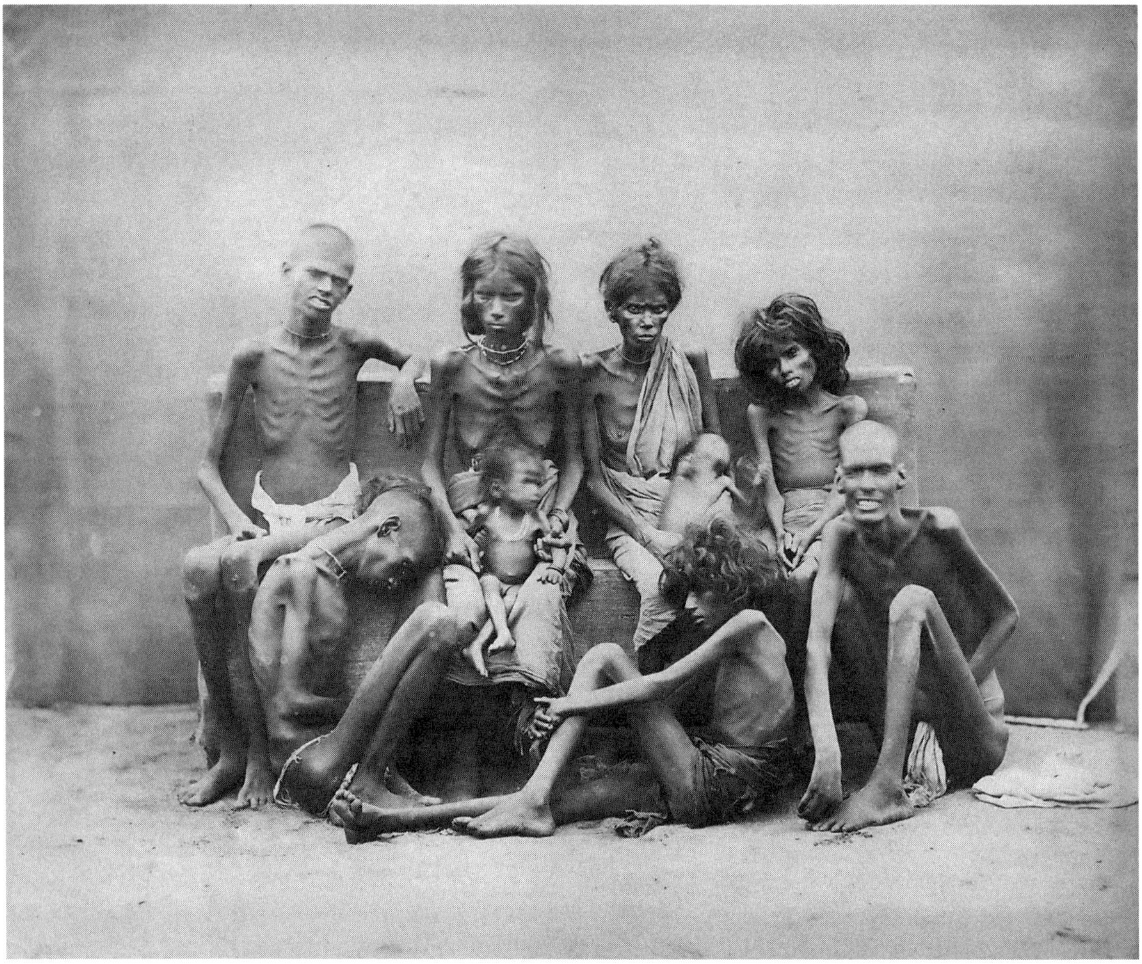

Figure 4.2. Willoughby Wallace Hooper, Madras famine of 1876–79. Royal Geographic Society (with the Institute of British Geographers).

before the pleasures and numbing gifts of effective anesthesia, shows the curious nature of "fellow feeling" as it meets bracing self-mastery (Figure 4.3). The spectator on the far right, himself missing a tooth, replicates the expression of the woman having her tooth pulled, and his expression is the precise inverse of the dentist's sadistic smile. Though suffering along with her, he holds himself back, knowing that the pain inflicted on the other is necessary and for an "ultimate good." The cartoon is pedagogical in several respects: it evokes fellow feeling in us for the woman whose tooth is being pulled, and implicitly it demonstrates that our sympathy can arise only because the woman in the picture suffers. Sympathetic suffering that leads to inaction, too, has its "virtues," as we will see.

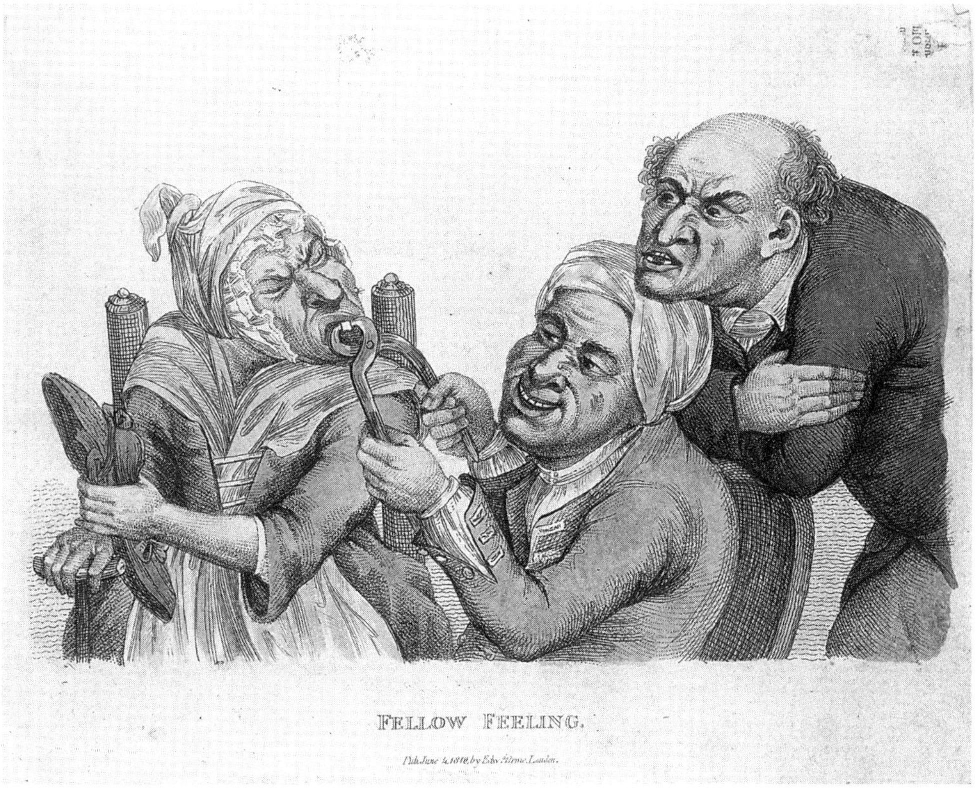

Figure 4.3. E. Orme, *Fellow Feeling*, London. 1810. Wellcome Library, London.

Memory's Page

This story begins at the end of the eighteenth century, with the Bengal famine of the 1770s, which killed about ten million people, one-third of the population of Bengal Province.[6] This catastrophe was witnessed by John Shore, who was serving as a colonial administrator, and was related by him in the following poem:

> Still fresh in Memory's eye, the scene I view,
> The shrivell'd limbs, sunk eyes, and lifeless hue;
> Still hear the mother's shrieks and infant's moans,
> Cries of despair, and agonizing groans.
> In wild confusion, dead and dying lie;—
> Hark to the jackall's yell, and vulture's cry,
> The dog's fell howl, as, midst the glare of day,
> They riot, unmolested, on their prey!
> Dire scenes of horror! Which no pen can trace,
> Nor rolling years from Memory's page efface.[7]

This poem, recording one of the most devastating famines that took place under the British administration, was written about forty years after the event. While the famine is still fresh in memory's eye, the scene that the poem describes is not primarily visual. After the second line ("The shrivell'd limbs, sunk eyes, and lifeless hue") the poem describes sounds rather than sights: mother's shrieks, infant's moans, cries of despair, groans, jackall's yell, vulture's cry, dog's howl. In a demonstration of synesthesia that memory perhaps accentuates, what the eye sees (sunken eyes, pale hue, glare of sunlight, dogs attacking human bodies) is interwoven with what the ear hears. And yet, throughout the poem, the flow of iambic pentameter breaks repeatedly with the profusion of commas, as if the constant shifting between sight and hearing results from a labored effort to describe the scene, compounded with hesitations about describing such violent moments.[8] Neither hearing nor sight can do the scene justice. The poem's form and content merge in the penultimate line, which abandons this tussle between the eye and the ear; both are inadequate because both must be rendered through language. Although the experience that memory evokes is one that no pen can trace, no number of years can efface these experiences from memory's page. Two decades after this poem was written, the book of memory would no longer be composed of figurative pages in the mind but would take the form of the private photographic album. The poem calls out for a medium of representation that would be adequate to the scenes of devastation; it places its faith in technologies other than language that may be adequate to the task. In its constant stops and fitful starts, its exclamations and breaks, it calls out to a form of representation beyond itself. Photography attempts to answer such a call.

Yet, about one hundred years and ten more Indian famines after the famine that John Shore witnessed, one colonial famine worker, Dr. Cornish, who worked as Madras's sanitary commissioner, bemoaned in the midst of the Madras famine of 1876–79:

> I often regret that I have not a photographer temporarily attached to my office while moving about amongst the famine-stricken people of this Presidency. Words, at best, can but feebly represent the actual facts, but if the members of Government could see the living skeletons assembled at feeding-houses as I see them, I do not think there would be much hesitation in arriving at a conclusion that the condition of the lower classes of the labouring poor of this district is most critical. . . . We saw children of all ages in such a condition of emaciation that nothing but a photographic picture could convey an adequate representation of their state.[9]

This frustration at the blindness of the official record also permeates the historiographies of nineteenth-century Indian famines, which seemed to happen like clockwork throughout the Indian subcontinent.[10] These historiographies

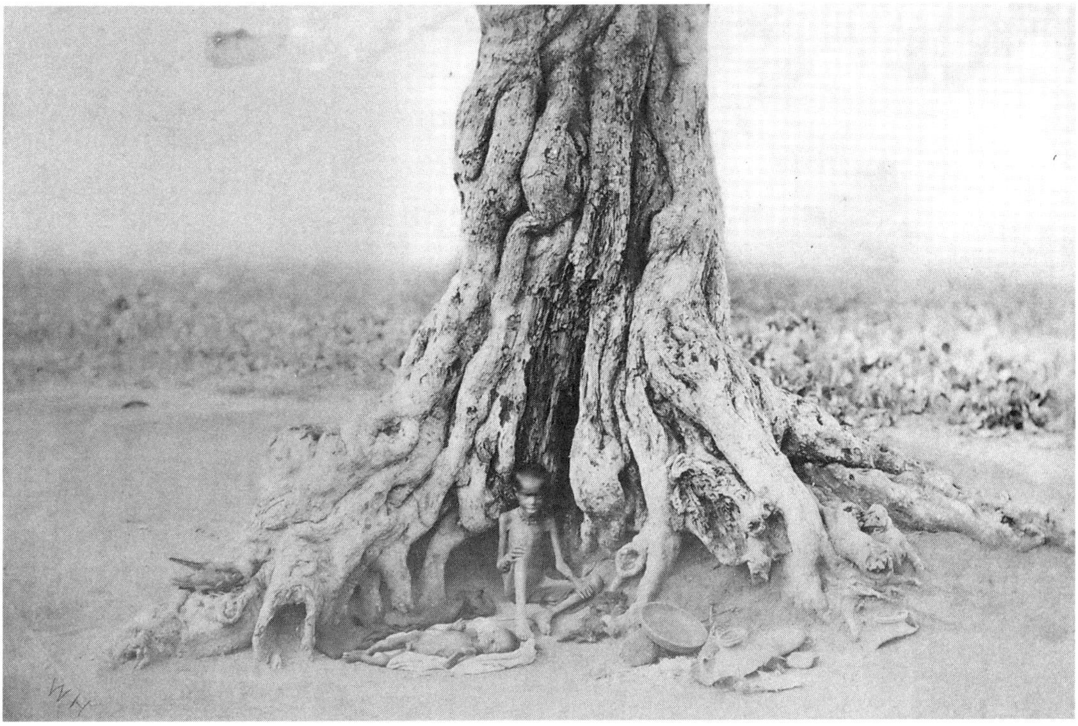

Figure 4.4. Willoughby Wallace Hooper, *Forsaken,* Madras, 1876–78. Royal Geographic Society (with the Institute of British Geographers).

Figure 4.5. Lithograph based on W. W. Hooper's photograph, from William Digby, *The Famine Campaign in Southern India,* 1878.

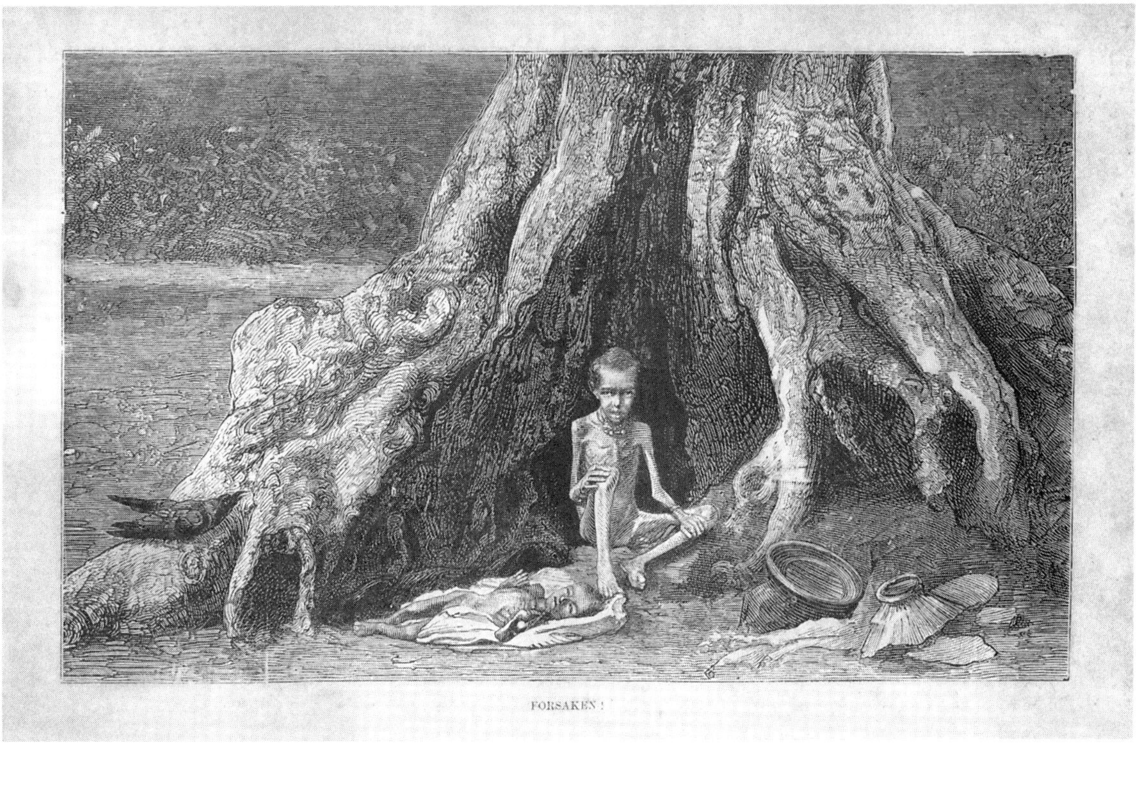

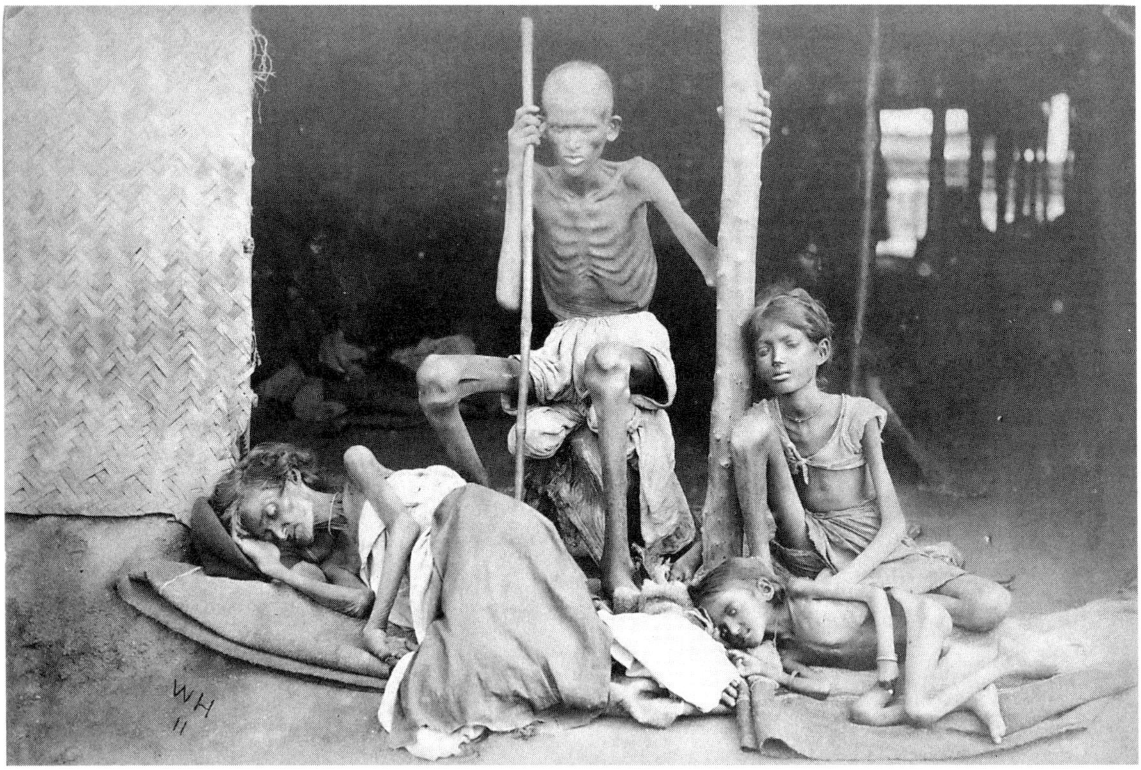

Figure 4.6. Willoughby Wallace Hooper, Madras famine of 1876–79. Royal Geographic Society (with the Institute of British Geographers).

are forced to parse words in the same vein as the imperial archive: famines pass under many names: drought, starvation, want, food shortage, scarcity. Often these various terms seek to render socially produced crises into the language of the natural, displacing the violence done by people onto the violence done by nature and effectively obfuscating the subtle processes of interdependence between natural and human-made crises.[11] With the rise of photographic technology, a whole new form of statements about famines became possible, though what these statements might say is less clear than would seem at the outset. The photograph seems to short-circuit the prolix discourse of officialdom, its wordplay, and speaks above and beyond the liberal pleas for identification with the victims. This happened, it says simply. Look what is happening.

While Dr. Cornish lamented the lack of a photographer at the height of the Madras famine, his contemporary, Captain Willoughby Wallace Hooper, a member of the colonial army, photographed that same famine while he traveled through the region. He had already contributed several photographs toward the collection *The People of India,* and his photographic oeuvre is among the most curious of all British photographers in India: in addition to ethnographic photographs (Figure 4.10), he took several photographs of tiger "hunts" in which the tiger, already dead or stuffed, is propped up for a dramatic scene (see Figure 4.11); staged domestic colonial scenes (Figure 4.12); and used taxidermy to orchestrate "natural" tableaux (Figure 4.13). Most controversially, in the Third Burmese War, Hooper took a series of photographs of prisoners as they were being executed (Figure 4.14). All of his photographs were taken for commercial ends and sold by various photographic studios in India as well as in England, with the London Stereoscopic Company as one of his most reliable clients. His photographs recording executions in Burma landed him in trouble, and the controversy, which began with newspaper articles discussing the cruelty of Hooper's photographic project, ended in Parliament.[12] In Burma, Captain Hooper summarily ordered executions and would set up his camera in order to record them. As journalist Edward Kyran Moylan recounts in his rather sensationalized coverage of Hooper's activities:

Figure 4.7. Willoughby Wallace Hooper, Madras famine of 1876–79. Digital image courtesy of the Digital Content Library, University of Minnesota.

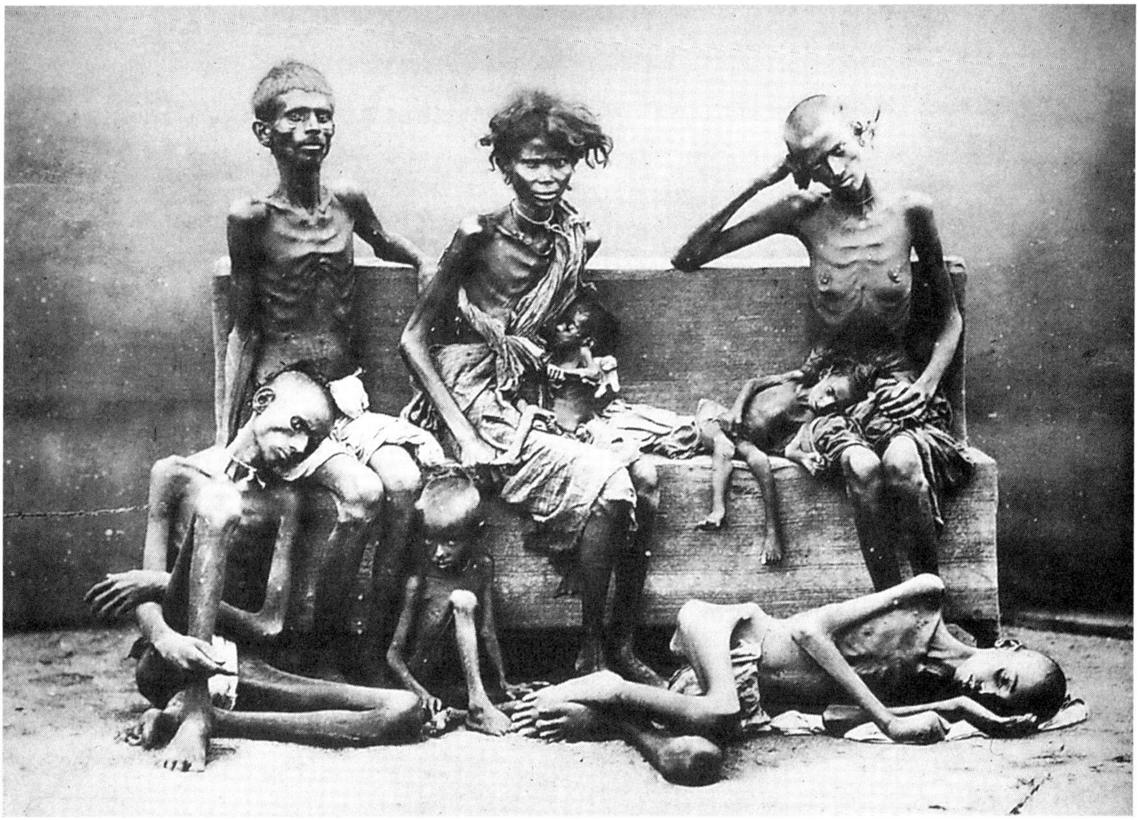

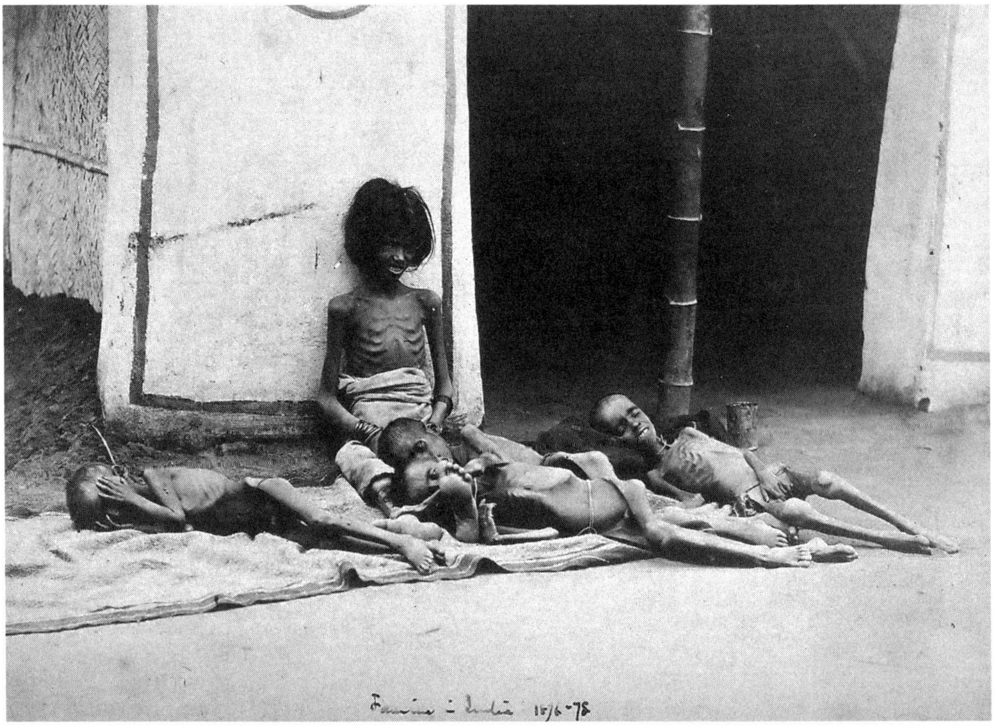

Figure 4.8. Willoughby Wallace Hooper, Madras famine of 1876–79. Wellcome Library, London.

Figure 4.9. Willoughby Wallace Hooper, Madras famine of 1876–79. Royal Geographic Society (with the Institute of British Geographers).

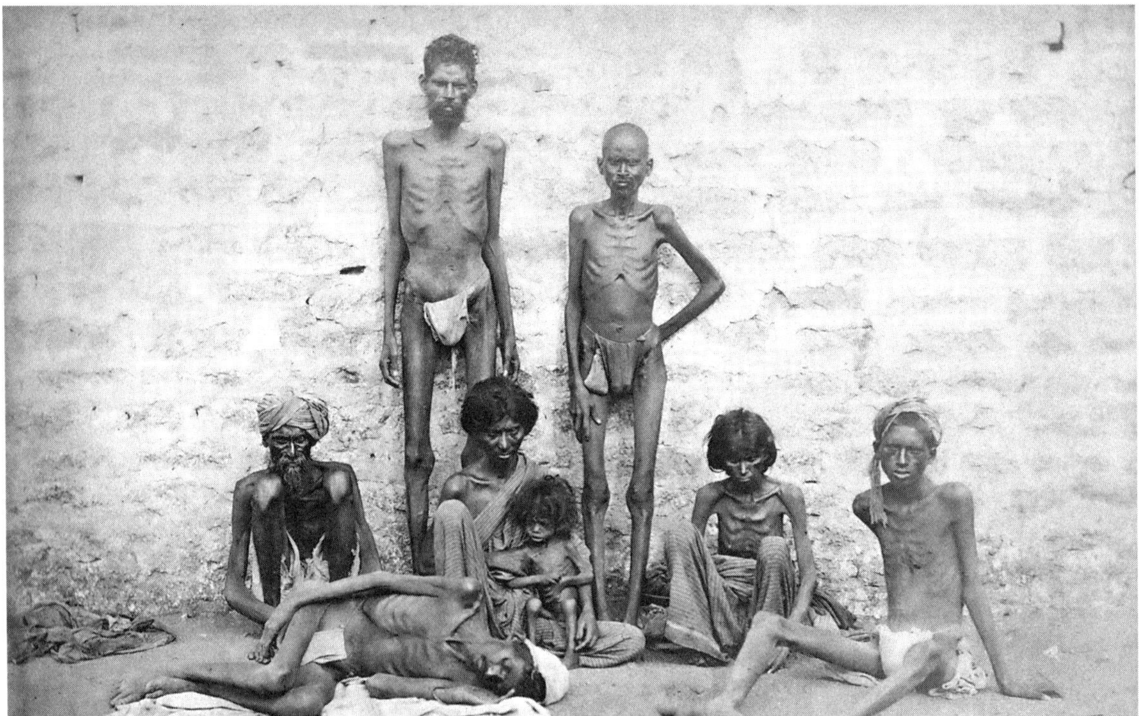

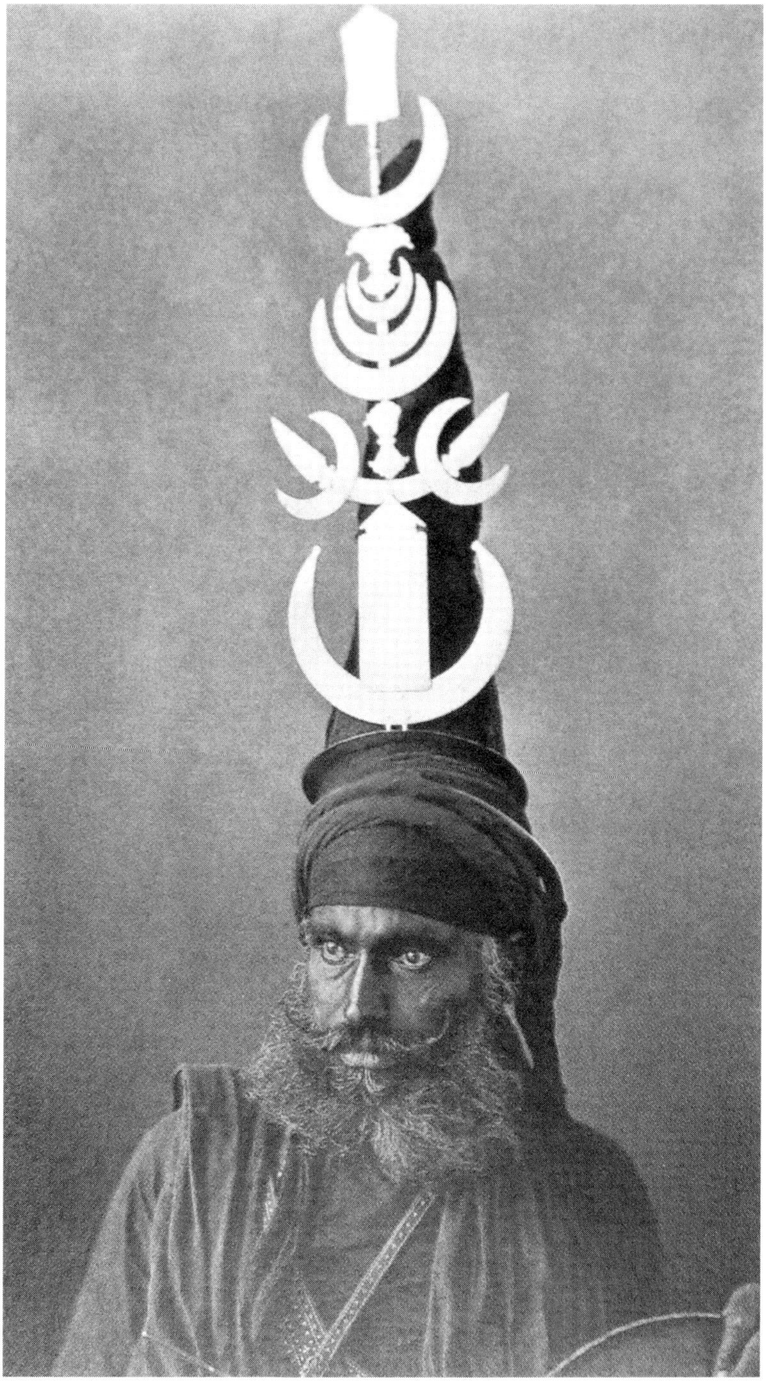

Figure 4.10. Willoughby Wallace Hooper, *A Sikh,* 1860s or 1870s. Digital image courtesy of the Digital Content Library, University of Minnesota.

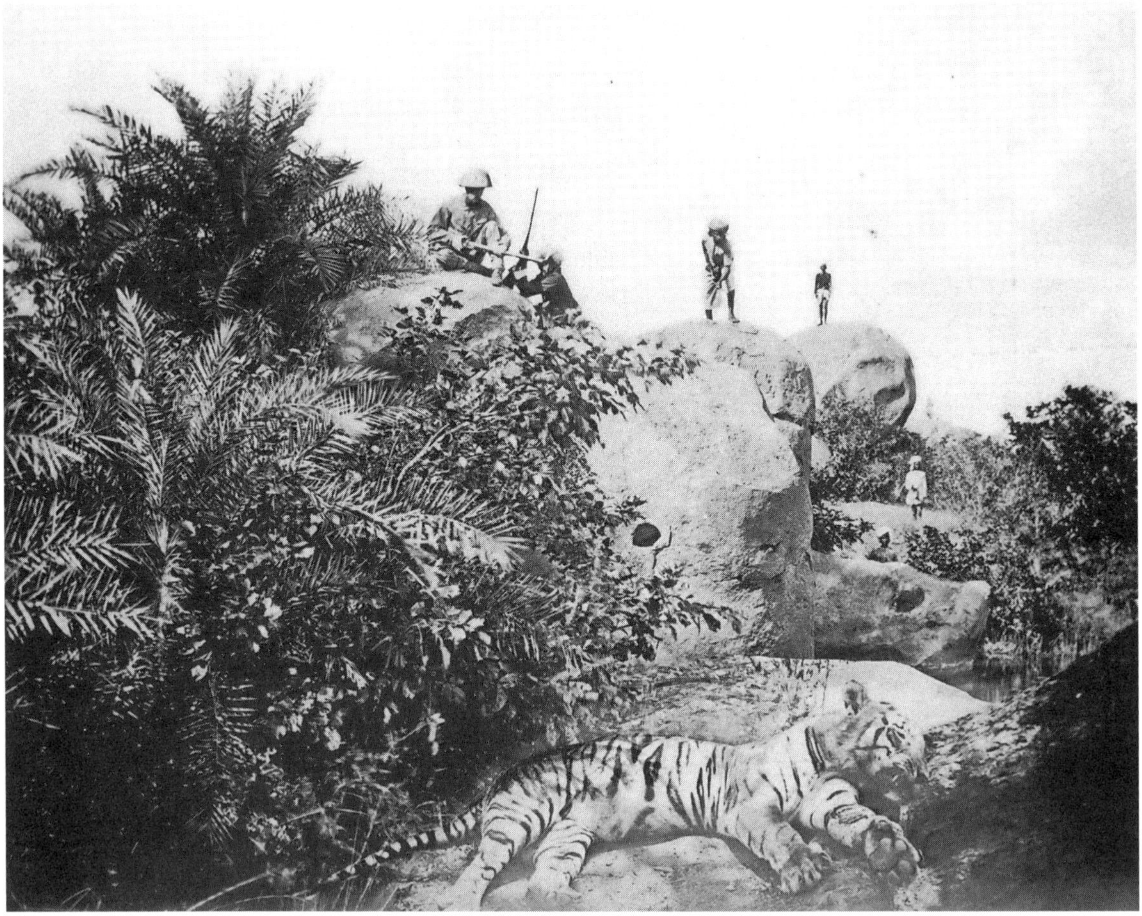

Figure 4.11. Willoughby Wallace Hooper, staged tiger hunt (tiger is already dead), 1870s or 1880s. Royal Geographic Society (with the Institute of British Geographers).

> The Provost Marshal, who is an ardent amateur photographer, is desirous of securing views of the persons executed at the precise moment when they are struck by the bullet. To secure this result, after the orders "ready," "present," have been given to the firing party, the Provost Marshal fixed his camera on the prisoners, who at times are kept waiting several minutes in that position. The officer commanding the firing party is then directed by the Provost Marshal to give the order to fire at the moment when he exposes his plates.[13]

The ensuing investigation made its way through the Parliament as well as the Court of Inquiry in Burma, where many details of Moylan's accounts were pondered in order to determine whether Hooper's actions could be deemed

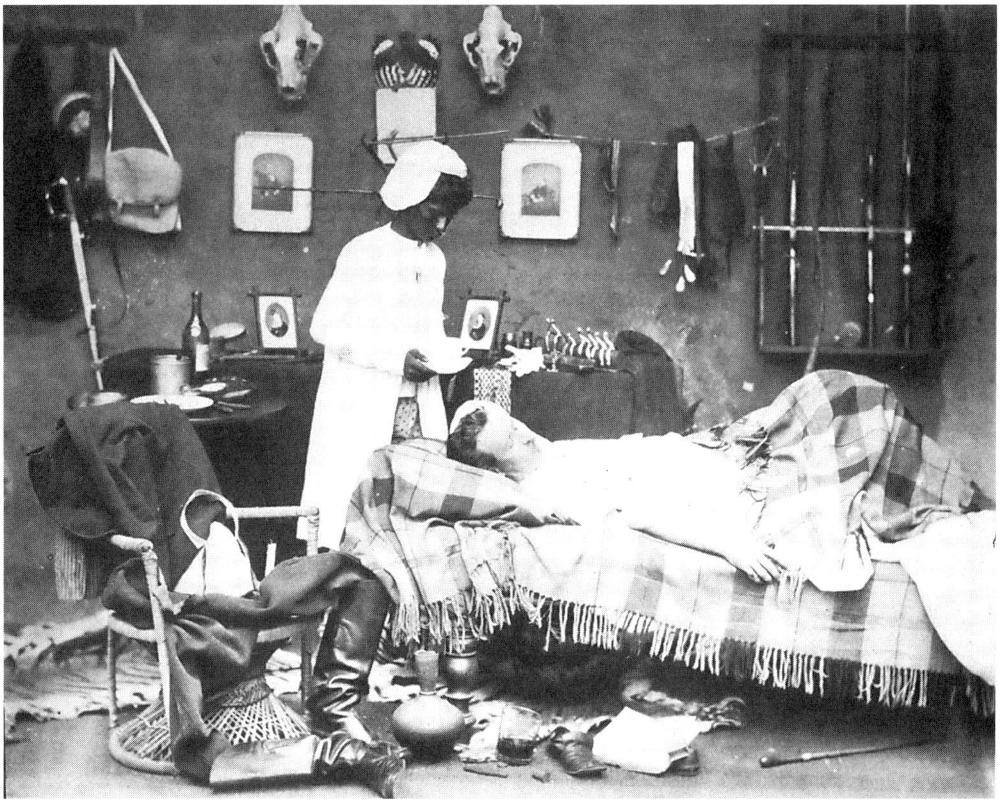

Figure 4.12. Willoughby Wallace Hooper, *Englishman Being Served Tea in Bed,* 1870. Digital image courtesy of the Digital Content Library, University of Minnesota.

cruel. The prisoners were in fact blindfolded, and there was not a delay, as Moylan attests, due to Hooper's photographic activities. Hooper was censured early on by a forced return to India from Burma, and the final verdict on his case deemed this punishment sufficient in spite of Hooper's "lamentable" actions.[14] The execution photographs were not, in the end, distributed as a part of the commercially produced album about Burma that Hooper composed.

The Mandalay execution photographs, though mired in controversy thanks to Moylan's coverage, remain a record of colonial brutality, whatever the ignoble or prurient aims of Hooper may have been. One of Hooper's own contemporaries, historian Grattan Geary, pointed out:

> It is open to doubt whether there is not something very pharasaical in the spirit which revolts at the operation of photographing a batch of men at the moment of their execution, when their execution in batches is accepted as an ordinary incident in the subjugation of a conquered people. . . . It is the custom to close the eyes and ears to the real nature of the "salutary

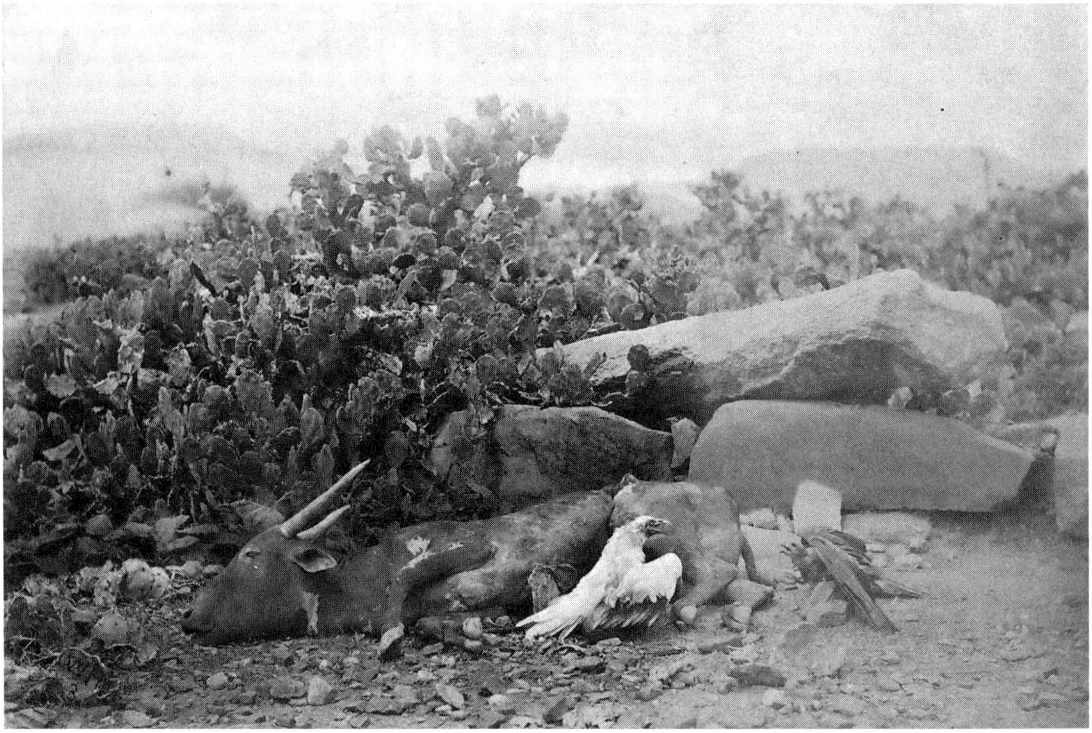

Figure 4.13. Willoughby Wallace Hooper, *Birds Eating Carrion* (staged scene with stuffed birds and carrion resulting from the Madras famine), 1878. Royal Geographic Society (with the Institute of British Geographers).

> severities" which are sparingly alluded to in narratives of military operations in a vanquished country. It would be a great gain to the cause of humanity if there were more Colonel Hoopers, who would focus and fix and make widely known, every horror which it is the custom to slur over in referring to incidents of this kind. If people at large realized with anything like exactitude, the real nature of the price which subjugated populations pay for the blessings of civilisation, sounder views on such subjects would perhaps become more prevalent. As has been said above, if the severities produced always and everywhere the tranquilizing effects which are generally expected from them, it might be a duty to acquiesce, as it is the duty of a surgeon to inflict pain as the price of an ultimate good.[15]

This remarkable passage from Geary's 1886 history of Burma is impressive in its equivocations. The passage immediately follows an observation that Hooper's photographing of execution victims is "undoubtedly reprehensible."[16] On the one hand, Geary recognizes that not only does photography record more than the intentions of the photographer but also that its meanings will

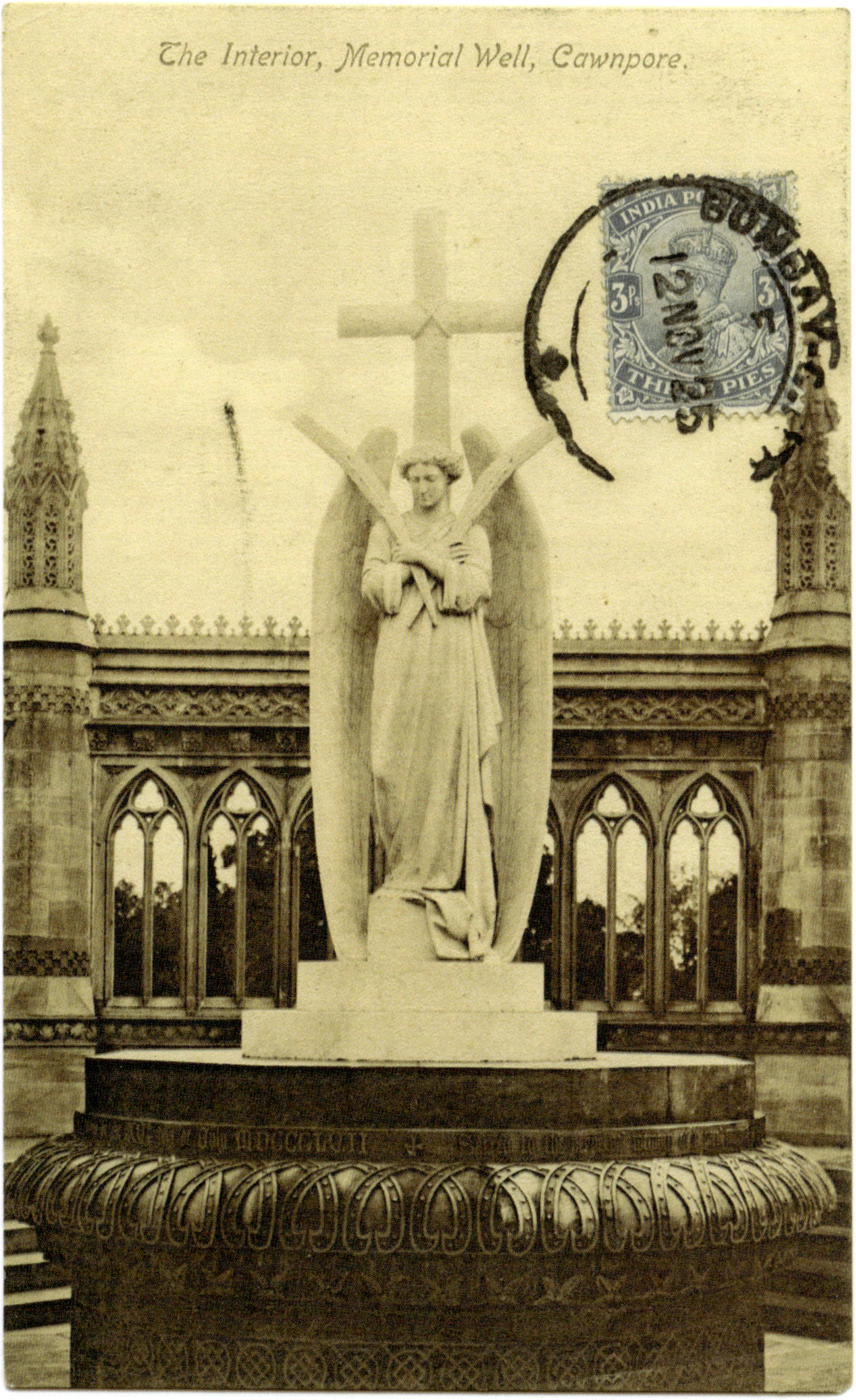

Plate 1. *The Angel at the Memorial Well,* Cawnpore, 1925. Postcard.

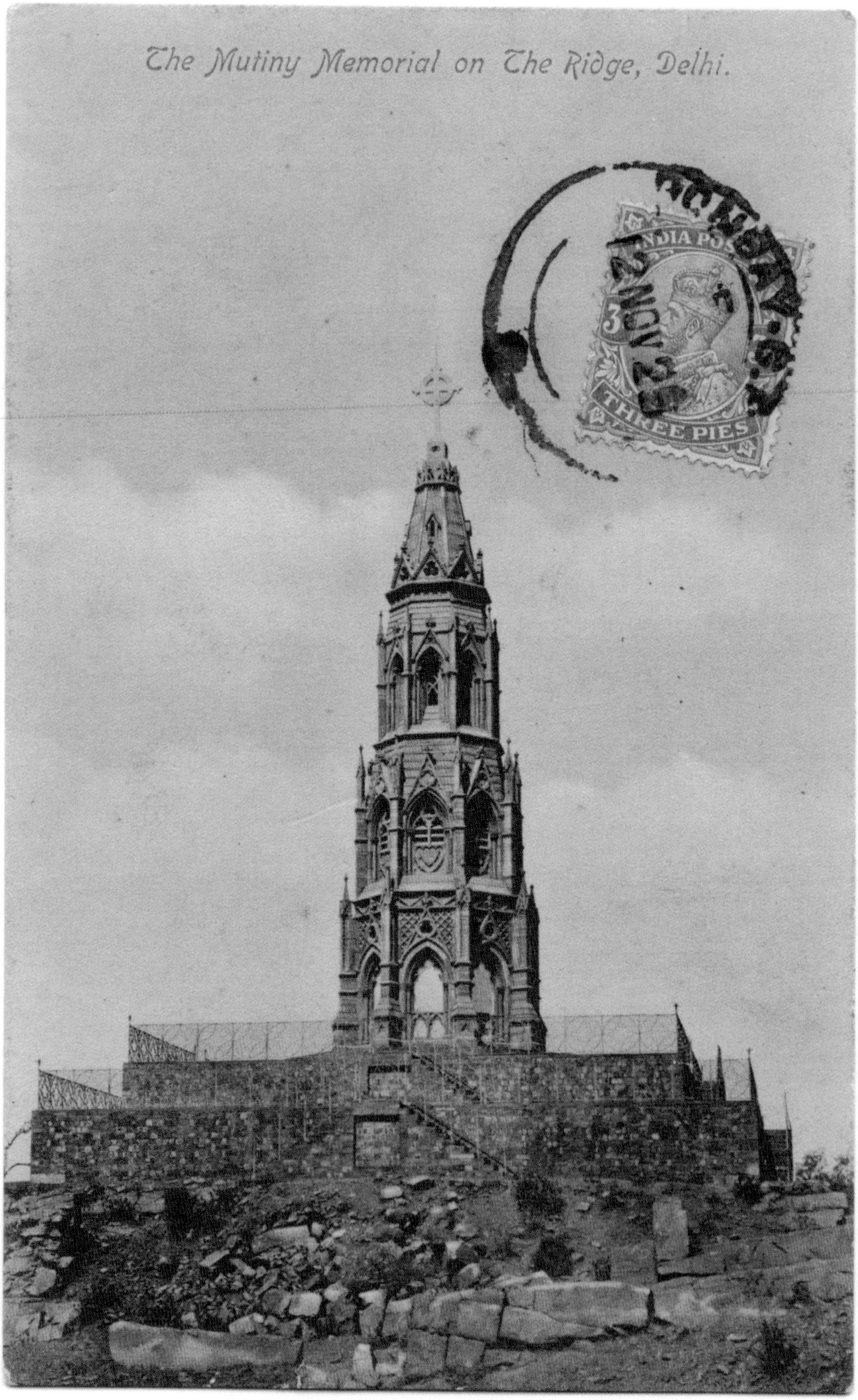

Plate 2. *The Mutiny Memorial on the Ridge,* Delhi, 1925. Postcard.

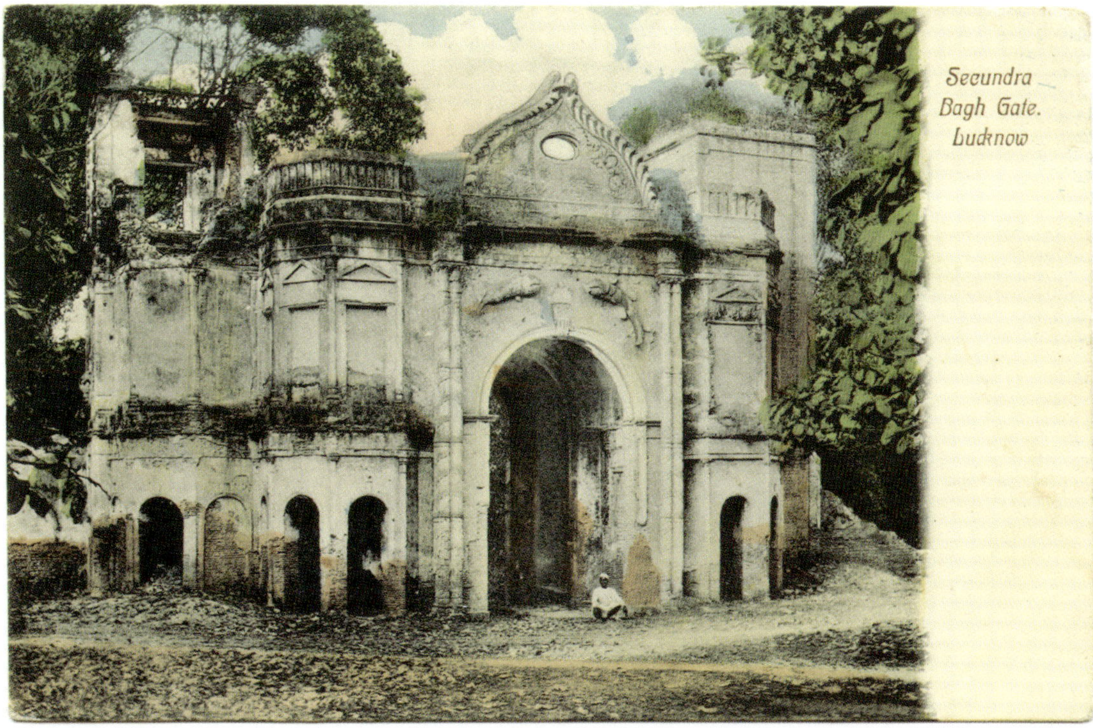

Plate 3. Colored photograph of Secundrabagh Gate, Lucknow, 1920s. Postcard.

Plate 4. Souvenir album cover. The Alkazi Collection of Photography.

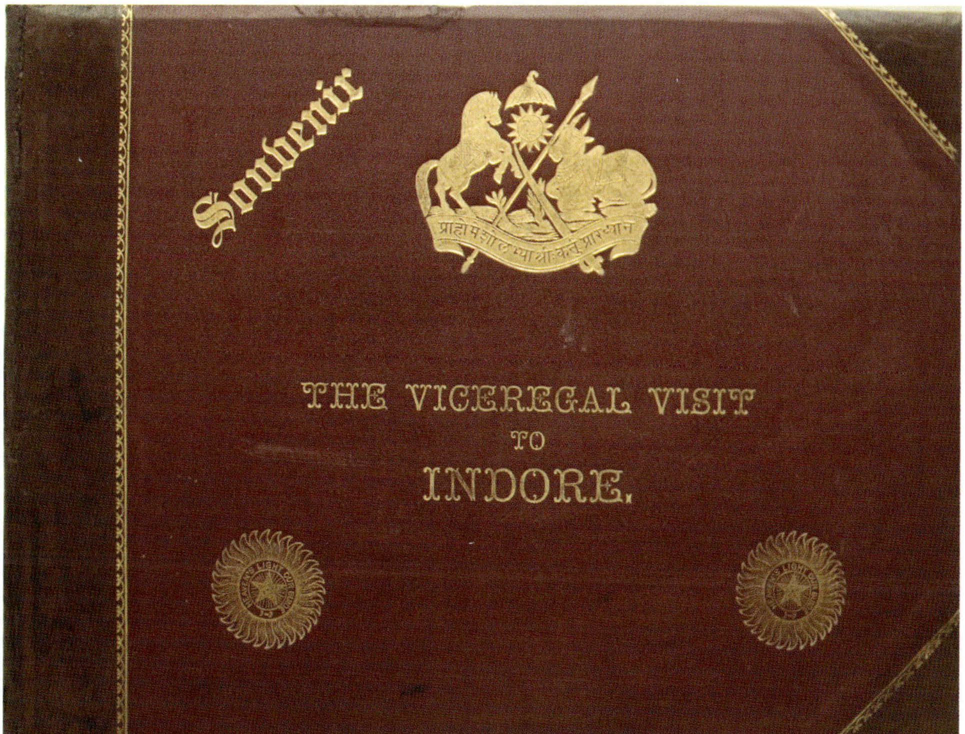

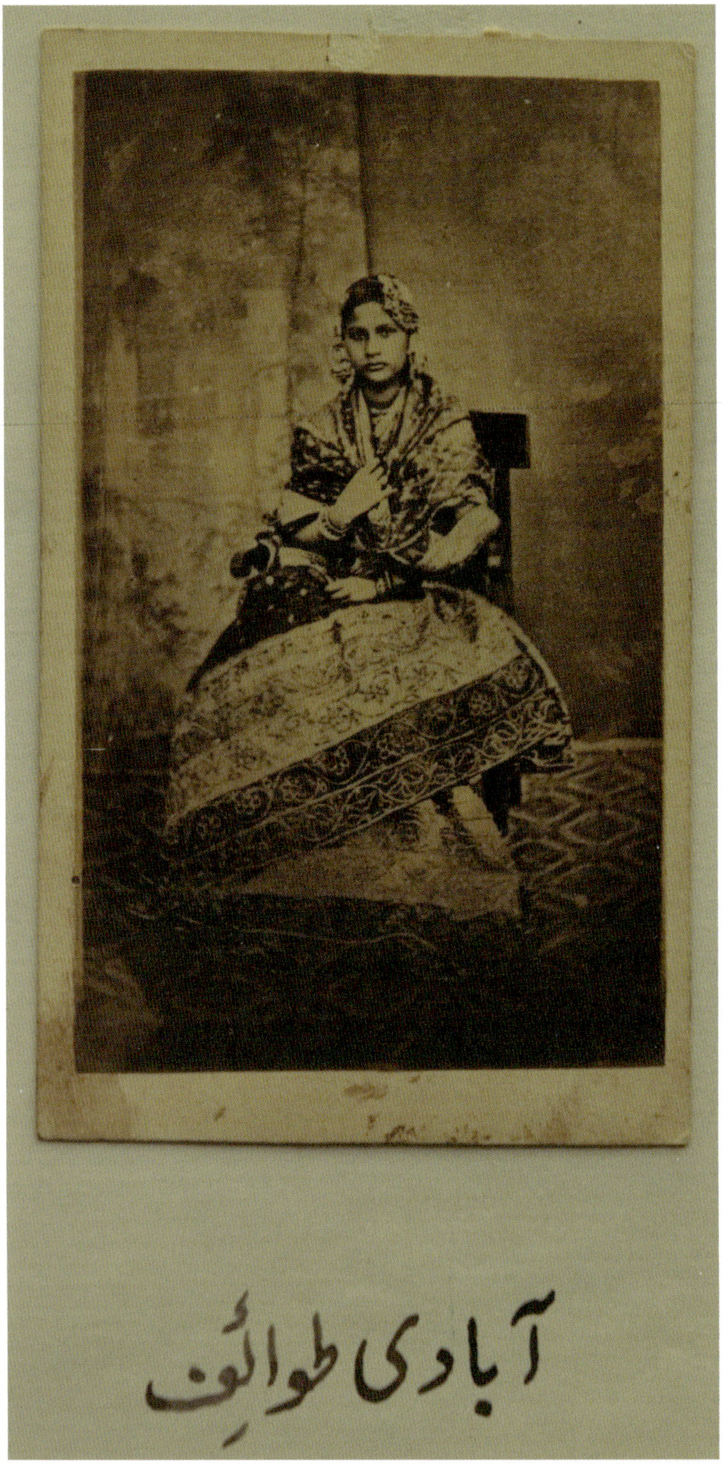

Plate 5. *"Abadi," Courtesan.* From Abbas Ali, *The Beauties of Lucknow,* 1874. "Abadi" means jovial, soothing, charming. The Alkazi Collection of Photography.

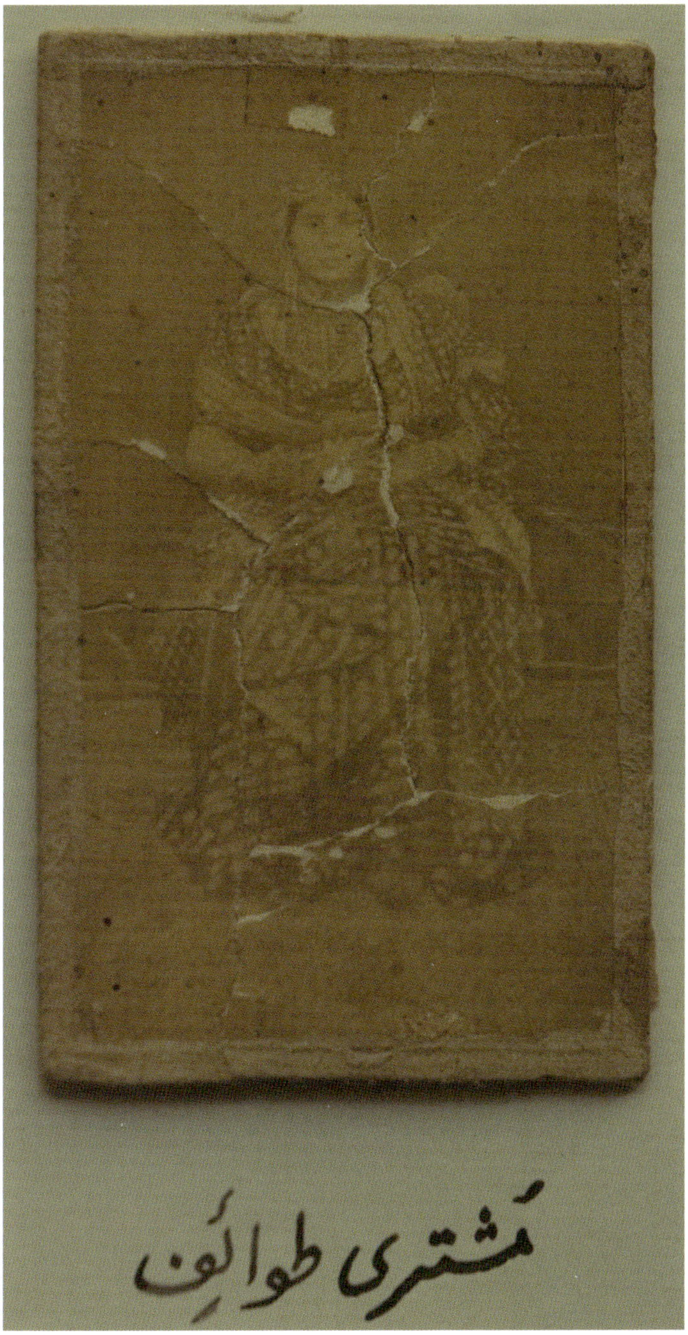

Plate 6. *"Mushteri," Courtesan.* From Abbas Ali, *The Beauties of Lucknow,* 1874. "Mushteri" was the name of a renowned Lucknow poet and courtesan. The Alkazi Collection of Photography.

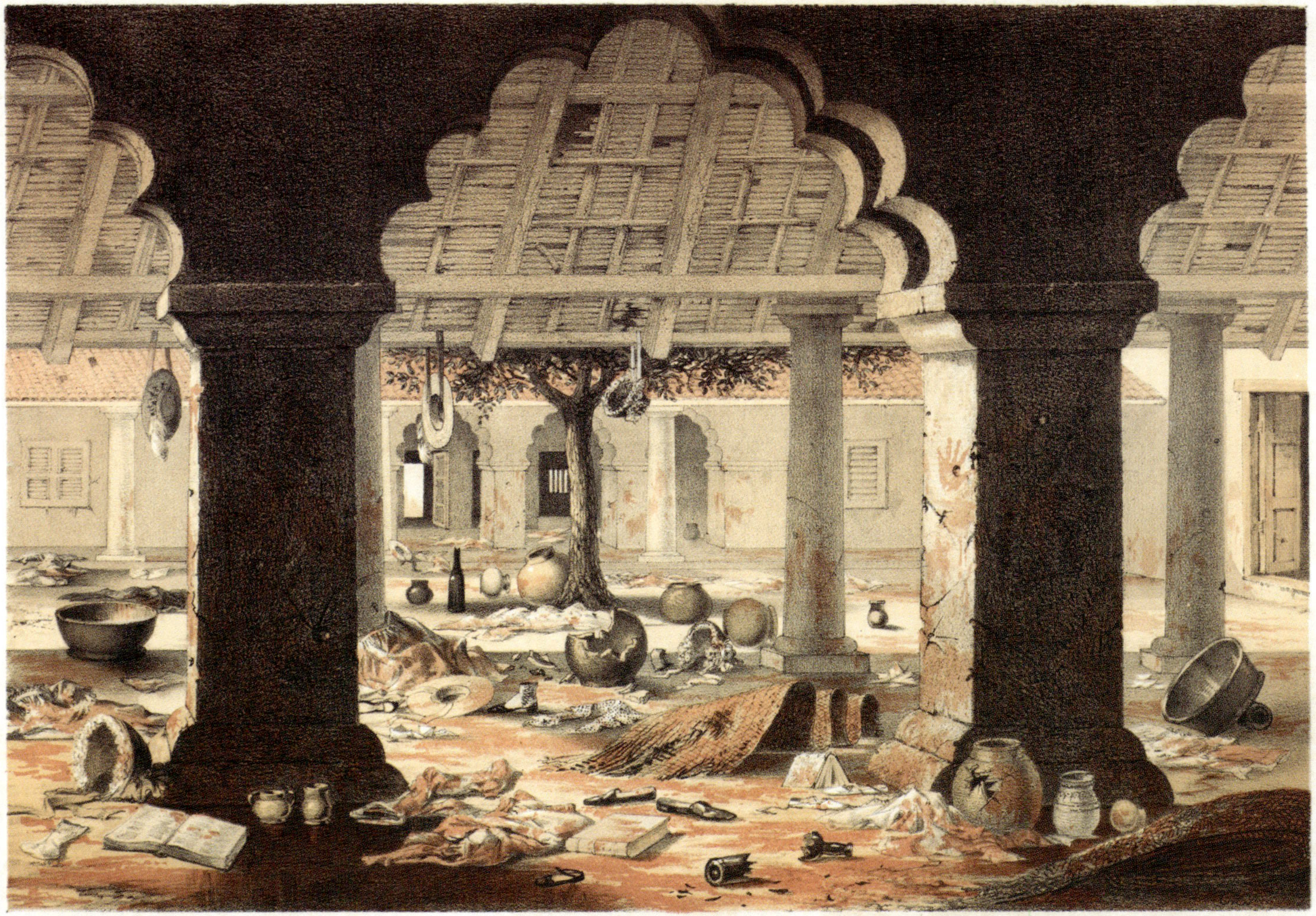

Plate 7. Vincent Brooks after Charles Wade Crump, *The Chamber of Blood.* Lithograph. Copyright British Library Board.

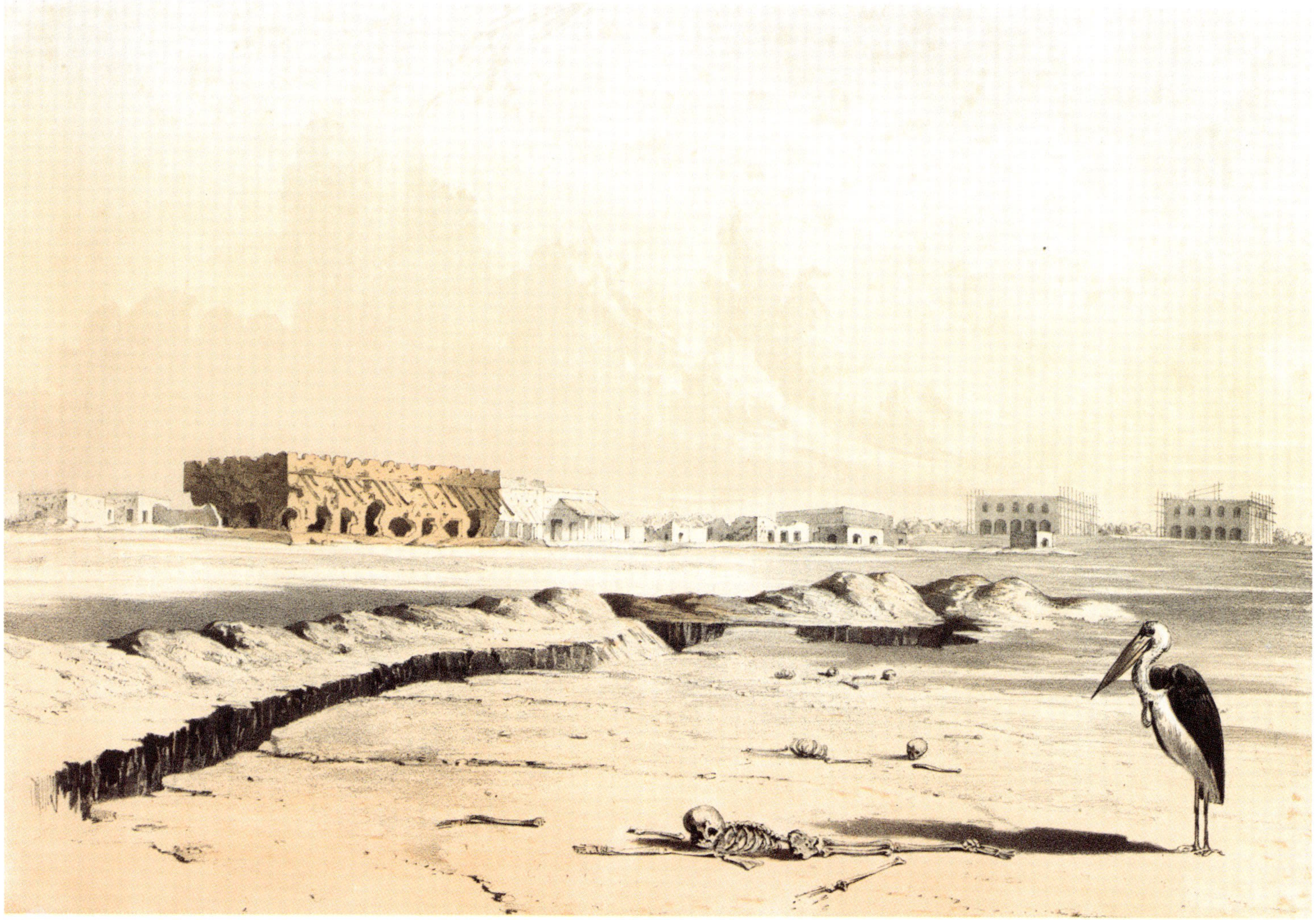

Plate 8. Vincent Brooks after Charles Wade Crump, *Battered Barracks*. Lithograph. Copyright British Library Board.

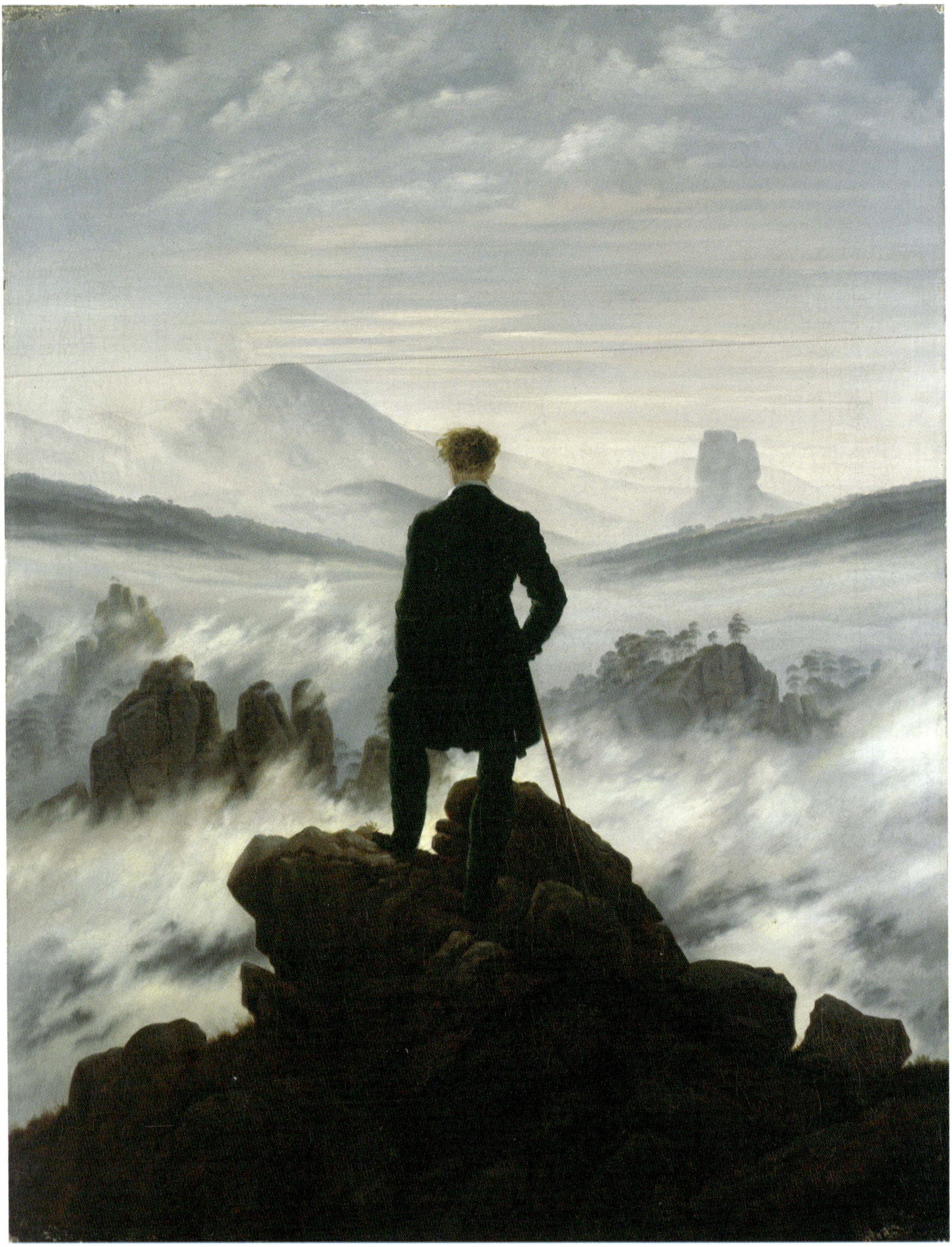

Plate 9. Caspar David Friedrich (1774–1840), *Der Wanderer über dem Nebelmeer* (Wanderer above a Sea of Fog), ca. 1817. Oil on canvas. Bildarchiv Preussischer Kulturbesitz/Art Resource, N.Y.

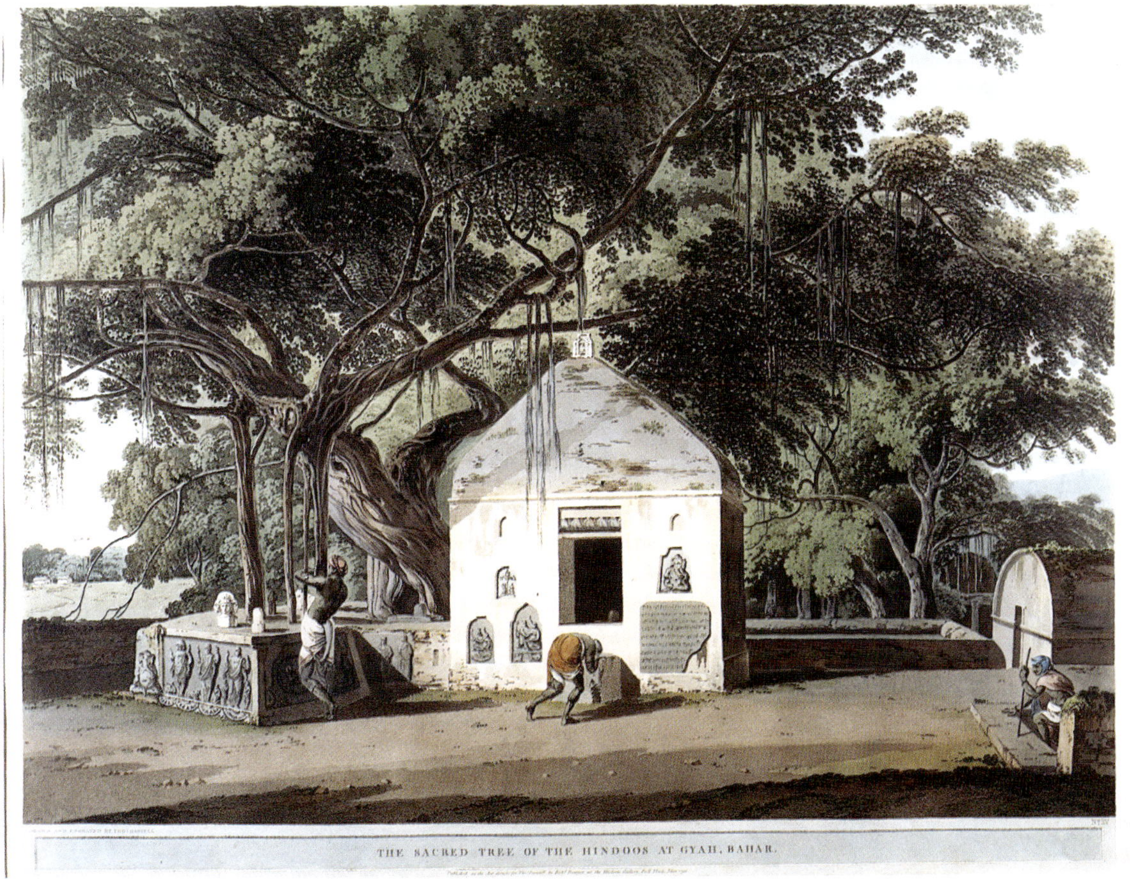

Plate 10. Thomas Daniell, *Banyan Tree with Hindu Shrine at Gaya,* Bihar, 1796. Wellcome Library, London.

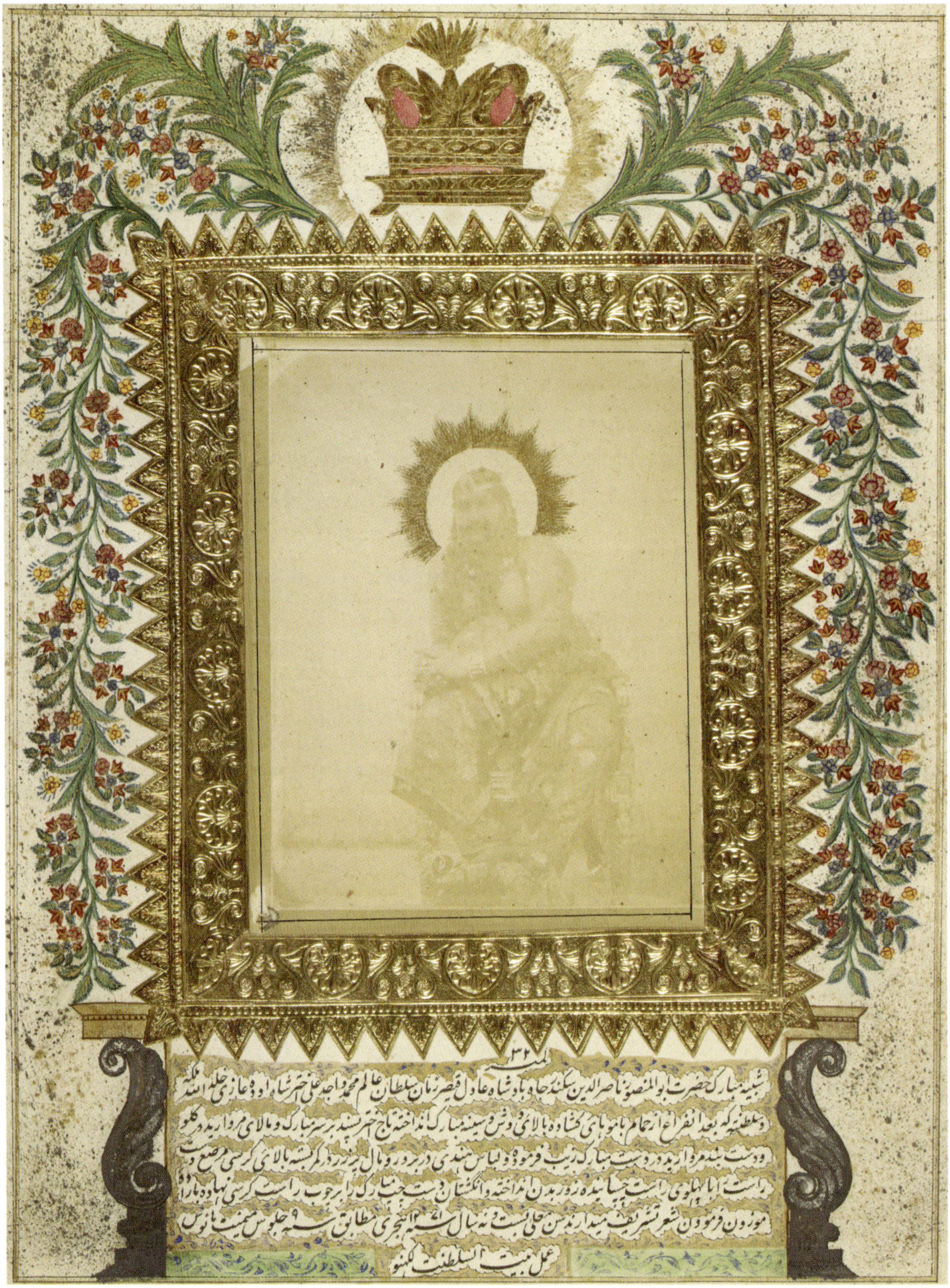

Plate 11. Ahmed Ali Khan, *Portrait of Wajid Ali Shah, King of Avadh 1847–56*, ca. 1855. Copyright British Library Board, Photo 500/(1). See Appendix for translation.

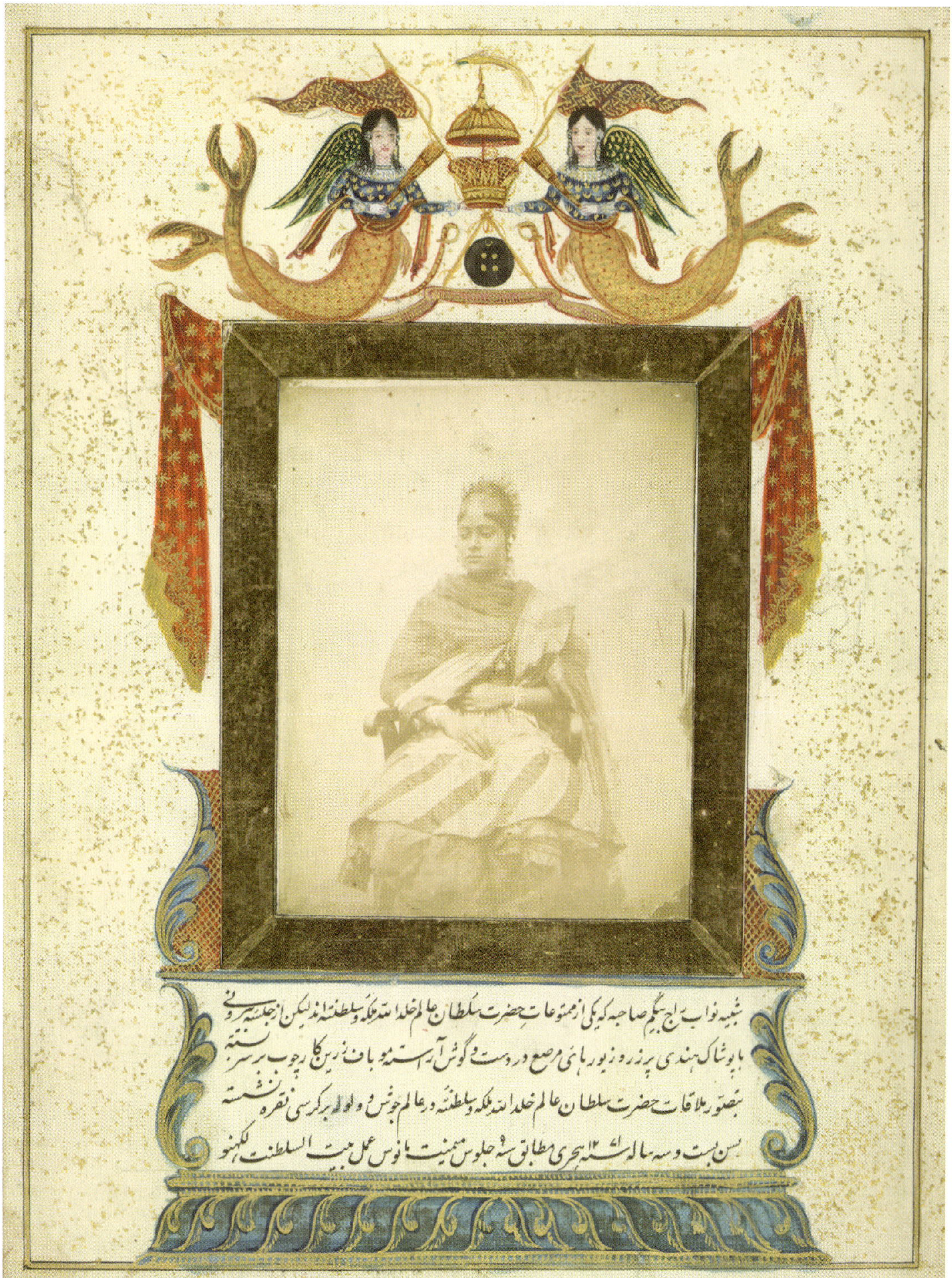

Plate 12. Ahmed Ali Khan, *Portrait of Nawaub Raj Begum Sahibah of Avadh,* ca. 1855. Copyright British Library Board, Photo 500/(3). See Appendix for translation.

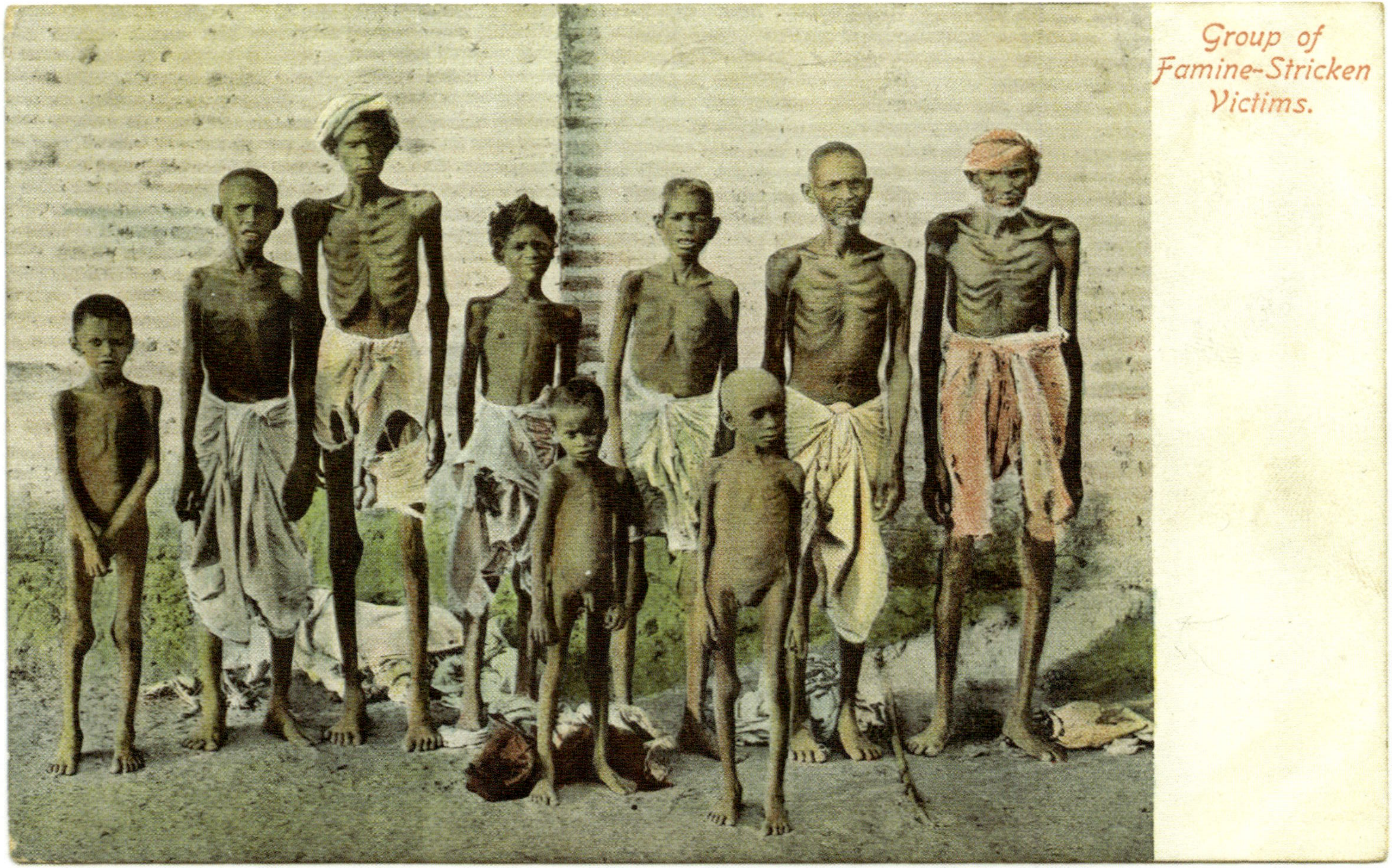

Plate 13. Postcard from the Allahabad famine (1900–1902).

continue to shift over time; what Hooper ends up recording, in Geary's view, is the violence upon which "civilization" itself depends. In other words, if we are offended by Hooper's execution photographs, our disgust may well serve the interests of the imperial state, which prefers that such scenes remain out of view in the first place. Our disgust would arise from sympathy for the victims, and yet sympathy would "misfire" (so to speak), creating the conditions for more victims to be executed but discreetly and away from cameras. And yet, Geary is prepared to accept such colonial violence under certain conditions, and the analogy he deploys of the surgeon being forced to inflict pain for the price of an ultimate good is a call for a social anesthetic. According to him, if such scenes, whether viewed or not, are the price of civilization, then "it might be a duty to acquiesce" in the face of the pain caused to another person, *if* it could be guaranteed that such colonial violence would have a tranquilizing effect and therefore hasten the end of war. ("Civilization" is always and necessarily the winner, because the winner sets the terms for what counts as civilization.) The conditional syntax in his text, the word *if*, upon which his whole

Figure 4.14. Willoughby Wallace Hooper, *Execution at Mandalay*, January 15, 1886. Copyright British Library Board, Photo 447/8(1).

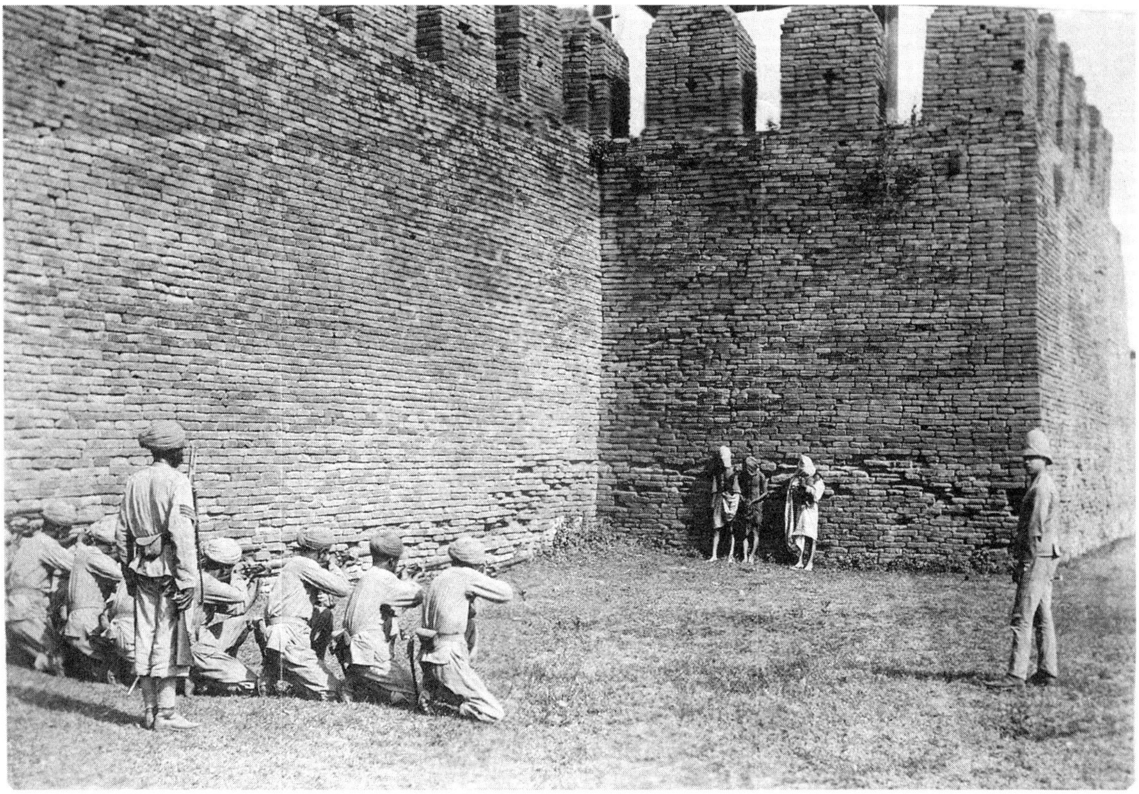

argument hangs, reproduces for us the dilemmas of the military leader in the field of battle, who must weigh the justification of ends and means with every action. But this conditional syntax is also a ruse, since it contains within it the possibility that severities in a time of war just might have the desired tranquilizing effect, in which case, as Geary states so vehemently, we must acquiesce to committing violence to others and hold our gut reactions in check. The ethical dilemma he paints already contains its solution, since it is freighted with the risk of losing "civilization" altogether, a risk that can never be taken when terms such as *civilization* and *barbarism* are invoked; these terms signify an ethical economy in which all such conundrums are in truth already solved. They mark a force of desire that provides the military commander and the reader of Geary's text with a clear map of this ambiguous and uncertain terrain.

This desire for civilization, the true north that leads out of uncertainty, entails curbing other desires and affects and mastering our reactions to scenes of violence. Social anesthesia is then a bulwark against the lapse into barbarism, and Geary implies that we must look at scenes of Hooper's executions, and sounder views on the necessity of civilization's violence can be made possible only by mastering our initial affective reactions to the views of that violence. Though such scenes might make us suffer, that suffering is the very bedrock of civilization. Joseph Conrad invokes this same structure of feeling when he notes, at the end of *Heart of Darkness,* that Kurtz's intended "had a mature capacity for fidelity, for belief, for suffering."[17] Though such a capacity is explicitly gendered as feminine in Conrad and remains unmarked in Geary, this capacity to suffer, the very kernel of civilizational affect, is a shuttling between feeling and anesthesia, emotional response and its mastery. This capacity allows a process of sympathetic renewal, whereby sympathetic feeling is persistently invoked, and any possible action resulting from that feeling is presistently deferred; sympathy as a technology of the self becomes the training ground for self-mastery.

At their core, both the controversy surrounding Hooper's execution shots from Burma and John Shore's poem about the Bengal famine of the 1770s are animated by sympathy. Shore feels for the suffering victims, and the legal inquiry that examines Hooper's photography of executions pivots on certain key facts: Could the condemned see that they were being photographed? Did the photographic process force the condemned to wait any longer than necessary before they were shot? In other words, sympathy for the condemned causes one to assess what kinds of cruelties may be permissible. In this regard, the famine photographs that Hooper took in 1876–79 in Madras have also circulated in contexts in which the images are intended to evoke sympathy for the suffering of famine victims, and no doubt they were also collected for sheer morbid curiosity: official and unofficial histories of the famines, in the form of etchings in newspapers and historical accounts in both India and England (see Figures 4.15 and 4.16), private photographic albums showing famine victims and colonial relief efforts, and so on.

Whether or not Hooper personally felt sympathetic or unsympathetic to any of his photographic subjects is, from an institutional as well as from a technophenomenological point of view, an irrelevant question. In fact, reports circulated in *Punch* and other publications that Hooper would group famine victims together, take his photograph, and then ask them to move along without providing any assistance. And yet not only are these photographs mobilized today in contemporary accounts that aim to foster sympathy with the famine victims;[18] they have also provided the basis for the entire tradition of famine photography, complete with repetitions of essentially the same ethical conundrums surrounding the documentation of suffering.[19]

Figure 4.15. Willoughby Wallace Hooper, *Madras Beach during the Famine, Showing Grain Piled for Export*, February 1877. Royal Geographic Society (with the Institute of British Geographers).

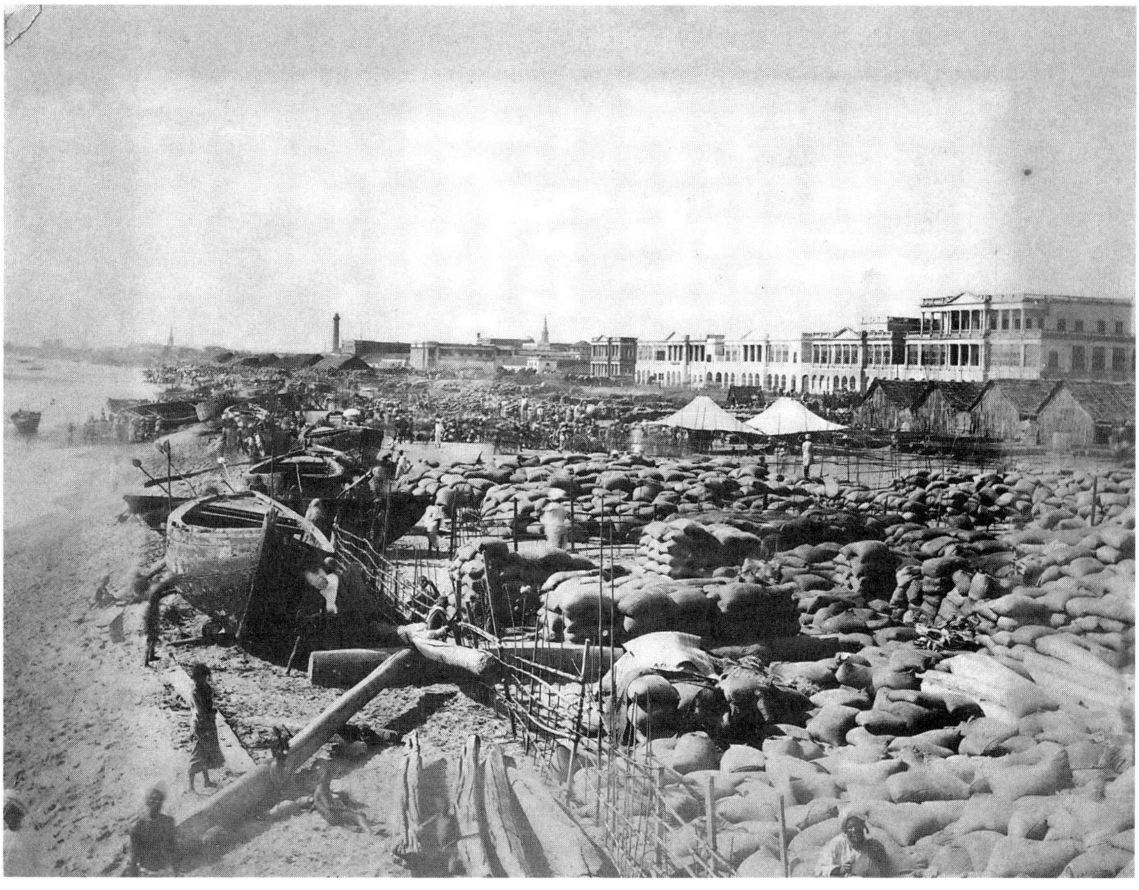

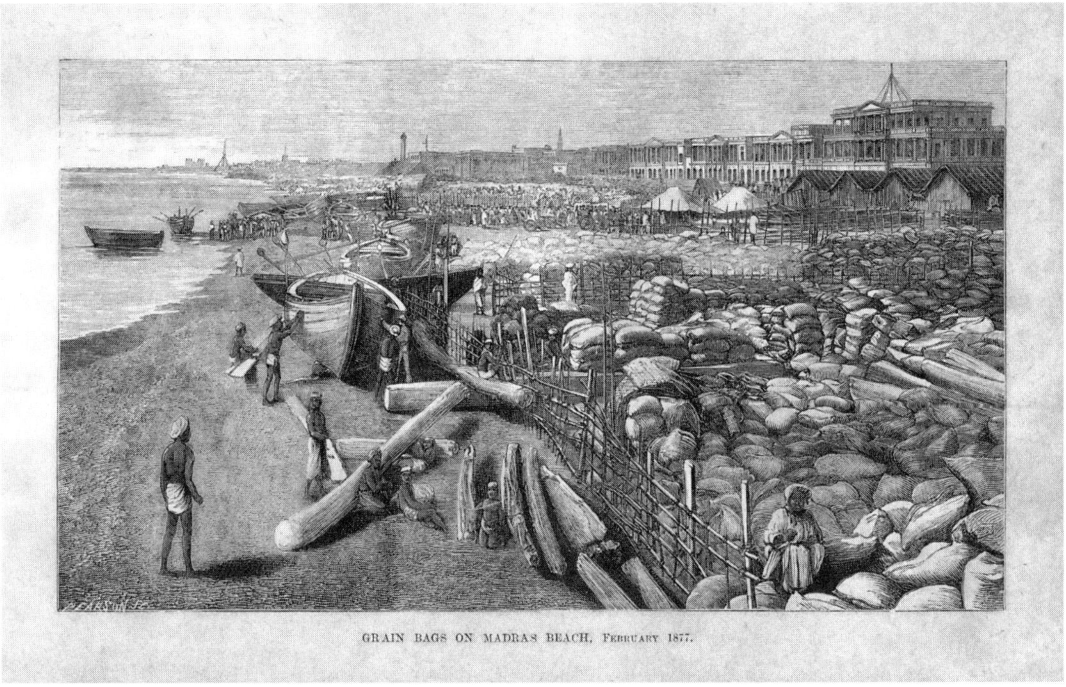

Figure 4.16. Lithograph based on W. W. Hooper's photograph, from William Digby, *The Famine Campaign in Southern India*, 1878.

Hooper's photographs are positioned at the beginning of this photographic tradition, which by now has grown rather familiar. Still, the specificities of the 1876–79 Madras famine merit some attention. As for the natural "cause" of the famine, the rains failed in the Madras region in 1876, resulting in skyrocketing prices for grains, in spite of the surplus production of wheat and other grains in the previous three months. This was in part because so much of the grain was shipped immediately to London; Figure 4.15 shows Hooper's shot of Madras beach piled with stacked grain bound for England at the height of the famine. As Mike Davis puts it, "Londoners were in effect eating India's bread."[20] The railroad was instrumental in shipping grains away from drought-stricken areas and into storage zones, the telegraph helped to raise prices uniformly across thousands of towns and cities, and financial speculation on the price of grain was encouraged as part and parcel of the business of extraction.[21] We are reminded here of Benjamin's warning that in the development of technology, even as we acknowledge the progress of science, we must observe the "concomitant retrogression of society" that technology under the rule of capitalism makes possible.[22] In Madras, when the poor began to die of malnutrition, newspapers in India as well as in England began to report scenes reminiscent of John Shore's poem: skeletal families, people dying of hunger in the streets, half-alive people attacked by jackals.[23] While these tragic scenes were mostly reported between 1876 and 1879, the scholarship on famines in India uniformly repeats the insight that fixed dates for "famine" conditions are notoriously difficult to assess.[24] The fact is that the populations most vulnerable to death lived with malnutrition as a quotidian experience, and this "normal" state of affairs is responsible for greater infant mortality than extreme situations of famine. Marking out certain dates as a distinct famine therefore falsely implies that the poor would otherwise normally be flourishing in good health, as if at the end of the famine food becomes plentiful and health is restored. In addition to regular, pervasive malnutrition, outbreaks of disease often followed periods of dearth and starvation.[25] As a result, the mortality figures of nineteenth-century famines are notoriously underreported in colonial ledgers. In his two-volume account of the Madras famine, William Digby, journalist and editor of the *Madras Times,* puts the figure at 10.3 million.[26]

Sympathetic Mimesis

"Poor heathen, famine-stricken India needs our truest sympathy!" beseeches one Jesse Hutcheon in an October 1877 issue of the *Weslyan Juvenile Offering,* a magazine printed in London for young children by the Weslyan Methodist Missionary Society. She encourages children to "practise a little self-denial this Christmas time" by donating some of their pocket money to the famine victims in Madras.[27] Modern humanitarianism, in the form of "benevolent institutions," was well-established by 1877, since it was in the eighteenth century that such institutions were founded in England. Charitable institutions founded for the sick included Westminster Hospital (1791), Guy's Hospital (1725), London Hospital (1740), Lock Hospital (1746), and Queen Charlotte Lying-in Hospital (1752). In the late eighteenth century, institutions were created to respond to other needs as well: the Climbing Boys Charity (benefiting chimney sweeps), the Royal Humane Society (for distributing information about resuscitating the drowned), the Society for the Discharge and Relief of Persons Imprisoned for Small Debts, various abolition and missionary societies (Quaker's London Meeting of Sufferings, 1783, and the Church Missionary Society, 1795), and also a literary fund to help struggling authors.[28] This was the context in which Adam Smith published *Theory of Moral Sentiments* to wide acclaim and, along with David Hume before him, made sympathy a cornerstone of his meditation on morality.

According to postcolonial critics, however, sympathy is a suspect sentiment. Amit Rai and others have rightly argued that sympathy is a conduit for imperial interventions that can be traced from the eighteenth century to the present day. Humanitarian aid can dispense help to suffering populations, but it also brings these populations under the sway of imperialist power, and the darker side of sympathy remains the secret sharer of contemporary liberalism.[29] The ethical minefield of sympathetic identification becomes clear when we compare, for example, Hooper's famine photographs with the postcard of the conversion in extremis (Figure 4.1). Both are scenes of sympathy, and if sympathy is a means of identification with the other, then ethically one can never be certain whether one is simply molding the other in one's own image, as the sympathetic nun does in Figure 4.1. Moreover, the sympathetic work of this photograph itself is uncertain: we might identify with the "sympathy" of the gentle nun, or we might identify with the dying Brahmin who is being converted at the last minute. Such sympathetic uncertainties are of a piece with photographic technologies, as we will see.

In Adam Smith's account, sympathy allows us, on the one hand, to imagine ourselves in the place of the other, providing the ground for all kinds of mimetic and mirroring processes: we "tremble and shudder" at the thought of another's agony, we return the facial expressions of joy at the sight of another's joy, and so on.[30] This would imply that sympathy is the means for escaping our own selves, a bodily and affective means for reaching out to another. But Smith's account is more complex than this: at the scene of our "brother's" suffering, "it is the impressions of our own senses only, not those of his, which our imaginations copy."[31] Smith provides an example:

> Sympathy, therefore, does not arise so much from the view of the passion, as from that of the situation which excites it. We sometimes feel for another, a passion of which he himself seems to be altogether incapable; because, when we put ourselves in his case, that passion arises in our breast from the imagination, though it does not in his from the reality. We blush for the impudence and rudeness of another, though he himself appears to have no sense of the impropriety of his own behavior; because we cannot help feeling with what confusion we ourselves should be covered, had we behaved in so absurd a manner.[32]

Here it seems that our own judgments prevent us from easy escape from ourselves. Only "when we put ourselves in his case," in the place of the other, however, can our imagination and our judgments enter into this experience. The mimesis of sympathetic feeling is a replication of the other that is indissociable from an affirmation of the self. In Adam Smith's account, the self paradoxically morphs through this extension toward another and yet remains to some extent self-same and identical.

This can happen, in part, because we grow up recognizing that in order to solicit others' sympathy for our emotions, we must modulate the show we make of our passions: "For if we are at all masters of ourselves, the presence of a mere acquaintance will really compose us, still more than that of a friend; and that of an assembly of strangers still more than that of an acquaintance,"[33] the aim being that we solicit the sympathy of an "impartial spectator" and therefore validate our original emotional state.[34] Among the dramatis personae of the hypothetical scenes of sympathy that Smith describes, the impartial spectator plays the leading part, because over the course of *Theory of Moral Sentiments* this figure, detached and external, becomes internalized in each of us. Standing in for the viewpoint of society at large, the impartial spectator is an imagined location from which we judge ourselves: "We examine our persons limb by limb, and by placing ourselves before a looking-glass, or by some such expedient, endeavor, as much as possible, to view ourselves at the distance and with the eyes of other people. . . . This is the only looking-glass by which we can, in some measure, with the eyes of other people, scrutinize the propriety of our own conduct."[35] This imagined standpoint, this trace of the other within us, is indispensable to our moral formation as subjects even if its nature is necessarily imaginary. Prefiguring the split subject of psychoanalysis, Smith locates a formative split at the moment of the subject's consolidation as a social agent:

> When I endeavor to examine my own conduct, when I endeavor to pass sentence upon it, and either to approve or condemn it, it is evident that, in all such cases, I divide myself, as it were, into two persons; and that I, the examiner and judge, represent a different character from that other I, the person whose conduct is examined into and judged of. The first is the spectator, whose sentiments with regard to my own conduct I endeavor to enter into, by placing myself in his situation, and by considering how it would appear to me, when seen from that particular point of view. The second is the agent, the person whom I properly call myself, and of whose conduct, under the character of a spectator, I was endeavoring to form some opinion.[36]

Unlike Buck-Morss's account of sensory splitting, Smith's notion of subjective splitting does not pivot on the displacement of pain or even of sensory stimuli but is akin to Freud's description of the critical self-censoring agency sometimes known as "the conscience."[37] Already in Smith, this capacity to split oneself into a spectator and an agent is what secures our sociability: "Nature . . . has endowed man not only with a desire of being approved of, but with a desire of being what ought to be approved of; or of being what he himself approves of in other men."[38] So for Smith sympathy is not simply an affect, though it is that too, but, as Jacques Khalip and Marc Redfield have argued, for Adam Smith sympathy is also a technology.[39] It is a mechanism that regulates our reaction to the other, to ourselves, and by extension to the social body at large. Because sympathy names a technology of the self, and does not itself contain any content, Adam Smith wagers that it is the suturing mechanism at the heart of society's regulation.

It is at this macrolevel, at the level of the socius itself, that a theological theme enters Smith's thought. While in his next work, *The Wealth of Nations,* this element would take the form of the famous "invisible hand," in *Theory of Moral Sentiments* Smith places his faith in what he sometimes calls "Nature" but more often "Author of Nature." This "all-wise" Author "has made man . . . the immediate judge of mankind; and has, in this respect . . . created him after his own image, and appointed him his viceregent upon earth, to superintend the behavior of his brethren";[40] our very capacity for sympathy for others (including sympathy for the dead) is made possible by this Author. Our actions in the world are mediated through the "looking glass" installed in each of us in the form of the impartial spectator, and we, who are already semblances of God, strive to resemble what we imagine is the standpoint of the impartial spectator within us, this replication of the society at large, all the while with a desire for approbation continually motivating the asymptotic movements of our strivings. Such is the mimetic and circular dance at the heart of the technology that is sympathy, a technology that in Smith's account aims at concord and harmony throughout society, and one that takes us out of ourselves only to return us to ourselves once again, chastened.

The links among sympathy, mimesis, and faith predate Adam Smith. *Sympathia* in Latin or *πάθος (pathos)* in Greek means "having fellow feeling," or "to feel with," complete with the double sense of feeling and suffering contained in the Greek roots *πενθ-, πονθ-, παθ-*. In the sixteenth and seventeenth centuries, one finds references to sympathy powder, a balm that could heal wounds through its application not on the wound but rather on a cloth stained with blood from the wound or even on the weapon that had inflicted it. Sympathy powder could work from great distances, although it depended on access to an indexical object like the cloth or the weapon that had had former contact with the victim. Traversing distances across the globe, between people, among parts of the body (which could stand in for other objects, even planets), sympathy names a phenomenon that has movement and replication as its basis. This magical basis of sympathetic effect, particularly in sympathy powder, is of a piece with what Foucault describes as the arrangement of the premodern episteme. Foucault names "sympathy" as one of the four forms of resemblances that anchor this episteme, and while sympathy can work through contact (as in sympathy powder), it does not require such touching and can draw the most distant objects together by forging resemblances among them (tuning their rhythms to one another, forming pictorial resemblances or resemblances in qualities of state such as heaviness, lightness, etc., or both). It is "a principle of mobility" that renders difference into sameness: "Sympathy is an instance of the *Same* so strong and so insistent that it will not rest content to be merely one of the forms of likeness; it has the dangerous power of *assimilating,* of rendering things identical to one another, of mingling them, of causing their individuality to disappear—and thus of rendering them foreign to what they were before. Sympathy transforms. It alters, but in the direction of identity."[41]

If one brackets the account of epistemic ruptures that Foucault traces in *The Order of Things,* then might not the mimesis of sympathy return in modernity as a kind of haunting? Such a mimesis nips at the heel of narratives of progress and rationality, because it manifests itself at the heart of those emblems of historical progress, like photography, that are meant to indicate a decisive break from premodernity.[42] Not only was spirit photography a craze in the early days of the medium, but a certain uncanniness resides at the heart of photographic mimesis itself: a strange mix of sympathetic production that is simultaneously contact and copy. Michael Taussig's accounts of sympathetic magic practices in postcolonial spaces note the incorporation of photographs;[43] Victorians famously held on to postmortem photographs because they believed that the photograph retained a trace of the departed; Hooper's photographs of military executions were scandalous because they magically transported the horror and anxiety of their victims;[44] and Dr. Cornish, who bemoans the lack of a photographer to take pictures of famine victims, wants all valences of sympathy (the power to be moved from a great distance, fellow feeling, identification) to reach the British public.

Sympathy, naming a neutral process—at its most elementary level, a tending toward another's feeling—does not come with a built-in ethical or moral compass. Smith details the process by which sympathy is felt as an affect, and in his account sympathy is the cement for social cohesion, and to that extent, it is good for society. But sympathy does not in itself guarantee good moral standing, because it is simply the name of a mobile tendency, and multiple and contradictory possibilities for action open up on its basis. Scenes of conversion in extremis (Figure 4.1) display most overtly the potentially dangerous powers of sympathy's capacity for assimilation and rendering similar. It is as if a desire for self-replication lies at the heart of the fellow feeling we share with others, and this sympathy in the face of another's torment comes with its own pleasures. Edmund Burke, in *A Philosophical Enquiry into the Origin of our Ideas of the Sublime and the Beautiful* (1757) and as we saw, in part, earlier in the opening epigraph, comments on the delight we find in scenes of other people's distress:

> As our Creator has designed we should be united by the bond of sympathy, he has strengthened that bond by a proportionable delight; and there . . . where our sympathy is most wanted, in the distresses of others. If this passion was simply painful, we would shun with the greatest care all persons and places that could excite such a passion; as, some who are so far gone in indolence as not to endure any strong impression actually do. But the case is widely different with the greater part of mankind; there is no spectacle

> we so eagerly pursue, as that of some uncommon and grievous calamity; so that whether the misfortune is before our eyes, or whether they are tuned back to it in history, it always touches with delight. This is not an unmixed delight, but blended with no small uneasiness. The delight we have in such things, hinders us from shunning scenes of misery; and the pain we feel, prompts us to relieve ourselves in relieving those who suffer; and all this antecedent to any reasoning, by an instinct that works us to its own purposes, without our concurrence.[45]

For Burke, scenes of social suffering and mass calamity, too, are experiences of the sublime and as destabilizing and threatening to self-mastery as awesome scenes of nature and historical events that terrify us even as they delight us. Susan Sontag repeats this Burkean insight when she writes, in *Regarding the Pain of Others,* "No moral charge attaches to the representation of these cruelties. Just the provocation: can you look at this? There is the satisfaction of being able to look at the image without flinching. There is the pleasure of flinching."[46] Both the mastery of one's reactions and the suffering caused by the initial reaction fulfill a need. As an aesthetic category, sympathy names one of the feelings, in Burke's words, antecedent to any reasoning, that acts a kind of instinct that works us to its own purposes, and we are carried away by this strange mixture of compassion and delight in the face of mass calamity.

In this light, Hooper's famine photographs, and possibly all famine photography, precariously serve two contradictory ends: they satisfy a latent sadistic desire even as they provide the basis for a sympathy that could lead to altruism. Just how much suffering needs to be made visible before we are moved to feel compassion?[47] The pleasure in looking, the delight in flinching, exists alongside the terror we feel at scenes of extreme violence and distress, and according to Burke's account of sympathy, it could not be otherwise. If Adam Smith is correct in noting that sympathy entails a return and consolidation of the self (the experience of the sublime, in both Burke and Kant, too, ultimately shores up the self after breaking it apart), then the impulse to stamp the other with one's own image, to assimilate him or her to oneself, is the result of the wish to escape the uneasiness caused by the scenes of distress. The pleasures of self-replication and self-consolidation draw their energies from the initial delight at the scenes of another's misery.

Sympathy's Intimate Publics

In light of Adam Smith's wager on sympathy as the conduit between the deeply personal and the most social, it is remarkable that the colonial state institutions meant to address the famine situation in India were void of any sympathetic consideration. Sir Richard Temple, who, as we've seen, waxed poetic about the picturesque nature of India, was the lieutenant-governor of Bengal at the time of the Madras famine and was asked to administer famine relief in Madras after his handling of the famine in Bengal. A letter dated January 16, 1877, from the secretary to the government of India dictates to Richard Temple:

> While it is the desire of the Government of India that every effort should be made, so far as the resources of the State admit, for the prevention of deaths from famine, it is essential in the present state of the finances that the most severe economy should be practiced. . . . The utmost care is necessary to restrict the expenditure to the absolute requirements of the case. . . . Considering that the revenues are barely sufficient to meet the ordinary expenditure of the Empire, and that heavy additional taxation is both financially and politically impracticable, we must plainly admit that the task of saving life, irrespective of the cost, is one which it is beyond our power to undertake.[48]

Richard Temple is being reminded here to adopt the strictest austerity in administering famine relief, because just four years earlier, after successfully overseeing the Bengal famine relief, he was admonished by the London administration for being extravagant, for allowing "the scale of wages paid at relief works to be determined by the daily food needs of the labourer and the prevailing food prices in the market rather than by the amount that the Government could afford to spend for the purpose."[49] Overcompensating for this previous "extravagance," Temple rigorously stuck to a regime of famine relief even stricter than that imposed by the government, becoming, as Mike Davis writes of him, "the personification of free market economics as a mask for colonial genocide," much like Charles Edward Trevelyan before him, in Ireland (who himself became governor of Madras later).[50] Davis is hardly exaggerating here, as Richard Temple, in his experiments to determine the minimal human subsistence diet, reduced the diet of coolies to one pound of rice per day, which was half their normal subsistence wages. This, as we've seen, came to be known as the "Temple wage" and contained less caloric value (1,627 calories) than the ration in Buchenwald would in 1944 (1,750 calories), all while the coolies were expected to engage in heavy labor toward famine relief projects.[51] Dr. Cornish was an outspoken critic of Temple's policies and reported the monthly mortality rate in relief camps at 94 percent: "The deaths are almost entirely due to disease which invariably, attack underfed and starving people, viz., extreme wasting of tissue, and destruction of the lining of membrane of the lower bowel. This is a simple statement of fact."[52] Such were the results of the colonial free market's operations, grounded as these were on the inexorable and self-contained logics of equations and ledgers, backed by administrative rationality.

As Parama Roy notes, popular Malthusian theories of demographic rise and fall, complete with the figuration of famine as a strangely apocalyptic phenomenon, only serve to foster acquiescence, even today. While Malthus, in *Essay on the Principle of Population,* combines seemingly contradictory figurations—theological as well as secular/rational—this unholy alliance between what Mary Poovey has called "figures of speech" and "figures of arithmetic" in Malthus's work renders extreme death and hunger inevitable.[53] The famine as eschaton is a figuration, then, that is both secular and religious, and, in turn, science in the form of instrumental reason finds its own eschatology. The mathematical and rational inexorabilities that are written into the Malthusian description of the world also make way for the performative actions or inactions that its account of the world enables in the face of mass calamity. Difference—in the case of the Madras famine, racial difference—ensures that economic policies can be conducted under the sign of such overdetermined eschatology; difference is the pivot that turns the management of life into the management of death.

What does one make, then, of the appeals to sympathy found in the letters about the Madras famine to newspaper editors, in publications for Christian children, and in newspaper editorials and periodicals during the Madras famine? While Amit Rai makes a convincing case that sympathy functions as window dressing for colonialist extraction, what interests me about sympathy is not its potential contradiction or contiguity with the bureaucratic–rational inexorabilities but its status as an affect and a technology of social cohesion.[54] The mass cultural discourse on sympathy was often but not always paired with appeals to Christian charity or Christian principles, but such appeals rarely entered the bureaucratic–rational sphere of existing government policy. In part this can be explained by the gradual secularization of the English state over the course of the nineteenth century, in which the state loosened restrictions barring non-Anglicans from holding office, attending certain universities, and so on, and citizenship rather than the religious fold increasingly became the "protective" mantle of state policy. In the colonies, England's official policy was always one of religious neutrality, and the colonial state distanced itself from the proselytizing efforts of missionaries. As Gauri Viswanathan puts it, England's policy "substituted 'Englishness' for 'Christianity' as the defining principle of subjecthood, even while retaining the moral foundations of Christianity."[55] Hence Macaulay's famous 1835 minute on Indian education, in which he exhorts the colonial state to adopt an education policy that would produce subjects who would be "Indian in blood and colour, but English in taste, in opinions, in morals, and in intellect."[56] In light of educational reform, the official aim of the civilizing mission, from the perspective of the colonial state in the nineteenth century, became molding subjects according to the dictates of Englishness. Religious subjectivity, in the view of administrative rationality, became a matter of private belief. Hence in England religious minorities previously excluded through various civil restrictions were emancipated into the English nation by the end of the nineteenth century.

Bureaucratic rationality became the purview of the state, and as Max Weber explains, such instrumental rationality seeks "the elimination of all those emotional and irrational manifestations of personal religion."[57] While faith, from the point of view of such an administrative attitude, becomes privatized, it does not disappear from public view. The appeals to sympathy and Christian benevolence in mass culture constitute a discourse similar to the phenomenon that Lauren Berlant has called the "intimate public," a sphere in which sentimentality reigns supreme, participants assume a common lived experience, and participation holds out the promise of a certain form of social belonging: the intimate public "flourishes as a porous, affective scene of identification among strangers that promises a certain experience of belonging and provides a complex of consolation, confirmation, discipline, and discussion about how to live as an *x*."[58] In true Smithian fashion, the appeals to sympathy in English newspapers and periodicals call out for identification with the other, and through this identification they secure and affirm a sense of belonging in a benevolent nation. The letters concerning the Madras famine from one Reverend Lord Sidney Godolphin Osborne of Durweston (Dorset), who regularly wrote as a concerned citizen to the *Times* between 1844 and 1888 on a variety of subjects, display a remarkable awareness of the place of faith, bureaucracy, and sympathy in England. In one letter published on March 11, 1874, at the height of the Bengal famine, Osborne writes:

> Official work leaves little margin for sentiment; it is not, perhaps, a hard and fast line of benevolent action, but it must in its nature be so far hard, so far limited, in that it has to guard, as a trustee of national funds, against anything and everything which may either foster imposition or lead to extravagant expenditure. . . .
>
> . . . Christian benevolence stops not to inquire whether famine or pestilence came on the sufferer through his own negligence or imprudence; it asks not how he came to be travelling the road which led to either; it finds him in want of bread or healing, it cannot let him die if it has bread or medicine to give him. . . .
>
> . . . I trust, then, English sympathy may now rouse itself to the high and holy task of seeking to aid [the vicerory's] efforts by supplementing the means [the viceroy in India] officially has to take to save life.[59]

Osborne's concatenation of premises ties the virtues of Christian benevolence to the discourse of sentiment and nationhood in one fell swoop: individual striving toward Christian virtue is an indispensable supplement to the nation's functioning (n.b., the sympathy to be attained is English sympathy), since bureaucratic state institutions (official work) must leave little margin for sentiment. Like the editorials on the Indian famines aimed at Christian children in the *Weslyan Juvenile Offering*, the aim here is to shape English subjects, who, even as they become legible as abstract citizens, can hone their affective connections with other virtuous citizen–subjects by sympathizing with dying Indians. Sympathetic mimesis ends in becoming a virtuous citizen–subject; sympathy as a technology of the self perfects that self's assimilation into the fold of (Christianized) citizenship, and to this end, scenes of Indian suffering provide opportunities for productive suffering that forges a better self who can lay claim to a place in the fold. The *Weslyan Juvenile Offering* and other publications of this intimate public of sympathy regularly printed drawings of famine victims based on Hooper's photographs.

Osborne also astutely compares victims of national wars to famine victims in India in an illuminating letter published on August 23, 1874, in the *Times*. Having witnessed the devastating effects of the Corn Law Act (1815) and the Acts of Enclosure, the death of servicemen in the Napoleonic Wars, and the terrible harvests of 1834–35, which exacerbated the condition of the already malnourished and starving farmworkers in his Dorset parish, he writes, "To myself . . . having had some little personal means of observation in scenes where war and famine have dealt thousands to death, the daily pictures of my daily papers appear in somewhat different lights from those in which many regard them."[60] He notes that pictures from the war front depict scenes of English courage, and though people are saddened by the death of soldiers, such sacrifices are acceptable, since war is seen by the public to stem "from causes held to be necessary," much like the social anesthesia called upon by Greary.[61] In contrast,

> I shall not wonder, Sir, if . . . the calmer wave of famine destruction may not carry the appeal to our hearts it ought to do. All that gilds over war—its reports of brave deeds and bold strategy—is here wanting; a people dies in silence save for the children's cry, who see not why they hunger. The victims fall here and there. Scarce sheltered by the home in ruin, they, like it, decay and fall; mere framework of the fed life, they faint to death; unwounded by the weapons of other war, want has poisoned the fountain of their life; yet these, thus fated in their tens of thousands—albeit not of our colour or our creed—*have the claim of countrymen on us, for they are fellow-subjects;* yes, and in all the dominions over which the British Queen rules, no subjects are to be found who more patiently have fought the battle of life under her rule.
>
> Let us then look to it, and that at once, that the compassion which can beget the charity which takes *English alms* to the victims of war, forget not that there is urgent need for its instant exercise, to the fullest, to aid that fund now raising, by which we may hope, with God's blessing, yet to snatch thousands of our kind from a fate, begotten not of national ambition

> or political intrigue, but simply from a visitation of Providence, to which we ourselves any year may be liable.[62]

Osborne notes that waging peace, in the sense of Baron von Clausewitz's notion of "Real War," in which war appears suspended ("peace time") but is in fact a kind of ever-present potentiality, has its own bleak images to show us. The victims of famines are the casualties of Real War as opposed to "Absolute War" (the deployment of armies, battles won and lost), and if sympathy extends easily to soldiers because ideologies of nationhood might secure it, then one must find grounds for sympathy with the victims of Real War as well. Osborne invokes the claim of countrymen, the fact of Indian famine victims being fellow subjects as the basis for extending to them English alms. But fellow feeling for dying Indians is also necessary, since both Indians and the English are subject to a deadly visitation of Providence. In the intimate public sphere of colonial sympathy, Osborne's argument relies on nation and God concurrently to legitimize the affect of sympathy he is simultaneously at pains to invoke and to produce in the reader.

Osborne produces sympathy through thick descriptions of famine's toll on the human body. Hunger reduces people to the sheer materiality of their bodily substance and lends a certain listlessness to their expression, draining it of affect altogether:

> [The] panic arising from the sense that what they [famine victims] now suffer from some want is but the foretaste of what they must come to from want of all, works to produce an apathy of mind, which, casting aside all hope, depressing all mental energy, becomes in itself a disease, as an auxiliary of death most powerful.[63]

> There is a listless apathy begotten of famine that seems to paralyse brain and limb. There is a stage when the heart cares not to seek the food to save the life, panic-stricken to a degree which almost courts death. It is a disease, this unfed hunger, which comes gradually on a whole household; they waste in common, and as they waste the fate which is on all seems to lose any terror for any one.[64]

This description of the loss of affect due to extreme hunger is meant to incite in us the affect of sympathy. Osborne's sympathy-inducing words, like the best kind of art according to Edmund Burke,[65] appeal to affect, bodily perception, and reason at the same time. While noting the reduction of the starving victim to his or her physical body, Osborne endows his readers with a whole body that is capable of linking together sensory perception, conceptual thought, and emotional response. The reader's body presumed by his text, in all of its experiential plenitude, is the opposite of the body presumed by a contemporary of his, the French physician Guillaume-Benjamin-Amand Duchenne de

Boulogne. Duchenne, as a part of his study of human facial expressions, experimented on his epileptic and mentally disabled patients at the Paris hospital La Salpêtrière by inducing certain emotional facial expressions in them by means of electrodes. His test subjects were reduced to a corporeal materiality, a point that Duchenne himself drives home by posing certain rhetorical questions. "Could not the isolated contraction of a muscle that presides over a particular emotion enable it to react on the soul, and produce an internal feeling that would provoke other involuntary contractions . . . ?" he asks in *The Mechanism of Human Facial Expression.*[66] If muscles, when stimulated, demonstrate a synergy with other muscles that are not actively stimulated, then might this be an index of deeper emotional shifts within the subject? Duchenne argues against this line of reasoning, pointing to his ample experiments conducted on the faces of cadavers, which yielded the same results given a particular point of muscle stimulation. By reducing the test subjects to sheer body (they may as well be dead), Duchenne lays the groundwork for a universalist argument: "The patterns of the human face cannot be changed, whether one stimulates them or actually produces them by an action of the soul; they are the same in all people, in savages and civilized nations, differing in the latter only by their moderation or exaggeration of certain traits."[67] The electrode is the earthly surrogate for the soul, not its replacement, and the experiments on cadavers prove that while the electrode cannot generate the soul, the universal nature of human expression is so deeply ingrained that it passes over into death.

Still, something about affect exceeds our narratives of it: Duchenne notes, regarding the look of sympathy (Figure 4.17), "When the smile of the lips is joined by the sweetest look that we have seen, in an instant we are irresistibly drawn by sympathy."[68] *We* the spectators, through some cause, are irresistibly drawn by the expression of kindness. Sympathy, employing a part of the face that Duchenne calls "the muscle of kindness," "is equally resistant to the will. It only obeys the sweet movement of the soul, which inspires a sympathetic gaze, as in [Figure 4.17]. This is one of nature's preventative measures, which has not permitted us to easily dissimulate or feign expressive lines, so that a man can distinguish his friends from his enemies."[69] The division of the socius between enemy and friend, that Schmittian figuration that proved so central to the cultural politics of the Sepoy Revolt, is congruent with the psychophysiological workings of sympathy, which, according to Duchenne, can help us regulate this division. Baruch Spinoza observed, about two hundred years before Duchenne's experiments, how sympathetic mirroring continues to affirm such divisions: "If we imagine someone like ourselves to be affected by an emotion, this thought will express an affection of our own body similar to that emotion. So from the fact that we imagine a thing like ourselves to be affected by an emotion, we are affected by a similar emotion along with

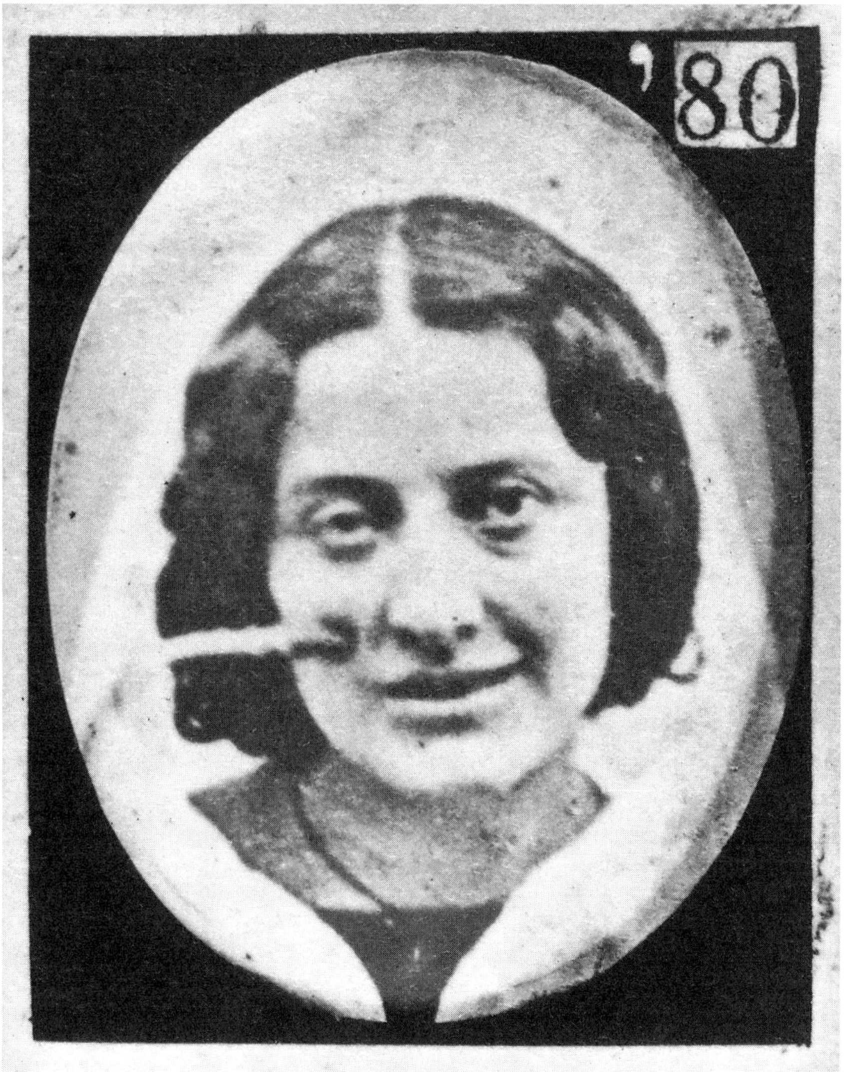

Figure 4.17. *Sympathy.* From Guillaume-Benjamin-Amand Duchenne, *Mécanisme de la physionomie humaine, ou, analyse électro-physiologique de l'expression des passions,* 1862. Wellcome Library, London.

it."[70] Hence the rhetorical strategies of Rev. Osborne's letters to the *Times,* making the case for Indian famine victims being on the "friend" side of the Schmittian divide, under the mantle of state and godly protection.

Such are the productive paradoxes of sympathetic identification: it is an irresistible tending toward the other and therefore an affirmation of the self; it acts as a binding agent within society and, as such, regulates the division of friends and enemies. Still, in all of these accounts of sympathy, from Smith and Burke to Osborne and Duchenne, as an affect, sympathy hovers in the space between perception and conception. If, as Burke says, sympathy is "antecedent to any reasoning," then where might the irresistible impulse we feel to mirror the expressions on another's face originate?

Affect and Referentiality

Whether the origin of emotions in the body is "the soul" (Duchenne) or the nourished bodily plenitude that can stitch together sensation and conception (Osborne), sympathy, as a shuttling between interior and exterior, makes it clear that however one imagines the origin of emotions, the body is a necessary but insufficient cause of them. Baruch Spinoza was among the first to claim this, starting with his elementary postulate in *The Ethics:* "The individual components of the human body itself, are affected by external bodies in a great many ways."[71] Spinoza uses the word *affectus,* often translated as *emotion* or *affect,*[72] to refer to a combination of a bodily state (perception) and its mental idea (conception), and made the study of *affectus* central to his discussion of ethics. If body and mind are, as Spinoza believes, two attributes of the same phenomenon and not separated as in a Cartesian fantasy, then the location of emotions in the interstices of bodily affections and mental ideas is hardly a mystifying observation.[73] Moreover, the "human body can undergo many changes and nevertheless retain impressions or traces of [external] objects." These traces take the form of physical changes or memory traces, and Spinoza refers to both kinds of traces as "images."[74] Given this subjection to the external world, in which sense perception actually begins (as trigger) and ends (as action), "those who believe that they speak, or keep silent, or do anything from free mental decision are dreaming with their eyes open."[75] The unity of sense perception and ideation, especially in the experience of *affectus,* highlights the subject's foundational lack of self-mastery, and the aim of *The Ethics* is to describe this lack of self-mastery and prescribe ways of working alongside it toward a conditioned form of freedom.

We are lacking in self-mastery because our freedom will always be checked, among other things, by emotional response, not because such responses are "antecedent to reason," as in Burkean aesthetics, but because they exist alongside reason, naming another dimension of experience and reminding us of our connection to the external world of objects and other people. Time and history are, in a certain sense, not operative in our emotional responses to stimuli, which always throw us into the present moment:

> As long as a man is affected by the image of a thing, he will regard the thing as present, even though it may not exist, and he does not think of it as past or future except in so far as its image is joined to the image of past or future time. Therefore the image of a thing, considered solely in itself, is the same

> whether it be related to the future, past, or present; that is, the state of the body, or the emotion, is the same whether the image be of a thing past or future or present. So the emotion of pleasure, and of pain, is the same whether the image be of a thing past or future or present.[76]

Our emotional responses reduce all time to the present time, and in the throes of a feeling, however fleeting, the image—whether it exists as an object in the world or is recalled by memory—insists on its simultaneity with us.

Spinoza's remarks allow us to locate the specificity of the photographic medium with respect to affective response; between words and photographs lies a vast difference in the functioning of sympathy. Compare, for example, Osborne's description of the effects of famine on the body and mind (the listless apathy, the draining of emotion) and John Shore's description of the Bengal famine in his poem, with Hooper's photographs of famine victims. Osborne's and Shore's words, insofar as they appeal to sympathy, presume that the person reading them can be appealed to on the level of both affect and reason simultaneously, that we readers, endowed with subjective plenitude, will in fact mirror the emotion of sympathy that produced these words in the first place. Sympathy is both a technology and an affect here; it is a technology because the words serve as access points through which we become similar to the writer, whom we experience as a string of words, and it is an affect because we are filled with a mixture of horror, sympathy, and possibly a willingness to act. In this relay of sympathetic replications, the writers themselves serve as the Smithian looking glass, the impartial spectator, in whom we are solicited to see ourselves. Like John Shore before him and like his contemporary Dr. Cornish in Madras, who bemoaned the lack of a photographer on hand, Rev. Sidney Osborne writes, "What I do feel is the difficulty of bringing home to the hearts and minds of my fellow-countrymen the real features of a famine-stricken people. No pen, I know, is really equal to the task."[77] As it happens, photography was already changing the very terms of sympathetic mimesis as Osborne wrote these words.

For example, Hooper's photographs of famine victims rely on a necessarily revamped order of sympathetic mirroring. In these photographs, the clear outlines of rib cages and the skeleton that lies beneath the skin, rather than the affectless faces, are the first things that strike our eyes. In Figures 4.4 and 4.6, our gaze settles first on the child sitting against the tree and on the group of victims in the foreground, respectively. In Figure 4.4, only if we look carefully do we see the emaciated baby at the foot of the child, and in Figure 4.6, the dark interior of the hut promises more scenes of starving bodies, whose outlines we can just barely discern. The more we look, in other words, the more we are reminded of additional victims not immediately present to the gaze, and the more we realize that we see only the most superficial, tiny aspect of a vast catastrophe. Looking at these bodies, we recognize how bodies, including our own, can be reduced to the merely physical and how this reduction is an ever-present possibility. Adam Smith notes that bodily feelings such as extreme hunger are not easily transmitted through the technology of sympathy: when we come across instances of others' extreme starvation, we sympathize with the experience, but because we "do not grow hungry" in reaction to such a scene, "we cannot properly, even in this case, be said to sympathize with their hunger."[78] And certainly the self-same view that all of Hooper's photographs of famine victims reveal to us can evoke only an ambivalent response that mirrors the paradoxical ambivalence of sympathy in the first place: although we are made aware of the finitude of our own embodied existence in the form of the "actually existing" emaciated bodies (the rhetoric of the indexical trace secures this fact), this recognition does not guarantee sympathy with the victims of the famine. The traces that these images leave on our own bodies are ambiguous. On the one hand, the extreme and sensational images accentuate the grotesque nature of the human body in extremis, displaying all that differentiates these bodies from the spectator, since the intimate publics in which these images circulate presume, like Osborne's letters to the *Times,* a whole and nourished spectator. On the other hand, the reduction to the body is a reminder, in the spirit of Duchenne, that the body with its unfortunate physical limits is that which we share with the famine victims. Famine photographs can begin the relay of sympathetic technology—the extension to the other that is an affirmation of one's self—but they do not in fact guarantee a referent for sympathetic mirroring.

A photograph does not provide a narrative, but only its opening terms—its stage, if you will. While actual narratives of sympathy inevitably provide an imaginary goal for our sympathetic mobility (the virtuous Christian subject, for example), the photograph does not provide a referent to be mirrored. *That* referent is the result of a narrative that might emplace the photograph in its own movement, but photographs of mass calamity, in themselves, do not guarantee such a referent. The textual figurations of the intimate public of colonial sympathy—poems about the famine, letters to newspaper editors, and so on—hail us to resemble as much as possible the sympathetic comportment of the writers (and by extension, the nation or the religious fold or both), and the famine victim is the critical point of mediation among a sympathetic, mobile, and intimate connection between writer and reader. This connection is forged through suffering: the suffering of the people described in the textual narrative also indicates the suffering of the writer who tells the narrative, and the reader is asked to mirror the writer's state. Such is the nature of language, which necessarily presumes a transaction between writer and reader, no matter how decentered the subjectivities of each. The point is not that words guarantee sympathetic identification (how could they?) but that the words of Osborne and Shore, for example, provide a referent and an end point for our sympathetic strivings, should such impulses be stirred. Sympathy in these famine photographs from the 1870s, remaining true to its ancient magical and mobile nature, traverses time and space to meet us in our own present moment, and if these photographs trigger an emotional reaction, then their subjects are, à la Spinoza, simultaneous with our present.

Yet the transformation that photography has effected in sympathy's technologies is that the mimetic referent that might guide our practices of emotional mirroring and resemblance has disappeared from the *structure* of the representation. As a result, these photographs unsettle us without offering the consolation of a completed sympathetic circuit. They confront us in the emotional simultaneity of our own present but without an attempt to mold the shape of our emotions. Such an open-ended affective response can transmute shock into horror or any form of (mis)recognition, of which sympathetic identification with the victims is only one possibility among many others. After all, if sympathetically suffering for the pain of others and bracing oneself in the face of such pain (because the other's pain may be seen to be inevitable, for example) are a hallmark of what some people call civilization or liberalism, then Hooper's famine photographs provide ample opportunities to practice one's civilizational or liberal drills. But nothing in the photographs determines the final destination of our sympathetic extension. If context, captions, and even a *sequence* of carefully selected photographs all attempt to provide such direction, to stabilize the mimetic referent of sympathetic mimesis, then this merely points to the differential nature of narrative (in the form of context and sequence) and text (in the form of captions) that attempt to reign in the open-endedness of photography's sympathetic magic.

One caption for any of Hooper's famine photographs could conceivably be these words from Walter Benjamin: "The deadening of the emotions, and the ebbing away of the waves of life which are the source of these emotions in the body, can increase the distance between the self and the surrounding world to the point of alienation from the body."[79] These words, which Benjamin used to describe melancholia, sound scandalously similar to the "listless apathy begotten of famine," which Osborne describes. Certainly the sympathetic relay that we encounter when we look at Hooper's famine photographs may well set us adrift in melancholia, producing an affect that is present in the frame but not in any literal sense. Photography enables sympathy to misfire like this because the referential status of its objects stands at the limits of meaning. Affects that result from photography are sympathetic mirroring, not necessarily in its perfected or failed form, but rather in its unforeseen form, and this is photography's danger and its saving grace.

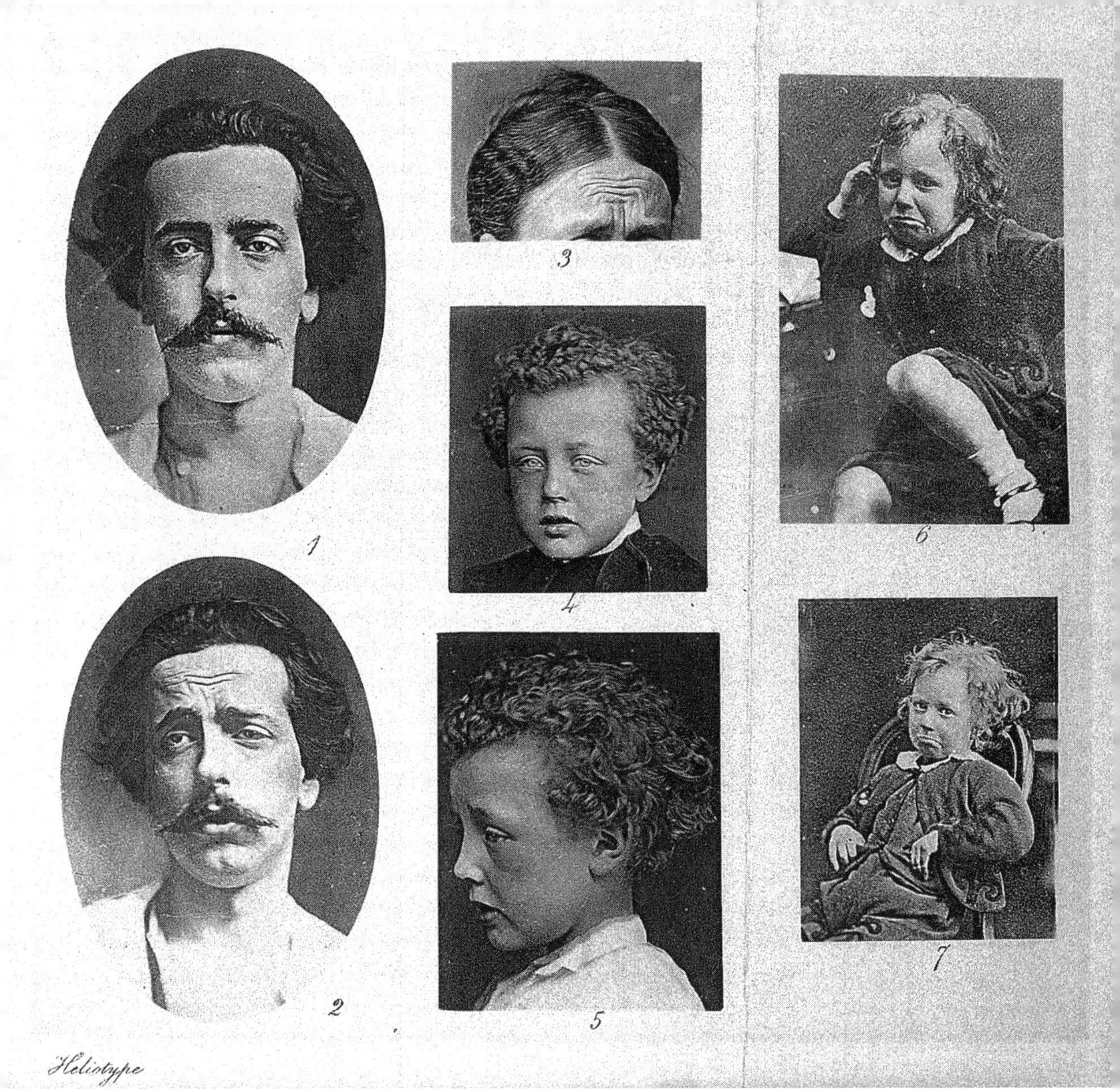

Figure C.1. *Grief.* From Charles Darwin, *The Expression of the Emotions in Man and Animals,* 1872. Wellcome Library, London. Figures 1 and 2 (on the left) are from Guillaume-Benjamin-Amand Duchenne, *Mécanisme de la physionomie humaine, ou, analyse électro-physiologique de l'expression des passions,* 1862. The man in the photographs is an actor, so there is no electrode in the image. Darwin notes that although his eyebrows do not contract as in unsimulated grief (shown in Figure 3, the upper image in the central column), the expression is "true" because audiences still read it as sorrowful.

CODA

Sensing the Past

> Knowledge is never categorical; it is always conditional. We can never be the past; it is only a spectacle before us, which is there for us to question. The questions come from us, and thus the responses in principle do not exhaust historical reality, since historical reality does not depend upon them for its existence.
>
> —Maurice Merleau-Ponty, "The Crisis of the Understanding"

> Instruction is the only nexus of the free union of the old with the new generation.
>
> —Walter Benjamin, letter to Gerhard Scholem, September 1917

THE PAST INCREASINGLY LEAVES ITS TRACES on our bodies in the form of images, and as Spinoza reminds us, we experience such traces as simultaneous with ourselves. Photography crystallizes some of these traces, and while it transforms our senses of truth, memory, and experience, it also relies upon and molds our affective capacities. Photographs are necessarily images of the past, and as we phenomenologically incorporate them into our bodily field, we do not necessarily feel this incorporation of the past as a fracturing of our present. We are accustomed to the simultaneity of our pasts with our present moment, because our bodies already inhabit a complex temporal field. Charles Darwin made this clear in his 1872 work, *The Expression of the Emotions in Man and Animals.* In this work he shares an anecdote at the end of his discussion on grief, concerning an old woman he observes on a train journey. She sits opposite him in the carriage, and as he looks at her he notices the contraction of the muscles around her lips—the *depressors anguli oris*—turning the ends of her lips downward, but the rest of her face remains perfectly placid. Darwin thinks to himself that the muscle contraction is in fact meaningless, and such twitches of the face can be misleading. However, he goes on to say:

> The thought had hardly occurred to me when I saw that her eyes suddenly became suffused with tears almost to overflowing, and her whole countenance fell. There could now be no doubt that some painful recollection, perhaps that of a long-lost child, was passing through her mind. As soon as her sensorium was thus affected, certain nerve-cells from long habit instantly transmitted an order to all the respiratory muscles, and to those around the mouth, to prepare for a fit of crying. But the order was countermanded by the will, or rather by a later acquired habit, and all the muscles were obedient, excepting in a slight degree the *depressors anguli oris.* The mouth was not even opened; the respiration was not hurried; and no muscle was affected except those which draw down the contours of the mouth.[1]

Although an account of grief, this is also an account of sympathy. In this woman's expression of grief Darwin sees his own, reflecting as he so often did on the death of his own long-lost child, ten-year-old Annie. Although the particular memory image that causes the woman's expression of grief is immaterial to Darwin's scientific observation, the sensitivity of that observation depends on Darwin's sympathetic extension to the woman. The source of her grief, of course, remains a mystery, but the manifestation of her memory triggers Darwin's own recollection, and the will that keeps closed the floodgates of grief, too, is intimately familiar to Darwin.[2] In his work on emotions Darwin relied extensively on Guillaume-Benjamin Duchenne's studies and even reprinted many of Duchenne's photographs (see Figure C.1), omitting the electrode when the photograph was rendered into a drawing. Darwin's account of human and animal emotions thus undeniably ties emotional responses, including responses of laughter and joy, to the past. Several pasts remain in play in any given expression of emotion, because these expressions are conditioned by phylogenetic as well as ontogenetic histories: the involuntary movements of humans' muscles obey a trajectory of time stretching back to the descent from older life forms (what Darwin calls "long habit" in the above passage); yet these involuntary responses are modified in the recent history of natural selection (so that screaming modulates into weeping, for example); over the course of a single lifetime one learns the mechanisms of control over the expression of emotions. While a bodily surplus occasionally may escape, the attempt at control might become a part of the emotion's expression. Our expression of emotions, including sympathy, invokes the time of the species and the time of the individual simultaneously; emotional expressions are complex snapshots of various times past that form the field of emergence for our individual paroxysms.

Walter Benjamin, in his concern with the historical transformation of perception, regenerated Darwin's project on a historical materialist ground.[3]

Benjamin notes in his reflections on modern experience that sympathetic mirroring in modernity can also take the form of the smile that crosses strangers' faces as they walk past each other on a busy street, a smile that Benjamin dubbed a "mimetic shock absorber."[4] Here sympathy becomes a form of mutual protection, since the smile is talismanic: it wards off contact, embodying an aversion to shock. Rather than a conduit for joy from one body to another, this smile serves as a social anesthetic. In this smile emotional expression does not match the feeling a smile would normally signify. In his experiments Duchenne discovered a disjuncture between the stimulation of facial muscles that produce expressions of joy or terror, even on the faces of cadavers, and the movements of the "soul" that flood the living body with emotion. Benjamin's account of the fragmentation of experience under modernity uncovers a similar and widening gap between bodily expression and feeling, and he famously placed his hopes in film and other visual technologies that he imagined could retrain the human sensorium for its changed environment, not to recover an Edenic plenitude of expressive feeling, but to forge ahead into new forms of sensory organization.

In Darwin's anecdote the visible expression of emotion exactly coincides with a feeling that was simultaneous with it, but Benjamin points to instances in which expression does not coincide with its proper feeling (or its "truth") as exemplary of modern experience. Shock threatens to transform forever the relation between expressions and emotions, which have coincided with one another throughout the long history of the species. Such a historical disjuncture, I would suggest, is contiguous with a simultaneous crisis in perception that created a cleavage between appearance and truth, and this crisis was already under way at the time that Darwin was writing. Fredric Jameson has described this crisis in terms of the developmental stages of capitalism (another narrative of the past and another explanation of how we came to be who we are). He argues that the deepest aesthetico-political problem of our contemporary age is a phenomenological one: the historical stages of capitalist development have caused a growing rift (starting with later stages of market capitalism) between experience and truth, such that our phenomenological experience of the world no longer coincides with the determinations that govern that experience. In earlier stages of market capitalism, immediately perceptible reality could encompass the "true economic and social form," but this begins to change as the organization of capitalism itself changes:

> At this point the phenomenological experience of the individual subject—traditionally, the supreme raw materials of the work of art—becomes limited to a tiny corner of the social world, a fixed-camera view of a certain section of London or the countryside or whatever. But the truth of that

> experience no longer coincides with the place in which it takes place. The truth of that limited daily experience of London lies, rather, in India or Jamaica or Hong Kong; it is bound up with the whole colonial system of the British Empire that determines the very quality of the individual's subjective life. Yet those structural coordinates are no longer accessible to immediate lived experience and are often not even conceptualizable for most people. There comes into being, then, a situation in which we can say that if individual experience is authentic, then it cannot be true; and that if a scientific or cognitive model of the same content is true, then it escapes individual experience.[5]

Hence, according to Jameson, the modernist experimentations with form and the continuing postmodernist experimentation are symptomatic of an acute crisis in perception. An imagination that can simultaneously map local political struggle onto the larger social and global totality in a reliable form would be an imagination equal to the aesthetic challenges of the most recent turns in capital's development. This is why Jameson writes that "achieved cognitive mapping will be a matter of form,"[6] since aesthetic forms are phenomenological templates for experience, molding it and reflecting it at the same time. Such a crisis in perception cannot be remedied at the level of empiricism—for example, by simply providing the "truth" of the nineteenth-century experience of London in the form of images and data from India, Jamaica, or Hong Kong. What is missing at the heart of modernity's experience is not a lack of information as such but the capacity to see how information coheres. Only an aesthetic of what Jameson calls "cognitive mapping" might be capable of showing, for example, how images of Victorian London are connected, precisely, to images of Cawnpore and Lucknow and how the last two cities might be linked to circuits other than those originating in London.

Benjamin's hermeneutical method would have us take such appearances themselves—in the form of photographs in examples I have provided in the preceding chapters—seriously: "Resolute refusal of the concept of 'timeless truth' is in order. Nevertheless truth is not—as Marxism would have it—a merely contingent function of knowing, but is bound to a nucleus of time lying hidden within the knower and the known alike. This is so true that the eternal, in any case, is far more the ruffle on a dress than some idea."[7] The cleavage between appearance and truth that Jameson diagnoses is real, but it need not discredit appearance, because, after all, appearances are what we have at hand: the ruffle on the dress, whose shape or absence shifts with the repetitive cycles of fashion, offers insight into the shape of history itself and our own present moment. Whether or not the gap between appearance and essence can be bridged through an aesthetics of cognitive mapping, appearances are so readily at our disposal, and, like expressions of emotions, appearances contain within them precipitates of various pasts even as we encounter them as simultaneous with us in the present.

This book was written in the United States after 9/11, in a period in which mourning yet again fell prey to its appropriation by war machines, when metropolitan cultures deemed only certain lives properly grievable, and photography from Abu Ghraib, in its advanced digital phase, revealed atrocities born of an age-old obsession with religious humiliation. None of this is news anymore. If, in Benjamin's words, our amazement that such things are "still possible" is not the "beginning of knowledge,"[8] then the start of the twenty-first century has already shown the additional relevance of Benjamin's related insight on the catastrophe that is history: "That it 'keeps going on like this' *is* the catastrophe."[9] How is one to approach, then, the treadmill of past failures that constitute history? If our phenomenological experiences can provide us with authenticity but not truth, then how do we go about refunctioning the pasts we have inherited? In the aggregation of the visual that is a hallmark of modernity, the problem for knowledge is not what this visual field conceals but the ways of being in the world that it makes possible and that it is the task of thought to excavate. What we must gaze upon is the silently stubborn past in the form of its appearances. The epigraph by Merleau-Ponty reminds us that the past, which is "only a spectacle before us," can never be exhausted by the questions we pose to it and the responses we mine from it.[10] It remains autonomous in spite of us, and this is why Benjamin had so little faith in a history that "showed things 'as they really were.'"[11] The recognition that we will never know the past as it really was also explains, in part, our current incapacity to map the present. Not only is lived experience no guarantee of truth, but the present itself has been transmitted by a past whose essence will elude us even if we were to suspect, as Benjamin does, that the past is unredeemed.

This obdurate and spectacular nature of the past and the forms of its transmission have been my primary concern in this book. The past may be a continuous tradition of catastrophe, but it is also a tradition that has a pedagogical dimension. In a 1917 letter to Gerhard Scholem, Benjamin describes the tradition of learning across generations:

> Knowledge becomes transmittable only for the person who has understood his knowledge as something that has been transmitted. He becomes free in an unprecedented way. The metaphysical origin of a Talmudic witticism comes to mind here. Theory is like a surging sea, but the only thing that matters to the wave (understood as a metaphor for the person) is to surrender itself to its motion in such a way that it crests and breaks. This enormous

> freedom of the breaking wave is education in its actual sense: instruction—tradition becoming visible and *free,* tradition emerging precipitously like a wave from living abundance.[12]

This enthusiasm for the historical passage of tradition seems, on the surface, to be discrepant with Benjamin's 1940 ruminations on the concept of history, in which he writes, "There is no document of culture which is not at the same time a document of barbarism, so barbarism taints the manner in which it was transmitted from one hand to another. The historical materialist therefore dissociates himself from this process of transmission as far as possible. He regards it as his task to brush history against the grain."[13] Brushing history against the grain is not to stand outside it but to surrender oneself, like the wave, to the tradition of education that history also contains. The nucleus of time that resides in the knower and the known, between the present and the past, allows truth to be revealed for the present. Benjamin placed his faith in technological reproducibility, since not only did this reproducibility make it possible to rip images from the past, from the burden of their discreet contexts, so their truth could be grasped for the present, but it also contained the potential to retrain the human sensorium itself. Photographs exemplify both the obdurate nature of the past and the productive mobility that technological reproducibility enables. Since this mobility also opens up photographs to heretofore unknown significations—in short, the future—visual technologies provide us with the mechanisms for working with the catastrophes that we inherit, and in this book I have sought to show how photography might have something to teach us about the political formation of our own senses in a period of more wars. If instruction is, as Benjamin says, "the only nexus of the free union of the old with the new generation,"[14] then perhaps photographs still hold the potential for grasping such freedom. Since photographs access conception, sensation, and emotion simultaneously, this learning is not wholly conceptual and abstract; photographs make demands on our bodies and emotions, and their circulation across generations mirrors the movements of Benjamin's Talmudic metaphor: "The generations are like waves that roll into each other and send their spray into the air."[15] The instruction to be gleaned from the past, which is always complete without us, is as delicate and forceful as this spindrift.

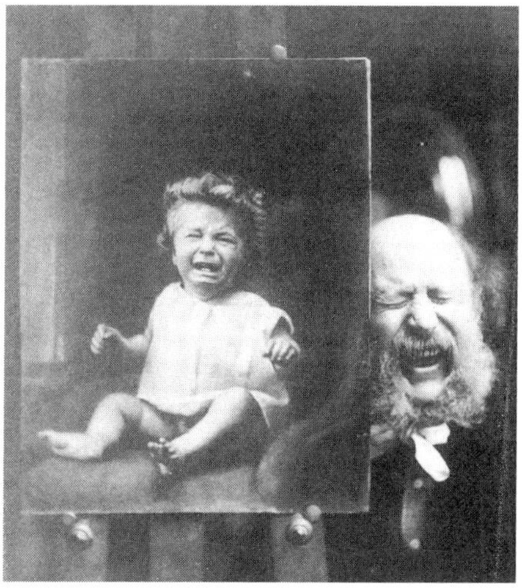

Figure C.2. Photographer Oscar Gustave Rejlander mirrors a baby in a photo session for Charles Darwin's *Expression of the Emotions in Man and Animals,* 1872. DAR 53.1 C.96. Reproduced by kind permission of the Syndics of Cambridge University Library.

Acknowledgments

THIS BOOK BEGAN with a conversation with Finbarr Barry Flood about Felice Beato's famous photograph from Sikanderbagh. The conversation snowballed into a graduate seminar paper for Natalie Melas and Susan Buck-Morss, both of whom kindly allowed me to submit the same paper for their seminars, thereby giving me the time to conduct extensive research and to fall under the spell of my first major academic obsession. I was soon writing a dissertation on colonial photography in India. I am grateful to Barry for sparking this interest in the first place and to Natalie and Susan for allowing me to explore where it might take me. I was fortunate to have the mentorship, encouragement, and patience of an eclectic and brilliant think tank as my dissertation committee at Cornell University: Susan Buck-Morss, Biodun Jeyifo, Natalie Melas, and Geoffrey Waite. None of these thinkers is known for following the paths of inherited doxa, and everything I have learned about the value of taking intellectual risks I learned from them.

Thanks are due as well to Sheetal Majithia, Lisa Brooks, and Joseph Campana for inspiring me since graduate school. A special thanks is due Iftikhar and Elizabeth Dadi, who followed this project from its first foray to its current form. Iftikhar has been a particularly important interlocutor and read multiple versions of the chapters. At the University of Washington (Seattle), my colleagues Eva Cherniavsky, Tom Foster, Gillian Harkins, Chandan Reddy, Caroline Simpson, Nikhil Singh, Alys Weinbaum, and Kathleen Woodward supported the book with their friendship and intellectual generosity.

At Princeton University, Eduardo Cadava, Anne Cheng, Jeff Dolven, Diana Fuss, Simon Gikandi, and Michael Wood generously shared their expertise and pushed the project forward at key moments. I will forever be grateful to Ben Conisbee Baer and Gayle Salamon, both for their friendship and for their feedback on the first draft of the Introduction; together, they grasped my intentions better than I had done myself and helped to reorient the project in an exciting direction. Daphne Brooks, Mia Fineman, Devin Fore, Sophie Gee, Brooke Holmes, Michael Jennings, Claudia Johnson, Deborah Nord, Jeff Nunokawa, Sara Rivett, Esther Schor, Joel Smith, Valerie Smith, Susan Stewart,

Alexandra Vasquez, and Tamsen Wolff supported the project in more ways than they know. Thanks are due, as well, to Patricia Doskoczynski, Christine Faltum, Pat Guglielmi, Kevin Mensch, Karen Mink, Marcia Rosh, and Nancy Shillingford for making it all run so smoothly—and for their good humor. I am grateful to Michael Barry for coming to the rescue with translations of the Farsi inscriptions in Plates 11 and 12, at short notice and with meticulous attention to details. Heartfelt thanks to my amazing fellow traveler and friend Meredith Martin. My tireless and brilliant research assistants and editors, Sarah Wasserman and Emily Hyde, went above and beyond the call of duty, not least by making themselves available at the last minute, especially in the final year of the manuscript preparation. Their own work, as well as that of Ellen Smith, continues to nourish me intellectually. I thank the graduate students in my seminars, who have taught me so much, both at the University of Washington and at Princeton.

Generous readers who took time to offer me feedback include Anjali Arondekar, Mrinalini Chakravorty, Rey Chow, Kajri Jain, Fredric Jameson, and Christopher Pinney. A special thanks is due Sangeeta Ray for her incisive feedback and her ample generosity with both her time and her intellect. Thanks to Robyn Wiegman's Seattle sojourns, I benefited from her feedback as well as her friendship during my time there. Thanks are in order for Dana Seitler's and Jonathan Flatley's exciting provocations and questions during a campus interview at Wayne State University, which became formative to the shape *Afterimage of Empire* would take. No words can convey the gratitude I owe Geeta Patel, an ideal interlocutor who can enter fully into any thought with someone, no matter how far removed from her own interests; conversations with her have been indispensable, from dissertation to this final publication.

Writing a book is like running a marathon: it requires people to cheer one on. For sustaining me with friendship and brilliance so that I could write at all, I am grateful to Albert Aurand, Ben Conisbee Baer, Hristina Dantcheva, Nishchaya Gera, Darlene Lee, Gerard Mannion, Meredith Martin, Tilar Mazzeo, Jesnee Mohamed, Gayle Salamon, Siona Wilson, and Catherine Zimmer. They are my bedrock and my home base. A special thanks to Darrell C. Greene for teaching me the importance of learning things outside the bounds of a book, so that I could finish writing this one. Hacho and Deanna Bohossian, Torrence Boone, Lucinda Broadbent, Ted Chapin, Krzysztof Czuba, Thomas Dobrowolski, Murad Hajeebhoy, Pejman Hanafi, James Hermelbracht, Aly Kassam-Remtulla, Mark Leininger, Irene Leung, Marc Marin, Graeme Napier, Geoffrey Prentiss, Jasbir Puar, Frank Joseph Rudy, and Louise Scott provided encouragement and much-needed diversion. Clark Worswick's generosity, with both his knowledge and his photograph collection, knows no bounds. Thanks to Mindy Bacharach, Jennifer Burch, and Nikki Costello for keeping me focused. Thanks to Daniel Hendrickson for sharing his expertise in the subtleties of German. A special thanks to Régina Aurand for her persistent queries about whether or not the book was finished and for sweetening her persistence with impeccably prepared meals in a Provençal home.

I am grateful to Philip Stearns, in memoriam, whose mentorship and friendship about twenty years ago showed me the way that led to an academic path. I miss him dearly. Thanks as well to Stephen Purdy for cheering me on alongside Philip. Thanks to Anindyo Roy for his brilliance and his mentorship. Thanks are due my family, those who have put up with my idiosyncrasies the longest: Saeeda and Ismail Syal, Sajida and Habib Chaudhary, Zahida and Shahzad Chaudhary, Ejaz and Kim Chaudhary, Sajjad and Asia Chaudhary, Imtiaz and Shamim Chaudhary, Javed and Shahida Chaudhary, and most recently, Hidayat ur-Rahman. This book is dedicated to my parents: my father, Chaudhary Muhammad Rafiq (1933–2009), who read chapter 2 in its published form years ago and looked forward to the publication of this book, and my mother, Razia Begum Rahman, who will be thrilled to hold it in her hands despite its imperfections.

I am grateful to the many patient librarians at Cornell, Princeton, the British Library (particularly the staff in the Prints, Drawings, and Photographs Division of the India and Africa Collections), the New York Public Library, and the Avery, Butler, and Burke libraries at Columbia University. Thanks to Rahaab Allana and Joyoti Roy at the Alkazi Foundation for the Arts in Delhi for their assistance and efficiency in providing so many photographs for the book. Marie-Louise Collard of the Wellcome Institute facilitated the copyright and permissions process.

I would like to thank the anonymous readers of Duke University Press, whose careful suggestions and encouragements made this a better book than it would have been, and to Ken Wissoker for his enthusiasm and understanding. I am grateful to the readers for the University of Minnesota Press (Marian Aguiar and an anonymous reader) for their meticulous and close reading of the manuscript and for their help in improving it. Marian kindly agreed to read more at my request during the revision process. I thank my editor, Richard Morrison, for his unwavering interest in this book, for engaged and invaluable conversations, and also lightning-fast efficiency in assisting me to bring the content to fruition. I am grateful to him and to Erin Warholm-Wohlenhaus, Laura Westlund, and Rachel Moeller: I could not have asked for a better team. Thanks to Robin Whitaker, copy editor extraordinaire, for significantly improving the book, and to Bonnie Hanks for compiling the index. All defects and imperfections in the book are, of course, my own doing.

Afterimage of Empire would not have been possible without the generous support of research grants: at Cornell University, from the Mario Einaudi

Center for International Studies, FLAS Fellowship, and the Sage Graduate Fellowship; at the University of Washington, the Simpson Center for the Humanities provided both time and research funds; at Princeton University, the University Committee on Research in the Humanities and Social Sciences funded research trips abroad, and the Donald A. Stauffer Bicentennial Preceptorship allowed a year off from teaching so I could finish the book. The American Council of Learned Societies (ACLS) also granted a year of support at a critical stage of writing, and a subvention from the Barr Ferree Foundation Fund for Publications, at Princeton University, helped to make publication possible.

Appendix: Translations

Translation of Proclamation Attributed to Nana Sahib (picked up by English troops in July 1857) (Figure 1.10)

Translation modified from Francis Cornwallis Maude and John Walter Sherer, *Memories of the Mutiny,* volume 2 (1894)

A traveller, who has just arrived in the city of Cawnpore from Calcutta, has informed that before serving out the cartridges for the purpose of taking away the religion of the people of India, the Sahibs met in council, and that this was the council's final decision. Since this is a matter of religion, [it was decided that] seven or eight thousand European soldiers and Englishmen, and fifty thousand Indians will be killed, and then the whole of India will be Christianized. A letter to this effect was sent to Queen Victoria, and her approval of the plan was received. A second council was held and some English merchants were also members of this Council.

This was determined: that assistance should be sought for English [*gora,* literally "white"] troops, in proportion to the strength of Indian troops; so that when the rebellion gained head the British would not get the worst of it. When that letter was read in England, thirty-five thousand English *[gora]* troops were quickly embarked in ships, and dispatched to India. The news of their departure reached Calcutta, and then the order was given out in Calcutta to distribute the cartridges, for the whole object was to Christianize the Indian army; once the army was Christianized, there would be no delay in Christianizing all the people of India, and the cartridges were made up with the fat *[charbi]* of pigs and cows. This information was received from the Bengalis who were employed in manufacturing the cartridges, and of those who blew the whistle on this plan, one was sentenced to death, and the remainder to imprisonment. So these people [the English] were making such plans here [in India]; while there [in London] the Ambassador of the Sultan of Turkey sent information from London to his Sultan, that 35,000 soldiers were about to be sent from England to India to Christianize it.

The Sultan of Turkey issued a *Firman* [royal request] to the Pasha of Egypt, of which the following was the report: "You are at peace with Queen Victoria. This is not a time for peace; because I have been informed by my Ambassador that 35,000 English troops have been dispatched to India to Christianize its army and its people. Under these circumstances if it is still possible to prevent them, and I am negligent, how shall I show my face before God? The same thing will happen some day to me; for, if the English Christianize India, they will also try to do the same to my country."

When the Pasha of Egypt received the *Firman* from the Sultan of Turkey, and before the arrival of English troops, he assembled and formed his own army near Alexandria—for that is the route to India. Immediately as the English troops arrived, the Pasha of Egypt opened fire on them with his cannons from all sides, and destroyed the ships and sank them, so that not a single European *[gora]* escaped. The English in Calcutta, after issuing the order for biting the cartridges, and in light of the intensifying rebellion, were in expectation of the troops from London, but God Almighty, in His mighty power, had already disposed of them. When the news of the troops' destruction arrived, the Governor General [of India] was extremely grieved, and beat his head. At night he was making plans for death and plunder; in the morning he had neither a body nor a head for a crown. By one turn of the lotus-like heavens, neither Nadir was its place, nor was there a Nadir.

Printed by the order of His Excellency the Peishwah, 13th Zilkadah, in the year 1273, Hijra.

Transliteration and Translation of Farsi Inscriptions in Plates 11 and 12

Courtesy of Michael Barry

Plate 11

Lambar 32: Shabîh-i mubârak-i Hazrat-i Abu-l-Mansûr Nâsiruddîn, Sikandar Jâh, Bâdshâh-i 'Âdil, Qaysar-i Zamân, Sultân-i 'Âlam, Muhammad Wâjid 'Alî Akhtar Shâh-i Oudh, Ghâzî, khallada Allâhu mulkahu wa saltanatahu, kih ba'd-i infirâgh az hammâm, bâ mû-hâ-yi gushâda bâlâ-yi dûsh-ô sînah-i mubârak andâkhta, Tâj-i akhtar-pasand bar sar-i mubârak-ô mâlâ-yi [?] marwârîd dar gulû-ô dastband-i marwârîd dar dast-i mubârak zayb farmûda, wa libâs-i Hindî dar bar-ô rû-mâl-i pur-zar dar kamar basta, wa bâlâ-yi Kursî-i murassa' dast-i râst-râ ba-pahlû-yi râst chaspânîda, zûr-i badan andâkhta-ô angushtân-i dast-i mubârak-râ bar chûb-i râst-i Kursî nihâda, ba-Irâda-yi mawzûn farmûdan-i shi'r tashrîf mîdârand. Sinn-i mu'allâ bist-o noh, sâl-i 1271-i Hijrî, mutâbiq-i sinna-yi 9-i julûs-i maymanat-i ma'nûs. 'Amal-i Bayt-us-Saltanat-i Lakhnaw.

Number 32: The blessed depiction of His Reverence Abu-l-Mansûr Nâsiruddîn, the Alexander in Majesty, the Just Emperor, the Caesar of the Age, the Sultan of the World, Muhammad Wâjîd 'Alî Akhtar, King of Oudh, the Victorious for the Faith, may God render forever his rule and sultanate, who after the cleansing of the bath, with hair unloosened over his blessed shoulders and breast, ordered his blessed head to be adorned with the crown pleasing unto the stars, along with a collar *[mâlâ]* of pearls about his neck, and a bracelet of pearls around his blessed hand, and Indian clothing upon his person [literally: chest or breast], and a gold-worked sash bound around his waist; upon the gem-studded throne he affixed his right hand, lodged thereupon his strong body, and placed the fingers of his blessed hand upon the right armrest of the throne. With weighty [or measured] will, he commands that the nobility of poetry be brought forth. The august age is twenty-nine, the year 1271 of the Hijra, corresponding to the 9th year of the auspicious and [divinely] beloved enthronement. Done in the Royal Palace, Lucknow.

Plate 12

Shabîh-i Nawwâb-i Râj Bêgum Sâhiba kih yakê az mamnû'ât-i Hazrat-i Sultân-i 'Âlam khallada Allâhu mulkahu wa saltanatahu and. Lêkin az jalsa-yi bêrûnî bâ pûshâk-i Hindî-i pur-zar-ô zêwar-hâ-yi murassa' dar dast-ô gûsh ârâsta, mû-bâf-i zarrîn-kâr chûb bar sar basta, ba-tasawwur mulâqât-i Hazrat-i Sultân-i 'Âlam khallada Allâhu mulkahu wa saltanatahu dar 'âlam-i jûsh-ô walwala, bar Kursî-i nuqra nishasta. Ba-sinn-i bîst-ô sih, sâla-yi 1271-i Hijrî, mutâbiq-i sinna-yi 9-i julûs-i maymanat-i ma'nûs. 'Amal-i Bayt-us-Saltanat-i Lakhnaw.

Depiction of the Deputized one [vicereine = *nawwâb*], Râj Bêgum Sâhiba, who is one of the Forbidden Ladies *[mamnû'ât]** of His Reverence the Sultan of the World, may God render forever his rule and sultanate. But she sits outside [the women's quarters] wearing a gold-encrusted Indian dress and her hands and ears adorned with studded gems, a wooden gold-work diadem comb affixed upon her head, having come forth into this world of boil-and-turmoil *[jûsh-ô walwala]* for the purpose of depiction *[tasawwur]* to meet His Reverence the Sultan of the World, may God render forever his rule and sultanate. She sits upon a silver throne at the age of twenty-three, the year 1271 of the Hijra, corresponding to the 9th year of the auspicious and [divinely] beloved enthronement. Done in the Royal Palace, Lucknow.

*This Farsi word is akin to *Pardanashin,* or "maintaining the veil," in Urdu.

Notes

Introduction

1. As Malcolm MacDougall writes, "Meaning is produced by our whole bodies, not just by conscious thought. We see with our bodies, and any image we make carries the imprint of our bodies; that is to say, of our being as well as the meanings we intend to convey." MacDougall, *The Corporeal Image,* 3.

2. Marx and Engels, *The Economic and Philosophic Manuscripts of 1844 and the Communist Manifesto,* 109, translation modified.

3. Graham, *The Life and Work of Sir Syed Ahmed Khan,* 188–89.

4. *Allygurgh Institute Gazette,* December 23, 1869.

5. For a recent and subtle discussion of the colonial archive, see Arondekar, *For the Record.*

6. Work on colonial discourse analysis is extensive, and some of the most astute examples of this line of thinking include Timothy Mitchell, Gyan Prakash, Anne McClintock, Zeynep Celik, and Paul Greenhalgh.

7. The following works on colonial photography show both the insight and limit of this line of thinking. See Hight and Sampson, *Colonialist Photography;* Maxwell, *Colonial Photography and Exhibitions;* and Edwards, *Raw Histories.*

8. For an alternate critique of this strand of postcolonial thought, see Dutta, *The Bureaucracy of Beauty,* 9–16.

9. Taylor and Great Britain, India Office, *The People of India,* i.

10. Pinney discusses at length the Indian-owned photographic studios of the nineteenth century, which sustained their business by making photographic portraits in fairly conventional forms borrowed from the British portraiture tradition. See Pinney, *Camera Indica,* 72–107.

11. Dobson, quoted ibid., 46.

12. Risley and Crooke, *The People of India,* Plate XX.

13. Ibid.

14. Ibid.

15. Anderson, *Imagined Communities,* 182–83.

16. Ibid., 184–85. Anderson is concerned with the production of the state-form under colonialism, a form that the postcolonial nation inherits, often without significant change in the geography, forms of local "heritage," and the systematic quantifications of the racial, ethnic, and religious contours of the population.

17. Benjamin, *Walter Benjamin: Selected Writings*, vol. 2: *1927–1934*, 328.

18. Barthes refers to the "punctum" as that element of a photograph that pierces the viewer, undoing both the scene of the photograph and the scene of viewing; Kracauer and Benjamin are interested in the spark of contingency in the photograph that is made possible only through a dialectic between the moment frozen in the frame and the moment of viewing. See, respectively, Barthes, *Camera Lucida;* Kracauer, *The Mass Ornament;* and Benjamin, *Walter Benjamin: Selected Writings*, vol. 2, "A Short History of Photography."

19. "It is through the camera that we first discover the optical unconscious, just as we discover the instinctual unconscious through psychoanalysis." Benjamin, *Walter Benjamin: Selected Writings*, vol. 4: *1938–1940*, 266.

20. This is as opposed to concepts preceding the object. Benjamin's approach is properly materialist and phenomenological.

21. Merleau-Ponty and Lefort, *The Visible and the Invisible*, 254, translation modified. In the original, "L'intouchable, ce n'est pas un touchable en fait inaccessible,—l'inconscient, ce n'est pas une representation en fait inaccessible. Le négatif n'est pas un *positif qui est ailleurs* (un transcendant)—C'est un vrai négatif." Merleau-Ponty and Lefort, *Le visible et l'invisible*, 307–8.

22. In an essay on Cézanne, Merleau-Ponty himself notes that looking through the camera means seeing a world whose subjective determination differs from the world we experience with the naked eye. He provides the example of a train, which, in a film, appears to approach and get bigger more rapidly than it would if seen without the camera's lens. The camera accentuates objective geometric relations among objects, relations that are not often visible to the naked eye: "To say that a circle seen obliquely is seen as an ellipse is to substitute for our actual perception what we would see if we were cameras: in reality we see a form which oscillates around the ellipse without being an ellipse." Merleau-Ponty, *Sense and Non-Sense*, 14. Also see Merleau-Ponty, *The Merleau-Ponty Aesthetics Reader*, "Eye and Mind."

23. Husserl, *The Essential Husserl*, 308.

24. Merleau-Ponty, *Phenomenology of Perception*, 167.

25. For the best account of *aisthēsis* in its Greek usage, see Heller-Roazen, *The Inner Touch*. Also see Eagleton, *The Ideology of the Aesthetic*.

26. The composite account I give here is based on the following: Trevelyan, *Cawnpore;* Shepherd, *A Personal Narrative of the Outbreak and Massacre at Cawnpore;* Thomson, *The Story of Cawnpore;* and A. Ward, *Our Bones Are Scattered*.

27. Trevelyan, *Cawnpore*, 229.

28. See Bernard Cohn's essay, "Representing Authority in Victorian India" in Cohn, *An Anthropologist among the Historians and Other Essays*. Ian Baucom notes, "In these acts of pilgrimage, the map of India was revealed not only as an instrument and product of war but as an artifact which, in wedding the emergent practices of tourism to the discourses of cartography and war, determined that the traveler in India was always the student of an imperial narrative of loyalty and betrayal." Baucom, *Out of Place*, 107.

29. Quoted ibid., 110.

30. Ibid., 101–35. For a corollary argument, also see Brantlinger, *Rule of Darkness*, "The Well at Cawnpore: Literary Representations of the Indian Mutiny," 199–226.

31. This theme is widespread in Kipling's stories, but especially foregrounded in "On the City Walls," "William the Conqueror," and "The Little House at Arrah." See chapter 4 in Arondekar, *For the Record,* 131–69. Also see Chakravarty, *The Indian Mutiny and the British Imagination.*

32. *Calcutta Review* (University of Calcutta, 1884), iv–v.

33. One eyewitness writes, "With merciless justice, the ten men were fastened to the muzzles of ten guns, which were charged with blank cartridge. The commanding officer directed the potfires to be lit. 'Ready! Fire!' and the drama was played out. The limbs of the slaughtered rebels were scattered, in all directions; their blood lay in one great pool under the cannon's mouth; and as the natives looked upon the scene, they 'not only shivered like aspen leaves, but changed into unnatural hues.'

"A lady, writing from Ferozepore, says: —'All the servants were compelled to witness the horrid scene; and though I naturally recoiled from the relation of it, one of my bearers insisted on giving a description to me in English, and said, 'Oh, mem-sahib, plenty of most fell on my shoulder—one man's leg!' I declined to hear the rest. Well were it if the mutiny then smouldering in other stations had also been suppressed by the blowing of ten men from the cannon's mouth, and the falling of a black man's leg upon a black man's shoulder. We were not always to get off so easy—nor were they." *Narrative of the Indian revolt from its outbreak to the capture of Lucknow,* 35.

34. Maude and Sherer, *Memories of the Mutiny,* vol. 1, 273.

35. Ibid., vol. 2, 467.

36. Dalrymple, *The Last Mughal,* 427. Sherer and Maude also record the particular brutality of Major Renaud: "In the first two days of our march towards Cawnpore we passed several dead bodies hanging from trees near the road. These had been executed by Renaud's men, presumably for complicity in the Mutiny; but I am afraid some innocent men suffered, for a comrade who ought to know says that 'Renaud was rather inclined to hang *all black creation.*' In every case, where the feet were near the ground, pigs (either wild or belonging to the villagers) had eaten the lower part of the bodies; the stench from the latter, in the moist still air, being intolerable." Maude and Sherer, *Memories of the Mutiny,* vol. 1, 41.

37. Taussig, *Mimesis and Alterity,* 67.

38. See ibid.

39. Stewart, *On Longing,* 138.

40. Susan Stewart explains, "You cannot make a copy of a scrapbook without being painfully aware that you possess a mere representation of the original. The original will supplant the copy in a way that is not open to the products of mechanical reproduction." Ibid., 139.

41. In Susan Stewart's words, "The nostalgic is enamored of distance, not of the referent itself." Ibid., 145. See chapter 3 for a discussion of Darogha Abbas Ali.

42. A detailed analysis of the photographic index will be presented in chapter 2.

43. No doubt these genres, too, demonstrate aspects of loss, but a too capacious understanding of loss renders the term meaningless.

44. Quoted in Morson and Emerson, *Mikhail Bakhtin,* 280.

45. Ibid., 106.

46. Also see Jameson, *The Political Unconscious,* 133–35. Given that genres are organs of memory, it makes sense that some early photographic genres relied on pictorial

tendencies inherited from painting and drama: staged historical scenes, mythological themes, still lifes, portraiture, etc.

47. Merleau-Ponty, *Phenomenology of Perception,* 167.

48. Ibid., 165. Gayle Salamon provides an innovative reading of this passage in Merleau-Ponty, in the context of racialized/colonized bodies. See Salamon, "'The Place Where Life Hides Away.'"

49. Merleau-Ponty, *Phenomenology of Perception,* 166.

50. Ibid., 165.

51. Bazin, "The Ontology of the Photographic Image," 7–8.

52. Bergson, *Matter and Memory,* ix.

53. Benjamin, *Walter Benjamin: Selected Writings,* vol. 2, 314.

54. For analyses of the photographic metaphor in Benjamin's critique of Bergson, see Marder, *Dead Time,* "Flat Death: Snapshots of History," 68–87. Also see Cadava, *Words of Light,* "Matter," 87–92.

55. This extract is from Benjamin, *Walter Benjamin: Selected Writings,* vol. 3: *1935–1938,* "Eduard Fuchs," 266.

56. Spivak, "Three Women's Texts and a Critique of Imperialism," 254.

57. Of course, Jain discusses the roots of Indian calendar art in the later nineteenth century, but her analysis of the vernacular focuses on the twentieth century. See Jain, *Gods in the Bazaar.* Interestingly, accounts of colonial photography in other colonial contexts also locate local differences of photographic practice in the twentieth century. See, among others, Gabara, *Errant Modernism;* Strassler, *Refracted Visions;* Lydon, *Eye Contact;* and Poole, *Vision, Race, and Modernity.*

58. See Stoler, *Along the Archival Grain.* Stoler's conclusions bear out Lenin's remarks in his 1917 work on imperialism, in which he argues precisely for the discontinuous and disorganized means by which imperialism functions. See Lenin, *Imperialism.*

59. Chow, *Sentimental Fabulations, Contemporary Chinese Films,* 148.

60. See Said, *Culture and Imperialism,* "Consolidated Vision."

61. Such histories have already been written with great rigor. See Dehejia, *India through the Lens;* Desmond and Great Britain, India Office, Library, *Victorian India in Focus;* Gutman and International Center of Photography, *Through Indian Eyes;* Ollman, *Samuel Bourne;* Pinney, *The Coming of Photography in India;* Pinney, *Camera Indica;* and Ryan, *Picturing Empire.* For an account of colonial Indian spectacle, see Mathur, *India by Design.*

1. Death and the Rhetoric of Photography

1. Tytler, *An Englishwoman in India,* 6.

2. Ibid., 149.

3. Ibid.

4. The game is a grisly form of the fort/da game that fascinated Freud in his ruminations on trauma, in *Beyond the Pleasure Principle,* except it is unclear in this case if the object is the blood of the mother or her capacity to be healed (and by extension, to heal).

5. Pinney, *The Coming of Photography in India,* 123.

6. Ibid., 132. But surely, as Eduardo Cadava notes, the object—even when "captured"—remains absent, since what one captures is an image, not an object. See Cadava, *Words of Light;* and Cadava and Cortés-Rocca, "Notes on Love and Photography."

7. See Peirce, Houser, and Kloesel, *The Essential Peirce.*

8. On situating the index as a deconstructive trace of absence-as-presence, see Cadava and Cortés-Rocca, "Notes on Love and Photography." On the intrusion of competing sign systems, see Mulvey, "The Index and the Uncanny." On the index as a false problem, see Elkins, *Photography Theory.* Also see *Differences: A Journal of Feminist Culutral Studies,* Special Issue on the Index, 18, no. 1 (2007); and Kelsey and Stimson, *The Meaning of Photography.*

9. Scholars of American Civil War photography, focusing on the work of photographers Matthew Brady and Alexander Gardner, demonstrate that even when dead bodies are present in the frame, they are in effect imagined, composed, and turned into spectacle. See Sweet, *Traces of War;* and Trachtenberg, "Albums of War."

10. Baer, *Spectral Evidence,* 181. Baer also writes compellingly about the work of Dirk Reinhartz and Mikael Levin, who photographed empty spaces that were the site of Nazi atrocities. See ibid., 61–85. On the photographic index and holocaust photography, see Didi-Huberman, *Images in Spite of All.*

11. As Eduardo Cadava's work persuasively shows, all photographs can be said to be figures of the corpse, and the link between photography and death can be made at multiple representational/affective registers. See Cadava, *Words of Light.*

12. "A very faithful drawing may actually tell us more about the model but despite the promptings of our critical intelligence it will never have the irrational power of the photograph to bear away our faith." Bazin, "The Ontology of the Photographic Image," 8.

13. I am influenced in my approach by Walter Benjamin's reading of the latest technological forms as refunctionings of archaic and mythic elements. This concern runs throughout Benjamin's oeuvre but is especially notable in *The Arcades Project.*

14. See the Introduction on Mikhail Bakhtin and genre theory.

15. "Description and Handlist 1892," in the British Library, London, Vibart Collection: The Dannenberg Album, Text, Photo 1, 245.

16. There is much dispute about what the writing on the wall means, but it has been identified as Masonic cipher. Because the wall from which the writing is transcribed/photographed (it is unclear which in fact was done) had chips of whitewash flaking away, the characters of the ciphers are ambiguous. The only (disputed) translation one can find of this is the following, from an entry in the *Encyclopedia of Freemasonry* (part 2): "Dear Jesus send His help soon and deliver us not into the enemy's hands. / The General's daughter is in this corner. / May God reward them according to the bloody deeds done to this innocent girl. / This is the corner General Wheeler occupied in his distress. / The General's wife is in this corner. / The P.M. in this. / This is the place where two soldiers [unintelligible] / Remember the innocent." For an account of this inscription and the various disputes it has provoked, see Mackey and Haywood, *Encyclopedia of Freemasonry,* 629–31.

17. "Description and Handlist," in the British Library, Vibart Collection: The Dannenberg Album.

18. *The Chamber of Blood* was originally drawn by one Lieutenant W. C. Crump in August 1857, allegedly recording the spectacle he encountered following the siege of Cawnpore. See Shepherd, *A Personal Narrative of the Outbreak and Massacre at Cawnpore,* frontispiece.

19. Benjamin, *The Origin of German Tragic Drama,* 166.

20. For a brilliant account of photography of ruins and its allegorical aspect in a different context, see Lloyd, *Irish Times: Temporalities of Modernity,* especially the chapter titled "Ruination: Partition and the Expectation of Violence."

21. Shepherd, *A Personal Narrative of the Outbreak and Massacre at Cawnpore,* 136.

22. As Eduardo Cadava and Paola Cortés-Rocca explain: "The confidence that what we call the referent or subject of an image is an entity that is stable and identical to itself, a full presence that exists before representation, that stands in front of the photographic apparatus and of which the camera (or language) gives a 'faithful' or 'true' representation, corresponds not to a characteristic proper to photography, but to a policing use of photographic technology. To naturalize a policial use of photographic technology and to convert this reading of the photograph into 'the' reading of it is, like any ideological operation, the result of a dehistoricization of the multiple modes in which the photographic image is circulated and read. Nevertheless, it is precisely because there is no single way to read indexicality that an index—for example, a photographic portrait or a lock of hair—says something different to a detective in a police story than to the protagonist of a romance novel." Cadava and Cortés-Rocca, "Notes on Love and Photography," 17–18.

23. Krauss, "Notes on the Index"; Krauss, "Notes on the Index, Part 2."

24. Of course, for Cadava and Cortés-Rocca, the desire at work here is the effect of a structure or institution rather than simply the individual desires of a person.

25. Gadamer, *Truth and Method,* 64.

26. Fletcher, *Allegory;* Teskey, *Allegory and Violence;* Benjamin, *The Origin of German Tragic Drama;* Eagleton, *Walter Benjamin.*

27. Benjamin, *The Origin of German Tragic Drama,* 166.

28. See the letter from Adorno in Adorno and Benjamin, *The Complete Correspondence, 1928–1940,* 114–15. Also see Benjamin, *The Arcades Project;* and Buck-Morss, *The Dialectics of Seeing.*

29. See Barthes, *Image, Music, Text,* "The Rhetoric of the Image," 44.

30. Walter Benjamin has noted that "the directives given by captions to those looking at images in illustrated magazines soon become even more precise and commanding in films, where the way each single image is understood seems prescribed by the sequence of all the preceding images." Benjamin, *The Work of Art in the Age of Its Technological Reproducibility, and Other Writings on Media,* 27.

31. Trevelyan, *Cawnpore,* 58.

32. Ibid., 60.

33. For a historical account of rumor, see Neubauer, *The Rumour.*

34. Sharpe, *Allegories of Empire.*

35. Thomson, *The Story of Cawnpore,* 31.

36. Ibid., 36.

37. On the friend/enemy distinction, see Schmitt, *The Concept of the Political.* For some recent analyses of rumor, see Froissart, *La rumeur;* Neubauer, *The Rumour;* and Fine and Turner, *Whispers on the Color Line.*

38. Kaye writes of the importance for the "natives" to be killed by hanging rather than by being blown apart, a practice preferred by many British generals. See Kaye and Malleson, *History of the Indian Mutiny of 1857–8.* Also, in Colonel Edward Vibart's memoir he reports: "During the course of this march I witnessed the execution of a notorious traitor by the dread ordeal of being blown from the mouth of a gun. The culprit was an old pensioned native officer who had served the Government for forty years, and was not only in receipt of the pension of his rank, but the emoluments derived from the order of British India as well. Notwithstanding this, he and his two sons had joined the rebel ranks on the outbreak of the mutiny, and all three had just fought against us at Puttialie. Thus he was no ordinary rebel, but a traitor of the deepest dye." Vibart, *The Sepoy Mutiny as Seen by a Subaltern,* 162.

39. "There are some acts of atrocity so abominable that they will not even bear narration. . . . We cannot print these narratives—they are too foul for publication. We should have to speak of families murdered in cold blood,—and murder was mercy!—of the violation of English ladies in the presences of their husbands, of their parents, of their children,—and then, but not till then, of their assassination. . . . What injury had the wretched English children inflicted upon the populations of British India . . . , they should be flung up in the air, and be caught as they descended upon the bayonet of their villains?" "Events in India," *Times,* August 6, 1857.

40. "These soldiers know that they have crossed the Rubicon, that they can never be friends with us again, that it is a death struggle now between us and them." *Times,* August 31, 1857.

41. She continues: "At any other time my heart would have been full of pity and sorrow at such awful sights, but after all we had suffered at the hands of our treacherous sepoys, pity had vanished and thirst for revenge alone remained. Such are effects of warfare upon the hearts of gentle, tender-hearted women." Tytler, *An Englishwoman in India,* 145.

42. Steel, *The Garden of Fidelity,* 15.

43. Thomson, *The Story of Cawnpore,* 245.

44. Quoted in Mason, *The Men Who Ruled India,* 125.

45. Ibid., 210–11.

46. Ibid., 211.

47. Trevelyan, *Cawnpore,* 298.

48. Ibid., 297.

49. Ibid., 299.

50. Ibid.

51. Steel, *The Garden of Fidelity,* 16.

52. Carey cited in Guha, *Elementary Aspects of Peasant Insurgency in Colonial India,* 239.

53. Kaye and Malleson, *History of the Indian Mutiny of 1857–8,* 418.

54. "[The *chapattis* travel] from village to village through the length and breadth of the North-West Provinces like the fiery cross that summoned the clans-men of

Roderick to battle." Holmes, *A History of the Indian Mutiny,* 90. Also, in Francis Cornwallis Maude and John Walter Sherer's *Memories of the Mutiny:* "The circulation of symbols in the form of cakes and lotus flowers throughout the Bengal army proved the existence of a general conspiracy" (19).

55. Guha, *Elementary Aspects of Peasant Insurgency in Colonial India,* 246.

56. "The chapati's circulation bears a contingent relation to the time-lag or temporal break in between sign and symbol, constitutive of the representation of the intersubjective, collective realm of meaning and action." Prakash, *After Colonialism,* "In a Spirit of Calm Violence," 336. This essay is a revision of Bhabha's earlier essay titled "By Bread Alone: Signs of Violence in the Mid-nineteenth Century," in Bhabha, *The Location of Culture,* 283–302.

57. After all, as Guha writes, "The proof of there being no causal connection between the relay of chapatis and the outbreak of the rebellion, as dreamt up in some Anglo-Indian circles, does not exhaust the question of their mutual association." Guha, *Elementary Aspects of Peasant Insurgency in Colonial India,* 242.

58. For detailed accounts of the uses of these signs, see ibid., 220–77.

59. For precisely this reason, Ranajit Guha (problematically) rejects the circulating *chapattis* as a sign of class consciousness: "It was this consciousness, an unquestionably false consciousness if ever there was one, which also generated a certain kind of alienation: it made the subject look upon his destiny not as a function of his own will and action, but as that of forces outside and independent of himself. The thinking which filled the void created thus by the displacement of the subject was, in its most general sense, religious—that is, to put it in Marx's words, 'a product of self-alienation.' . . . What was political came thus to be regarded as religious." Ibid., 268.

60. Kaye and Malleson, *History of the Indian Mutiny of 1857–8,* 420. J. W. Sherer also noted, "And it must be remembered that the circulation of chupatties is a superstitious practice not unknown in Central India, resorted to, we are told, in the hope of passing on epidemics." Maude and Sherer, *Memories of the Mutiny,* 8.

61. Crooke, *The Popular Religion and Folk-Lore of Northern India,* 164.

62. Guha, *Elementary Aspects of Peasant Insurgency in Colonial India,* 244.

63. Ranajit Guha: "The vague and indefinite character of the message carried by the *[chapatti]* keeps it wide open to various degrees of semantic modification at each point of its passage between communicators. It is no wonder, therefore, that the circulating chapati, as a witness at Bahadur Shah's trial testified, 'had different meanings for different people.'" Guha, *Elementary Aspects of Peasant Insurgency in Colonial India,* 245, 246.

64. Vibart, *The Sepoy Mutiny as Seen by a Subaltern,* 98.

65. *The Delhi Massacre,* 2.

66. "The retention of the image, its development and multiplication, form an ordered succession of steps which composed the photographic act, taken as a whole. History determined, however, that this act would find its goal in reproduction, much the way the point of film as spectacle was established from the start. . . . So that photography's contribution, to use the terms of classical economy, is less on the level of *production,* properly speaking, than on that of *consumption.*" Damisch quoted in Trachtenberg, *Classic Essays on Photography,* 290.

67. Kant, *Prolegomena to Any Future Metaphysics,* 129.

68. For a recent account of analogy that aims to rescue it as a form of reasoning, see Silverman, *Flesh of My Flesh,* especially the Introduction and the chapter on Gerhard Richter, "Photography by Other Means."

69. Print culture, also similar to these archaic forms yet radically different from photography in its economy of certitude, also does not exhaust these patterns of relations.

70. Steel, *On the Face of the Waters,* "Preface."

71. Sharpe, *Allegories of Empire;* Ray, *En-Gendering India.*

72. In her memoir, Steel writes, "Nothing is more remarkable, nothing is more sad, than to look through the newspapers of that time [1857] and note the bloodthirsty tone of the letters to the editors, especially those of many Christian clergymen." Steel, *The Garden of Fidelity,* 15.

73. Sharpe, *Allegories of Empire,* 109.

74. Steel, *On the Face of the Waters,* 431.

75. Such a presentation of the Sepoy Revolt forecloses many Indians from a reading of the events of 1857, in whose point of view the revolt signified a war of independence. See Sharpe, *Allegories of Empire,* 109, 113.

76. Gadamer, Weinsheimer, and Marshall, *Truth and Method,* 63.

77. Barthes and Heath, *Image, Music, Text,* 272.

78. Peirce, *Collected Papers of Charles Sanders Peirce,* 414.

79. Ibid., 211.

80. "In both [the symbolic and iconic aspects], the index is defined by a physical, material connection to its object. . . . In its intimacy with the symbolic, the index as shifter (or *deixis*) forces language to adhere to the spatiotemporal frame of its articulation. As photographic trace or impression, the index seems to harbor a fullness, an excessiveness of detail that is always supplemental to meaning or intention. Yet the index as deixis implies an emptiness, a hollowness that can only be filled in specific, contingent, always mutating situations. It is this dialectic of the empty and the full that lends the index an eeriness and uncanniness not associated with the realms of the icon or symbol. At times, the disconcerting closeness of the index to its object raises doubts as to whether it is indeed a sign, suggesting that the index is perched precariously on the edge of semiosis." Doane, "Indexicality," 2.

81. Bazin, "The Ontology of the Photographic Image," 8.

82. Maude and Sherer, *Memories of the Mutiny;* Trevelyan, *Cawnpore.* See also, for example, Vibart, *The Sepoy Mutiny as Seen by a Subaltern.*

83. Sells, *Mystical Languages of Unsaying,* 2.

84. Bazin, "The Ontology of the Photographic Image," 8.

85. Trevelyan, *Cawnpore,* 363.

86. Ibid., 341–42.

87. "Description and Handlist," British Library, London, Vibart Collection: The Dannenberg Album.

2. Anaethesis and Violence

1. Sammy House was a military outpost on the route between Lucknow and Delhi. Trevelyan, *Cawnpore,* 365.

2. Marx and Engels, *The First Indian War of Independence,* 94.

3. Hilton, *The Mutiny Records,* 20.

4. See Pal et al., *From Merchants to Emperors,* 79.

5. Marx and Engels, *The First Indian War of Independence, 1857–1959,* 38.

6. Ibid.

7. See Pal et al., *From Merchants to Emperors,* 82.

8. Hilton, *The Mutiny Records,* 122.

9. Quoted in Verney, *The Devil's Wind,* 75.

10. Quoted in Fraser, "Beato's Photograph of the Interior of the Sikanderbagh at Lucknow," 51.

11. Quoted ibid., 53.

12. Clarke, Fraser, and Osman, "A Revised Chronology of Felix (Felice) Beato (1825/34?–1908?)." Because Beato was from Corfu and of Italian heritage (though technically a British subject), some readers and conference audiences have objected that his photographic project cannot be assimilated to a "colonial project" in any easy way, especially since he was a commercial photographer looking to make a profit and unconcerned with the policies of the colonial state. Some critical facts—two of them historical, and the other, as their result, theoretical/methodological—are worth signposting at the outset: Beato's photographs circulated in British compendiums of memory, so his work is a part of the cultural circuits of British colonialism. Also, in the colonies governing a people and running a commercial enterprise have always gone hand in hand. (Hence the East India Company's infrastructure in India seamlessly became inhabited by official state institutions after 1857, when control of India shifted to the crown.) This is why I find the work of Michel Foucault on governmentality productive for an analysis of colonial photography, since "governmentality" names the linkages between technologies of caring for the self and the management of populations. Such management is, of course, not the exclusive affair of the state. And finally, the personal motives of Beato can hardly control or predetermine the uses to which his images are put.

13. Sir George Campbell, judicial commissioner at Lucknow, said: "The great pile of bodies had been decently covered before the photographer [Beato] could take them, but he insisted on having them uncovered to be photographed before they were finally disposed of." Quoted in Desmond and Great Britain, India Office, Library, *Victorian India in Focus,* 64.

14. Fraser, "Beato's Photograph of the Interior of the Sikanderbagh at Lucknow," 51. The intricate and intentional grouping of the human remains is not the only constructed aspect of this photograph; instantaneous photography was not invented at the time this scene was captured, so it took some time—and frozen patience on the part of Beato's live background subjects—to make this photograph.

15. Desmond India Office Library, *Victorian India in Focus,* 64.

16. For a description of such albums, see Lifson, "Beato in Lucknow."

17. See Benjamin, *Walter Benjamin: Selected Writings,* vol. 4, "The Work of Art in the Age of Its Technological Reproducibility," 251–83.

18. Alluding to Henri Lefebvre, one might say that the phantasmagoric aesthetic facilitates the shift from the production of physical space to its psychological aspect.

See Lefebvre, *The Production of Space.* This, as we will see, is linked in colonial India with the rise of statistics.

19. For a relevant account of a similar structure of colonial governmentality in the Sri Lankan context, see Scott, *Refashioning Futures.*

20. Foucault, *The Foucault Effect,* 93.

21. Ibid.

22. Ibid., 103. An earlier translation of this passage reads: "Maybe what is really important for our modern times, that is, our actuality, is not so much the State-domination of our society, but the 'governmentalisation' of the State." Foucault, "Governmentality," 20.

23. Foucault writes, "We all know the fascination which the love, or horror, of the state exercises today; we know how much attention is paid to the genesis of the state, its history, its advance, its power and abuses, etc. [One way of attributing value] to the problem of the state [is] the form of analysis that consists in reducing the state to a certain number of functions, such as the development of productive forces and the reproduction of relations of production, and yet this reductionist vision of the relative importance of the state's role nevertheless invariably renders it absolutely essential as a target needing to be attacked and a privileged position needing to be occupied. But the state, no more probably today than at any other time in its history, does not have this unity, this individuality, this rigorous functionality." Foucault, *The Foucault Effect,* 103. Foucault's critique here is aimed not at a consideration of the development of productive forces or at the reproduction of the relations of production. Instead, he critiques an understanding of the state that reduces its functions to these two modes. The implication here is that both the development of productive forces and the reproduction of the relations of production are processes that exceed state governance, perpetuated as they are within and without the purview of the state. In the case of India, the colonial state before 1857 was hardly unified, since it consisted mainly of three loosely connected "presidencies" (Bombay, Calcutta, Madras) of the East India Company, and after 1857 these presidencies, although they came under the jurisdiction of the English crown, faced the divergent interests of competing industries that threatened to undermine the unity of the colonial state itself. On the fragmentary nature of the colonial state in India, see Sharma, *Famine, Philanthropy, and the Colonial State;* Chatterjee, *The Nation and Its Fragments;* and Guha, *Dominance without Hegemony.* Given this historical context, "governmentality" rather than "governance" describes more accurately the overlapping bureaucratic, administrative, and commercial structures that are not reducible to the colonial state. This is not to say that the state is a wholly discursive structure or that governmentality is an absolutely discursive practice. To read Foucault's work on governmentality in this way means to lose sight of the aims of discursive practices insofar as these practices are intertwined with material necessities and material effects. So in colonial India the ownership of the means of production remained squarely within the purview of British interests before and after 1857, and this ownership was defended brutally by the use of arms. However, the necessity of such violence (which is, I argue below, a quotidian state of affairs, especially under colonialism) marks the intersection of competing political, economic, and cultural struggles that extend outside the contours of state power.

24. Foucault, *The Foucault Effect,* 99.

25. See Prakash, *Another Reason.* Also see Anderson, *Imagined Communities,* "Census, Map, Museum."

26. Sekula, "The Body and the Archive," 56.

27. Thurn, "Anthropological Uses of the Camera," 184.

28. Ibid.

29. Ibid., 188.

30. Bourne, "Photography in the East," 268.

31. For an extended discussion on the uses of photography in warfare in a different colonial context, See Ryan, *Picturing Empire,* 73–98.

32. Clausewitz elaborates: "*War is only a branch of political activity; it is in no sense autonomous.* . . . We maintain that war is simply a continuation of political intercourse, with the addition of other means. We deliberately use the phrase 'with the admixture of other means' because we also want to make it clear that war in itself does not suspend political intercourse or change it into something entirely different." Clausewitz, *On War,* 605.

33. Benjamin, *The Arcades Project,* 14.

34. Crystal Bartolovich, in an instructive reading of Benjamin's *Berlin Chronicle,* interprets the sculpture of a Moor that Benjamin finds as a child in his father's house as a reminder that "the dream of capital is global, not merely local, in its desires and effects"—this is the context in which Benjamin was writing. Bartolovich, "Figuring the (In)Visible in an Imperial Weltstadt," 172. She adds: "Although [Benjamin's] texts don't announce an anti-imperial agenda as such, they can still be understood as providing an anti-imperialist reading practice—or at least demanding such a reading practice from inhabitants of an imperialist world to which his texts are offered as counterpoint" (191). Imperialism here is understood in Leninist terms: "Imperialism is the global form of capital, by no means reducible to colonialism alone; rather it encompasses the networks of banking, production, and trade established to benefit some peoples over others at the global level—'the struggle for economic territory,' not only colonies" (ibid., 177–78).

35. Benjamin, *The Arcades Project,* 19. In addition to his basic description of the arcades, Benjamin notes, "The first department stores appear to be modeled on oriental bazaars." Benjamin, *The Arcades Project,* A7,5. (In citations to *The Arcades Project,* when a particular section of a convolute is cited, the precise passage number is given, as it is here in the latter citation. When one of the essays is cited, simply the page number is given, as in the former citation.)

36. Ibid.

37. Benjamin cites Chenoue and H.D., 1827: "It was not until after the exhibition to Egypt, when people in France gave thought to expanding the use of precious cashmere fabric, that a woman, Greek by birth, introduced it to Paris. M. Ternaux . . . conceived the admirable project of raising Hindustani goats in France. Since then, . . . there have been plenty of workers to train and trades to establish, in order for us to compete successfully against products renowned through so many centuries!" Ibid., A6,1. On the Cairo street scene in the Paris Exposition of 1889, see Mitchell, *Colonising Egypt.*

38. Benjamin, *The Arcades Project,* G16,6.

39. Buck-Morss, *The Dialectics of Seeing,* 86.

40. Bartolovich, "Figuring the (In)Visible in an Imperial Weltstadt," 194.

41. Marx, *Capital,* 162.

42. Ibid., 165.

43. For a historical account of the production of vision in the nineteenth century, see Crary, *Techniques of the Observer.*

44. See Buck-Morss, *Dialectics of Seeing,* 216–52.

45. Outlining the "method of this project," Benjamin writes, "I needn't *say* anything. Merely show. I shall purloin no valuables, appropriate no ingenious formulations. But the rags, the refuse—these I will not inventory but allow, in the only way possible, to come into their own: by making use of them." Benjamin, *The Arcades Project,* N1a,8. The use of these fragments takes many possible forms, from photo montage to dream interpretation, but the aim of each method is to "demonstrate a historical materialism which has annihilated within itself the idea of progress." Ibid., N2,2.

46. Quoted in Buck-Morss, "Aesthetics and Anaesthetics," 4. This is Buck-Morss's modified translation, significantly different from the once-standard English translation by Henry Zohn, which appears in Benjamin and Arendt, *Illuminations.* The more recent translation by Edmund Jephcott and Henry Zohn reads as follows: "'Fiat ars—pereat mundus,' says fascism, expecting from war, as Marinetti admits, the artistic gratification of a sense perception altered by technology. This is evidently the consummation of *l'art pour art.* Humankind, which once, in Homer, was an object of contemplation *[Schauobjekt]* for the Olympian gods, has not become one for itself. Its self-alienation has reached the point where it can experience its own annihilation as a supreme aesthetic pleasure. *Such is the aestheticizing of politics, as practiced by fascism. Communism replies by politicizing art.*" Benjamin, *Walter Benjamin: Selected Writings,* vol. 4, 270. By translating *Schauobjekt* as "object of spectacle," Buck-Morss foregrounds Benjamin's emphasis on the exhibitionary aspect of modernity, an aspect minimized in this Jephcott–Zohn translation. This emphasis is critical to my reading of colonial photography as phantasmagoria.

47. Buck-Morss, "Aesthetics and Anaesthetics," 4. Buck-Morss is interested in exploring what Benjamin sees as the communist, or revolutionary, response to aestheticized politics. The politicization of art surely cannot mean that art becomes a vehicle for communist propaganda, as that would amount to art aestheticizing politics once again. "[Benjamin] is demanding of art a task far more difficult—that is, to *undo* the alienation of the corporeal sensorium, *to restore the instinctual power of the human bodily senses for the sake of humanity's self-preservation,* and to do this, not by avoiding the new technologies, but by *passing through* them. . . . [However,] if we were really to 'politicize art' in the radical way he is suggesting, art would cease to *be* art as we know it. Moreover, the key term 'aesthetics' would be transformed, indeed, redeemed, so that, ironically (or dialectically), *it* would describe the field in which the antidote to fascism is deployed as a political response." If this point is allowed to develop, says Buck-Morss, "it changes the entire conceptual order of modernity." Ibid.

48. Ibid., 6.

49. The synaesthetic system of the body is prelinguistic, regardless of the possibilities

for the acculturation of senses: "The expressive face is, indeed, a wonder of synthesis, as individual as a fingerprint, yet collectively legible by common sense. On it the three aspects of the synaesthetic system—physical sensation, motor reaction, and psychical meaning—converge in signs and gestures comprising a mimetic language. What this language speaks is anything but the concept." Ibid., 14.

50. Ibid., 22.

51. *Phantasmagoria* comes from Greek *phantazein,* meaning "to present to the world," or from Latin *phantasma,* "phantom," and the Greek *ageirein,* "to assemble." So a phantasmagoria is an assemblage of phantoms (mere appearances in the world), and these shows were often accompanied by eerie music and sound effects. Figures projected onto a screen would rapidly increase and decrease in size, advance, retreat, dissolve into one another, or vanish. An account from 1831 by David Brewster describes phantasmagorias as "an exhibition depending on . . . principles [of projection]. . . . Spectres, skeletons, and terrific figures . . . suddenly advanced upon the spectators, becoming larger as they approached them, and finally vanished by appearing to sink into the ground." Quoted in Castle, *The Female Thermometer,* 18.

52. World exhibitions were a phantasmagoria of sight and sound on a gigantic scale. Theodor Adorno reads Richard Wagner's operas, designated by himself as *Gesamtkunstwerk* (total artwork), as precisely such examples of phantasmagoria, in their combination of music, poetry, and theatre that would harmonize into "a permanent invitation to intoxication, as a form of 'oceanic regression.'" Buck-Morss, "Aesthetics and Anaesthetics," 24.

53. A watercolor of the entrance to this panorama is shown in Hyde, *Panoramania!*

54. Although the sense of sight was privileged in phantasmagorias of the nineteenth century, it was not the only sense affected by this phenomenon: "Perfumeries burgeoned in the nineteenth century, their products overpowering the olfactory sense of a population already besieged by the smells of the city. Zola's novel *Le bonheur des dames* describes the phantasmagoria of the department store as an orgy of tactile eroticism, where women felt their way by touch through the rows of counters heaped with textiles and clothing. In regard to taste, Parisian gustatory refinements had already reached an exquisite level in post-Revolutionary France, as former cooks for the nobility sought restaurant employment." Buck-Morss, "Aesthetics and Anaesthetics," 24.

55. Lala Deen Dayal and colonial difference will be discussed in chapter 3.

56. Buck-Morss, "Aesthetics and Anaesthetics," 23.

57. Ibid., 33.

58. Ibid., 30.

59. Ibid.

60. Ibid., 31.

61. "At the same time, surface pattern, as an abstract representation of reason, coherence, and order, became the dominant form of depicting the *social* body that technology had created—and that in fact could not be perceived otherwise." Such aesthetics give each individual member of the social body a "reassuring perception of the rationality of the whole of the social body," justifying their own individual place within it. Ibid., 35. Buck-Morss gives the example of the Soviet organization plan (1921) showing the "general scheme of organization of the Supreme Council of National Economy."

Also, Leni Riefenstahl's film *Triumph of the Will* (1935) represents a public mass phantasmagorically, in such a way that the surface patterns of the mass at the Nuremberg Stadium provide "a pleasing design of the whole, letting the viewer forget the purpose of the display, the militarization of society for the teleology of making war. . . . the aesthetics allow an *an*aesthetization of reception, a viewing of the 'scene' with disinterested pleasure, even when that scene is the preparation through ritual of a whole society for unquestioning sacrifice and ultimately, destruction, murder, and death" Ibid., 38.

62. Prakash, *Another Reason,* 3.

63. Eagleton, *The Ideology of the Aesthetic,* 13.

64. Statistics also made health insurance companies possible at the end of the nineteenth century. For these companies—founded upon a calculation of human suffering and death—"whoever dies is unimportant; it is a question of ratio between accidents and company's liabilities." Adorno and Horkheimer quoted in Buck-Morss, "Aesthetics and Anaesthetics," 32.

65. Marx, *Capital,* 552.

66. Benjamin, *Walter Benjamin: Selected Writings,* vol. 4, "On Some Motifs in Baudelaire," 328.

67. Ibid., 331.

68. To ask whether this clock is material or discursive shows the limits of both categories. The temporality of labor, at the heart of Marx's labor theory of value—arguably a central contribution to the critique of political economy—reveals itself to be profoundly "dematerial," like the commodity that "transcends sensuousness." I am indebted to Geeta Patel for this insight.

69. Photography also serves as an essential aid for legitimating state repression. See Tagg, *The Burden of Representation.*

70. See Bhabha, *The Location of Culture.*

71. Prakash comes to a similar conclusion in the realm of colonial science and education. Under the aegis of the civilizing mission, the British sought to instruct the "natives" in Western scientific knowledge that claimed universality. However, because the tools of this universal science were intended for local objects and practices in India, "the British were compelled to represent the universality of science in the particularity of the imperial mirror." The universality of science is thus hatched from its "particular, colonial double." Prakash, *Another Reason,* 20.

72. One instance in which a sector of the colonized mass approves its own manipulation is the case of the indigenous bourgeoisie, molded in India to the instructions of Thomas Macaulay's famous "Minute on Indian Education" (1835): "I feel . . . that it is impossible for us, with our limited means, to attempt to educate the body of the people. We must at present do our best to form a class who may be interpreters between us and the millions whom we govern; a class of persons, Indian in blood and colour, but English in taste, in opinions in morals, and in intellect. To that class we may leave it to refine the vernacular dialects of the country, to enrich those dialects with terms of science borrowed from the Western nomenclature, and to render them by degrees fit vehicles for conveying knowledge to the great mass of the population." Macaulay, *Selected Writings.*

73. See Saunders, "The Agony and the Allegory"; and Saunders, *The Concept of the Foreign.*

74. Colonial advertisements, frequently using photography as well as drawings, affirmed the legitimacy of the colonial endeavor. Pear Soap ads often remarked on the ability of the company's mission to "lighten the dark recesses of the world." For a discussion of "commodity racism," see McClintock, *Imperial Leather.*

75. See Anderson, *Imagined Communities,* 182.

76. Foucault, *Technologies of the Self,* 18–19. Spivak takes Foucault to task for his "sanctioned ignorance" of the colonial genealogies of Western discursive production. See Spivak, "Can the Subaltern Speak?"

77. Lifson, "Beato in Lucknow," 101. Transliterations of "Sikanderbagh" vary from writer to writer.

78. Bergland, *The National Uncanny,* 36. See Castle, *The Female Thermometer,* for an extended discussion of the content of early phantasmagorias.

79. In my research, I came across the following excerpts from Beato's "diary" on Lucknow:

"In a way this place is almost too easy, a tautology; the bespoken picturesque. It's a good thing that I can document my journey here day by day. Otherwise I might stand accused of supervising the demolition: blast a little more of the east wing. A trench there will complete the view.

"This is architecture at its most provisional. Walls reverting to masonry, beams to timber, windows to gaps and emptinesses. Architecture is cut loose and remanded to the imagination's custody to lay down principles of a new picturesque. In places it is almost like some tuneless passages in Berlioz or Liszt—almost abstract. Its elements and its materials are at my disposal, its halting rhythms and half-formed pictures mine to delineate. Photograph a building and you've made its portrait, located it within its lifetime. But these British have given me better materials. What can sketch like gunpowder, and propose such architecture to the imagination?

"Most contenders for the Mediterranean overran Corfu at one time or another. Venice, the Normans, Byzantium, Corinth, and in my lifetime these English. Most left ruins there. Thucydides tells us how first the Spartan, then the Athenian party leveled my city and laid the countryside waste, how the aristocrats tore the roof off the temple to shoot arrows and fling javelins down on the democrats who were taking sanctuary there. So why weep here, biting the hand that feeds me. Absorbing my island's history, I knew Lucknow. I have no tears for it now. Better to exult in form" (quoted in Lifson, "Beato in Lucknow," 103).

However, Ben Lifson, who quotes these "diary entries" as Beato's meditations "on the architecture of war," in a 1988 *Artforum* article on Beato's Lucknow photographs, does not provide a reference for Beato's diary. After searching in vain for it, I contacted Lifson, who confessed that he was not aware if Beato ever kept a diary, and he had made up these meditations himself as a form of a sort of poetic criticism, since this seemed to him to be the best way to represent certain feelings that Beato's Lucknow photographs evoke. Interestingly enough, it seems from his fictional journal entries that Lifson reads these photographs as phantasmagoric, though he does not mention phantasmagoria or aesthetic alienation in his article.

80. For an excellent recent account of the place of railways in colonial and postcolonial imaginaries, see Aguiar, *Tracking Modernity.*

81. "The postcard would be a resounding defense of the colonial spirit in picture form. It is the comic strip of colonial morality. But it is not merely that; it is more. It is the propagation of the phantasm of the harem by means of photography. It is the degraded, and degrading, revival of this phantasm." Alloula, *The Colonial Harem,* 4.

82. "The aperture of the camera corresponds to a single mathematically definable point of view from which the world could be logically deduced and re-presented. Founded on laws of nature—that is, geometrical optics—the camera provided an infallible vantage point on the world. Sensory evidence that depended in any way on the body was rejected in favor of the representations of this mechanical and monocular apparatus, whose authenticity was placed beyond doubt." Crary, *Techniques of the Observer,* 32. Also see chapter 1.

83. Fanon, *The Wretched of the Earth,* 29–30.

84. Ibid., 30.

85. Ibid.

86. The works of Fanon and Memmi remain the most cogently polemical elaboration of this colonial dynamic. See ibid.; Fanon, *Black Skin, White Masks;* and Memmi, *The Colonizer and the Colonized.* I am leaving aside questions of hybridity and colonial ambivalence in order to emphasize the material, rather than symbolic, relations between the colonizer and the colonized. I am influenced in this choice by Pheng Cheah's critique of hybridity; see Cheah, *Cosmopolitics,* 290–328.

87. Marshall explained, "[The English are] the resultant breed of several distinct races [whereas the Todas] are all of the same type" as a result of their practice of endogamy, so there is "an extreme simplicity and uniformity." Quoted in Pinney, *Camera Indica,* 51.

88. Fanon, *The Wretched of the Earth,* 31.

89. Ibid., 29–30. For an elaboration of this in various colonial contexts, see Pierce and Rao, *Discipline and the Other Body.*

90. Chatterjee, *The Nation and Its Fragments,* 19.

91. Benjamin, *Walter Benjamin: Selected Writings,* vol. 4, 338. The more or less self-reflexive connection of photography itself to death has been repeated by contemporary theorists. Thus, Roland Barthes sees it as "a figuration of the motionless and made-up face beneath which we see the dead," and the figures in virtually any given photograph are "anesthetized and fastened down, like butterflies." Barthes, *Camera Lucida,* 32, 57. Elaborating Benjamin's theory, Eduardo Cadava writes, "Rather than reproducing, faithfully and perfectly, the photographed as such, the photographic image conjures up its death." Cadava, *Words of Light,* 3. Further extending the well-nigh Orphic properties alluded to here, Paul Virilio emphatically questions the destructiveness not only of photography but also of vision per se: "The pilot's hand automatically trips the camera shutter with the same gesture that releases his weapon. *For men at war, the function of the weapon is the function of the eye.*" Virilio, *War and Cinema,* 20. These significations of the opposition between the subject and the camera cannot be universalized across all contexts, however, and in turn, the location of violent "agency" (assuming one can speak of agency in a violence perpetrated by the camera) cannot be

reduced to, or fixed within, the dark confines of the camera. Photography—or, rather, the camera qua camera—does not always gesture to the death of its subjects, not just by itself. In the specific context of colonial photography, in any event, the opposition of the subject and the camera breaks down in the overdetermined axes of material exploitation, including epistemic, psychological, and bodily violence. In a context in which unquestioned binary distinctions such as colonizer and colonized translate to distinctions between the technologized, "rational" human and its "sense-driven" other, economic–political inquiry must at least be brought into discussions of photographic representation, which is not at all the same as reducing the latter to this questioning: Who has the means to represent whom? What is the purpose (conscious and ideological) of the representation? What is ultimately at stake in a given representation, also for us viewers? Such questions relocate the purported violence of the camera, arguably even the violence of vision itself, in an uncannily symbiotic relation among the *photographer,* the technology of representation, the represented and subjected subject, and the viewer of that representation, rather than simply between the camera and its subject.

92. See the Sladen Collection (British Library Oriental and India Office Photographic Collection), Photo 1100/(4), 1866. "Pandy" designated a Sepoy who had mutinied. The *Hobson-Jobson* dictionary of Anglo-Indian words contains the following entry under "Pandy":

"The most current colloquial name for the Sepoy mutineer during 1857–58. The surname *Pande* [Skt. *Pandita*] was a very common one among the high-caste Sepoys of the Bengal army, being the title of a *Jot [got, gotra]* or subdivisional branch of the Brahmins of the Upper Provinces, which furnished many men to the ranks. 'The first two men hung' (for mutiny) 'at Barrackpore were Pandies by caste, hence all Sepoys were Pandies, and ever will be so called' (*Bourchier,* as below). 'In the Bengal army before the Mutiny, there was a person employed in the quarter-guard to strike the gong, who was known as the *gunta* Pandy' *(M.-G. Keatinge). Ghanta,* 'a gong or bell.'

"1857.—'As long as I feel the entire confidence I do, that we shall triumph over this iniquitous combination, I cannot feel gloom. I leave this feeling to the Pandies, who have sacrificed honour and existence to the ghost of a delusion.'—*H. Greathed, Letters during the Siege of Delhi,* 99.

"'We had not long to wait before the line of guns, howitzers, and mortar carts, chiefly drawn by elephants, soon hove in sight. . . . Poor Pandy, what a pounding was in store for you! . . .'—*Bourchier, Eight Months' Campaign against the Bengal Sepoy Army,* 47 (Cited in Henry Yule, Sir [1968] 667–8)."

93. Memmi, *The Colonizer and the Colonized,* 119.

94. Ibid., 25–26.

3. Armor and Aesthesis

1. Bourne, "Ten Weeks with the Camera in the Himalayas," 51. Bourne writes during another expedition, "How often have I lamented that the camera was powerless to cope with these almost ideal scenes, and that with all its truthfulness it can give no idea of the solemnity and grandeur which twilight in a vast mountainous region

reveals partly to the sense and partly to the imagination." Bourne, "Narrative of a Photographic Trip to Kashmir (Cashmere) and Adjacent Districts," 560.

2. See Merleau-Ponty, *Sense and Non-Sense,* "Cézanne's Doubt," 15. Merleau-Ponty's own comments on photography in this essay are remarkably naïve. For example, he aligns photography with a scientific and rational perspective, as opposed to the phenomenologically more accurate expression of the world in painting: "By remaining faithful to the phenomena in his investigations of perspective, Cézanne discovered what recent psychologists have come to formulate: the lived perspective, that which we actually perceive, is not a geometric or photographic one. The objects we see close at hand appear smaller, those far away seem larger than they do in a photograph. (This can be seen in a movie, where a train approaches and gets bigger much faster than a real train would under the same circumstances)" (14). While these observations are technically correct, it is also the case that photography, in the historical aggregation of visual technologies of reproduction, conditions phenomenological experience and is itself among the objects of our experiential field and phenomenological incorporation.

3. Bourne, "Ten Weeks with the Camera in the Himalayas," 69.

4. Ibid. See also, Bourne's narrative from Kashmir: "What a scene was the whole to look upon! And what a puny thing I felt standing on that crest of snow!—a mere atom, and scarcely that in so stupendous a world! To gaze upon a scene like this till a feeling of awe and insignificance steals over you, and then reflect that in the midst of this vast assemblage of sublime creations you are not forgotten, cannot fail to deepen the veneration of every right-feeling man for that Almighty, but Beneficent Power, who upreared the mountains, and in whose hand is the breath of every living thing." Bourne, "Narrative of a Photographic Trip to Kashmir (Cashmere) and Adjacent Districts," 564.

5. Sampson, "Photographer of the Picturesque," 165. Also see Sampson, "The Success of Samuel Bourne in India"; Sampson, "Samuel Bourne and 19th-Century British Landscape Photography in India"; Falconer, *India;* Ollman, *Samuel Bourne;* Gordon, *The Imperial Gaze;* and Kabir, *Territory of Desire,* "Framing Fantasy," 54–79.

6. Mitchell qualifies the claims made on behalf of landscape's imperial missions: "Imperialism is clearly not a single, homogenous phenomenon but the name of a complex system of cultural, political, and economic expansion and domination that varies with the specificity of places, peoples, and historical moments. . . . Landscape, understood as a concept or representational practice, does not usually declare its relation to imperialism in any direct way; it is not to be understood, in my view, as a mere tool of nefarious imperial designs, nor as uniquely caused by imperialism." Mitchell, *Landscape and Power,* 10.

7. Emerson, *Essays and Lectures,* 42; Williams, *The Country and the City,* 120; Barrell, *The Dark Side of the Landscape.*

8. See, for example, Barrell, *The Dark Side of the Landscape;* Cherry, "Earth into World, Land into Landscape"; Bermingham, *Landscape and Ideology;* and W. J. T. Mitchell, *Landscape and Power.* In his "Orientalism and the Exhibitionary Order," Timothy Mitchell develops an argument that links the detached and elevated spectator to the colonial presence.

9. Of course, the afterlife of the picturesque—for example, in Walker Evans—extends this incidental nature of the photographic gaze even as it revises ideas about both nature and beauty. See Kemp and Rheuban, "Images of Decay."

10. Gilpin, *An Essay upon Prints,* 33.

11. Gilpin, *Observations on the River Wye,* 33. Violence often underlay the production of the picturesque. For example, in another essay, Gilpin comments upon Scaleby Castle: "What share of picturesque genius Cromwell might have, I know not. Certain however it is, that no man, since Henry the Eighth, has contributed more to adorn this country with picturesque ruins. The difference between these masters lay chiefly in the style of ruins, in which they composed. Henry adorned his landscapes with the ruins of abbeys; Cromwell, with those of castles. I have seen many pieces by this master, executed in good style; but seldom a finer monument of his masterly hand than this. He has rent the tower, and demolished two of its sides; the edges of the other two he has shattered into broken lines." Gilpin, *Observations, relative chiefly to picturesque beauty, made in the year 1772,* 122–23.

12. Gilpin, *An Essay upon Prints,* 2.

13. See Budge, *Aesthetics and the Picturesque.*

14. See Andrews, *The Search for the Picturesque;* Barbier, *William Gilpin;* Bermingham, *Landscape and Ideology;* Copley and Garside, *The Politics of the Picturesque;* Percy, *In Pursuit of the Picturesque;* and Richards, *The Free Fantasia and the Musical Picturesque.*

15. Bourne, "Photography in the East," 345–46.

16. Ollman, *Samuel Bourne,* 8.

17. Bourne, "Narrative of a Photographic Trip to Kashmir (Cashmere) and Adjacent Districts," 560, italics added.

18. Bourne makes a distinction here between the "photographer" and the "artist," which is quite obviously a distinction between photography and painting. Working during the beginnings of the debate about photography's status as documentary or art or both, Bourne notes elsewhere, "I am happy to inform you that, unlike the treatment which photography received last year at the hands of the Commissioners in London, it is here [in India] classified as one of the *fine arts;* and I was told yesterday by the gentleman who is superintending the erection of the building, and who will have the arrangement of the Exhibition [of the fine arts of the Punjab], that it will be so placed as to have the best light which the building affords." Bourne, "Ten Weeks with the Camera in the Himalayas," 70.

19. Bourne, "Narrative of a Photographic Trip to Kashmir (Cashmere) and Adjacent Districts," 560.

20. Rodin quoted in Merleau-Ponty, *The Merleau-Ponty Aesthetics Reader,* "Eye and Mind," 145.

21. Alluding to Eadweard Muybridge, Maurice Merleau-Ponty compares his photographs to paintings of horses in motion: "When a horse is photographed at that instant when he is completely off the ground, with his legs almost folded under him—an instant, therefore, when he must be moving—why does he look as if he were leaping in place? And why, by contrast, do Géricault's horses really *run* on canvas, in a posture impossible for a real horse at a gallop? It is because the horses in *Epsom Derby* bring

me to see the body's grip upon the ground and that, according to a logic of body and world I know well, these 'grips' upon space are also ways of taking hold of duration. . . . The photograph keeps open the instants which the onrush of time closes up forthwith; it destroys the overtaking, the overlapping, the 'metamorphosis' of time. This is what painting, in contrast, makes visible, because the horses have in them that 'leaving here, going there,' because they have a foot in each instant." Ibid.

22. Bourne, "Narrative of a Photographic Trip to Kashmir (Cashmere) and Adjacent Districts," 560, italics added.

23. Pinney, *The Coming of Photography in India,* 29.

24. My implication here is not that with sufficient technomaterial progress, the sublime can be captured but rather that the sublime is perhaps best thought of as that experience beyond the horizon of any given technomaterial limit.

25. Daniell and Daniell, *A picturesque voyage to India,* ii.

26. Ibid., 1–2.

27. For a genealogy of vision and corporeality in Europe, see Crary, *Techniques of the Observer.*

28. Price, *An Essay on the Picturesque,* 105.

29. Leask, *Curiosity and the Aesthetics of Travel Writing,* 174. Also see Ray, "The Painted Raj."

30. Bourne, "Photography in the East," 208.

31. Hunter and Great Britain, India Office, *Imperial Gazetteer of India,* 356.

32. Kemp and Rheuban, "Images of Decay," 110.

33. Mitchell, *Colonising Egypt.*

34. Bourdieu, *Outline of a Theory of Practice,* 86. Bourdieu borrows the term *habitus* from Marcel Mauss and reelaborates it. See Mauss, "Les techniques du corps." For a reading of Mauss's influence on Bourdieu, see Chow, "Reading Derrida on Being Monolingual," 229n16. Chow also provides an intriguing account of the habitus and its relationship to postcolonial theory. For an account of Bourdieu's concept as it articulates with Husserl's and Merleau-Ponty's notions of habit, see Crossley, *The Social Body.*

35. Bourdieu, *Distinction,* 474.

36. Bourdieu, *Outline of a Theory of Practice,* 78.

37. Ibid., 95.

38. See Bourdieu, "Making the Economic Habitus."

39. Ibid., 18. Bourdieu continues: "This mismatch forced one to discover that access to the most elementary economic behaviours (working for a wage, saving, credit, birth control, etc.) is in no way axiomatic and that the so-called 'rational' economic agent is the product of quite particular historical conditions. That is precisely what is ignored both by the economic theory which records and ratifies a particular, historically situated and dated, case of the economic habitus under the name 'rational action theory,' without any consideration of the economic and social conditions that make it possible, because it takes it for granted, and the 'new economic sociology' which, for lack of having a genuine theory of the economic agent, adopts 'rational action theory' by default and fails to *historicize economic dispositions* which, like the economic field, have a social genesis." Ibid.

40. Pinney, *The Coming of Photography in India,* 23, 30.

41. However, Pinney makes a suspect symmetrical claim that "the changing technological base of photography—its increasing miniaturization and cheapness—propelled a disengagement from the colonial *habitus*." Ibid., 30. This implies, via a Kittlerian understanding of technology, not only that politics is determined by technological limits but also that colonial arrangements of power are now made obsolete in the contemporary acceleration of image-making technologies. Following from this logic, Pinney ends his argument with the implication that the functioning of faster visual technologies in India in the twenty-first century makes possible the rise of a truly democratic state.

42. Quoted in Luther, *Raja Deen Dayal*, 81.

43. Judith Gutman includes Deen Dayal in her account of the "Indian way of seeing," in Gutman and International Center of Photography, *Through Indian Eyes*.

44. See Demmerling, *Sprache und Verdinglichung*.

45. Martin Jay explains, "The word 'imitation' *(Nachahmung)*, [Adorno] implies, suggests too active a role for the subject, whose making alone cannot be the source of the meaning it finds in the mimetic relation with the other. Instead, Adorno prefers the verb *anschmiegen* (to snuggle up or mold to) to stress a relationship of contiguity." Jay, "Mimesis and Mimetology," 32.

46. On such instances of mimetic replication, Adorno writes, "If mimetic comportment does not imitate something but makes itself like itself, this is precisely what artworks take it upon themselves to fulfill. *In their expression, artworks do not imitate the impulses of individuals, nor in any way those of their authors; in cases where this is their essential determination, they fall as copies precisely to the mercy of that reification that the mimetic impulse opposes.* Artistic expression enforces on itself history's judgment that mimesis is an archaic comportment, *that as an immediate practice mimesis is not knowledge, that what makes itself like itself does not become truly alike, that mimetic intervention failed.* Thus mimesis is banished to art that comports itself mimetically, just as art absorbs the critique of mimesis into itself by carrying out the objectivation of this impulse." Mimetic intervention fails in part because history intervenes so that what may appear truly alike is not identical, and such failures point to possibilities of a nondominative relationship to the object of mimesis. Adorno, *Aesthetic Theory*, 111, italics added.

47. Fredric Jameson's account of aesthetic form remains among the subtlest treatments of form and causality. See Jameson, *Marxism and Form*.

48. Benjamin, *Walter Benjamin: Selected Writings*, vol. 2, 720.

49. Merleau-Ponty, *Sense and Non-Sense*, "Cézanne's Doubt," 25.

50. "Oudh" and "Avadh" are transliterations of the same name.

51. Benjamin, *The Arcades Project*, Y4a,1.

52. My reading of *The Arcades Project* here is a paraphrase of Susan Buck-Morss's reading in Buck-Morss, *The Dialectics of Seeing*.

53. Walter Benjamin was among the first to note that visual technologies operate by means of endless procedures of testing and experimentation, changing the very notions of permanence and truth even as these technologies equip the human body with new forms of sensing. The second version of the "Work of Art" essay is markedly optimistic about the possibilities of such experimentation. See Benjamin, *Walter Benjamin: Selected Writings*, vol. 3, 101–33.

54. Benjamin, *The Arcades Project,* Y7,5.

55. My argument is not that Abbas Ali and Ahmed Ali Khan replicate a historical template that has already played out in Europe and that such universal and world-historical shifts subsume the regional, the indigenous, or the local. Instead, I conceive of Ali's and Khan's aesthetic differences as having a nonidentical relationship with the general and the universal; such an assertion is not a statement of their "resistance" to the general, but rather it highlights the relationship between the universal and the particular as one between the shape of a constellation and a nonidentical element within in it. Through such grounds of comparison, Disderi meets Ali and Khan on an equal aesthetic footing. I elaborate this relationship between the particular and the universal in the context of postcolonial critique and mimesis in my essay "Subjects in Difference."

56. Some of the most compelling accounts of the twentieth-century flowering of region-specific photographic practices and visual economies include Jain, *Gods in the Bazaar;* Pinney et al., *Photography's Other Histories;* Pinney, *Photos of the Gods;* and Strassler, *Refracted Visions.*

57. A hundred years after Dayal and in the aftermath of British colonialism, the afterlife of the picturesque in South Asian kitsch and in the alpine settings of some Bollywood cinema would show the differential ways in which aesthetic forms are inhabited and transmitted.

58. Temple is perhaps best known for his handling of the famine in Bengal and Bihar in 1873–74, when he imported large quantities of rice from Burma to offset the failed local crops. The expenditure proved to be too costly in the eyes of his superiors, even if it did prevent mass mortality, so in order to conserve his position in the administration Temple found opportunity during the catastrophic famine of 1877 to rectify his record. During his tenure as finance minister in 1876–78, he placed the famine "under control" by enforcing what came to be known as the "Temple wage," which restricted the diet of workers to such an extent that people literally fell dead in the middle of the workday. In his memoir *Men and Events of My Time in India,* Temple details at great length his successes during the 1873–74 famine but is circumspect about the loss of thousands of lives in the 1877 famine, attributing many of them to smallpox and cholera. See chapter 4 on famine photography and for more on the Temple wage.

59. Temple, *Men and Events of My Time in India,* 133–34, italics added.

60. Ibid., 139.

61. Temple, *A Bird's-Eye View of Picturesque India,* 17.

62. Ibid., 2.

63. Rowlandson, *Narrative of the Captivity and Removes of Mrs. Mary Rowlandson,* 26. Emphasis added. Also see Anderson, *The Spectre of Comparisons,* 60–70.

64. Knight, *An Analytical Inquiry into the Principles of Taste,* 101–2.

65. Ibid., 136.

66. Alison, *Essays on the Nature and Principles of Taste,* 20.

67. This dynamic is not precisely the same as that described by Heidegger in "The Age of the World Picture" (in his *Question concerning Technology, and Other Essays*) or expounded by Mitchell in *Colonising Egypt.*

68. Bourdieu, *Outline of a Theory of Practice,* 86.

69. See letter dated March 18, 1936, in Adorno and Benjamin, *The Complete Correspondence, 1928–1940,* 127–34.

70. Benjamin, *Walter Benjamin: Selected Writings,* vol. 1, 476. Also, as Miriam Hansen puts it, "Just as script has entered a new phase of 'eccentric pictoriality' and graphic mobility, . . . images, instead of hanging on museum and collectors' walls, have come to inhabit a three-dimensional and public space, the space of the collective." Hansen, "Room-for-Play," 21.

71. Benjamin traces this, however, back to the original reproducibility of print and script. See Benjamin, *Walter Benjamin: Selected Writings,* vol. 1, "Attested Auditor of Books" (from *One-Way Street*), 456–57.

72. For a thorough historicist reading of this photograph, see Sampson, "Unmasking the Colonial Picturesque."

73. For an account of the tree's erstwhile positive representations, see Almeida and Gilpin, *Indian Renaissance.* For an account of the tree's newly sinister nature, see Pinney, "Underneath the Banyan Tree."

74. Sampson, "Unmasking the Colonial Picturesque."

75. Dalhousie to Sir George Couper, February 1848, quoted in Curzon, *British Government in India,* 21, italics added.

76. Parks, *Wanderings of a Pilgrim,* 63.

77. Quoted in Canning, *A Glimpse of the Burning Plain,* 43.

78. Barrackpore Park itself contained a menagerie that in 1837 was "quite full" with a collection of rhinos, tigers, sloths, black bears, a cheetah, a white monkey, a baboon, a giraffe, and a "number of birds." This collection was in decline by the time the Cannings lived at Barrackpore. Curzon, *British Government in India,* 24–27.

79. Sampson writes, "The image of a white woman amid tropical foliage indicates that this particular jungle has been subdued." Sampson, "Unmasking the Colonial Picturesque," 99.

80. See Sharpe, *Allegories of Empire.*

81. Levine, *The Realistic Imagination,* 17.

82. Ibid., 21.

83. The phrase is from Benjamin's essay "Little History of Photography," in Benjamin, *Walter Benjamin: Selected Writings,* vol. 2. However, Siegfried Kracauer makes a similar point in his essay "Photography," in Kracauer, *The Mass Ornament.* Roland Barthes refers to something similar in his discussion of the "punctum," which pierces the spectator of the photograph. See Barthes, *Camera Lucida.*

84. "Barrackpore was also the first scene in the Mutiny of 1857, the famous incident of Mungul Pandy and the heroic conduct of General Hearsey having been enacted on the Parade Ground in the Cantonement." Curzon, *British Government in India,* 45.

4. Famine and the Reproduction of Affect

1. See Jean-Paul Sartre's preface in Fanon, *The Wretched of the Earth;* and Nandy, *The Intimate Enemy,* for accounts of such intimacy.

2. Foucault, *Ethics,* 263.

3. Berlant, *Intimacy;* Giddens, *The Transformation of Intimacy.*

4. Tytler, *An Englishwoman in India,* 9–10.

5. Ibid., 10.

6. Roy, *Alimentary Tracts,* 116.

7. Teignmouth, *Memoir of the Life and Correspondence of John, Lord Teignmouth,* 25–26.

8. I am indebted to Meredith Martin for pointing me to the metrical subtleties of this poem.

9. Digby, *The Famine Campaign in Southern India,* 112.

10. The eighteenth century closed with famines in Bengal (1769–70) and Madras (1781–82), and the following famines were recorded in the nineteenth century: Bombay (1802–3); Doab (1803–4); Agra (1812–14); Delhi (1824–25); Cawnpore, Farrukhabad, and Bundelkhand (1833–34); Agra (1837–38); Doab and Delhi (1860–61); Orissa (1865–67); Rajputana (1868–70); Bihar (1873–74); Madras and Bombay (1876–79); Ganjam and Bihar (1888–89); Madras, Bombay, Deccan, Bengal, the United Provinces, and the Central Provinces (1896–97); and Bombay, the Central Provinces, Berar, and Ajmer (1899–1900). See McAlpin, *Subject to Famine;* Sharma, *Famine, Philanthropy, and the Colonial State;* and Davis, *Late Victorian Holocausts.*

11. According to Sanjay Sharma, not only is the supposedly sharp disjunction between a famine situation and a "normal" circumstance the product of a certain state archival discourse, but also "in the early accounts we find that terms like 'drought,' 'scarcity,' 'distress,' 'dearth,' and 'famine' are generally used interchangeably." Sharma, *Famine, Philanthropy, and the Colonial State,* 6.

12. A detailed account of this controversy is presented in Falconer, "Willoughby Wallace Hooper."

13. London *Times,* January 21, 1886.

14. See Falconer, "Willoughby Wallace Hooper."

15. Geary, *Burma, after the Conquest,* 244–45.

16. Ibid., 243.

17. Conrad, *Heart of Darkness,* 206. I am grateful to Marian Aguiar for pointing me to this connection to Conrad.

18. For example, see Davis, *Late Victorian Holocausts.*

19. See www.imaging-famine.org/.

20. Davis, *Late Victorian Holocausts,* 26.

21. Ibid.

22. Benjamin, *Walter Benjamin: Selected Writings,* vol. 3, "Eduard Fuchs," 266.

23. Jackal attacks on dying famine victims are a recurring motif, from John Shore's late eighteenth-century memories to the great famine in Gujarat in 1900–1902. One missionary pamphlet includes a photograph of a child rescued from jackals' attack. See R. Ward, *Some Fruits of the Great India Famine.*

24. McAlpin, *Subject to Famine;* Sharma, *Famine, Philanthropy, and the Colonial State;* Dutt, *Indian Famines, Their Causes and Prevention;* Davis, *Late Victorian Holocausts;* Hall-Matthews, *Peasants, Famine and the State in Colonial Western India;* Roy, *Alimentary Tracts.*

25. An 1877, article in *Punch* notes, "[England] has not yet shaped into a fact in her rather slow imagination the horrible truth that the slow sure hand of Hunger has already wiped out of life more than half a million men, women, and children—the population of Liverpool; that Pestilence dogs the steps of Famine to glean the blighted life she leaves." See "The Cry of India."

26. Digby, *The Famine Campaign in Southern India,* vol. 2, 377–94.

27. Wesleyan Methodist Missionary Society, *Wesleyan Juvenile Offering,* October 1877, 134.

28. Ellis, *The Politics of Sensibility,* 15.

29. Rai, *Rule of Sympathy;* Stoler, "On Degrees of Imperial Sovereignty," 125; Fassin, "Compassion and Repression"; Boltanski, *Distant Suffering.*

30. "Though our brother is upon the rack, as long as we ourselves are at our ease, our senses will never carry us beyond our own person, and it is by the imagination only that we can form any conception of what are his sensations. . . . By the imagination we place ourselves in his situation, we enter as it were into his body, and become in some measure the same person with him, and thence form some idea of his sensations, and even feel something which, though weaker in degree, is not altogether unlike them. His agonies, when they are thus brought home to ourselves, when we have thus adopted and made them our own, begin at last to affect us, and we then tremble and shudder at the thought of what he feels. For as to be in pain or distress of any kind excites the most excessive sorrow, so to conceive or to imagine that we are in it, excites some degree of the same emotion, in proportion to the vivacity or dullness of the conception." Smith, *The Theory of Moral Sentiments,* 13–14.

31. Ibid., 13.

32. Ibid., 16.

33. Ibid., 30.

34. Ibid., 33.

35. Ibid., 134–35. Smith elaborates: "Our first moral criticisms are exercised upon the characters and conduct of other people; and we are all very forward to observe how each of these affects us. But we soon learn, that other people are equally frank with regard to our own. We become anxious to know how far we deserve their censure or applause, and whether to them we must necessarily appear those agreeable or disagreeable creatures which they represent us. We begin, upon this account, to examine our own passions and conduct, and to consider how these must appear to them, by considering ourselves the spectators of our own behavior, and endeavor to imagine what effect it would, in this light, produce upon us." Ibid., 135.

36. Ibid., 135–36.

37. Freud first discusses this critical agency in his 1914 paper on narcissism and then expands it in his discussion of the "ego-ideal" and "super-ego" in *Group Psychology and the Analysis of the Ego* (1921, chapter 11) and in *The Ego and the Id* (1923, chapter 3). His formulation of this agency in the essay "The Uncanny" (1919) is strikingly close to Adam Smith's conception of the impartial spectator: "A special agency is slowly formed [over the course of the ego's development], which is able to stand over against the rest of the ego, which has the function of observing and criticizing the self and of exercising a censorship within the mind, and which we become aware of as our 'conscience.'" Freud, *Writings on Art and Literature,* 211.

38. Smith, *The Theory of Moral Sentiments,* 140.

39. Khalip, *Anonymous Life,* 96–132; Redfield, *Phantom Formations,* 134–70. Also see Schor, *Bearing the Dead,* 19–47, 73–115.

40. Smith, *The Theory of Moral Sentiments,* 152.

41. Foucault, *Order of Things,* 23–24. The world does not reduce itself to the self-

same, because the principle of antipathy holds things apart, according to Foucault's account of the premodern episteme.

42. I am echoing here Horkheimer and Adorno's concerns in *Dialectic of Enlightenment,* in which they demonstrate how the legacy of the enlightenment continues to be haunted by the forms of mimesis it seeks to banish, because these magical forms of mimesis lie at the heart of modernity: "Civilization replaced the organic adaptation to otherness, mimetic behavior proper, firstly, in the magical phase, with the organized manipulation of mimesis, and finally, in the historical phase, with rational praxis." Horkheimer and Adorno, *Dialectic of Enlightenment,* 148. These replacements are subject to dialectical reversals at every turn; the magic of mimesis transforms as a result but is never effectively banished. For a reading of this dynamic in colonial contexts, see Taussig, *Mimesis and Alterity.*

43. Taussig, *Mimesis and Alterity;* see also Taussig, *The Magic of the State.*

44. The judge who passed the verdict on Hooper notes, "In thus photographing the criminals, Lieutenant Colonel Hooper did not in effect do more than has frequently been done by special war artists, who have employed pencil and brush to depict executions, and whose productions have been printed in newspapers and published to the world. . . . But I have never seen that they have been criticized, much less condemned, in Parliament or elsewhere; whilst the artists are men usually well received in society." Quoted in Falconer, "Willoughby Wallace Hooper," 283–84.

45. Burke, *A Philosophical Enquiry into the Origin of Our Ideas of the Sublime and Beautiful,* 42–43. Also see Gibbons, *Edmund Burke and Ireland,* "The Sympathetic Sublime," 83–120.

46. Sontag, *Regarding the Pain of Others,* 41.

47. Perhaps a question equally relevant to our contemporary televisual world would be: If "compassion fatigue"—a sort of apathetic attitude produced by a media saturated with pictures of social suffering—is a uniquely modern affect, then how have visual technologies recast the problem of sympathy? See Moeller, *Compassion Fatigue.*

48. Digby, *The Famine Campaign in Southern India,* vol. 2, 397–98.

49. Quoted in Davis, *Late Victorian Holocausts,* 36.

50. Ibid., 37.

51. Ibid., 39.

52. See Digby, *The Famine Campaign in Southern India,* vol. 2, 203–4.

53. Roy, *Alimentary Tracts,* 125–26; Poovey, *A History of the Modern Fact,* 307–28.

54. Of course, Adam Smith himself wrote about the marked lack of sympathetic capacity in "savages and barbarians," or the inhabitants of "rude and barbarous nations": in such places "the virtues of self-denial are more cultivated than those of humanity." Smith's account is, like much racialist discourse, inherently self-contradictory. Although Smith notes that "savages" cultivate self-denial, a paragraph later he writes, "All savages are too much occupied with their own wants and necessities, to give much attention to those of another person. A savage, therefore, whatever be the nature of his distress, expects no sympathy from those about him." Smith's ethnocentrism and racism are not in doubt. Smith, *The Theory of Moral Sentiments,* 239–40.

55. Viswanathan, *Masks of Conquest,* 14.

56. Macaulay, *Macaulay,* 729.

57. Weber, *The Sociology of Religion,* 90.

58. Berlant, *The Female Complaint*, viii. Where the comparison with Berlant's notion of "intimate publics" falls short is that in her account, these publics are composed of consumers, and participation in the intimate public sphere requires consumption of commodities that secure a sense of belonging to that sphere. The intimate public of mass cultural colonial sympathy also calls out for money, but money spent on procuring virtue by giving to charity.

59. Osborne, *The Letters of S.G.O.*, 62–63.

60. Ibid., 64.

61. Ibid., 65.

62. Ibid., 66, italics added.

63. Ibid., 64.

64. Ibid., 62.

65. "It is by [sympathy] that poetry, painting, and other affecting arts, transfuse their passions from one breast to another, and are often capable of grafting a delight on wretchedness, misery, and death itself." Burke, *A Philosophical Enquiry into the Origin of Our Ideas of the Sublime and Beautiful*, 41.

66. Duchenne de Boulogne, *The Mechanism of Human Facial Expression*, 20.

67. Ibid., 30.

68. Ibid., 128.

69. Ibid., 126.

70. Spinoza, *The Ethics; Treatise on the Emendation of the Intellect; Selected Letters*, 119 (II. Prop. 27. proof).

71. Ibid., 76.

72. I use *emotion*, *affect*, and *feeling* interchangeably here with the understanding that these terms roughly designate what Spinoza means by *affectus*. Within the growing and varied scholarship on affect, there is an increasing investment in differentiating among these terms, without a clear agreement on what these differences might be but with a vague worry that one of these terms might presume that the subject is the source of emotion/feeling/affect. Brian Massumi and Lawrence Grossberg have made these distinctions central to their arguments. See Massumi, *Parables for the Virtual;* and Grossberg, *We Gotta Get Out of This Place*, "Mapping Popular Culture," 69–87. For my purposes, the various differentiations among these terms are not central to the account of *affectus* that I present here; once the Spinozan understanding of this word is clear, there is no danger of smuggling in the myth of the autotelic subject merely with the use of a corresponding term. For some recent interventions in the affective turn, see K. Stewart, *Ordinary Affects;* Ngai, *Ugly Feelings;* Clough and Halley, *The Affective Turn;* and Gregg and Seigworth, *The Affect Theory Reader*.

73. "For each man's actions are shaped by his emotion; and those who furthermore are a prey to conflicting emotions know not what they want, while those who are free from emotion are driven to this or that course by a slight impulse. Now surely these considerations go to show clearly that mental decision on the one hand, and the appetite and physical state of the body on the other hand, are simultaneous in nature; or rather, they are one and the same thing which, when considered under the attribute of Thought and explicated through Thought, we call decision, and when considered under the attribute of Extension and deduced from the laws of motion-and-rest, we

call a physical state" (III. Prop 2. Scholium). Spinoza, *The Ethics; Treatise on the Emendation of the Intellect; Selected Letters,* 106.

74. Ibid., 103.

75. Ibid., 107.

76. Ibid., 114 (II. Prop. 18).

77. Osborne, *The Letters of S.G.O.,* 67–68.

78. Smith, *The Theory of Moral Sentiments,* 35.

79. Benjamin, *The Origin of German Tragic Drama,* 140.

Coda

1. Darwin, *The Expression of the Emotions in Man and Animals,* 180.

2. Darwin writes repeatedly and over many years of his grief over Annie. See Henrietta Litchfield, *Emma Darwin, a Century of Family Letters.*

3. Benjamin learned a great deal from Darwin's writings but distanced himself from the strain of Marxism that adopted Darwinism as a theory of social development. In *The Arcades Project,* Benjamin invokes prehistory and geological time in order to interrupt the narrative that weds technological progress with progress for humanity. Reading Darwin in a Benjaminian tone means attending to the multiple temporalities that simultaneously determine the present. For Benjamin's distrust of the Darwinian strain in Marxism, see Benjamin, *Walter Benjamin: Selected Writings,* vol. 3, "Eduard Fuchs," 260–304. For an account of the baleful effects of Darwinism on working-class movements in Germany, see Kelly, *The Descent of Darwin.* For a reading of Benjamin's politicized notion of natural history, see Buck-Morss, *The Dialectics of Seeing,* 58–77.

4. The phrase occurs in Benjamin's reading of Edgar Allan Poe's short story "Man of the Crowd." See Benjamin, *Walter Benjamin: Selected Writings,* vol. 4, "On Some Motifs in Baudelaire," 313–55.

5. Jameson, "Cognitive Mapping," 347.

6. Ibid., 360.

7. Benjamin, *The Arcades Project,* N3,2.

8. "The current amazement that the things we are experiencing are 'still' possible in the twentieth century is *not* philosophical. This amazement is not the beginning of knowledge—unless it is the knowledge that the view of history which gives rise to it is untenable." See Benjamin, *Walter Benjamin: Selected Writings,* vol. 4, "On the Concept of History," 392.

9. In the original, "Daß es 'so weiter' geht, *ist* die Katastophe" (Benjamin, *Das Passagen-Werk,* 592). The English translation renders this as "That things are 'status quo' *is* the catastrophe" (Benjamin, *The Arcades Project,* N9a,1), which, although correct, diminishes the aspect of continuation from the past.

10. Merleau-Ponty, *The Primacy of Perception,* "The Crisis of the Understanding," 194.

11. Benjamin, *The Arcades Project,* N3,4.

12. Benjamin, *The Correspondence of Walter Benjamin,* 94.

13. Benjamin, *Walter Benjamin: Selected Writings,* vol. 4, 392.

14. Benjamin, *The Correspondence of Walter Benjamin,* 94.

15. Ibid., 94.

Bibliography

Adorno, Theodor W. *Aesthetic Theory.* Minneapolis: University of Minnesota Press, 1998.

———. *Minima Moralia.* Trans. E. F. N. Jephcott. New York: Verso, 2005.

Adorno, Theodor W., and Walter Benjamin. *The Complete Correspondence, 1928–1940.* Edited by Henri Lonitz. Cambridge, Mass.: Harvard University Press, 2001.

Aguiar, Marian. *Tracking Modernity: India's Railway and the Culture of Mobility.* Minneapolis: University of Minnesota Press, 2011.

Alison, Archibald. *Essays on the Nature and Principles of Taste.* Edinburgh: Harper and Brothers, 1853.

Alloula, Malek. *The Colonial Harem.* Minneapolis: University of Minnesota Press, 1986.

Almeida, Hermione De, and George H. Gilpin. *Indian Renaissance: British Romantic Art and the Prospect of India.* Aldershot, U.K.: Ashgate Publishing, 2006.

Anderson, Benedict. *Imagined Communities: Reflections on the Origin and Spread of Nationalism.* New York: Verso, 1991.

———. *The Spectre of Comparisons.* New York: Verso, 1998.

Andrews, Malcolm. *The Search for the Picturesque: Landscape Aesthetics and Tourism in Britain, 1760–1800.* Stanford, Calif.: Stanford University Press, 1989.

Arondekar, Anjali R. *For the Record: On Sexuality and the Colonial Archive in India.* Durham, N.C.: Duke University Press, 2009.

Baer, Ulrich. *Spectral Evidence: The Photography of Trauma.* Cambridge, Mass.: MIT Press, 2005.

Barbier, Carl Paul. *William Gilpin: His Drawings, Teaching, and Theory of the Picturesque.* Gloucestershire, U.K.: Clarendon Press, 1963.

Barrell, John. *The Dark Side of the Landscape: The Rural Poor in English Painting, 1730–1840.* Cambridge: Cambridge University Press, 1983.

Barthes, Roland. *Camera Lucida: Reflections on Photography.* 2nd ed. Trans. Richard Howard. New York: Hill and Wang, 1982.

———. *Image, Music, Text.* Trans. Stephen Heath. New York: Hill and Wang, 1977.

Bartolovich, C. "Figuring the (In)Visible in an Imperial Weltstadt: The Case of Benjamin's Moor." *Cultural Critique* (2002): 167–208.

Baucom, Ian. *Out of Place.* Princeton, N.J.: Princeton University Press, 1999.

Bazin, André. "The Ontology of the Photographic Image." *Film Quarterly* 13, no. 4 (Summer 1960): 4–9.

Benjamin, Walter. *The Arcades Project.* Edited by Rolf Tiedemann. Cambridge, Mass.: Harvard University Press, 1999.

———. *The Correspondence of Walter Benjamin, 1910–1940.* 1st ed. Chicago: University of Chicago Press, 1994.

———. *Das Passagen-Werk.* Edited by Rolf Tiedemann. Frankfurt am Main: Suhrkamp, 1982.

———. *One-Way Street and Other Writings.* New York: Verso, 1979.

———. *The Origin of German Tragic Drama.* New York: Verso, 1998.

———. *Walter Benjamin: Selected Writings.* Vol. 1: *1913–1926.* Edited by Marcus Bullock and Michael William Jennings. Cambridge, Mass.: Harvard University Press, 1996.

———. *Walter Benjamin: Selected Writings.* Vol. 2: *1927–1934.* Edited by Marcus Paul Bullock, Michael William Jennings, Howard Eiland, and Gary Smith. Cambridge, Mass.: Harvard University Press, 1999.

———. *Walter Benjamin: Selected Writings.* Vol. 3: *1935–1938.* Edited by Michael William Jennings and Howard Eiland. Cambridge, Mass.: Belknap Press of Harvard University Press, 2002.

———. *Walter Benjamin: Selected Writings.* Vol. 4: *1938–1940.* Edited by Michael William Jennings and Howard Eiland. Annotated ed. Cambridge, Mass.: Belknap Press of Harvard University Press, 2003.

———. *The Work of Art in the Age of Its Technological Reproducibility, and Other Writings on Media.* Edited by Michael William Jennings, Brigid Doherty, and Thomas Y. Levin. Cambridge, Mass.: Harvard University Press, 2008.

Benjamin, Walter, and Hannah Arendt. *Illuminations.* New York: Knopf Doubleday Publishing Group, 1969.

Bergland, Renée L. *The National Uncanny: Indian Ghosts and American Subjects.* Hanover, N.H.: University Press of New England, 2000.

Bergson, Henri. *Matter and Memory.* London: Allen and Unwin, 1962.

Berlant, Lauren Gail. *The Female Complaint: The Unfinished Business of Sentimentality in American Culture.* Durham, N.C.: Duke University Press, 2008.

———. *Intimacy.* Chicago: University of Chicago Press, 2000.

Bermingham, Ann. *Landscape and Ideology: The English Rustic Tradition, 1740–1860.* Berkeley: University of California Press, 1989.

Bhabha, Homi K. *The Location of Culture.* New York: Routledge, 2004.

Boltanski, Luc. *Distant Suffering.* Cambridge: Cambridge University Press, 1999.

Bourdieu, Pierre. *Distinction: A Social Critique of the Judgement of Taste.* Translated by Richard Nice. Cambridge, Mass.: Harvard University Press, 1984.

———. "Making the Economic Habitus: Algerian Workers Revisited." Translated by Richard Nice and Loic Wacquant. *Ethnography* 1, no. 1 (2000): 17–41.

———. *Outline of a Theory of Practice.* Cambridge: Cambridge University Press, 1995.

Bourne, Samuel. "Narrative of a Photographic Trip to Kashmir (Cashmere) and Adjacent Districts." *British Journal of Photography* 13–14 (1866).

———. "Photographic Journey through the Higher Himalayas." *British Journal of Photography* 16 (1869): 13–14, 28–29, 79–80, 570, 603; 17 (1869): 15–16, 39–40.

———. "Photography in the East." *British Journal of Photography* 10 (1863): 268–70, 345–47.

———. "Ten Weeks with the Camera in the Himalayas." *British Journal of Photography* 11 (1864): 50–51, 69–70.

Brantlinger, Patrick. *Rule of Darkness: British Literature and Imperialism, 1830–1914.* Ithaca, N.Y.: Cornell University Press, 1990.

Buck-Morss, Susan. "Aesthetics and Anaesthetics: Walter Benjamin's Artwork Essay Reconsidered." *October* 62 (Autumn 1992): 3–41.

———. *The Dialectics of Seeing: Walter Benjamin and the Arcades Project.* Cambridge, Mass.: MIT Press, 1991.

Budge, Gavin. *Aesthetics and the Picturesque, 1795–1840.* Bristol, U.K.: Thoemmes, 2001.

Burke, Edmund. *A Philosophical Enquiry into the Origin of Our Ideas of the Sublime and Beautiful.* Reprint. New York: Oxford University Press, 2009.

Burnell, Arthur Coke. *Hobson-Jobson: A Glossary of Colloquial Anglo-Indian Words and Phrases, and of Kindred Terms, Etymological, Historical, Geographical and Discursive.* London: J. Murray, 1903.

Cadava, Eduardo. *Words of Light: Theses on the Photography of History.* Princeton, N.J.: Princeton University Press, 1998.

Cadava, Eduardo, and Paola Cortés-Rocca. "Notes on Love and Photography." *October* (April 1, 2006): 3–34.

Canning, Charlotte. *A Glimpse of the Burning Plain: Leaves from the Indian Journals of Charlotte Canning.* London: M. Joseph, 1987.

Castle, Terry. *The Female Thermometer: Eighteenth-Century Culture and the Invention of the Uncanny.* New York: Oxford University Press, 1995.

Chakravarty, Gautam. *The Indian Mutiny and the British Imagination.* Cambridge: Cambridge University Press, 2005.

Chatterjee, Partha. *The Nation and Its Fragments: Colonial and Postcolonial Histories.* Princeton, N.J.: Princeton University Press, 2007.

Chaudhary, Zahid R. "Subjects in Difference: Walter Benjamin, Frantz Fanon, and Postcolonial Theory." *Differences: A Journal of Feminist Cultural Studies* 23, no. 1 (forthcoming 2012).

Cheah, Pheng. *Cosmopolitics: Thinking and Feeling beyond the Nation.* Minneapolis: University of Minnesota Press, 2000.

Cherry, Deborah. "Earth into World, Land into Landscape: The 'Worlding' of Algeria in Nineteenth-Century British Feminism." In *Orientalism's Interlocutors: Painting, Architecture, Photography,* ed. Jill Beaulieu and Mary Roberts, 103–30. Durham, N.C.: Duke University Press, 2002.

Chow, Rey. "Reading Derrida on Being Monolingual." *New Literary History* 39 (2008): 217–31.

———. *Sentimental Fabulations, Contemporary Chinese Films.* New York: Columbia University Press, 2007.

Clarke, John, John Fraser, and Colin Osman. "A Revised Chronology of Felix (Felice) Beato (1825/34?–1908?)." Unpublished, n.d.

Clausewitz, Carl von. *On War.* 1st ed. Princeton, N.J.: Princeton University Press, 1989.

Clough, Patricia Ticineto, and Jean O'Malley Halley. *The Affective Turn: Theorizing the Social.* Durham, N.C.: Duke University Press, 2007.

Cohn, Bernard S. *An Anthropologist among the Historians and Other Essays.* New York: Oxford University Press, 1998.

Conrad, Joseph. *Heart of Darkness.* Plain Label Books, 1975.

Copley, Stephen, and Peter Garside. *The Politics of the Picturesque: Literature, Landscape and Aesthetics since 1770.* Cambridge: Cambridge University Press, 2010.

Crary, Jonathan. *Techniques of the Observer: On Vision and Modernity in the Nineteenth Century.* Cambridge, Mass.: MIT Press, 1992.

Crooke, William. *The Popular Religion and Folk-Lore of Northern India.* Westminster, London: A. Constable, 1896.

Crossley, Nick. *The Social Body: Habit, Identity and Desire.* Thousand Oaks, Calif.: Sage Publications, 2001.

"The Cry of India." *Punch,* August 25, 1877.

Curzon, Marquis. *British Government in India: The Story of the Viceroys and Government Houses, by the Marquis Curzon of Kedleston.* London: Cassell and Company, 1925.

Dalrymple, William. *The Last Mughal: The Fall of a Dynasty: Delhi, 1857.* New York: Vintage, 2008.

Daniell, Thomas, and William Daniell. *A picturesque voyage to India: By the way of China, by T. and W. Daniell.* London: Thomas Davison, Whitefriars, 1810.

Darwin, Charles. *The Expression of the Emotions in Man and Animals.* London: Penguin Classics, 2009.

Davis, Mike. *Late Victorian Holocausts: El Niño Famines and the Making of the Third World.* London: Verso, 2002.

Dehejia, Vidya, ed. *India through the Lens: Photography 1840–1911.* Munich: Prestel, 2001.

The Delhi Massacre. A narrative. By a Lady. Reprinted from the *Indian Daily News,* etc., 1870.

Demmerling, Christoph. *Sprache und Verdinglichung: Wittgenstein, Adorno und das Projekt einer kritischen Theorie.* Frankfurt am Main: Suhrkamp, 1994.

Desmond, Ray, and India Office Library. *Victorian India in Focus: A Selection of Early Photographs from the Collection in the India Office Library and Records.* London: Her Majesty's Stationery Office, 1982.

Didi-Huberman, Georges. *Images in Spite of All: Four Photographs from Auschwitz.* Chicato: University of Chicago Press, 2008.

Digby, William. *The Famine Campaign in Southern India (Madras and Bombay Presidencies and Province of Mysore) 1876–1878.* 2 vols. London: Longmans, Green, and Co., 1878.

Doane, Mary Ann. "Indexicality: Trace and Sign: Introduction." *Differences: A Journal of Feminist Cultural Studies* 18, no. 1 (Spring 2007): 1–6.

Duchenne de Boulogne, G.-B. *The Mechanism of Human Facial Expression.* New York: Cambridge University Press, 2006.

Dutt, Romesh Chunder. *Indian Famines, Their Causes and Prevention.* Westminster, U.K.: P. S. King, 1901.

Dutta, Arindam. *The Bureaucracy of Beauty: Design in the Age of Its Global Reproducibility.* New York: Routledge, 2007.

Eagleton, Terry. *The Ideology of the Aesthetic.* 1st ed. Malden, Mass.: Wiley-Blackwell, 1991.

———. *Walter Benjamin: Or, Towards a Revolutionary Criticism.* New York: Verso, 2009.

Edwards, Elizabeth. *Raw Histories: Photographs, Anthropology and Museums.* 1st ed. London: Berg Publishers, 2001.

Elkins, James. *Photography Theory.* New York: Routledge, 2007.

Ellis, Markman. *The Politics of Sensibility: Race, Gender and Commerce in the Sentimental Novel.* New York: Cambridge University Press, 2004.

Emerson, Ralph Waldo. *Essays and Lectures.* Edited by Joel Porte. Des Moines, Iowa: Library of America, 1983.

Falconer, John. *India: Pioneering Photographers: 1850–1900.* London: The British Library and the Howard and Jane Ricketts Collection, 2001.

———. "Willoughby Wallace Hooper: A Craze about Photography." *Photographic Collector* 4 (Winter 1983): 258–85.

Fanon, Frantz. *Black Skin, White Masks.* Translated by Charles Lam Markmann. New York: Grove Press, 1967.

———. *The Wretched of the Earth.* New York: Grove Press, 2005.

Fassin, D. "Compassion and Repression: The Moral Economy of Immigration Policies in France." *Cultural Anthropology* 20, no. 3 (2005): 362–87.

Fine, Gary Alan, and Patricia Ann Turner. *Whispers on the Color Line: Rumor and Race in America.* Berkeley: University of California Press, 2001.

Fletcher, Angus. *Allegory: The Theory of a Symbolic Mode.* Ithaca, N.Y.: Cornell University Press, 1970.

Foucault, Michel. *Ethics: Subjectivity and Truth.* 1st ed. New York: New Press, 2006.

———. *The Foucault Effect: Studies in Governmentality.* Edited by Graham Burchell, Colin Gordon, and Peter Miller. Chicago: University of Chicago Press, 1991.

———. "Governmentality." *Ideology and Consciousness* 6 (1979): 5–22.

———. *Order of Things: An Archaeology of the Human Sciences.* 2nd ed. New York: Routledge, 2001.

———. *Technologies of the Self: A Seminar with Michel Foucault.* Edited by Luther H. Martin, Huck Gutman, and Patrick H. Hutton. Amherst: University of Massachusetts Press, 1988.

Fraser, J. "Beato's Photograph of the Interior of the Sikanderbagh at Lucknow." *Journal of the Society for Army Historical Research* 59 (1981): 51–55.

Freud, Sigmund. *Beyond the Pleasure Principle.* CreateSpace, 2010.

———. *The Ego and the Id.* First Edition Text. Eastford, Conn.: Martino Fine Books, 2010; originally published 1923.

———. *Group Psychology and the Analysis of the Ego.* New York: W. W. Norton and Company, 1975; originally published 1921.

———. *Writings on Art and Literature.* 1st ed. Stanford, Calif.: Stanford University Press, 1997.

Froissart, Pascal. *La rumeur: Histoire et fantasmes.* Paris: Belin, 2002.

Gabara, Esther. *Errant Modernism: The Ethos of Photography in Mexico and Brazil.* 1st ed. Durham, N.C.: Duke University Press Books, 2008.

Gadamer, Hans-Georg. *Truth and Method.* Translation revised by Joel Weinsheimer and Donald Marshall. New York: Continuum, 2004.

Geary, Grattan. *Burma, after the Conquest: Viewed in Its Political, Social, and Commercial Aspects, from Mandalay.* London: S. Low, Marston, Searle, and Rivington, 1886.

Gibbons, Luke. *Edmund Burke and Ireland: Aesthetics, Politics and the Colonial Sublime.* Cambridge: Cambridge University Press, 2003.

Giddens, Anthony. *The Transformation of Intimacy: Sexuality, Love and Eroticism in Modern Societies.* Stanford, Calif.: Stanford University Press, 1993.

Gilpin, William. *An Essay upon Prints.* London: printed for J. Robson, 1768.

———. *Observations on the River Wye.* London: Woodstock Books, 1991.

———. *Observations, relative chiefly to picturesque beauty, made in the year 1772: On several parts of England; particularly the mountains, and lakes of Cumberland, and Westmoreland.* 3rd ed. London: printed for R. Blamire, 1792.

Gordon, Sophie. *The Imperial Gaze: The Photographs of Samuel Bourne, 1863–1870.* London: Alkazi Collection of Photography, 2000.

Graham, George Farquhar Irving. *The Life and Work of Sir Syed Ahmed Khan.* New York: Oxford University Press, 1974.

Gregg, Melissa, and Gregory J. Seigworth. *The Affect Theory Reader.* Durham, N.C.: Duke University Press, 2010.

Grossberg, Lawrence. *We Gotta Get Out of This Place: Popular Conservatism and Postmodern Culture.* New York: Routledge, 1992.

Guha, Ranajit. *Dominance without Hegemony: History and Power in Colonial India.* Cambridge, Mass.: Harvard University Press, 1997.

———. *Elementary Aspects of Peasant Insurgency in Colonial India.* Durham, N.C.: Duke University Press, 1999.

Gutman, Judith Mara, and International Center of Photography. *Through Indian Eyes.* Oxford: Oxford University Press, 1982.

Hall-Matthews, David Nicolas John. *Peasants, Famine and the State in Colonial Western India.* New York: Palgrave Macmillan, 2005.

Hansen, Miriam Bratu. "Room-for-Play: Benjamin's Gamble with Cinema." *October* 109 (Summer 2004): 3–45.

Heidegger, Martin. *The Question concerning Technology, and Other Essays.* New York: Harper Perennial, 1982.

Heller-Roazen, Daniel. *The Inner Touch: Archaeology of a Sensation.* New York: Zone Books, 2007.

Hight, Eleanor M., and Gary David Sampson. *Colonialist Photography: Imag(in)ing Race and Place.* New York: Routledge, 2002.

Hilton, Edward H. *The Mutiny Records: Oudh and Lucknow (1856–57).* Lahore: Sang-e-Meel, 1975.

Holmes, Thomas Rice. *A History of the Indian Mutiny: And of the Disturbances Which Accompanied It among the Civil Population.* London: Macmillan and Co., Ltd., 1904.

Horkheimer, Max, and Theodor W. Adorno. *Dialectic of Enlightenment.* 1st ed. Stanford, Calif.: Stanford University Press, 2007.

Hunter, Sir William Wilson, and Great Britain, India Office. *Imperial Gazetteer of India. . . .* London: Clarendon Press, 1908.

Husserl, Edmund. *The Essential Husserl: Basic Writings in Transcendental Phenomenology.* Edited by Donn Welton. Bloomington: Indiana University Press, 1999.

Hyde, Ralph. *Panoramania! The Art and Entertainment of the "All-Embracing" View.* London: Trefoil in association with Barbican Art Gallery, 1988.

Jain, Kajri. *Gods in the Bazaar: The Economies of Indian Calendar Art.* Durham, N.C.: Duke University Press, 2007.

Jameson, Fredric. "Cognitive Mapping." In *Marxism and the Interpretation of Culture*, ed. Cary Nelson and Lawrence Grossberg, 347–60. Champaign-Urbana: University of Illinois Press, 1988.

———. *Marxism and Form: Twentieth-Century Dialectical Theories of Literature.* Princeton, N.J.: Princeton University Press, 1974.

———. *The Political Unconscious: Narrative as a Socially Symbolic Act.* New ed. New York: Routledge, 2002.

Jay, Martin. "Mimesis and Mimetology: Adorno and Lacoue-Labarthe." In *The Semblance of Subjectivity: Essays in Adorno's Aesthetic Theory*, ed. Tom Huhn and Lambert Zuidervaart, 29–54. Cambridge, Mass.: MIT Press, 1999.

Kabir, Ananya Jahanara. *Territory of Desire: Representing the Valley of Kashmir.* Minneapolis: University of Minnesota Press, 2009.

Kant, Immanuel. *Prolegomena to Any Future Metaphysics.* London: Open Court Publishing, 1912.

Kaye, William, and G. B. Malleson. *History of the Indian Mutiny of 1857–8.* London: Greenwood, 1971.

Kelly, Alfred. *The Descent of Darwin: The Popularization of Darwinism in Germany, 1860–1914.* Chapel Hill: University of North Carolina Press, 1981.

Kelsey, Robin Earle, and Blake Stimson. *The Meaning of Photography.* New Haven, Conn.: Yale University Press, 2008.

Kemp, Wolfgang, and Joyce Rheuban. "Images of Decay: Photography in the Picturesque Tradition." *October* 54 (Autumn 1990): 103–33.

Khalip, Jacques. *Anonymous Life: Romanticism and Dispossession.* Stanford, Calif.: Stanford University Press, 2008.

Knight, Richard Payne. *An Analytical Inquiry into the Principles of Taste.* London: T. Payne, 1808.

Kracauer, Siegfried. *The Mass Ornament: Weimar Essays.* Cambridge, Mass.: Harvard University Press, 2005.

Krauss, Rosalind. "Notes on the Index: Seventies Art in America." *October* 3 (Spring 1977): 68–81.

———. "Notes on the Index: Seventies Art in America. Part 2." *October* 4 (Autumn 1977): 58–67.

Leask, Nigel. *Curiosity and the Aesthetics of Travel Writing, 1770–1840: "From an Antique Land."* Oxford: Oxford University Press, 2004.

Lefebvre, Henri. *The Production of Space.* Malden, Mass.: Wiley-Blackwell, 1999.

Lenin, V. I. *Imperialism: The Highest Stage of Capitalism.* London: Pluto Press, 1996.

Levine, George. *The Realistic Imagination: English Fiction from Frankenstein to Lady Chatterley.* Chicago: University of Chicago Press, 1983.

Lifson, B. "Beato in Lucknow." *Artforum International* 26 (1988): 98–103.

Litchfield, Henrietta Emma Darwin. *Emma Darwin, a Century of Family Letters, 1792–1896.* New York: D. Appleton, 1915.

Lloyd, David. *Irish Times: Temporalities of Modernity.* Dublin: Field Day Publications, 2008.

Luther, Narendra. *Raja Deen Dayal: Prince of Photographers.* Hyderabad, India: Creative Point, 2003.

Lydon, Jane. *Eye Contact: Photographing Indigenous Australians.* Durham, N.C.: Duke University Press Books, 2005.

Macaulay, Thomas Babington. *Macaulay: Poetry and Prose.* Edited by G. M. Young. Cambridge, Mass.: Harvard University Press, 1967.

———. *Selected Writings.* Edited by John Leonard Clive and Thomas Pinney. Chicago: University of Chicago Press, 1972.

MacDougall, David. *The Corporeal Image: Film, Ethnography, and the Senses.* Princeton, N.J.: Princeton University Press, 2006.

Mackey, Albert G., and H. L. Haywood. *Encyclopedia of Freemasonry.* New York and Chicago: Masonic History Company, 1921.

Marder, Elissa. *Dead Time: Temporal Disorders in the Wake of Modernity (Baudelaire and Flaubert).* Stanford, Calif.: Stanford University Press, 2001.

Marx, Karl. *Capital: A Critique of Political Economy.* Translated by Ben Fowkes. Harmondsworth, U.K.: Penguin Books in association with New Left Review, 1976.

Marx, Karl, and Friedrich Engels. *The Economic and Philosophic Manuscripts of 1844 and the Communist Manifesto.* 1st ed. Amherst, N.Y.: Prometheus Books, 1988.

———. *The First Indian War of Independence, 1857–1959.* Moscow: Foreign Languages Publishing House, 1960.

Mason, Philip. *The Men Who Ruled India: The Founders.* New York: Schocken Books, 1964.

Massumi, Brian. *Parables for the Virtual: Movement, Affect, Sensation.* Durham, N.C.: Duke University Press, 2002.

Mathur, Saloni. *India by Design: Colonial History and Cultural Display.* Berkeley: University of California Press, 2007.

Maude, Francis Cornwallis, and John Walter Sherer. *Memories of the Mutiny.* London: Remington, 1894.

Mauss, Marcel. "Les techniques du corps." *Journal de Psychologie* 32, no. 3 (1936). Reprinted in Marcel Mauss. *Sociologie et anthropologie.* Paris: Presses universitaires de France, 1968.

Maxwell, Anne. *Colonial Photography and Exhibitions: Representations of the Native and the Making of European Identities.* Leicester, U.K.: Leicester University Press, 2000.

McAlpin, Michelle Burge. *Subject to Famine: Food Crises and Economic Change in Western India, 1860–1920.* Princeton, N.J: Princeton University Press, 1983.

McClintock, Anne. *Imperial Leather: Race, Gender, and Sexuality in the Colonial Contest.* New York: Routledge, 1995.

Memmi, Albert. *The Colonizer and the Colonized.* Boston: Beacon Press, 1991.

Merleau-Ponty, Maurice. *The Merleau-Ponty Aesthetics Reader: Philosophy and Painting.* Edited and with an introduction by Galen A. Johnson; Michael Bradley Smith, translation editor. Chicago: Northwestern University Press, 1993.

———. *Phenomenology of Perception.* 2nd ed. New York: Routledge, 2002.

———. *The Primacy of Perception: And Other Essays on Phenomenological Psychology, the Philosophy of Art, History and Politics.* 1st ed. Chicago: Northwestern University Press, 1964.

———. *Sense and Non-Sense.* Chicago: Northwestern University Press, 1964.

Merleau-Ponty, Maurice, and Claude Lefort. *Le visible et l'invisible.* Paris: Gallimard, 1964.

———. *The Visible and the Invisible.* Chicago: Northwestern University Press, 1968.

Mitchell, Timothy. *Colonising Egypt.* Berkeley: University of California Press, 1991.

———. "Orientalism and the Exhibitionary Order." In *The Art of Art History: A Critical Anthology,* ed. Donald Preziosi. New York: Oxford University Press, 2009.

Mitchell, W. J. Thomas. *Landscape and Power.* Chicago: University of Chicago Press, 2002.

Moeller, Susan D. *Compassion Fatigue: How the Media Sell Disease, Famine, War and Death.* New York: Routledge, 1999.

Morson, Gary Saul, and Caryl Emerson. *Mikhail Bakhtin: Creation of a Prosaics.* Stanford, Calif.: Stanford University Press, 1990.

Mulvey, Laura. "The Index and the Uncanny." In *Time and the Image,* ed. Carolyn Bailey Gill, 139–48. Manchester, U.K.: Manchester University Press, 2000.

Nandy, Ashis. *The Intimate Enemy: Loss and Recovery of Self under Colonialism.* 2nd ed. Oxford: Oxford University Press, 2010.

Narrative of the Indian revolt from its outbreak to the capture of Lucknow. London: G. Vickers, 1858.

Neubauer, Hans-Joachim. *The Rumour: A Cultural History.* Trans. Christian Bauer. London: Free Association Books, 1999.

Ngai, Sianne. *Ugly Feelings.* Cambridge, Mass.: Harvard University Press, 2005.

Ollman, Arthur. *Samuel Bourne: Images of India.* Carmel, Calif.: Friends of Photography, 1983.

Osborne, Sidney Godolphin. *The Letters of S.G.O.: A Series of Letters on Public Affairs Written by the Rev. Lord Sidney Godolphin Osborne and Published in The Times, 1844–1888.* London, 1890.

Pal, Pratapaditya, Vidya Dehejia, Pierpont Morgan Library, and Los Angeles County Museum of Art. *From Merchants to Emperors: British Artists and India, 1757–1930.* Ithaca, N.Y.: Cornell University Press, 1986.

Parks, Fanny. *Wanderings of a Pilgrim, in Search of the Picturesque, during Four-and-Twenty Years in the East; with Revelations of Life in the Zenana.* 2 vols. London: Richardson, 1850.

Peirce, Charles Sanders. *Collected Papers of Charles Sanders Peirce.* Cambridge, Mass.: Belknap Press of Harvard University Press, 1987.

———. *The Essential Pierce: Selected Philosophical Writings, 1893–1913.* Edited by the Pierce Edition Project. Bloomington: Indiana University Press, 1998.

Percy, Joan. *In Pursuit of the Picturesque: William Gilpin's Surrey Excursion: The Places He Passed and Their Claims to Fame.* Surrey, U.K.: Surrey Gardens Trust, 2001.

Pierce, Steven, and Anupama Rao. *Discipline and the Other Body: Correction, Corporeality, Colonialism.* Durham, N.C.: Duke University Press, 2006.

Pinney, Christopher. *Camera Indica: The Social Life of Indian Photographs.* Chicago: University of Chicago Press, 1997.

———. *The Coming of Photography in India.* London: British Library, 2008.

———. *Photos of the Gods: The Printed Image and Political Struggle in India.* Chicago: Reaktion Books, 2004.

———. "Underneath the Banyan Tree: William Crooke and Photographic Depictions of Caste." In *Anthropology and Photography, 1860–1920,* ed. Elizabeth Edwards, 168–72. New Haven, Conn.: Yale University Press, 2005.

Pinney, Christopher, Nicolas Peterson, Nicholas Thomas, Jo-Anne Driessens, and Michael Aird. *Photography's Other Histories.* Durham, N.C.: Duke University Press Books, 2003.

Poole, Deborah. *Vision, Race, and Modernity: A Visual Economy of the Andean World.* Princeton, N.J.: Princeton University Press, 1997.

Poovey, Mary. *A History of the Modern Fact: Problems of Knowledge in the Sciences of Wealth and Society.* 1st ed. Chicago: University of Chicago Press, 1998.

Prakash, Gyan. *After Colonialism: Imperial Histories and Postcolonial Displacements.* Princeton, N.J.: Princeton University Press, 1995.

———. *Another Reason: Science and the Imagination of Modern India.* Princeton, N.J.: Princeton University Press, 1999.

Preziosi, Donald, ed. *The Art of Art History: A Critical Anthology.* New York: Oxford University Press, 2009.

Price, Sir Uvedale. *An Essay on the Picturesque: As compared with the sublime and the beautiful; and, on the use of studying pictures, for the purpose of improving real landscape.* Rev. ed., London: printed for J. Robson, 1796; originally published 1794.

Rai, Amit. *Rule of Sympathy: Sentiment, Race, and Power, 1750–1850.* London: Palgrave Macmillan, 2002.

Ray, Romita. "The Painted Raj: The Art of the Picturesque in British India, 1757–1911." Ph.D. dissertation, Yale University, 1999.

Ray, Sangeeta. *En-Gendering India: Woman and Nation in Colonial and Postcolonial Narratives.* Durham, N.C.: Duke University Press, 2000.

Redfield, Marc. *Phantom Formations: Aesthetic Ideology and the Bildungsroman.* Ithaca, N.Y.: Cornell University Press, 1996.

Richards, Annette. *The Free Fantasia and the Musical Picturesque.* Cambridge: Cambridge University Press, 2006.

Riddett, A. P. "Saved from Famine." *Weslyan Juvenile Offering,* April 1, 1878.

Risley, Herbert, and W. Crooke. *The People of India.* London: W. Thacker and Co., 1908.

Rowlandson, Mary White. *Narrative of the Captivity and Removes of Mrs. Mary Rowlandson: Who was Taken by the Indians at the Destruction of Lancaster, in 1676.* Lancaster, U.K.: Carter, Andrews, and Co., 1828.

Roy, Parama. *Alimentary Tracts: Appetites, Aversions, and the Postcolonial.* Durham, N.C.: Duke University Press Books, 2010.

Ryan, James R. *Picturing Empire: Photography and the Visualization of the British Empire.* Chicago: University of Chicago Press, 1997.

Said, Edward W. *Culture and Imperialism.* New York: Vintage, 1994.

Salamon, Gayle. "'The Place Where Life Hides Away': Merleau-Ponty, Fanon, and the Location of Bodily Being." *Differences: A Journal of Feminist Cultural Studies* 17, no. 2 (Summer 2006): 96–112.

Sampson, Gary David. "Photographer of the Picturesque." In *India through the Lens: Photography 1840–1911,* ed. Vidya Dehejia, 163–97. Munich: Prestel, 2001.

———. "Samuel Bourne and 19th-Century British Landscape Photography in India." Ph.D. dissertation, University of California, Santa Barbara, 1991.

———. "The Success of Samuel Bourne in India." *History of Photography* 16, no. 4 (1992).

———. "Unmasking the Colonial Picturesque." In *Colonialist Photography: Imag(in)ing Race and Place,* ed. Eleanor Hight and Gary Sampson, 84–106. New York: Routledge, 2004.

Saunders, R. "The Agony and the Allegory: The Concept of the Foreign, the Language of Apartheid, and the Fiction of J. M. Coetzee." *Cultural Critique* (2001): 215–64.

———. *The Concept of the Foreign: An Interdisciplinary Dialogue.* Lanham, Md.: Lexington Books, 2003.

Schmitt, Carl. *The Concept of the Political.* Chicago: University of Chicago Press, 2007.

Schor, Esther H. *Bearing the Dead: The British Culture of Mourning from the Enlightenment to Victoria.* Princeton, N.J.: Princeton University Press, 1994.

Scott, David. *Refashioning Futures: Criticism after Postcoloniality.* Princeton, N.J.: Princeton University Press, 1999.

Sekula, Allan. "The Body and the Archive." *October* 39 (Winter 1986): 3–64.

Sells, Michael Anthony. *Mystical Languages of Unsaying.* Chicago: University of Chicago Press, 1994.

Sharma, Sanjay. *Famine, Philanthropy, and the Colonial State: North India in the Early Nineteenth Century.* New York: Oxford University Press, 2001.

Sharpe, Jenny. *Allegories of Empire: The Figure of Woman in the Colonial Text.* Minneapolis: University of Minnesota Press, 1993.

Shepherd, W. J. *A Personal Narrative of the Outbreak and Massacre at Cawnpore: During the Sepoy Revolt of 1857.* Printed at the London printing press, 1879.

Silverman, Kaja. *Flesh of My Flesh.* Stanford, Calif.: Stanford University Press, 2009.

Smith, Adam. *The Theory of Moral Sentiments.* New York: Penguin Classics, 2010.

Sontag, Susan. *Regarding the Pain of Others.* New York: Picador, 2004.

Spinoza, Baruch. *The Ethics; Treatise on the Emendation of the Intellect; Selected Letters.* 2nd ed. Indianapolis, Ind.: Hackett Publishing Company, 1991.

Spivak, Gayatri Chakravorty. "Can the Subaltern Speak?" In *Marxism and the Interpretation of Culture,* ed. Cary Nelson and Lawrence Grossberg, 271–313. Champaign-Urbana: University of Illinois Press, 1988.

———. "Three Women's Texts and a Critique of Imperialism." *Critical Inquiry* 12, no. 1 (Autumn 1985): 243–61.

Steel, Flora Annie. *The Garden of Fidelity: Being the Autobiography of Flora Annie Steel 1847–1929.* London: Macmillan and Co., 1930.

———. *On the Face of the Waters.* London: W. Heinemann, 1897.

Stewart, Kathleen. *Ordinary Affects.* Durham, N.C.: Duke University Press, 2007.

Stewart, Susan. *On Longing: Narratives of the Miniature, the Gigantic, the Souvenir, the Collection.* Durham, N.C.: Duke University Press Books, 1993.

Stoler, Ann Laura. *Along the Archival Grain: Epistemic Anxieties and Colonial Common Sense.* Princeton, N.J.: Princeton University Press, 2010.

———. "On Degrees of Imperial Sovereignty." *Public Culture* 18, no. 1 (2006): 125–46.

Strassler, Karen. *Refracted Visions: Popular Photography and National Modernity in Java.* Durham, N.C.: Duke University Press Books, 2010.

Sweet, Timothy. *Traces of War: Poetry, Photography, and the Crisis of the Union.* Baltimore, Md.: Johns Hopkins University Press, 1990.

Tagg, John. *The Burden of Representation: Essays on Photographies and Histories.* Minneapolis: University of Minnesota Press, 1993.

Taussig, Michael. *The Magic of the State.* 1st ed. New York: Routledge, 1997.

———. *Mimesis and Alterity: A Particular History of the Senses.* New York: Routledge, 1993.

Taylor, Meadows, and Great Britain, India Office. *The People of India: A Series of Photographic Illustrations, with Descriptive Letterpress, of the Races and Tribes of Hindustan, Originally Prepared under the Authority of the Government of India, and Reproduced by Order of the Secretary of State for India in Council.* London: India Museum, 1868.

Teignmouth, Baron Charles John Shore. *Memoir of the Life and Correspondence of John, Lord Teignmouth.* London: Hatchard, 1843.

Temple, Sir Richard. *A Bird's-Eye View of Picturesque India.* London: Chatto and Windus, 1898.

———. *Men and Events of My Time in India.* London: J. Murray, 1882.

Teskey, Gordon. *Allegory and Violence.* Ithaca, N.Y.: Cornell University Press, 1996.

Thomson, Mowbray. *The Story of Cawnpore.* London: R. Bentley, 1859.

Thurn, E. F. "Anthropological Uses of the Camera." *Journal of the Anthropological Institute of Great Britain and Ireland* 22 (1893): 184–203.

Trachtenberg, Alan. "Albums of War: On Reading Civil War Photographs." *Representations* 9 (1985): 1–32.

———. *Classic Essays on Photography.* New Haven, Conn.: Leete's Island Books, 1980.

Trevelyan, George Otto. *Cawnpore.* London: Macmillan, 1866.

Tytler, Harriet. *An Englishwoman in India: The Memoirs of Harriet Tytler, 1828–1858.* Oxford: Oxford University Press, 1986.

Verney, Gerald Lloyd. *The Devil's Wind: The Story of the Naval Brigade at Lucknow, from the Letters of Edmund Hope Verney and Other Papers concerning the Enterprise of the Ship's Company of H.M.S. Shannon in the Campaign in India, 1857–58.* London: Hutchinson, 1956.

Vibart, Edward Daniel Hamilton. *The Sepoy Mutiny as Seen by a Subaltern: From Delhi to Lucknow.* London: Smith, Elder and Co., 1898.

Virilio, Paul. *War and Cinema: The Logistics of Perception.* New York: Verso, 1989.

Viswanathan, Gauri. *Masks of Conquest: Literary Study and British Rule in India.* New York: Columbia University Press, 1989.

Ward, Andrew. *Our Bones Are Scattered: The Cawnpore Massacres and the Indian Mutiny of 1857.* New York: H. Holt, 1996.

Ward, Robert. *Some Fruits of the Great India Famine, Being Pen Pictures and Photographs by Robert Ward, 1900–1902.* Madras: M. E. Publishing House, Mount Road, 1902.

Weber, Max. *The Sociology of Religion.* Boston: Beacon Press, 1993.

Williams, Raymond. *The Country and the City.* New York: Oxford University Press, 1975.

Index

Zahid R. Chaudhary is assistant professor of English at Princeton University.